The Good o

God, Life
and
the Basis of Ethics

For Luke
from

Stephen C. Lovatt

with my
fond regards

Feb 2013

The Good of Being
God, life and the basis of ethics

CreateSpace
Seattle, WA USA

ISBN-10: 1480224111
ISBN-13: 978-1480224117

First Edition

https://www.createspace.com

For Henry Christopher Milton

When one who lacks skill in arguments puts his trust in an argument as being true, then shortly afterwards believes it to be false – as sometimes it is and sometimes it is not – and so with another argument and then another. You know how those in particular who spend their time studying contradiction in the end believe themselves to have become very wise and that they alone have understood that there is no soundness or reliability in any object or any argument; but that all that exists simply fluctuates up and down as if it were in the Euripus[1] and does not remain in the same place for any time at all!...

We should not allow into our minds the conviction that argumentation has nothing sound about it; much rather we should believe that it is we who are not yet sound and that we must take courage and be eager to attain soundness... The uneducated, when they engage in argument about anything, give no thought to the truth about the subject of discussion, but are only eager that those present will accept the position they have set forth...

I am thinking.... that if what I say is true, it is a fine thing to be convinced; if, on the other hand, nothing exists after death, at least for this time before I die I shall distress those present less with lamentations, and my folly will not continue to exist.... but will come to an end in a short time...

Give but little thought to Socrates, but much more to the truth. If you think that what I say is true, agree with me; if not, oppose it with every argument and take care that in my eagerness I do not deceive myself and you.
[Plato "Phaedo" (90b-91c)]

---

1 A narrow channel of water separating the island of Euboea from Boeotia in mainland Greece. It is subject to strong tidal currents which reverse direction several times a day.

Table of Contents

Introduction

The business of this book is to elucidate the connection between "goodness, value and worth" on the one hand and "life, being and existence" on the other. This may seem like an abstruse academic project, but I believe it to be of great practical importance. I think that a careful consideration of this topic results in a clear vision of what it means to be a living human being; how we ought to live our lives, and so be happy; and what fulfilment we can reasonably hope for.

In the first part of this book (Chapters One to Nine) I argue that mortal existence can only be rationally accounted for and made sense of on the prospect of union with God; as envisaged by Plato of Athens and promised by Jesus of Nazareth.

First I discuss rationality, truth, logic and reality; showing how these ideas are interconnected. I then move on to consider physical existence in general before reflecting on the kind of existence which we identify as life, and in particular the life of sentient[1] and sapient[2] beings. Next, I discuss the ideas of beauty, justice, love and value. I argue that they are intimately connected, and ultimately united in the single idea of "the Good" or God. I then consider the relationship between human beings and God: characterized on the one hand by sin, death and futility; and on the other by mercy, love and immortality.

Now, if God is no more than a figment of human imagination, my claim that sense can be made of our mortality by referring it to eternity would not amount to much. Hence, the second part of this book (Chapters Ten to Fourteen) deals with reasons for believing that God is real and that therefore the idea of human immortality is reasonable.

After identifying some wrong reasons for believing in God I address the issue of suffering which legitimately calls God's reality into question. In doing so, I offer a view of the Fall and of Original Sin which casts light on the fundamental purpose of mortal existence and makes it possible to account for why God generally deals with us remotely and obscurely. I then present critical accounts of four potentially sound reasons for believing in the reality of God.

---

1 Sentience is "personal subjective experiential consciousness."
2 Sapience is sentience together with the knowledge of good and evil.

The third part of the book (Chapters Fifteen to Seventeen) addresses more carefully the relationship between mortal existence and Eternal Life. I discuss the notion of freewill which underpins much of what has gone before and then turn to consider more strictly theological matters: the vocation to enlightenment communion and fellowship with God; the significance of the life and death of Jesus of Nazareth, and how this relates to the Eucharist; and the mission, purpose and business of the Church.

I write as a Physicist by education, a Platonist by outlook and a Catholic by conviction. Many of the ideas presented here have developed as a result of conversations and dialogues with friends and acquaintances and I am indebted to various correspondents; in particular: Aaron Feldman, Abid Siddiqui, Andrew Narvaez, Gabriel Bodeen, Henry Christopher Milton, Jake Kramer, Jean-François Garneau and Paul Miller.

Dates are given in accordance with the Gregorian Calendar, with AD implied unless BC is specified.

Chapter 1 Knowledge and Truth

> For the Lord gives wisdom; from His mouth come knowledge and understanding. [Prov 2:6 RSV]

> For this I was born, and for this I have come into the world, to bear witness to the truth. [Jn 18:37 RSV]

Motivation

This book is an enterprise of intellectual architecture. It is going to build tall. Like the engineers of Babel,[1] I am going to attempt to connect the Earth with the Heavens; though with better motivation and outcome, I hope. In order to stand any chance of success in this enterprise it is necessary to establish sound foundations. Hence the first few chapters of this book are concerned with philosophical fundamentals. Once they would have been common currency, but due to the predations of Subjective Relativism they are now less generally appreciated and understood.

What is knowledge?

Curiosity is one of the distinguishing marks of human beings. It is especially characteristic of children, who generally enjoy learning about new things. Adults are less keen on learning and discovery, they tend to believe either that they already know it all, or that they will never understand some topic and so don't bother to try.

Plato believed that every worthwhile aspect of what it is to be human could be identified with knowledge or expertise, in one way or another. To the degree that he is right in this belief, epistemology (the study of what knowledge is and how it can be obtained) is of central importance. Conventionally, knowledge has been linked with the notions of belief, reality, truth and certainty. So, to know something is to believe, with justification, that it is certainly true and that it is real. Before proceeding further, it is therefore appropriate to consider these notions.

---

1 Gen 11:1-9.

What is Reality?

Reality is a difficult concept, but no less important for that. As an Objective Realist, I want to say that reality is the object of our knowledge. It is that which is actual, entirely independent of our perception and impervious to our will or desire. Reality is the context in which we live. It would continue to exist should all sentient beings cease to exist; changed only by the factual loss of those sentient beings – being no less real for that real deprivation.

Reality is made up of what we call "things" or "objects" which *exist*, "events" which *occur* and "processes" which *persist* in space and time .

> Here, we will understand by realism not so much the hypothesis that there is an autonomous external world known as "physical reality" (the overwhelming majority of physicists would agree with this assumption) but rather the stronger idea that the concepts of physical theories refer to "things" existing in the real world, i.e. physical theories and concepts are more than convenient manners of organizing the data obtained from observation. Indeed, if that were to be the case, that is if physical theories and concepts spoke of objects that do not really exist, then, as Putnam put it, "only a miracle could account for the success of Science".[2]
> [A. Matzkin "Realism and the wave function" (2002)]

Reality doesn't let us have our own way with it, but rather insists on having its way with us. It is independent of us. It is given and not negotiable, "it is kickable and able to kick back if kicked".[3]

> After we came out of the church, we stood talking for some time together of Bishop Berkeley's ingenious sophistry to prove the non-existence of matter, and that every thing in the Universe is merely ideal. I observed, that though we are satisfied his doctrine is not true; it is impossible to refute it. I never shall forget the alacrity with which Johnson answered, striking his foot with mighty force against a large stone, till he rebounded from it, "I refute it THUS."[4]
> [J. Boswell "Life of Johnson" (1791)]

---

2 H. Putnam "Philosophical Papers Vol 1" (1975)

3 K.R. Popper in "Quantum theory and reality" (1967)

4 This is, of course, not a valid refutation, but see page 250.

The only viable option for a living being is to base their aspirations and actions on reality, simply because if they don't do so they will suffer harm and die. Wishful thinking does not produce success, whereas realistic thinking does. If I walk off the edge of a precipice (on the strength of a firm belief that I can fly) I shall fall to my death; whereas if I construct a strong bridge to walk upon (basing its design on a sound understanding of Physics and of engineering principles) I will reach the far side in safety.

What is Truth?

Two kinds of truth are commonly discussed. The first kind is "coherence truth". This is the truth of a proposition defined in terms of some axiomatic system, which may or may not relate to anything beyond itself. Such a proposition is true or *coherent* if it is consistent with the axioms of the system. Equally, the axioms themselves are coherent (or self-consistent) if asserting them together as a group does not entail any contradiction. Statements whose truth is coherent are called "analytic statements". Coherence truth is characteristic of mathematics. Coherence truth is pretty much a matter of definition, and so its nature is not controversial – at least among those who aspire after rationality.

The second kind of truth is "correspondence truth". This pertains to the correlation of an idea: a memory, impression, belief or theory with some aspect of reality which is supposed to be associated with it. If the idea corresponds closely to some external fact (an object or event, say) then it has a high degree of "verisimilitude"; if it corresponds only slightly then it is pretty much false. Statements whose truth is correspondent are called "synthetic statements". Correspondence truth is characteristic of Science, History and everyday experience.

Now if (as might seem obvious) actual facts can never be in conflict with each other, any theory which corresponds fully with the actual facts of objective reality must itself be coherent; so it is first necessary that a theory be coherently true – that is, it must "make sense" – before it can possibly be correspondently true – that is, tell us anything about existent, physical, reality.[5]

In as far as truth is the correspondence of an idea with reality, it is what living and thinking beings are always after. It is the possession

5 This amounts to the assumption that the world we live in is itself coherent. This is a foundational premise of Science; but one that cannot be established as true, either analytically or synthetically.

of "some truth he can use"[6] that enables a human being to live a relatively successful and secure life.

> The advantage of knowledge is that wisdom preserves the life of him who has it. [Eccl 7:12 RSV]

Unfortunately, we can never enjoy the luxury of uncompromised truth, because we are finite beings with a limited capacity for comprehension; and with distorting and misleading senses to boot. Life involves a continual search for truth, but this quest cannot possibly be completed in this life. All of our truths are mixed with error and our best belief is accompanied by doubt. Indeed, I shall in due course argue that it is precisely because of this dichotomy that we are able to grow and mature as ethical beings.

What is Certainty?

One is certain of some proposition if one definitely knows that it is right to think it to be true; in other words, that belief in the truth of the proposition is justified. Sadly, it is unclear that one can ever be certain about anything. The result of a mathematical proof is certain; but only on the understanding that the axioms on which it is based are themselves true; and generally this is only conventionally so. Euclid's famous geometrical axioms were accepted as being correspondently true for two thousand years; but while they are coherent, in actual fact they do not correspond to the real world – at least not on a large scale, Einstein taught us this.[7] In the real world very little – if anything at all – is certain; not even our most cherished and well-established beliefs.

Cardinal Newman invented the idea of "certitude" in an attempt to mitigate this problem. He proposed that one might obtain enough certitude for action from the cumulative evidence of independent testimony and arguments, none of which was an adequate basis for certainty.[8] This suggestion brings us to one of the basic questions in epistemology, This is, the validity or invalidity of induction. Before tackling this, however, it is necessary to consider deductive or inferential reasoning.

---

6 Emerson, Lake & Palmer "Hallowed be thy Name." (1977)

7 Until the beginning of the Nineteenth Century, it was assumed that Euclid's parallel-lines axiom could be derived from his other, simpler, axioms. Only when it was shown that coherent geometries existed which contradicted this axiom was the belief that Euclid's geometry described the physical world called into question.

8 J.H. Newman "An Essay in aid of a Grammar of Assent" (1870)

Deduction

Deductive reasoning is based on some system of inference, by means of which the truth of one proposition (the conclusion) can be shown to inevitably follow from the truth of other propositions (the premises) on which it is then seen to depend. If an argument can be created using such inferential rules, and if those rules are themselves trustworthy; then the conclusion obtained by this argument is as true as the premises. This means that truth can be propagated from a set of axioms (the basic premises of a system) to a wide range of conclusions. This is the business of mathematics; which is at root the investigation of what consequences follow when a set of axioms is postulated.

Various systems of inference have been invented by logicians, but the one which appears to apply to our mundane experience was first codified by Aristotle and is called "Classical Inference". In this system, disproof is just as important as proof, and is generally easier to obtain. Often, a proposition can be disproved by demonstrating that it is incoherent or self-contradictory; in which case it is said to be absurd. Now, according to Aristotle's "Law of the Excluded Middle", if a proposition is shown to be false then its exact opposite must be true. So, if it is incoherent to say "such and such" then "*not* such and such" must necessarily be true. Hence, in Classical Inference, disproof is an effective means of proof.

The origin of Truth

Mathematical axioms are true simply because they are axioms and have been shown not to be mutually inconsistent. The *idea* of the axiom corresponds precisely to its associated objective *reality*, because the objective reality of the axiom is not anything other, more than or beyond the idea which it is. In the physical world, however, deduction runs up against two serious problems. First, how can one first obtain true basic premises from which conclusions may be inferred? Second, how can one know that the rules of Classical Inference are applicable to reality? These questions are popularly answered by the following proposals:

1. The truth of a first category of basic premises is self-evident or "a priori", it cannot be challenged.
2. The truth of a second category of basic premises can be discovered "a posteriori", on the evidence of experience, by a process called "induction".
3. The truth of a third category of basic premises is known by the exercise of "faith".

Induction

Induction depends on the acceptance of some system by which a probability or plausibility can be assigned to a proposition, based on those evidences which are construed as supporting it. Such a system might be called a "Probability Calculus".[9] The idea is that as evidence in favour of some proposition accumulates, the degree of confidence which it is rational to have in the truth of the proposition increases.

Unfortunately, Popper has shown "inductive reasoning" to be invalid. He points out that no matter how much evidence exists which is consistent with (and so supports or corroborates) a proposition; once a single fact which is inconsistent with it is discovered, then the proposition is known to be false. Therefore, it is palpably not true that the more evidence we have in favour of a proposition, the more sure we can be of its truth.

Conjecture and Refutation

Moreover, Popper claims that induction is never used in the formal development of theories. It is thought to be employed in this enterprise because it is easily confused with what actually takes place.[10] When faced with an open question, a researcher first guesses, postulates or conjectures an answer and then checks to see whether their guess ties in with common experience, experimental results and other generally accepted ideas.

This process, called the Scientific Method, can never establish truth with certainty. First, because the interpretation of facts is influenced by the expectations of the observer; so the import or significance of some observation may easily be misconstrued. Second, as we have seen, no level of corroboration of a theory can ever establish its certain truth: there could always be some untried situation in which it fails.

> No amount of experimentation can ever prove me right; a single experiment can prove me wrong. [A. Einstein (c 1920)[11]]

Coming to a view of the real world is an untidy process. Induction is untrustworthy and therefore misleading. Deduction, while trustworthy, requires axioms and these are simply not to hand. Knowledge can still advance,[12] but only by means of intuition and imagination.

---

9 K.R. Popper "The Logic of Scientific Discovery" (1934, 1968)
10 K.R. Popper "Conjectures and Refutations" (1963)
11 In "The New Quotable Einstein" (2205)
12 K.R. Popper "Objective Knowledge" (1972, 1979)

Hysteresis in Physics

Hysteresis is an effect common to many branches of Physics and Mathematics. A commonplace example is the electrical switch. This has two stable configurations, namely "on" and "off". It is possible to flip between them by pushing a short lever. The switch resists any attempt to change its state, however. This is because a spring is attached to the lever (internally to the mechanism of the switch) so as to hold it in place until a significant force is applied.

Consider the process by which a switch which is "off" comes to become "on". At first, a small force is applied; but the spring resists it, the lever does not move and the switch stays off. Then a moderate force is applied. The spring continues to resist it; the lever moves a little and the switch remains off. Then a larger force is applied. The spring cannot resist it and instead buckles. The lever abruptly changes its position and the switch turns on. When the force is taken away the spring keeps the lever secure in its new position and the switch stays on.

Such behaviour is typical of systems which obtain part of their input, premises or motivation from their output, conclusion or result in such a way as to reinforce and stabilise their present state. This *positive feedback* biases them in favour of whatever state they happen to be in. A large opposing stimulus is needed to overcome this bias and make them change state.

There are two complementary aspects to hysteresis. First, there is the tendency to maintain an established stance against present incentives to change that stance. This might be called stubbornness. Second, there is the tendency to adopt a position in a more definitive manner than is strictly justified by the force that favours that position. This might be called conviction.

Epistemological hysteresis

A theory which makes many accurate and pertinent predictions is worthwhile precisely because it does so. It may enable the life-form that has developed or adopted it to anticipate external threats and opportunities and so to "live long and prosper". It is, on this basis, a *helpful* or *useful* belief.

As a theory successfully withstands yet more and more provocative and stringent tests, then the psychological impression that it is trustworthy builds up. One might call this subjective judgement the evidential weight in favour of the new theory. Once a certain (somewhat arbitrary) tipping-point is reached, one dispenses with an old or competing theory (known to be less adequate in some way) and adopts the more successful theory as part of one's general account of the world. This sudden transition (or paradigm shift) is an example of a *catastrophic* change and is characteristic of hysterical systems.

The change is sudden, definite and resolute because once made it affects ones view of the world. According to the newly adopted perspective, certain observations and experiences are more significant than they were according to the old world-view, and others less so. Hence the overall evidential weight is more favourable to the new paradigm once it has been adopted than it was before the transition was made. This is a form of *positive feedback.* So, while one thinks that the moon glows by its own light, the fact that it shows phases has no particular significance – it is just part of the occult lunar nature – and eclipses are entirely unaccountable. Once one comes to believe that the moon glows only by reflected light, its phases and eclipses become crucial evidence in support of this theory.

I call this kind of behaviour epistemological hysteresis. Other more common names for it are *courage* and *loyalty.* These emphasise its tendency to ignore evidence which calls into question a decision already taken in favour of some proposition, course of action, or person. Epistemological hysteresis is also known as *faith, zeal,* and *conviction.* These terms highlight its tendency to invest confirmatory evidence with a higher degree of significance than it strictly warrants; which, analytically, is always precisely zero.

Faith and Wishful Thinking

Those who are opposed to faith, typically identify it as a kind of self-deception. They argue that one should not believe something simply because it is congenial or comforting; but that one should believe whatever seems most reasonable and most in accord with the evidence, even if this is troublesome or distressing. For example, it is imprudent to discount the evidence which is accumulating in favour of human agency being behind Global Warming. To do so is an example of wishful thinking and so is immoral: in particular because it makes us complacent and de-motivates us from taking action which would mitigate the disaster which we seem to be bringing on ourselves. Similarly, they argue that belief in God, or objective morality, or life after death is simply wishful thinking and that such comforting ideas make us complacent and distract us from the real business of life,whatever they may claim this to be.

Now I shall later argue that "wishful thinking" is the basis of wickedness,[13] so I must take this charge against faith seriously. If faith is a species of self-deception, it must be eschewed at all costs. However, this charge against faith is false. Faith can be distinguished from "wishful thinking" by its rationale. Whereas "wishful thinking" is motivated by the desire to minimize suffering and maximize happiness (and even, perhaps, to keep hope alive when no hope is justified) faith is motivated by the desire to make things coherent and to underpin rationality: "to make sense of stuff".

Now this motivation can easily be misplaced. This is because some "stuff" does not make sense: it is just what it is. The glowing embers of a fire do not objectively represent grinning faces; it is only the imagination of the observer which projects this meaning onto them. Similarly, when the innocent suffer there is no purpose or meaning to be found in this fact: it is simply unjust and deeply regrettable. Any "faith" which tries to rationalise such suffering is no more than "wishful thinking". It is wicked and devalues the human spirit. However, the fact that faith can be misplaced does not invalidate the idea of faith. When faith is exercised to allow rational discourse, or to serve as the foundation for value and justice, it is not simply "wishful thinking"; rather it is the necessary basis for the entire enterprise of being human.

Science and Religion

It is commonly thought that Science deals with public certainties, whereas religion deals with private sentiment. In fact, nothing could be further from the truth. Science never deals with proofs, but only with disproofs. No scientific proposition is definitive or certain; though many are promoted zealously as such by their supporters. All scientific theories are provisional and subject to reformulation (if not outright rejection) with the passing of time.

Even the most deeply held principles of Physics (such as relativity, locality, the non-existence of magnetic monopoles, or the conservation of electric charge) are subject to continual re-evaluation, doubt and dispute. Scientific empiricism is itself an act of faith. It is based on the pre-scientific and indeed pre-rational conviction that the world is comprehensible, coherent and lawful; unlike a nightmare or a "Tom and Jerry" cartoon. This metaphysical conviction is justified only by the fact that it seems to work: to the extent that it is the basis and motivation of all the Science and technology of Western Civilization.

---

13 See page 160.

In every aspect of human knowledge of the real world, faith precedes understanding:

> For understanding is the recompense of faith. Therefore, seek not to understand so that you may believe, but believe that you may understand; for unless you believe, you will not understand. [Augustine of Hippo "Tractates on the *Gospel of John"*]

Hence, Physics is as dependent on faith as is Theology. Indeed, there is a close correspondence between the scientific method and the life of faith. Both Science and Religion are based on evidence. In neither case is the evidence conclusive, because empirical evidence never can be so. In both it is necessary to adopt as working certainties (that is, on faith) conclusions which are not formally certain. In both is it necessary to remain open to other unimagined possibilities if progress is to be made.

The conventional view is contrary to this. It sets up an unhealthy dichotomy at the heart of epistemology. Science is seen as incontrovertible and as able to objectively validate, whereas religion is personal and able only to subjectively affirm.

> Only the kind of certainty resulting from the interplay of mathematical and empirical elements can be considered scientific… this method excludes the question of God, making it appear an unscientific or pre-scientific question. Consequently, we are faced with a reduction of the radius of Science and reason – one which needs to be questioned… from this standpoint any attempt to maintain Theology's claim to be "scientific" would end up reducing Christianity to a mere fragment of its former self the questions raised by religion and ethics… must thus be relegated to the realm of the subjective. [Benedict XVI "Faith, Reason and the University" (2006)]

On the contrary, religious faith is no different in species than any other kind of belief. It is a hysterical[14] opinion (based on substantial, but not overwhelmingly conclusive, evidence) concerning matters that are sufficiently important, and which is held with sufficient conviction, as to motivate action.

> Where we are asked to form a judgement which is based on any kind of hearsay evidence, we shall not have the… courage, to form such a judgement unless we are prepared to make an effort

14 In the sense discussed on page 15.

> of the will[15]... there is a prejudice which lurks deep in our natures at all times… against affirming anything, against identifying ourselves with a positive judgement, when it is so much simpler to take refuge in humming and hawing and saying, "Yes, I suppose so."
>
> There is all the difference in the world, practically, between saying, "Yes, I suppose that is true," and saying, "By Gad, that's true!" And the difference… arises… out of our willingness to identify ourselves with the judgement which our reason ratifies[16]...
>
> Faith comes in to encourage us, when we are hesitating to make an affirmation; and that is why we can say that faith is a gift: there is a bestowal of grace which confirms our wills, and makes it possible for us to assert, and to go on asserting, truths of religion over which, if we were left to our indolent and cowardly selves, we might be tempted to suspend judgement.
>
> [R.A. Knox "In Soft Garments" Ch 12 (1941)]

Science and religion are mainly distinguished by the fact that it is not generally practical or appropriate to test theological ideas experimentally. Similarly, it is not right to conduct psychological tests on a friendship; for to do so would be to undermine the very thing which one was attempting to study.

> You say that all knowledge must stem from faith based axioms, I think it might be helpful to discuss in further detail the fact of our senses. Insofar as that our senses determine much of what it is logically tenable to have faith in. In other words, to make an attempt to minimize what it is necessary to have faith in. Many times have Christians said that their faith and mine is similar, because I "have faith in logic" and they

15 Though I reject this Aristotelian analysis (see page 22) the import of what Knox has to say remains. As a Platonist, I would replace "make an effort of the will" with "think carefully and clearly".

16 I would say "the clarity with which we apprehend this judgement." The Aristotelian thinks that the reason is always clear in its judgement and therefore has to find an extra reason why it is troublesome to obey reason's authoritative diktat. The Platonist thinks that the reason is generally far from clear in its conclusions (because the evidence available for it to work on is so indefinite) and so has no need to look for any additional explanation as to why the reason is not automatically absolutely sovereign in the soul.

> "have faith in God". The major difference here is that faith in God is not an *axiomatic* position, but something that must be determined from prior logical steps. That is, it is not something clear from our senses, it is not a foundational assumption. I think it would be helpful to distinguish between faith that is built upon a reliable relationship with our senses, and a faith that masquerades conclusions as axioms.
> [J. Kramer "Private Communication" (2012)]

I discuss the role of the senses and the problems associated with Empiricism in Chapter Two of this book.[17] It is not true to say that anything is "clear from our senses" or that "our senses determine much" – or even anything. However, it is true that our interpretations of sensory experience make it difficult to believe in those theories which make predictions which do not seem to be born out by experience or experiment.[18]

While there is no call to minimise what it is necessary to have faith in, it is very important not to invoke faith when it is not needed. This is because every matter of faith is an independent basic premise, and to have a good account of reality it is important not to multiply such axioms without need. Every time faith is invoked, the extent to which it is possible to explain and understand how and why things fit together as they do is reduced. Similarly, every fundamental physical constant (such as the speed of light and the electronic charge) the value of which is not explained in terms of other yet more basic ideas represents a limit on the intelligibility of the Cosmos. The important thing is to identify those physical constants and beliefs which do characterise the Cosmos and reject those (such as the length of a day, the acceleration due to gravity at sea level on Earth, and Aristotelian ontology) which do not.

The way in which one has faith in logic and faith in God is very different. God's reality need not be a matter of faith. It can be proved in terms of other premises.[19] Faith in God relates to God's nature as trustworthy and beneficent; which propositions cannot be clearly deduced from uncontentious premises. Faith in God is akin to faith in a friend, parent or lover. It is based on what they say, promise and have done. It is based "on a reliable relationship with our senses". Faith in logic does in a sense "masquerade a conclusion as an axiom", for after a cursory analysis it becomes clear that one cannot sustain logic without faith[20] and so one takes as an axiom of faith that logic is trustworthy.

---

17 See page 27.
18 See page 14.
19 See Chapter Fourteen of this book.
20 At least when one tries to apply logic to the real world; see pages 30-43.

Episteme and Doxa

The best kind of knowledge that anyone can normally have of anything is at the very least compromised and prejudiced by one's one subjective assumptions, expectations and viewpoint. This kind of knowledge is called "doxa" in Greek and "belief" or "opinion" in English. Sometimes, one's belief can (with high accuracy) correspond to objective reality. In such a case the belief is true and the term "orthodoxy" is appropriate. In contrast with "doxa", Plato championed "understanding" or "episteme".

Episteme can be defined as "justified orthodoxy", in which case the key aspect of episteme is "justification". Different people give different accounts of what constitutes "justification". An empiricist might claim that it is the existence of "sufficient experimental evidence". A romantic might say that a belief is justified if it "feels right". A theorist might say "whatever agrees with my equations" is justified. A mystic might say that a belief is justified if it brings harmony, peace and joy to the soul.

Plato does not give an explicit specification of what justifies a belief; but suggests that episteme is an intuitive apprehension of some aspect of reality which can be expressed in terms of an exhaustive, rational and coherent account or narrative of how things come to be exactly as they are in fact found to be.[21] In which case, one knows that one has the truth when it is entirely obvious that one's theory is a complete explanation of what it seeks to account for, with no loose ends.

Plato was committed to the notion that doxa (even orthodoxy[22]) was untrustworthy and that only episteme was worthwhile. I concur with him that a smattering of episteme (were it to be available) is eminently preferable to dollops of orthodoxy. However, if some ideal thing is unavailable, then one must make do with what is to hand. After all "True opinion is in no way a worse guide to correct action than knowledge."[23] Moreover, I think that Plato was too dismissive of orthodoxy. He only really conceived of it as *accidentally* correct belief. His problem with such knowledge was that its possessor would have no reason for committing themselves to it and would as likely reject it at some point in favour of error as maintain it.

> True opinions, as long as they remain, are a fine thing and all that they do is good, but they are not willing to remain long... they are not worth much until one ties them down by an account

21 Plato "Theaetetus" (201-210)

22 In the case of orthodoxy, although one holds a correct opinion, one has no certainty that it is in fact correct.

23 Plato "Meno" (97c)

> of the reason why… After they are tied down, in the first place they become knowledge, and then they remain in place.
> [Plato "Meno" (98a)]

According to Plato, then, orthodoxy always results from the naïve acceptance of the persuasive words of some salesman, politician or preacher; or else from an accidental discovery. It never results from a rigorous and systematic attempt to answer the question "Why?" so it can never bring with it any kind of understanding of reality. In both cases, the "true opinion" can only be asserted as a slogan, with no "rational account" to back it up.

I think that there are two kinds of orthodoxy: first, the kind which Plato identified and second, what might be called *scientific orthodoxy.*[24] I believe that the Popperian dialectic of conjecture and refutation tends to result in a belief on the part of those engaged in the process which conforms ever closer to reality.[25] If so, the limit of scientific orthodoxy is episteme; because it has been reached by the systematic and rigorous exercise of reason, rather than by either indoctrination or accident.

Knowledge of the good

Plato believed that for a person to be virtuous it was enough that they should have a clear knowledge of what was for the best[26] and behave rationally. He dismissed the notion of willpower[27].

---

24 By "scientific orthodoxy" I do not mean the "platonic orthodoxy" which just happens to characterize the scientific establishment.

25 This belief – which I suppose is shared by all scientists – is itself a matter of faith. I have no idea how to set out any kind of proof that the scientific method can be expected (let alone be guaranteed) to tend towards truth. The difficulty is that the scientific method can do no more than systematically eliminate error; and there are so many wrong beliefs (potentially an infinite number) to be eliminated, that any process which simply enables one to identify and reject error is entirely inadequate to the task of identifying truth.

I don't think that Occam's Razor is about "the probability of a hypothesis being true" at all. In particular, it doesn't tell us that "the simplest hypothesis is the most probable." It is simply a guide to action. It tells us that it is most expedient to attempt to eliminate those vaguely interesting hypotheses which are most conveniently falsified before bothering to consider other more complex ones.

26 The question of what is "good" or "for the best" or what one "ought to do" is covered in detail in Chapter 7. Suffice to say here, that the idea of "the good" and "value" is foundational to Plato's philosophy.

27 Hence my comments on the R.A. Knox passage, quoted above.

> Isn't the expression "self-control" ridiculous? The stronger self that does the controlling is the same as the weaker self that gets controlled, so that only one person is referred to in all such expressions. [Plato "Republic" (IV 430e)]

He argued that the basis of wickedness was two-fold. Either a sinner was confused about what was right,[26] and so acted out of ignorance; or else their nature was *immoderate*, with the lower functions of the mind – the affections and appetites[28] – not being governed by reason.

> Moderation[29] spreads throughout the whole. It makes the weakest, the strongest, and those in between… all sing the same song together. [Plato "Republic" (IV 432a)]

Even the immoderation of a wicked human being was a kind of ignorance, because it was a malformation of their soul. It was as if the established patterns of thought which governed their decision making were inappropriate, and either erratically (or even consistently) ignored or undervalued factors which ought[26] to have been taken into account. Hence, these patterns of thought did not produce results in accordance with their supposed purpose.

> The evil of a robber does not lie in the fact that he pursues his own interest, but in what he regards as to be his own interest; not in the fact that he pursues his values, but in what he chooses to value; not in the fact that he wants to live, but in the fact that he wants to live on a subhuman level.
> [A. Rand "The Virtue of Selfishness" (1964)]

On this analysis, while immoderation is a defect of the soul, it is not some mysterious weakness of character to be overcome by suffering or exercise. The dysfunctionality results from the presence of incorrect information[30] (defective habitual thought patterns, comparable to a

---

28 For Plato's division of the soul into gut, heart and head, see page 105.

29 By "moderation" Plato does not mean "neither too hot nor too cold". His meaning is closer to "integrity", "harmony" or "coherence". He uses the word, more or less as a synonym for "justice", where either can be a property of a soul or of a society. Hence he talks of those who are joined in moderation "singing the same song together", each playing their part.

30 There are two kinds of information. The first is data. This provides the contingent premises of any argument. The second comprises rules, algorithms and models. These provide the means for drawing conclusions from premises. That the second category is information is demonstrated by the fact that computer programmes are stored as data.

bug-ridden suite of computer software) and so ignorance in the soul. It comes about largely as the habitual legacy of a history of individual blameworthy acts which have set a precedent for future wickedness.[31] Platonic immoderation is a malformation or sickness of the soul and should be corrected by a regime of training or moral reformation intended to habituate wholesome decision making processes. The techniques most apt to achieve this outcome are gentle ones such as role-play, meditation, dialogue, and encouragement. This is not to deny that discipline has a role in the gaining of moderation.

> My son, do not despise the Lord's discipline or be weary of His reproof, for the Lord reproves him whom He loves, as a father the son in whom he delights. [Prov 3:11-12 RSV]

Immoderation is regularly corrected by the person suffering from it having to contend with the demands of reality. For example, the spendthrift will either have to find honest ways of earning the money they want to spend, in which case what seemed to be a vice has in fact spurred them on to virtue; or have to accept that they are headed for trouble and reform their ways, in which case they have had a happy escape; or have to stop their profligacy because they run out of money, in which case their vice has been forcibly replaced by prudence; or else become a thief. In the last case, it is to be hoped that they will be apprehended and suffer punishment which will bring them to penitence and correct their character.

According to Plato, therefore, all wickedness was ignorance in one way or another. Negative ignorance (the mere absence of truth, the lack of any precedent to guide future response) was, however, only the possibility of wickedness or "concupiscence". Positive ignorance (the presence of falsehood, which is often the legacy of previous wrong actions) was real wickedness or vice.

For Plato, a rational being who was entirely moderate and had access to definite information would, in an important sense, have no freewill. This is because they would always know clearly what choice was right and understand exactly why it was so; being aware of the precise outcome that would result from each and every departure from it – with all the attendant consequences. Arguably, this is the agony of Paul Mau'dib.[32] Paul has the "gift" of prescience and suffers greatly for it. He is forced to acquiesce both in the death of his beloved concubine

31 I do not here wish to take sides on the "nature" versus "nurture" debate. Some immoderation is undoubtedly genetic and some vicious habits can be imposed upon individuals by malign and coercive external conditioning.

32 F. Herbert "Dune" (1966)

Chani, and the prosecution of a blood-thirsty jihadic revolutionary war; because he is sure that all the alternatives to these two highly disagreeable options are much worse.

Now, if the freewill or autonomy of some rational agent is in any way important, and if Plato is right about knowledge being incompatible with freewill; it follows that it is necessary that such an agent operates with a degree of ignorance or uncertainty. Indeed, it is only when a free agent is unsure of what is for the best that they can develop what would ordinarily be understood to be autonomous virtues – based on a internal personal model, theoretical account or narrative of what is the case.[33]

> You are expounding some of Plato's ethics here. If you are intending to start with the foundations, perhaps it would be best to first explain why the enemies you mention (the relativists) are in fact wrong *before* you begin building your "tower". As a reader who is not already convinced of your moral principles, it would constantly nag at me, as I continue reading, that you have not yet vanquished the position that might nullify a large portion of what you declare.
> [J. Kramer "Private Communication" (2012)]

My main critique of Subjective Relativism is in Chapter Two. I discuss Plato's linking of knowledge with virtue here, rather than later, because anyone familiar with Plato would castigate me for not doing so. It is important that I present this theory at some point as it underpins part of my subsequent argument. In as far as I have not yet discussed what "the good" or "value" is, the reader must treat these terms as place holders for concepts which will be substantiated later on, in Chapter Seven[34] and for the time being interpret them in accordance with their own ideas.

---

33 It can be asked: "What is the value of autonomous virtues? Would it not be better if everyone was programmed to act justly from the start?" My response is that I suspect that it is only possible for a moral agent to be virtuous as a result of trial and error learning and self-motivated discovery. More of this when I discuss "original sin" and "freewill" in some depth; see Chapters 12 and 15.

34 The title of this book anticipates the conclusions which are reached there.

Chapter 2 Reason and Objectivity

> You shall not hate your brother in your heart, but you shall reason with your neighbour, lest you bear sin because of him. [Lev 19:17 RSV]
>
> Reason is the beginning of every work, and counsel precedes every undertaking. [Sir 37:16 RSV]

Motivation

In this chapter, I want to explore in more detail what rationality amounts to and why one should be bound by it; that is, why one ought to be reasonable. I am indebted to two correspondents whose ideas I use as foils for the argument I am going to develop in this chapter. Although I disagree with both of them, I have the greatest respect for each as an individual and for the integrity with which they address the matters at issue. I have learned a lot from the dialogue I have had with them. My intention here is to allow others to share in that learning process.

I shall argue: first, that reason arises from a belief in objective reality and that without such a belief there can be no motive for being reasonable; and second, that strict adherence to reason is necessary if either the individual or society is to survive or prosper. Hence, the basic justification of reason is that it is *useful* for human life. In preparation for these arguments, it is opportune to discuss epistemology further. A number of epistemological theories are in general circulation.

Theories of knowledge[1]

The first theory of knowledge is **Foundationalism**. This asserts that there exist certain fundamental propositions (such as "any and every thing must be exactly and precisely whatever it is"[2] and "I think, therefore I am."[3]) which are "a priori" or self-evident and so of

---

1 This section is based on an original treatment by A. Feldman.

2 This apparently trivial proposition (known as the Law of Identity) is called into serious question by all of the commonly accepted interpretation of the formalism of Quantum Mechanics.

3 René Descartes "Discourse on Method of Rightly Conducting the Reason, and Seeking Truth in the Sciences" Ch 4 (1637)

themselves certain. Other truths can come to be known by deriving conclusions from these foundational truths by the application of reason. The problem with this position is two-fold. First, what seems self-evident to one person does not necessarily seem so to another. Hence Foundationalism has something of Subjectivism about it. Second, it seems to produce certainty and knowledge from nothing. Plato answered this second difficulty by hypothesising that all knowledge and learning was a disguised form of remembrance of things previously experienced in a life before conception.[4] The extravagance of Plato's answer to this problem should indicate the profundity of the difficulty involved.

The second theory of knowledge is **Empiricism**. This claims that sense experiences constitute the category of unquestionable truths. The most obvious problem with this naïve claim is that human senses cannot always be trusted. Clear examples of such unreliability occur when one is intoxicated, sick, dreaming or presented with an optical illusion. If an Empiricist was asked to provide a specimen statement for which they held there was conclusive sensory evidence, they might volunteer: "I have ten fingers, including two thumbs." However, when asked to explain how they came to know this, they would have to fall back on the supposed reliability of the senses, which they have not demonstrated, and their ability to count, which is also questionable. So any reasons the Empiricist gives for accepting some experiential data as definitive will rely on other reasons and so on... which rather undermines the plausibility of the proposition that: "sense experiences constitute the category of unquestionable truths." The alternative option (of asserting that any proposition supposed to be empirical is unquestionable and basic simply because it is supposed toe be empirical) is also most unsatisfactory. This is a viciously circular argument hardly differing from "Z is true because Z is true."

The third theory of knowledge is **Coherentism**. This is based on the idea that a set of propositions is acceptable if and only if it can be shown (on the basis of some deductive system, typically Classical Inference) to be free from contradictions. When asked about the truth or falsehood of some proposition, the Coherentist will test whether it is consistent with whatever body of coherent propositions they are currently using. If it is compatible with this "background knowledge" they will accept the new proposition as true, if not they will reject it as false. The problem with Coherentism is that there is no reason to think that there is a unique system of belief which is self-consistent. Indeed, the existence of Solipsism (the theory that only I am real and the entirety of the observed world is nothing other than a figment of my imagination;

4 Plato "Meno" (80-81, 85-86, 89)

which system of belief is coherent and irrefutable) shows the converse proposition to be true. Because of this, Coherentism cannot (even in principle) unambiguously assign a truth-value to any proposition. Only if one particular system is chosen, arbitrarily, can it escape this difficulty; and such a choice transforms a Coherentist into a kind of Foundationalist. Coherentists are often accused of preferring large circles over small ones, when it comes to arguments.

The fourth theory of knowledge is **Infinitism**. The Infinitist claims that the basis of truth is an infinite string of reasons that never loops back on itself. In effect this is a form of Coherentism, with the added propositions that the set of consistent propositions is necessarily unique and has an infinite membership. The purpose of the second proposition is to exclude trivial systems such as Solipsism as possibilities. The basic hypothesis here is that everything which is true (no matter how arbitrary or accidental it might seem) is true precisely because it is utterly inevitable and absolutely necessary. However, the truth of this seemingly extravagant hypothesis cannot itself be established, so this theory is no more soundly based than Coherentism.

The fifth theory of knowledge (which has been lurking in the shadows throughout all of the previous discussion) is **Skepticism**. This claims that there is no way to attain certain knowledge of anything. The weakest variant of Skepticism only makes a claim about generalities, hence: "No universal means or general criterion can be used either to obtain, determine or manifest certainty regarding propositions." This variant doesn't deny the possibility of episteme (rather, it is compatible with the existence of any number of self-evident propositions) it simply denies the existence of any systematic means by which certainty can be attained. This proposition is a version of Gödel's first incompleteness theorem,[5] which tells us that there are some propositions which are definitely true but nevertheless cannot be demonstrated to be true. This version of Skepticism is pretty much established as itself true, in so far as any propositions can be proved.

The strongest variant of Skepticism is irrational. It claims that: "No proposition can be known to be 'true', as there is no such thing as 'truth'." It does not really matter whether this proposition is self-consistent or incoherent; because the proposition disclaims the notion of 'truth', of which coherence is no more than an aspect. Any-one committed to rationality must reject this form of Skepticism while being aware of its existence as a possibility.

---

5 Goedel published this in 1931. A good treatment is given in: S.C. Kleene, "Mathematical Logic" (1967)

The strongest rational variant of Skepticism claims that only its own foundational proposition can be known for certain, namely: "This is the only proposition which can be known with certainty." Now this is unsatisfactory because it is impossible to account for this singular exception and especially for its "a priori" nature.

The final variant claims that: "It is impossible to know anything for sure, that is: to have episteme of anything." Now it is impossible to hold this proposition as certainly true, for the proposition itself excludes this possibility. Hence the most that can be claimed for this proposition is it is in fact true, but can never ever be known to be so: that it can only be postulated to be true, as a matter of faith. Arguably, this is the most plausible form of Skepticism and it is the form which I adhere to.

Theories of rationality

There are three approaches to rationality. The first amounts to the idea that any thinking being is bound to be reasonable by necessity, and that the question "Why be reasonable?" either does not arise, or else is trivial. This approach is typical of Infinitism, Coherentism and Foundationalism. I shall call it Rationalism.

Rationalism

A Rationalist might say that the reason that reason should be trusted is that it is reasonable to do so. The problem with this kind of circular argument is that it relies entirely on the truth of its conclusion for its premise and so establishes neither. In this regard it is Foundationalist. However, it is at least some kind argument; for it sets out an ordered account of the relationships between a number of ideas or propositions, showing how they depend on each other. In this regard it is Coherentist.

A Rationalist might attempt to establish their position more soundly by trying to prove that the converse position is absurd and then relying on the rule of Classical Inference that the negation of an absurd proposition is necessarily true. Their argument might go something like this: "If I doubt the validity of reason, and attempt to take a neutral position, I immediately find that I cannot sensibly even be a Skeptic. This is because Skepticism itself uses reason to express itself. A Skeptic who simply says: 'I don't believe that I can know anything,' won't thereby convince anyone else to adopt this same view. The bold assertion of Skepticism doesn't provide a listener with any motive for paying it any attention. It is simply no argument."

"Unless reasons are given why a position ought to be adopted, that position has no credibility. Without adequate reason, there can be no motive to either believe or else disbelieve any proposition. One might 'just believe' with no reason; but why would one ever do so? Such a belief cannot be taken seriously by anyone – not even the believer themselves. Moreover, without reason a belief cannot have any application, but must remain simply a set of inchoate sounds or symbols. Without reason, how can a belief be connected with or applied to the real world? How can the believer recognise when the conditions for some action to be taken are fulfilled, if the very idea of 'truth-value' is not available to them?"

"Furthermore, every person who wants to take their life seriously, has no choice but to depend on some form of reasoning to support and implement their beliefs. No belief system of any kind can exist without relying on some kind of logic. Indeed it is logic which always systematises belief. Finally, reason is a prerequisite if we are ever to cooperate with each other, or have any kind of meaningful interaction. What else do we have absolutely in common other than reason? Whenever two people disagree, they have two choices: violent conflict or peaceful and reasonable dialogue. The supposed problem of circularity is not a problem if there is no alternative to rationality."[6]

Existentialism

The second approach to rationality amounts to the idea that "being reasonable" is the personal construct of each individual. Hence, each person claims to be reasonable; but is reasonable in their own unique way: a way that is their own business and is not subject to scrutiny or critique by any other individual. This approach is typical of an existentialist[7] philosophy.

> What is rational for one person may be considered irrational by another, hence the importance of subjectivity. I can provide my account and then you can claim that it is not rational and then a person may read our debate and think that my account is rational. So in your mind your contention is still true, while in another's it is false. Therefore you should never claim that all rational people should reach your conclusion, because rationality is completely subjective. It is irrational for you to claim that anyone who does not share your view is irrational

6 These paragraphs summarise an argument due to A. Feldman.
7 As pioneered by S. Kierkegaard, F. Nietzsche and later developed by M. Heidegger, A. Camus and J.P. Satre.

while believing that you are rational. This is the problem when people believe in objectivity; once you are convinced that things are definitely one way, then everyone else in your mind is wrong, which is arrogant unless you can completely demonstrate why your position is indeed correct.
[A. Narvaez #1 (Aug. 2008)]

An objective standard for morals and values does not exist; they are subjective and generally relative to culture. The same thing goes for what we view as rational; an objective standard for being rational does not exist. The way we interpret what is right or wrong, funny or stupid, just or unjust, is all dependent on the subjectivity that we cannot tear ourselves away from.
[A. Narvaez #2 (Oct. 2008)]

Devout Skepticism

The third approach to rationality is my own; though I do not claim to have originated it. It is intermediate between Rationalism and Existentialism. It takes from the first approach the idea that rationality is not a subjective construct, but instead has a definite and non-negotiable constitution. It takes from the second approach the idea that each individual has to discover for themselves (that is, to learn from the experiences of their own existence) what logic and rationality are, how to be reasonable and why they should be so. I like to describe this position as Devout Skepticism.

Does belief in objective reality necessitate conflict?

If one believes in objective reality and that one has a half-decent account of it, then one has to believe that any other seemingly contradictory narrative is liable to be mistaken. This may seem like a basis for contention rather than pacific dialogue;[8] and I think that what motivates many Existentialists in their choice of epistemology is a heart-felt desire to avoid such conflict. However, if one doesn't believe in objective reality and the possibility of a proposition being either true or false, then what is the point of having a discussion about any idea or notion?

Belief in objective reality should not give rise to acrimony. Being absolutely convinced that things are definitely the way that one believes them to be is a barrier to learning; but this attitude is characteristic of the

8 Especially in the realm of morality, discussion of which is largely postponed to Chapter 7.

bigot, not of the Objective Realist as such. An Objective Realist should always remain open to the possibility that their account of reality is less adequate than they suppose it to be,[9] as also to the idea that a number of narratives which seem to contradict each other might somehow be synthesised into an even better account of reality. The beginning of wisdom is the recognition of one's own ignorance.[10]

The marks of rationality

A rational person detests absurdity above all else. They embrace challenge and criticism; for it helps them to clarify their thoughts and to identify and correct any errors they have made. They can calmly entertain the possibility that they might be mistaken. They welcome the opportunity to test their ideas against experience and experiment. They take into account all relevant information. Rationality is, therefore, the idea that what one does and says and thinks ought to be characterized by the following "Marks of Rationality".

First, it should be coherent or internally self-consistent according to the rules of Classical Inference; as far as these can be applied or coherently extended.

Second, it should be subject to continual re-evaluation and challenge, both from oneself and from other competent and serious persons. When an idea, model or theory fails, it should be rejected and replaced by some other one which seems more liable to serve. This approach was championed by Plato as the dialectical method.

Third, it should be subject to empirical testing, in as far as this is possible. Ideas should not only be coherent, but also have some connexion with real-life (experiential) and laboratory (experimental) facts. Some theories make immediately testable predictions, these are "scientific" theories. Other theories are more "metaphysical" and only relate to reality by providing the context in which other theories can be tested. An example of the latter kind of theory is the proposition "all events and things have causes and require explanation."

An Inductive Empiricist will hold that experimental evidence can establish (at least in a probabilistic sense) the truth of properly posed theories. A Deductive Empiricist will deny this and claim, along with Popper, that the paramount purpose of experimentation is to weed-out the chaff; much in the way that Plato has Socrates describe his role in exposing error as a philosophical midwife.

---

9 Plato "Phaedo" (90b-91c) see the dedication of this book, page 3.

10 There is no record that Socrates ever said this, to the best of my knowledge; but it is typical of his thought.

> The most important thing about my art is the ability to apply all possible tests to the offspring, to determine whether the young mind is being delivered of a phantom, that is, an error, or a fertile truth… when I examine what you say, I may perhaps think that it is a phantom and not truth, and proceed to take it quietly from you and abandon it. Now if this happens, you mustn't get savage with me… because it is not permitted to me to accept a lie and put away truth.
> [Plato "Theaetetus" (150c-151c)]

Both Rationalism and Devout Skepticism agree as to what reason is; namely the application of Classical Inference to a situation. In order to deal with practicalities this is either augmented by the addition of an inductive principle or else tempered by a Popperian acceptance of the provisional nature of empirical truth. Rationalism involves the notion that the option to be rational is inevitable and that any other possibility is absurd. Devout Skepticism, while accepting that this option is the correct one, denies that it is obviously so; saying rather that: first, it is a matter of faith and, second, it is corroborated by experience and therefore is itself empirical and provisional.

Existentialist Rationality

Many Existentialists in practice also base their rationality on Classical Inference; but they claim to do so as a matter of subjective free choice and feel no need to justify this choice. Indeed, from their point of view this choice is unjustifiable; because before the choice has been made to be rational, how could anything be justified?

It seems to me that the Existentialist has to answer the following questions. First: "Is rationality anything more than an arbitrary convention or political consensus as to what is acceptable, which itself is only understood in terms of deviations from the average?" Second: "What makes superstition irrational, if rationality is completely subjective?" Third: "The lunatic will claim to be rational. His incoherent account of reality will seem reasonable enough to him. Is he therefore justified in claiming to be rational? Are we justified in claiming that the paranoid schizophrenic is not rational?" In practice, the Existentialist is unable to respond to these inquiries without borrowing ideas from Rationalism. So, for example:

> When I think of "rational", I think of something that I can take and put into "deduction form", since a deduction with a valid form and valid premises will always provide a sound or rational argument. [A. Narvaez #3 (Sept. 2008)]

Moreover, my existentialist correspondent conceded this point for a while, saying of my three marks of rationality:

> I cannot see how somebody could deny any of these. On that note, I agree with you that it is just our application of rationality that is subjective. Rationality itself, should not be open for interpretation in the same way as triangularity should not be. [A. Narvaez #4 (Sept. 2008)]

However, this concession did not last. Subsequently, he wrote:

> It is very clear that our application of rationality and justice is relative, as you have admitted; but it is also very clear that people have vastly different ideas of exactly what it means to be rational… For a moment, I agreed with you that rationality should not be open for interpretation, but I do not agree with that any more. This is clearly a change in my position. Rationality and justice are [themselves] open for interpretation, along with their application. [A. Narvaez #5 (Oct. 2008)]

> I cannot explain why my idea of rationality should be a certain way, for I could easily conceive of a different way of constructing it... My idea of rationality is self-consistent because it only claims that I will not believe anything to be true unless I find reasons to do so; it guards against contradictions... Since I do not believe my idea of rational to be true or false, but only useful, I do not have to worry about the formation of my idea of rational to be subject to its own claim.
> [A. Narvaez #6 (Jan. 2009)]

> Our conceptions do not need to be based on objectivity in order to be necessary and clearly useful for society. People need to collectively agree… on things in order to function together... If we all have different ideas of what justice or truth is, then of course we are going to come across problems. All we can really do is explain to each other what our personal views are, and hopefully an agreement or compromise can be made so that we can function together. [A. Narvaez #7 (Feb. 2009)]

Different people certainly vary in their understandings of rationality, and therefore apply it in different ways; in particular when evaluating evidence and deciding what conclusions to draw from it. Moreover, I concede that it is inevitable that ones notion of what it is to be rational is personal and subject to change. This is inevitable, as there is always liable to be a difference between the objective *actuality* of any thing – rationality being no exception – and an individual's subjective *notion* of that thing. However, to admit this is quite different from asserting that the thing itself has no definite reality beyond an individual's idea of it; which then becomes a whim, desire or arbitrary choice.

I approve of the idea that *usefulness*[11] is a criterion which can usefully be invoked; but I don't think that *useful* is synonymous with *consensual*.[12] The fact that a group of people agree to perform a ritual dance in order to obtain rain in a drought doesn't make it useful for them to do so; leastwise not useful for the use they intended it to be useful for. Things are useful they advance a worthwhile purpose, and they can usually only do so if they relate to a reality beyond the subject.

> When it is a question of what things are good, we no longer find anyone so heroic that he will venture to contend that whatever a community thinks useful, and conventionally establishes as such, really is useful (just so long as it is the established order) unless, of course, he means that it is simply called "useful"; but that would be making a game of our argument, wouldn't it?
> [Plato "Theaetetus" (177d)]

I then pointed out to my correspondent that no-one who believes that rationality is subjective (and hence fundamentally arbitrary) can be trusted to adhere faithfully to its principles. They will always feel free to deviate from them as soon as the argument stops going their way. Hence, even though he had claimed to be committed to rationality, his view of rationality as being fundamentally subjective meant that this commitment had no content. It amounts to no more than: "I am committed to whatever I chose to be committed to, and this commitment means whatever I chose it to mean." He replied to this as follows:

> This is a good point, but I am well aware of it… There is a possibility that I can decide not to be consistent with my views of rationality or even to change them and "deviate from them as soon as the argument stops going" my way, but I can do the very same thing even if I believe that rationality is objective… However, do you honestly think that just because I think rationality is subjective that I am going to go against what I think it is and not accept its conclusions?
> [A. Narvaez #8 (Oct. 2008)]

11 As introduced in quotes #6 and #7 on page 35.

12 As implied in quote #7, on page 35.

This is a clever debating stance, for two reasons. First, it deflects attention from matters of truth to the question of personal integrity. Second, it ensures that however it is attacked there is a plausible defence at hand. To the charge of unreliability, he replied:

> I hope you are not claiming that my *commitment* to being rational (not accepting beliefs without proper reasons[13] to do so) will be abandoned if that leads me to an "inconvenient truth". Of course, I cannot even imagine that my *commitment* to my rationality could ever lead me to inconvenient truth.
> [A. Narvaez #9 (Dec. 2008)]

To the charge that his reliability can only be justified on the basis of an objective standard,[14] the Existentialist can justly reply that even those who claim to believe in objective standards can deviate from them when they don't like where the argument takes them. Hence a profession of Rationalism does not make the professor constitutionally reliable.

A redirection from external truth to interior sincerity is typical of Existentialism. Sorrowfully rejecting belief in objectivity as untenable, or even harmful (as leading to conceit and intolerance of diversity) the existentialist attempts to irrigate the aridity of Subjective Relativism with "personal integrity".

> My opinion of what being rational amounts to is my commitment to "not accepting beliefs without first seeing what I believe to be *valid* reasons[15] for doing so." Just because I believe my position is subjective, does not mean that I cannot be committed to it... I can disbelieve in objectivity while being committed to what I perceive to be a rational attitude.
> [A. Narvaez #10 (Dec. 2008)]

The Existentialist does this with the most admirable of intentions. He wants first to be honest and second to be humble; not claiming to know more than he is certain of. He can see that an uncompromising

---

13 It is difficult to understand how "proper reasons" might differ from improper ones if there is no objective standard for rationality.

14 To write of a thing "what I think it is" carries the implication that it has a given nature which I am trying to grasp. If it has no such objective character, I ought to write "what I make or wish it to be", not "what I think it is".

15 Now my correspondent has inserted "believe to be" and changed "proper" to "valid". In doing so he has removed any reference to objectivity and put all the emphasis on personal commitment.

reliance on "pure reason" avails to nothing, so he makes what can only be understood as a step of faith; committing himself (without any rationale other than an implicit desire for meaning) to that very form of rationality which belief in objective reality necessarily engenders.

> I think it is rational (of sound mind) to apply our subjective views to the *world*,[16] because otherwise we are left with nothing[17]... We can be curious about the *world*[16] and ask questions without asserting that there is absolute truth... Can we not ponder about human life without asserting that everything we believe must or must not correspond to... [something] which exists outside of us?[16] [A. Narvaez #11 (Dec. 2008)]

However, the Existentialist does not acknowledge that this conviction is any kind of faith; insisting rather that all faith is irrational and to be avoided at any cost. Yet Existentialism is itself based on a personal commitment to something which it supposes to be not at all knowable, even if it exists – namely rationality. How does this differ from an exercise of blind faith? Existentialism does not allow for the possibility that there is a kind of faith which is reasonable; yet how is it right to reject all faith as unreasonable before one has established a basis for rationality which is independent of faith?

My correspondent then argues that Objective Realists are no better off, even in their own terms:

> If you hold the view that something can only be rationally accounted for if it corresponds to something which exists objectively, then you have no way to know if you are rational since you have no way of knowing if Objective Realism is a reflection of reality. [A. Narvaez #12 (Dec. 2008)]

However, he fails to notice that without an objective standard the very idea of "personal integrity" itself has no content. When the position he is intent on adopting is pursued to the point where it is claimed that rationality itself is subjective, then "personal integrity" cannot be understood (by anyone else) to mean even as little as merely "being self-

---

16 One might ask what "the world... which exists outside of us" is (and how one might be curious about it) if our opinions are all that there is and these do not relate to any objective reality.

17 I agree with this conclusion and believe that it serves as a good reason to accept that rationality is objective: that is, not subject to personal specification. From an Existentialist perspective, it would seem that it wouldn't matter if one was "left with nothing".

consistent". This is because what "is self-consistent" has itself become subjective and arbitrary, so that anyone can maintain that anything is "self-consistent for them", no matter how absurd it is according to the standards of Classical Inference.

> If whatever the individual judges by means of perception is true for him; if no man can assess another's experience better than he, or can claim authority to examine another man's judgement and see if it be right or wrong; if, as we have repeatedly said, only the individual himself can judge of his own world, and what he judges is always true and correct: how could it ever be, my friend, that Protagoras was a wise man...?
>
> To examine and try to refute each other's appearances and judgements, when each person's are correct – this is surely an extremely tiresome piece of nonsense, if the Truth of Protagoras is true, and not merely an oracle speaking in jest.
> [Plato "Theaetetus" (161d-162a)]

On the one hand my Existentialist correspondent maintains his conviction that rationality is subjective, while on the other hand professing his absolute commitment to the same standard of rationality which I uphold. He claims to have thoughts about what rationality actually is[18] (rather than simply his personal specification of rationality) at the same time as denying that rationality is anything other than whatever he specifies it to be.[19] This is incoherent.

My Existentialist friend seems to concede that there *could* in principle be such a thing as an objective basis for rationality; but believes that no-one has any way of coming to know what this is, and so that this possibility is irrelevant. Moreover, he gives no account of how it comes to be the case that his (supposedly whimsical) concept of Rationality is so very similar to the one that an Objective Realist would argue is required by a belief in objective reality.[20]

> Rationality, I own, comes down to opinions of what is rational or not (whether or not an objective reality exists) because we are only aware of our opinions. [A. Narvaez #13 (Dec. 2008)]

---

18 See quote #3 on page 34.

19 See quotes #5 and #6 on page 35.

20 See page 44.

His criterion for determining whether some idea is admissible or not is "validity". When pressed, he explains this in the following way:

> You asked me, "Where do you obtain your criterion of validity from?" As you suspected, I was not referring to truth; I was referring to legitimate or lawful. That which is legitimate or lawful passes the tests of logic, which means that they do not present contradictions and correctly follow from deductive syllogisms... I use words like acceptance and valid, rather than truth and real, because the latter requires a correspondence with something which exists outside of human conception... So when I say a person's conception of justice is acceptable or valid, I mean that their idea of it is not violating any logical rules and is, therefore, non-contradictory and consistent.
> [A. Narvaez #14 (Feb. 2008)]

This coherence criterion cannot be used to reject beliefs that are self-consistent, such as Solipsism or the simplistic and inhumane creed of some religious cult or totalitarian political party.

Existentialism is incoherent

While professing a commitment to rationality, Existentialism makes "rationality" into an arbitrary specification or personal whim, which can only correspond by happenstance to the stipulations of Classical Inference and its extensions. How then can this "rationality" be said to be rational in any definite sense?

While admitting that analysis alone is insufficient to do justice to the entirety of human experience, Existentialism insists that any complementary system must be fully justified as analytically true; even if that system explicitly involves the notion that many important truths cannot be proven. This is unreasonable. What reason does the Existentialist have for believing that anything (let alone everything) can be proved or even that "to prove" has any significance beyond "to persuade"?

The Existentialist's commitment to rationality is motivated by the judgement that if it is not made then no progress can be made.[21] Why is this argument from utility or necessity not admitted as significant evidence for the objectivity of rationality?

21 See quote #11 on page 38.

Existentialism refers to the world and allows that certain ideas are useful while others are not.[22] However, it refuses to concede that the world is more than the subjective experience of the individual. In the absence of an objective standard for rationality how does a con-artist differ from a logician?

Existentialism refuses to offer any solid proof of itself, even in its own terms. The best it does is to proceed from the unwarranted supposition that "no alternate system based on objective reality could ever be proved to be true", to the conclusion that "therefore Existentialism is justified." How, then, is Existentialism not guilty of applying double standards and of demanding more of other systems than it requires of itself?

The Existentialist asserts that "all ideas and notions are subjective and cannot be said to be true or false, but only accounted as valid or acceptable."[23] Now, to be self-consistent, this judgement must be applied rigorously to the idea of Existentialism itself; with the immediate conclusion that the assertion: "All ideas and notions are subjective and cannot be said to be true or false, but only accounted as valid or acceptable," has no truth-value[24] and can itself be no more than useful, at best. In which case this proposition has no logical force behind it, but only political force, and one is not rationally obligated to adopt it.

For Existentialism to be justified in its own terms it would actually have to be *found* to be useful and not just stated to be so by its proponents. Now, usefulness might arise in one of two ways. First, Existentialism might be useful in completing some larger self-consistent philosophical scheme, or at least in motivating its development. Second, it might be useful in solving some social, scientific, engineering or otherwise practical problem; or at least in identifying some problem which is in need of solution.

Now, on the first count, the Existentialist makes no claim that their belief contributes to the coherence of any larger mental project which without Existentialism is somehow incomplete. Moreover, on the second count, were they to propose some practical or even political justification of their conjecture this very attempt at empirical validation would contradict their basic premise; namely, that there is no objective reality against which an idea can be tried. How, then, can Existentialism even be said to be useful?

---

22 See quotes #5 and #6 on page 35 and quote #11 on page 38.
23 See quote #14 on page 40.
24 See quote #6 on page 35.

Rationalist rationality[25]

Most Rationalists believe strongly in Classical Inference. They claim, however, that this is not a question of faith, conviction or experience; but that it is self-evident. Typically, they argue that it is demonstrably certain that rationality is valid; because Classical Inference is an internally consistent set of rules which is indispensable if coherent thought or any kind of discourse or communication is to be undertaken and because it is hugely successful in its application.

A Rationalist would say that reason has coercive power over them and that they have no choice about what it is or what it demands of them. One of these demands is that a proposition should be accepted as provisionally true if it has sufficient supporting evidence to make this reasonable. Another is that such a proposition should be set aside as soon as it is disproved. The Rationalist would further say that those propositions which appear to be highly dubious but which can nevertheless not be absolutely disproved, ought not to be entertained; on the basis that they tend to conflict with the body of background knowledge which has already been accumulated. To accept such a proposition as true would potentially entail calling into question the entire edifice of established knowledge and reasoning.[26] Of course, to be justified in taking this attitude, one has to be reasonably satisfied that one's present body of background knowledge is itself sound.

I agree with the Rationalist that reason has coercive power; is our most important and fundamental tool in communicating and cooperating with others; and that without it we would have no connection to the objective world. However, I do not agree that there is *conclusive* evidence for the reliability of reason – or for its validity or applicability. I disagree with the Rationalist on this point first, because their argument is circular and second, because there is an alternate coherent position.

Is reason merely a whim?

This alternate position is the assertion that reason is a figment of the imagination and so a whim. This position cannot be disproved; because it excludes the possibility of proof or disproof, in principle. Moreover, it doesn't even require to be shown to be useful. It stands starkly by itself and is entirely self-adequate.

---

25 These paragraphs are a summary of the Rationalist position as presented to me by A. Feldman.

26 Such a revolution is called a Paradigm Shift. [T. Kuhn "The Structure of Scientific Revolutions" (1962)]

If the only reality is oneself and one's own imaginings, then there is no reason to fear any external threat,[27] for there is nothing other then oneself to fear. In this case, survival is certain and both pain and prosperity no more than phantasms. Hence there is no need for anything to be useful, for the very idea of utility has no content. Further, there is no reason to attempt to conform one's thoughts to any thing or standard other then oneself, because there is nothing other then oneself for one to conform to.

Finally, there is no reason why one's thoughts ought to be consistent with each other; for they have no purpose other than to be themselves. The thoughts of the Subjective Relativist are free to be as whimsical or paranoid as the rantings of a lunatic or the expostulations of a surrealist poet, and may explore and extol contradiction and absurdity (if indeed these can be recognised as differing from concord and congruity) without let or limit.

It simply has to be admitted that the composite choice to be an irrational Subjective Relativist is an option which cannot in its own terms be shown to be wrong. Hence the alternate composite choice (to be a rational Objective Realist) can never be established as the only one open to a person;[28] but only that it be the only one open to a *rational* person – such a person having, however, already made the faith-choice in favour of rationality.

Devout skepticism

Although Rationalism and Existentialism are oppositional, they have a lot in common. Both involve commitments to rationality; but whereas the Existentialist founds their commitment on their personal integrity, the Rationalist prefers a circular coherence argument. Both are antipathetic to what they perceive as faith and involve a commitment not to accept any belief until acceptable or valid reasons for doing so have been provided. Both appeal to the coherence criterion as a necessary condition for the validity of any idea; but both also admit that this is insufficient to address facts of practical reality.

In order to augment the coherence criterion, the Existentialist appeals to his own subjective judgement or will as a criterion of what is valid, invoking the ideas of usefulness or consensus – which ideas he tends to blur together. The Rationalist rejects this proposal; pointing out

27 There is still, of course, the internal threat of psychological disintegration and insanity; but one would have to question whether there could be any difference between sanity and insanity in the absence of an objective reality.

28 The option of being a rational Subjective Relativist has been shown to be at best implausible, see page 40.

that usefulness is not synonymous with truth, and that many ideas are useful, expedient or politically correct in a restricted context while being based on entirely false (and even execrable) world-views.

The Rationalist therefore chooses to supplement the coherence criterion with a test of compatibility with whatever body of knowledge has already been established as trustworthy. They cannot, however, explain how this body of background knowledge was itself established as trustworthy and admit that it might have to be rejected – or at least substantially modified.[29]

As a Skeptic, it seems to me that neither the Rationalist nor the Existentialist have managed to establish their epistemology in a way that is consistent with their own criteria. Moreover, it strikes me on a more fundamental level that there can be no way of proving that rationality is trustworthy without either assuming (without reason – because before this assumption is made there can be no sound reasons for anything) that it is so; or else choosing to believe in objective reality.

Adopting the second option, as being less viciously circular, it seems to me that all one can say for sure is: "If one chooses to believe in an objective reality about which it is worth trying to learn (so as to come up with useful ideas which will enable one to better survive and prosper) and so of which it is worth talking with others; then one has no choice but to be rational."

Belief in objective reality automatically gives a basis for rationality. This is because factual things are real – that is, they exist "out there" independently of myself;[30] whereas fictional suppositions are not real, but only imaginary; that is, they do not exist apart from myself. It is from this duality of possibility (existence and non-existence) that truth and falsehood arises. Similarly, it is from the fact that existence absolutely precludes non-existence (and vice-versa) that the idea of "self-consistency" arises. These two ideas (truth and self-consistency) are constitutional of what rationality is. Hence, the notion of reason flows directly, immediately and inevitably from that of objective reality.

However, the choice to believe in objective reality is itself an act of faith, and is not demanded of one on any grounds other than that it is "reasonable" or "promises to be useful". It is because I am willing to make this step of faith – and explicitly admit to making it – that I call myself a Devout Skeptic.

---

29 K.R Popper "Objective Knowledge." (1972, 1979).

30 I shall later argue that God is not a "factual thing" and "does not exist" but is nevertheless real, see Chapter 14.

Coherence, utility and faith

I agree with the Rationalist that rationality is more about checking that a principle of thought or system of belief is coherent, rather than about proving that it is necessarily true. I also agree with them that this is the main criterion which rationality itself should fulfil. However, I do not agree that once this is done one should rest content in circularity; claiming that one's circle is somehow large enough and therefore not vicious. Moreover, I agree with the Existentialist that usefulness (but not consensus) is the key issue here. While agreeing with the Rationalist that usefulness cannot possibly supply necessary truth, I would point out that it can readily supply usefulness – and that the primary motivation which underlies and accounts for man's pursuit of knowledge is the "search for some truth he can use."[31]

Once, then, one has shown that a system, proposition or concept is internally coherent one ought to move on to consider its usefulness. This amounts first, to its scientific utility: that is its predictive or explanatory power and empirical falsifiability; and second, to its metaphysical utility or fruitfulness: that is the degree to which it motivates, suggests or provides for further possibilities.[32] Choosing one set of beliefs over another, because the former helps you to understand or engage with the world in a productive way which the latter excludes is definitely sensible; if, that is, one is trying to do anything useful.

This is a crucial criterion when considering certain premises of a religious or ethical character which can only be evaluated in terms of what they motivate, allow for and facilitate. Solipsism is irrefutable, but gives one no indication of how to progress in understanding one's experience; hence it should be rejected in favour of Objective Realism, which does offer a way forward. Similarly, Nihilism is an arguable position; but as it necessitates the idea that life and thought (including this thought) are futile and valueless it ought to be rejected in favour of an outlook which acknowledges the existence of value and so allows life and thought to be purposeful.[33] When one is presented with a choice between one premise which allows for and facilitates life and another which implies death, one should prefer the former; for if one does not, one is not able to make any more choices.[34]

---

31 Emerson, Lake & Palmer "Hallowed be thy Name" (1977)

32 Misapplying the criterion proposed by Jesus of Nazareth: "You will know them by their fruits." [Mat 7:16 RSV]

33 This is a version of "Pascal's Wager." See page 264.

34 Deut 30:19-20, quoted on page 119.

As a man of faith, it seems to me that belief in objective reality is not rational in the sense of being deducible from other premises which are more foundational. After all, what could these premises possibly be? This belief is, however, rational in the sense that without it rationality is itself rendered irrational.

Sadly, as there can be no reason to believe that things should be reasonable if rationality is itself invalid, the mere demonstration that Subjective Relativism is incompatible with Rationality does not prove that Subjective Relativism is wrong or even "invalid". This is because, as we have previously noted,[35] there is a ghastly alternative; which is to say, in effect: "Nothing is right or wrong and no thought can possibly signify anything other than an arbitrary and non-negotiable desire or appetite, which is to be socially and politically managed on some basis (such as that of democracy or dictatorship) if conflict is to be avoided."

I am not sure that my belief in objective reality is correct, in the sense of having analytically proved that it is so. I am not even sure that there is no means to establish a basis for rationality other than a belief in objective reality. I cannot myself conceive of any other way, however; and so I have no choice but to believe in objective reality, since I very much wish to hold to rationality as the basis of all I do. I have no problem with this belief, as it seems to me to be by far the simplest and most straight-forward hypothesis to adopt.

A note on Empiricism

It is worth considering to what extent and in what manner our senses are valid and reliable sources of information.

> It seems to me that our senses are in fact what allows us to confirm a rational reality. Without them we would have no reason to think of such a thing. If I try to imagine being without senses, it seems to me that I would then not be able to know of anything and so it would be rational for me to say that there was no outside reality. Moreover, if a person was mentally ill and constantly living in a "dream world", it seems to me that this would be their "actual reality". In our reality we are able to examine such people and notice deformities in their brains, and we are led to conclude that we are aware of the "real reality" and they are not. Even so, it must still be admitted that it is proper and sensible for that ill person to believe that their reality is real.

35 See page 42.

> Now, what are the consequences of this position, for the theory that our reality is limited to our senses and derivatives of them? It implies that we do not have to think that there is in fact an "objective reality" in order to take note of the fact that the "reality" which almost every person perceives behaves in consistent and coherent ways. It is not necessary to believe in an "objective reality" in order to think that our reality has certain rules and to know that within the reality which we perceive there can be a thing called "truth". In other words, in as far as our senses tell us that there is an outside world, we cannot but comply. [J. Kramer "Private Communication" (2012)]

I agree with the first paragraph of this quotation, except that I think we have reasons in addition to anatomical ones for concluding that certain individuals have defective world-views. Mentally ill people often hold opinions which conflict with each other and also with whatever empirical evidence that is presented to them. They are always more willing to invoke conspiracies to explain away evidence which conflicts with their theories than to accept it as refuting them. Of course, the dividing line between delusional belief and reasonable faith is a fine one. In the end, I think one has to fall back on the "utility criterion" and judge all attitudes and beliefs in terms of their helpfulness.

I also agree with the last paragraph of the quotation, but think that it misses the point. It is true that one can recognise and acknowledge a commonality of experience without hypothesising an objective reality as an explanation of this commonality. However, this begs two questions. First why is it that there is so much commonality of experience? In particular, why is it that the same laws of Physics describe every personal reality, and even the personal realities of those very many persons who have no understanding whatsoever of these laws? Second, what is the meaning of "truth"?

It seems to me that the simplest explanation for the commonality of subjective experience – most obviously manifested in the fact that we regularly talk to each other about things and tend to understand what we mean – is that there is in fact a single reality "out there", apart from and beyond and underlying all personal subjective experience and that it is this single objective reality that is the explanation for all that is experientially common and shared. All science is based on this hypothesis and every success of science and engineering corroborates it – though never proving that it is absolutely true.

It seems to me that without the notion of "objective reality", one can have no notion of correspondence truth; but only coherence truth. Philosophically, this is not problematic; but psychologically it is deeply problematic. It is not enough to acknowledge that everything that a person has done and said is consistent with the proposition that they love you; what really matters is that in fact they actually do love you – even if they sometimes behave in ways which seem to be (or in fact are) inconsistent with this fact. One can tolerate a level of human weakness and fallibility when it comes to being loved, one cannot tolerate any level of hypocrisy. Without depth, appearances are devoid of meaning. Without being, they are devoid of value.

A Note on Logical Positivism[36]

Logical Positivism amounts to the apparently sensible position that no meaning, validity, significance or importance should be attached to any statement that does not correspond directly to actual events or things which can be observed and measured. The goal of its proponents, generally known as the Vienna Circle[37] was to characterize Metaphysics (which primarily concerns itself with those supposed aspects of reality which are unobservable and immeasurable) as nonsensical: devoid of any possible meaning.

This sounds very scientific, and was an epistemology favoured by the pioneers of Quantum Theory – especially Neils Bohr and the Copenhagen School. It subsequently become popular in psychology (where it is called "behaviourism") and from thence entered education and management theory. Logical Positivism, however, is trivially incoherent; for it is itself a metaphysical position and its statement does not correspond – even indirectly – to any actual events or things which could be observed and measured. Hence, according to its own validity criterion, Logical Positivism is irrational and nonsensical – devoid of any possible meaning.

The futility of the Vienna Circle's programme should have became clear when Gödel published his incompleteness theorems in 1931.[5] However, those who are less philosophically or mathematically oriented typically not only fail to grasp the basic decrepitude of the Logical Positivist position but also often fail to recognise even that they have themselves adopted it. Hence it remains deeply embedded in popular thought and academic psychology.

36 J. Powers "Philosophy and the New Physics" (1982)

37 Foremost of whom were Richard Carnap and Ludwig Wittgenstein. David Hilbert's programme to reduce all Mathematics to arithmetic was a parallel and linked endeavour.

Chapter 3 Order and Existence

> In the beginning was the Logos, and the Logos was with God, and what God was the Logos was. The same was the origin, together with God, of the becoming of things. Nothing came to be without Him. The Logos enlightens mankind and is the basis of life itself. [Jn 1:1-4, my own rendering]

Order, chaos and spontaneity

Later on I will have cause to call upon the ideas of Beauty and Justice. In this chapter I prepare the ground by discussing what they are. I shall contend that they are both forms of harmony or orderliness. Hence the first topic of this chapter is the nature of order. In general, what it means for a thing to be ordered is that it is understandable. In other words, that it is possible to give a rational account of it (instructions for how it could be made, perhaps; or an explanatory history of how it came to be what it is) using much less data than the whole thing itself represents.

Random numbers don't obey or arise from any kind of formula or algorithm. If they did (and if the formula or algorithm was known) the next number could be predicted, and so it wouldn't be random. This means that it is impossible to give any rational account of a set of truly random and spontaneous numbers and it is impossible to have any understanding of them. The conventional view of Quantum Mechanics is that all fundamental events are absolutely random in this sense.

> You say that for something to be random means that it is not possible to give a rational account of it. Now, I may be misunderstanding you, but I don't think this sort of thing exists. I am under the belief that every single event happens for a directly physical reason, and thus is rational. You said that in Quantum Mechanics it is conventionally thought that random events occur. Does this mean that they do not happen because of precise physical causes, and if so, what is the evidence for this? I wouldn't consider an event random simply because it would take many, perhaps thousands, of formulas to determine its causes or effects. For even a great number of formulae would still be much less information than the total possible set of information. [J. Kramer "Private Communication" (2012)]

I concede that it is very difficult, if not impossible, to understand how a physical event can occur apart from "a directly physical reason"; but this is how Quantum Mechanics seems to work.[1] There are various accounts of the basic problem, which is called "the collapse of the wave-packet";[2] but they are all different ways of saying the same thing: that in as far as one accounts of the world in terms of particles (and it is particles that we regularly observe in experiments, so this seems to be the sensible outlook) there can never be a fully satisfactory explanation as to why any particle does what it does in fact do. There is no set of formulae which accounts for individual events; but only statistically significant populations of events. It is not that such set of formulae are unknown, or even unknowable, but that they simply do not exist at all. The very best that theory can hope to achieve is an accurate specification as to the frequencies with which various particular occurrences occur.

Quantum Mechanics can, in principle, predict how frequently a piece of blue cheese will spontaneously materialise out of the vacuum onto a plate provided to receive it. Quantum Mechanics may even be able to give some guidance as to how best to arrange the plate and its environment so as to minimise the mean waiting time between such spontaneous materialisations. However, Quantum Mechanics cannot predict when a piece of blue cheese will actually materialise.

Einstein understood this clearly, as did Bohr. They took opposite sides in the argument which ensued. Einstein held firmly to the belief that beneath the probabilistic formulation of Quantum Mechanics there must lie a properly causal account which is as yet hidden from us – and might even be hidden from us in principle, and so permanently. Einstein's belief came to be called "Locally Realistic Hidden Variable Theory". Bohr dismissed this idea, taking a Logical Positivist[3] stand and insisted that all there was to reality was what Quantum Mechanics allowed one to know.

Einstein, Podolsky and Rosen proposed an experiment which they thought could distinguish between Bohr's metaphysical world-view and Einstein's.[4] It didn't serve to determine what the *hidden variables* were or how they could make rational what appeared to be spontaneous; but only that these mysterious variables did in fact exist and did in fact have this effect, even though they were hidden from direct observation. A version of the experiment was conducted in 1982, long after Einstein's

---

1 P. Davies "The Matter Myth" (1992) p214-215
J. Powers "Philosophy and the New Physics" (1982) p130-138

2 K.R. Popper "Quantum Theory and the Schism in Physics" (1982) p121-125

3 See page 48.

4 P. Davies "The Matter Myth" (1992) p215-216
K.R. Popper "Quantum Theory and the Schism in Physics" (1982) p147-150

death. The data obtained very strongly supported the conclusion that Bohr was right and Einstein was wrong.[5]

Subsequently it has been suggested that this conclusion is flawed[6] as it rests on three questionable assumptions. The first is that causality only works forwards in time, so that later events do not constrain earlier events in the way that earlier events constrain later ones.[7] This is equivalent to the axiom that signals cannot travel faster than the speed of light. This idea is commonly accepted as foundational; but is not, in fact, necessitated by any principle more basic than itself.[8] Moreover, although it is in accordance with common sense, it has no solid foundation in any part of Physics apart from Quantum Mechanics itself; and there only in exactly that part of the theory which is problematic. The second tacit assumption is that the *hidden variables* commute with each other,[9] when there is no reason to expect them to do so – especially as the manifest variables of Quantum Mechanics often do not. The third assumption is to do with how averages are to be taken and amounts to the idea that the world is not deterministic and that the notion of "could have been the case" means something,[10] which is a contention that I very much doubt.

At present, therefore, the jury is still out on the question as to whether the basic constitution of the Cosmos – all the microscopic events which come together to make up the macroscopic events of everyday experience – is spontaneous, absolutely random and unaccountable or whether it is causal. What is absolutely clear, however is that these two alternatives can be proposed as distinct possibilities and that there is some hope of deciding between them on the basis of experimental evidence.

---

5 P. Davies "The Matter Myth" (1992) p217-218.

6 V.J. Stenger "The Unconscious Quantum" (1995) p145-155.

7 If this is false, Physics must become much more complicated; as it must explain how retro-temporal causality can be ubiquitous while never obvious. [H. Price "Time's Arrow and Archimedes' Point" (1997)]

8 J.G. Cramer "The transactional interpretation of quantum mechanics" Reviews of Modern Physics Vol 58, #3 pp.647-687 (1986)

9 When two things A and B commute, this means that the order in which they appear, happen or are executed does not matter. This can be represented symbolically as "$AB = BA$". A simple example of two things not commuting occurs when rotating a six-sided die. Rotating it first 90° clockwise about the vertical axis (let us designate this rotation "V") and then 90° clockwise about one of the two horizontal axes (let us designate this rotation "H_1") it finishes up in one orientation. Rotating it first 90° clockwise about the same horizontal axis and then 90° clockwise about the vertical axis it finishes up in a different orientation. Hence "$H_1V \neq V H_1$".

10 K. Brown "Reflections on Relativity" lib 9 cap 6.

Kinds of order

Some kinds of order, such as that of simple geometrical shapes is apparent, but others are not. The infinite sequence of numbers:

0, 1, 1, 2, 3, 5, 8, 13, 21, 34, 55, 89, 144, 233, 377, 610…

is called the "Fibonacci sequence". It is defined and generated by the following formula:

$$X_{(N+1)} = X_N + X_{(N-1)} \quad : \quad X_1 = 0 \quad : \quad X_2 = 1$$

This formula means that the first number in the sequence, X_1, is zero; that the second, X_2, is one and every subsequent number in the sequence is given by the sum of the previous two numbers "$X_{(N+1)} = X_N + X_{(N-1)}$". No matter how one looks at this, the formula itself represents much less data than the infinite sequence of numbers which it generates. Hence, the Fibonacci sequence is highly ordered.

The motion of the planets baffled astronomers for centuries. Until Copernicus conjectured that the Earth moves around the Sun, it was impossible to give a concise narrative of what was observed. Once the Earth's own movement was accepted, the obscure planetary movements became easier to understand and soon it was discovered that all planetary motion is governed by Newton's laws of gravity and mechanics.[11] Finally, it was discovered that all the tables of detailed observational records could be summarised in two simple equations:

$$F = m.a \qquad \text{and} \qquad F = (G.m.M) / R^2$$

Fractal order

The Mandelbrot set of complex numbers,[12] $\mathcal{M}$ is generated by the following formula:

$$X_{(N+1)} = X_N^{\,2} + X_0 \quad : \quad X_0 \in \mathcal{M} \text{ if } \mathrm{Lim}_{N\to\infty}\{X_N\} < \infty$$

11 In the case of Mercury, the Newtonian account proved inadequate.

12 Complex numbers involve the "square root of minus one". This is designated as "i" and is defined by the relationship "$i^2 = -1$". Any complex number, Z, is made up from an ordinary or "real" part, "P", and an "imaginary" part, "i.Q"; such that "$Z = P + i.Q$", where "P" and "Q" are themselves ordinary numbers. Examples of complex numbers are "$Z_1 = 3 + i.7$", where "$P = 3$" and "$Q = 7$" and "$Z_2 = i.\pi - \sqrt{2}$", where "$P = \sqrt{2}$" and "$Q = \pi$".

In other words, X_0 belongs to the Mandelbrot set, $\mathcal{M}$, if squaring it and adding X_0 to the result to obtain another number, X_1 which in turn one squares and augments by X_0, obtaining X_2 and so on… never results in a number which is infinite.

"$X_0 = 1$" gives the sequence: "1, 2, 5, 26, 677…", which gets remorselessly large. Hence, "1" is not an element of $\mathcal{M}$.

"$X_0 = -i$" gives the sequence: "$-i$, $(-1 + i)$, $-i$, $(-1 + i)$…", which repeats endlessly. Hence "$-i$" does belong to $\mathcal{M}$.

"$X_0 = 1/2$" gives the sequence: "1/2, 3/4, 17/16…". Hence, "1/2" is not an element of $\mathcal{M}$.

"$X_0 = -1/2$" gives the sequence: "–1/2, –1/4, –7/16, -79/256…", which tends to a limit of "$(1-\sqrt{3})/2$". Hence, "-1/2" is an element of $\mathcal{M}$.

The Mandelbrot set can be plotted out as a graph. Every complex number "P + *i*.Q" corresponds to a point on the graph, with its real part, P, constituting the x-coordinate of the point and its imaginary part, Q, constituting the y-coordinate of the point. Every complex number which belongs to the set can be indicated by a red dot and every one which does not belong to the set can be indicated by a blue dot. The complete Mandelbrot set would then be composed of all the red points taken together as a whole.

The Mandelbrot set is an example of a fractal shape. It is very complex in appearance when it is plotted out, and its boundary does not become smooth (or simplify in any way) when it is inspected at any level of magnification. Even on the closest and most careful inspection, the boundary of the Mandelbrot set will seem to be entirely unpredictable, and to specify it in any direct way would require an infinite amount of information. Nevertheless, we have seen that the constitution of the set can be summarised in a very simple formula. Hence it is highly ordered.

Fractal shapes are characterized by intricate complexity on every possible scale; so to a casual observer it is far from obvious that they have any order at all. No matter how carefully a fractal object is inspected, it never becomes overtly simple. Only when one knows how they arise (when one is in possession of the generating formula: the account as to how they come to be exactly what they are) can one recognise the underlying simplicity and order that is present. Very many physical and biological structures are fractal. At first sight they seem disordered and complex, but a deeper mathematical analysis reveals patterns, structure and a basic simplicity which are not immediately apparent.

Order, information and disorder

A system (such as a set of child's building bricks or a jigsaw puzzle) is said "to have no entropy" when its arrangement or configuration is unique; in other words, does not belong to a set of similar states. A system is said to be in a state of "high entropy" (or to be "disordered") when its configuration belongs to a set of many similar states; but the question then arises: "which states are to be counted as similar?"

Generally speaking, states count as similar when they have overall characteristics in common, such as their temperature,[13] pressure, chemical composition and volume in the case of gasses; or word-count, mean word-length, mean sentence length or vowel-frequency in the case of texts. The "bottom up" question as to which states should be counted as similar does not generally arise; as some high-level characteristic (such as the temperature of a gas or mean word-length of a text) will have already been shown to be important for some reason, and this will dictate those states which belong together in a "top-down" manner.

A correctly assembled jigsaw has no configurational entropy; whereas a jumbled set of jigsaw pieces contained within a large box has a lot of configurational entropy; as the relative position and orientation of each and every piece has to be specified, and there is an extremely large set of possible configurations of jumbled-up pieces to chose from.

In technical jargon, each specific, individual and particular jumble is termed a "micro-state". Every one of these is unique. A number of unique micro-states make up a set of similar states (this set is called a "macro-state") if they all share certain easily identifiable and measurable properties such that one can classify them all together. So, in the case of the jumbled jigsaw puzzle the total mass of the puzzle is the same however its pieces are arranged in the large box. In this sense any and all arrangements of the puzzle pieces are equivalent and every possible micro-state belongs to one all-encompassing macro-state.

Entropy is a property of a macro-state, not of a micro-state. Consider the puzzle pieces to be laid out higgledy-piggledy, but without overlap, on the flat surface of a tray, all turned face up. We are now selecting out a tiny sub-set of all the possible arrangements of the jigsaw pieces: those with the pieces arranged in a flat two-dimensional configuration, face up, with no overlapping edges. Every micro-state which conforms to our new prescription is a member of this new macro-state. This new macro-state has considerably less configurational entropy than the original macro-state defined by the capacious box, precisely because it is constituted from considerably fewer micro-states.

13 The most common form of entropy is heat-entropy, which is the disordered movement of molecules, atoms and sub-atomic particles.

If the area of the tray were to increase, the configurational entropy of the jigsaw pieces would increase, because the larger tray would allow for the pieces to be arranged in a greater variety of ways. If the area were to reduces, the configurational entropy of the jigsaw pieces would decrease, because the smaller tray would more strictly constrain the arrangement of the pieces. If the specification of the arrangement allowed some or all of the pieces to be placed face down, its configurational entropy would be much larger. If the specification of the arrangement of the pieces allowed their edges to overlap, the the configurational entropy of the jigsaw pieces would also be much larger.

Macro-states arise in our account of reality all the time because we are usually in no position to either fix or know of the exact arrangement of all those particles which make up any object or system. The best we can usually do is to specify some obvious constraint or notice some obvious large-scale property. In doing so we are identifying a macro-state not a micro-state. Thermodynamics is the study of how the large-scale properties of systems only "roughly specified" in terms of macro-states change with time.

Entropy and Information

Generally speaking, the more information a system contains the higher will be its entropy. A blank sheet of paper has a word count of zero and is unique when viewed as a text, with no literary entropy at all. Shakespeare published one hundred and fifty-four sonnets, so the fact that someone is in possession of a sealed envelope containing a sheet of paper with one of them printed on it makes their state one out of one hundred and fifty-four possibilities. Hence they have a significant literary entropy. If they open their envelope and discover which sonnet it contains, their literary entropy immediately decreases to zero.

This might seem to contradict the famous Second Law of Thermodynamics, which states that entropy always increases.[14] It does not do so because the act of opening the envelope means that the identity of the sonnet is now known to its possessor, and this fact will be reflected in the state of their brain, with an attendant increase in its informational entropy. This will exactly compensate for their loss of literary entropy. Moreover, the act of identifying the poem will be inefficient (involving the production of waste heat) and the decrease in their literary entropy will be very much less than the increase of their heat and informational entropy added together.

---

14 See page 78.

The more ordered a system is in terms of it containing significant information, the less ordered it is liable to be in terms of any reductionist analysis of its state. Indeed, it is possible to construe all disorder as information and to claim that the only difference between randomness and significance is the lack of a suitable code key, or other means of understanding. On this basis, the Second Law of Thermodynamics becomes easy to understand, for it says no more than that "as history progresses the amount of information increases"; but this is a truism, as more events will have occurred and so have to be accounted for.

It may be that at some time in the future a method of deciphering the positions and trajectories of the molecules in a bottle of gas at any moment will be found, such that the entire prior history of that bottle will be laid bare to the decrypter. If this does happen, then the randomness of such a bottle of gas will cease to be truly random, but be revealed as richly informative. I do not expect this ever to happen, however, as I believe that the effects of non-linearity[15] will make it impossible to ever play-back the changes that any real system has undergone in order to find its state at an earlier time with any reliability.

What is existence?

The basic idea of a field of Physics called Scattering Theory is that one can give a full account of a thing in terms of its response to all possible stimuli. Once one has done this, there is nothing else to know about that thing. Of course, compiling a list of all responses to all stimuli is in principle impossible; but for simple systems (the kind that mainly interest physicists) the most important stimuli can be identified and so a summary list of all the most important behaviour be compiled.

Now, unsurprisingly, it turns out that for a thing to have any identifiable response, it has to be different from its context or surroundings. In other words for it to have any properties at all it must "stand out from" its environment.[16] So, it is impossible to notice a particular flake in a drift of snow. Only when one looks very closely, with a magnifying glass perhaps, and sees the edges of the flake can one identify the flake. This line of thought tends to the view that a thing has existence only in as far as it differs from its context; and hence that the existence of any thing will always be an organisation of some sort or other. After all, how else could any thing exist, other than by being a patterning of being?

---

15 See footnotes on page 275.

16 "Existence" is often used as a synonym for "being"; but "to exist" originally meant "to stand out proud from", as a pattern embossed on a shield protrudes from the background metal.

For existence, intelligibility is necessary and this is not compatible with spontaneity, randomness or "absolute chaos". In Platonic thought the Logos (the fundamental account of and rationale for the Cosmos) is close to the root of being. In other words, intelligibility is at the basis of existence. The more ordered something is, the more there is to its existence. Physics only knows of energy which is organised in one way or another. One can say the words "random matter"; but as a physicist I can't give this phrase any significance. As soon as I start to think about "random matter" I necessarily start to make it "non-random"; constituting it from arrangements of electrons and quarks, each of which is a repetition of exactly the same pattern of fields and charges.

The hierarchy of existence

Now, a poem has more existence than a random collection of words. Both exist as a set of words, but the poem also exists as an intelligible message. If it is a good poem it also exists as a work of art. It is therefore beautiful. Its message is conveyed on more than one level of patterning and can only be fully appreciated in its proper context where all of its order is made clear.

Similarly, a living creature has more existence than the mere accumulation of all the chemicals of which it is constituted. First, its molecules are physically organised in a systematic manner. Second, the whole assemblage is in motion. It is characterized by a set of processes all interacting with each other so as to constitute a single self-sustaining coherent reality – which set of processes can conveniently be referred to as its soul. Without the soul the living creature does not exist, but only its dead corpse.

A perfect diamond is just that – and no more. A diamond with a flaw has more information to it. The flaw itself exits and has its own form; an ordering which is at odds with that of the general crystal. Hence, the flawed diamond has a greater existence than the perfect one. Similarly, an engraved ring has a greater existence than a plain one. In each case, there is more to the "less ordered", and less simple object than to its pristine equivalent. Existence is quantifiable as information. A tree and a rock of similar size will be described by similar amounts of information. A complete specification of the tree would involve many exact repetitions of molecular structures and cellular organelles. An exhaustive specification of the rock might involve a variety of crystal structures representing a wide range of different minerals.

Even the sub-atomic particles of which the tree and rock are composed can be understood in terms of information. Every such particle is fully specified by a set of "quantum numbers", such as electric charge, quark flavour and gluon colour. The only aspect of existence which cannot clearly be specified in terms of information is the mass-energy which seems to give a basic reality to every particle. Now that the Higgs boson has definitely been identified it may be possible to give a complete account of existence in terms of only two ideas. First, that of "potentiality" or "materiality", as represented by fields; and second, that of "actuality" or "information", as represented by the excitations (quantum vibrations) of these fields.

In general, existence builds up as a hierarchy of information or ordering. Non-physicists don't notice this is, I suspect, because they are not conscious of the huge hierarchy of patterned organisation (and so existence) already present in the simplest of raw materials. This means that the *extra existence* (which is the kind of order, form and pattern imposed by human beings on matter by their skill) goes unmarked in their view of things. They do not notice the occasional new-sprung sapling amidst the confused tangle of all the old established trees.

Typically this *extra existence* is given another name entirely, namely: significance. Significance is not usually recognised as being *extra existence* because it is swamped out by the enormous background of material organisation which it sits on top of; which organisation is itself not usually recognised as ordering, but rather something entirely different: namely "substance" – or even matter itself. Significantly, the word "significance" indicates that something has value or, as one might say, that it *matters*. Hence, the English language itself suggests that physical matter and informational or epistemic significance are closely related to each other.

What is beauty?

If something is perceived as beautiful, we are attracted to it, and tend to stare at or listen to it: we show an interest in it. When a mathematician or physicist discovers something interesting they find it attractive and describe it as beautiful. I therefore contend that beauty is a property of interesting, subtle and deep forms of order and that the words "beautiful", "attractive" and "interesting" differ only as having different (but overlapping) fields of conventional applicability.

Whereas my theory accounts for the perception of beauty in situations of extreme order, it may seem to be incompatible with the perception of beauty in chaotic situations. It isn't at all obvious that order is the root of all beauty. Conventionally, beauty is found both in regularity: as in geometrical decoration, classical architecture and the symmetry of a daisy, and also in irregularity: as in the ragged clouds of a stormy sky or a troubled sun-set; the scattering of buttercup flowers across a lawn; the erratic growth of the branches and twigs of a tree; the flickering of a camp-fire or the fluctuating cascades of a water-fall.

However, it must be noted that for something to be beautiful it is first necessary for it to exist: it must stand out proud from its context and so be identifiable as being what it is; else it is (at most) disorganised, formless, random matter. Now without order and intelligibility there is nothing to be perceived and so nothing to be attractive. Hence, order is at least a prerequisite for beauty.

Now, order is of paramount necessity in providing for life. Life requires sources of low entropy (highly ordered) energy and matter, otherwise known as "food". Rationally, therefore, a living being should find such sources attractive; because they tend to be good for it by facilitating its continued existence. Hence one should expect that any living being will find order attractive on a very basic level, and especially any form of order which is associated with food or shelter; that is instances of order which it is equipped to benefit from. Now, if such a being was intelligent one should expect it to give *some* account of this basic attraction; even if it had not yet developed the idea of entropy or order. It seems to me that this is what talk of beauty is all about. It is a way of referring to an intuitive perception or instinctive recognition of order without mentioning the idea of order.

This isn't to devalue beauty. Rather, it is to elevate beauty to the highest place possible. For any living being, all that in the end matters to it is its own life. After all, its concern for any other thing necessarily terminates the very moment that it itself ceases to be. Now, a living being's life is facilitated by all those things which are good for it, and beauty (an intuitive and informal evaluation of order) is a very helpful (but not infallible) indicator of what is of benefit. Hence as Plato tells us, beauty is very close to "the Good" in the scheme of things.

> Beauty was radiant to see at that time when the souls… were ushered into the mystery that we may rightly call the most blessed of all… Now beauty, as I said, was radiant among the other objects, and… here we grasp it sparkling through the clearest of our senses. Vision, of course, is the sharpest of our bodily senses, although it does not see wisdom. It would awaken a terribly powerful love if an image of wisdom came through our sight as clearly as beauty does… but now beauty alone has this privilege, to be the most clearly visible and the most loved. [Plato "Pheadrus" (250b-e)]

> If we cannot capture the Good in one form, we will have to take hold of it in a conjunction of three: beauty, proportion and truth... Any-one should by now be able to judge between pleasure and intelligence, which of these is most closely related

> to the supreme good... first comes what is somehow connected with measure... the second rank goes to the well-proportioned and beautiful, the perfect, the self-sufficient... the third rank, as I divine, to reason and intelligence... the fourth rank to... right opinions... the fifth kind will be those pleasures we set aside and called painless. [Plato "Philebus" (65a-c)]

Beauty and disorder

A tree is an ordering of matter. It has a beauty that is partly to do with regularity, as in the uniform colour and shape of its leaves and the symmetrical outline of its foliage; and partly to do with irregularity, as in the unpredictable positions and shapes of its twigs and branches. This kind of irregularity is part and parcel of what it is to be a tree. It is fractal order and far from random; being governed on the one hand by general mathematical principles, and on the other by the genome of the tree species in question. It definitely contributes to the beauty of the tree.

A second form of disorder is not part and parcel of what it is to be a tree. It comes about because of adverse extrinsic influences such as disease, gales and lightning-strike. This kind of disorder is present in any real tree, but is a derogation from its treeness. It conflicts with and compromises the pattern which the tree follows in as far as it is a tree. Such distortions are all evils as far as the tree is concerned, because they result in a diminution of the order which is properly characteristic of the tree. We would say that they are ugly and that they mar its beauty.

If one packages these two kinds of disorder together (on the basis that both are unpredictable and superficially random) one will tend to speak of the tree as having disorder (unqualified) as part of itself and come up with the ideas that disorder (and so evil) is intrinsic to being (and contributes to beauty) rather than that it is an extrinsic and avoidable failing, sickness or deficiency.

Ironically, ugliness (and so disorder) can itself be beautiful in a way. So, though the scars on the body of a heroic military veteran (obtained as the wages of valour and courage) are ugly on a merely physical level; when considered in terms of the story which they tell they take on a certain beauty – because of the habitual pattern of virtue which they exemplify. Similarly, the horrors of Piccaso's painting "Guernica" are intended to communicate the disorder of war so as to emphatically recommend its exact opposite: peace. Similarly, the blurring of line in an impressionist painting may communicate the frailty of human life and perception and so direct the soul towards realities which are more robust, definite and clear.

Beauty and non-biological randomness

The account I have so far given of beauty does not allow for the beauty associated with *random* motion. Stationary fish, birds or flames are, or would be, less beautiful than moving ones; and it would seem that the flickering of flames and fluctuations of water flow (in a fountain or over a weir, say) are pretty much devoid of order – but are they?

Water flows erratically because the equations of fluid dynamics are non-linear.[17] This means that the consequences of any disturbance are not strictly proportional to the size of that disturbance. The truth of this can be established by pouring water from a wine bottle. If one tilts the bottle gently, the water dribbles out, down the side; if one inclines the bottle more abruptly, it pours steadily and uniformly; and if one tips the bottle on its side, the water glugs out in seemingly irregular bursts. The non-linearity of liquid flow can also be seen in the way that water leaves a tap as it is slowly turned on. At first, drips form regularly. Then, as the water flow increases, the rhythm takes on a "one-**two**, one-**two**" beat. Then the pattern of dripping becomes more complex – and apparently irregular – before the drips merge together into a continuous flux.

In general, it is found that all non-linear physical systems (not just those involving fluid flow) exhibit what is called "chaotic" rather than "random" behaviour. This behaviour is mathematically related to fractals. Indeed, most (if not all) of what one takes to be irregular or random occurrences can be traced back to non-linear effects and so found to be mathematically chaotic rather than absolutely random. The difference between mathematically chaotic behaviour and absolutely random behaviour is that there is a rationale behind the former, which often manifests at a high level in terms of various averages being predictable even though individual events are not; while the latter has no pattern whatsoever – hidden or otherwise.

Now all the examples I have given of random beauty arise from the non-linearities of fluid dynamics. Hence, their beauty can be attributed to the underlying chaotic order which they represent, in the same way as the apparently random beauty of living beings can be attributed to fractal order. I suspect that if truly random behaviour was extrinsically imposed upon a flame or water-flow, much of the beauty of its motion would be lost; and also that it would be difficult for any observer to say exactly what was wrong: why the randomness which they were accustomed to think of as beautiful had become crass, inept and ugly.

---

17 See footnotes on page 275.

Pristine beauty

Which is the more ordered, a blank sheet of paper; or the same sheet once one of Shakespeare's sonnets has been inscribed upon it? If beauty is order, then what of a blank canvas or the works of Mondrian and similar minimalist artists? Now it cannot be denied that a blank canvas is highly ordered and so is in a state of low entropy. However, this does not of itself make us typically think of it as beautiful. By way of contrast, a blank white wall may strike us as beautiful, and similarly a very plane article of white clothing may be judged as beautiful precisely because of its simplicity. We call such beauty "pristine".

A virginal drawing book may have a certain pristine beauty, but when assaulted by the pencil of an accomplished artist its beauty will be enhanced, not reduced. Contrariwise, if the same book were to be given into the tender clutches of some juvenile dauber its original stark simplicity will be spoiled by their additions. Hence, the beauty of a thing can crucially depend on the skill and intentionality of its constructor.

A blank sheet of paper is not typically recognised as beautiful – and so exhibited in a gallery – because it is not acknowledged as a thing in itself; but only as a background against which some thing is supposed to stand out. Although physically the sheet does undoubtedly exist, conventionally it does not do so; and its edges and surface (the only features of its reality which make it what it is, indeed which make it any thing at all) are discounted. The ideal blank canvas, after all, would have no texture or colour or size or shape; in fact it would be pure nonentity – into which an artist might intrude and impose whatever thing(s) they might wish, free of the constraint of any pre-existing medium. Understood in this way, a blank canvass is only a thing in as much as it is imperfect; and its imperfections are of no significance, unless an artist chooses to make them significant by featuring them in their work.

Of course, a cartoonist in need of paper might well account the find of a supply of crisp white leaves most beautiful. Similarly a sculptor might reasonably describe a flawless slab of marble as beautiful before they impose their will upon it. The artisan and artist each appreciate the beauty of their raw materials because they perceive and value them as such: these are the "food" by which they live as creative agents.

Pristine beauty is the beauty of a single thing which cannot sensibly be decomposed into simpler things. Indeed, its beauty consists of this very fact: that it has an integrity or interior unity which defies analysis. This is its glory – and at the same time its poverty. Other, richer, forms of beauty are found in the harmonious relationships among simple things and have more reality and significance precisely because they represent subtly ordered complexity rather than regimented simplicity.

Contextual Beauty

A uniformly white wall can be construed as beautiful only when it is understood to be a wall, and its uniformity is recognised as supporting and stressing its integrity as the wall that it is; when its low information content is itself acknowledged as referring to its existence as a wall. Similarly, the whiteness of the bride's dress is beautiful when it is understood as symbolic of her virginal dedication to her husband.

In both cases, pristine beauty takes its existence from a clear and concise contextual reference to an important idea[18] which has its formal reality quite apart from the matter of the beautiful object itself. The object is given extrinsic significance by the contextual reference made to the idea which it manifests and it gains much of its beauty as a result of the communication of this significance; which may be symbolic or – as in the case of a wall – arise from a practical utility, namely shelter.

Clearly, this kind of beauty can only exist when the artist and the admirer of their work share common theoretical referents, background knowledge or a culture; but a moment's reflection will show that this requirement is not limited to the appreciation of minimalist art or simple technology. A sequence of letters is so much gibberish unless one recognises and is conversant with the language it exemplifies. A Morse-coded poem – which has no beauty when viewed as unintelligible dots and dashes – manifests its art once the secret of its encryption is discovered and its occult meaning revealed. Hence, the beauty of a thing can depend crucially on its admirer possessing a key of interpretation.

So beauty is, to a degree, contextual, but no context could make a random collation of matter beautiful; though even such a mess might be redeemable if enough effort were expended on organising it and so reducing its entropy. In this sense – that any matter, no matter how corrupt, is capable of being organised, set straight and given significance – all existence is good and has a basic and inalienable beauty.

Beauty is the comprehensible ordering of things

Beauty is not *quite* the same as order, then. The blank sheet of paper is perfectly ordered but not particularly beautiful – except to the artist who wants to draw on it and relative to whom it has a purpose or teleos. A coded message might be beautiful once decoded; but without knowledge of how it is to be decoded it appears as nothing more than random noise and its beauty remains hidden – perhaps forever.[19]

---

18 An idea is itself an ordering of being.

19 The beauty of a good encryption scheme lies in it disguising the presence of any meaning whatsoever; not just the presence of the particular meaning. A well encrypted signal should look like background noise.

Beauty depends upon there being a multiplicity of identifiable things organised according to an identifiable pattern or rationale. So a blank piece of paper is ordered, but is only one thing. Hence it is not very beautiful. Contrariwise, a random pile of bricks is many things (each brick having a definite identity) but is disordered. A regimented array of bricks is more beautiful; but not very much so, as its order is easily accounted for and the number of identifiable things involved is not particularly large: arguably the number of bricks plus one – the whole array itself being a thing apart from and above the individual bricks.

Arranging the same number of bricks in a set of similar arrays, in accordance with an abstract rule, will result in a system with considerably more identifiable things in it. Each separate array counting as a thing and the law linking them altogether being a thing also. If that rule is mathematical, it may refer to and imply a plethora of related rules; in which case the system of bricks will implicitly exemplify all those other rules and so its overall significance be difficult to fathom.[20]

A representative painting clearly contains many things and shows them as co-existing with each other, whether or not they are arranged in accordance with any geometrical or fractal scheme. Moreover, natural objects are themselves composed of sub-units (such as leaves, flowers, legs and eyes) in accordance with an order and purpose. The beauty of such a representation lies in it displaying the naturally existing order well, or else in it communicating some other ordering or significance intended by the artist and imposed by them on their subject matter.

For the beauty of an object to be appreciated, the observer has first to recognise the things from which that object is constructed and second the rationale or pattern in accordance with which it is constructed. In order to appreciate the beauty of a poem, the listener must recognise the sounds as words, be conversant with the vocabulary and grammar of the language in which the poem is being read and be aware of the conventions of rhyme and metre.

What is justice?

The purpose or business of any being is simply "to be" – and to be all that it can be. This is especially true of God[21] whose nature is "Being-in-Itself" and couldn't possibly have any purpose other than simply "to be". Justice (or righteousness) is fundamentally about allowing and enabling each and every agent and thing the freedom, resources and scope which will enable it to fulfil itself (to actualise all of its potentiality) without being constrained, interfered with or harmed by any other agent or thing.

---

20 Thanks to S. James for explaining this to me.

21 Whether God is real or not is the subject of Chapter 14.

> There shall come forth a shoot from the stump of Jesse… With righteousness he shall judge the poor, and decide with equity for the meek of the earth… Righteousness shall be the girdle of his waist, and faithfulness the girdle of his loins. The wolf shall dwell with the lamb, and the leopard shall lie down with the kid, and the calf and the lion and the fatling together, and a little child shall lead them. The cow and the bear shall feed; their young shall lie down together; and the lion shall eat straw like the ox. The sucking child shall play over the hole of the asp, and the weaned child shall put his hand on the adder's den. They shall not hurt or destroy in all my holy mountain; for the earth shall be full of the knowledge of the Lord as the waters cover the sea. [Is 11:1-9 RSV]

> Justice is doing one's own work and not meddling with what isn't one's own. [Plato "Republic" (IV 433a)]

Justice is a harmony and organisation of being. A just order or organisation is one which facilitates the thriving and fulfilment of being. Injustice frustrates this. The Hebrew word "shalom" (poorly translated into English as "peace") encapsulates this idea. Where there is shalom, moderation or justice, there is no conflict but only cooperation; with every agent "minding their own business" and respecting the expertise of others as each makes their contribution to the common life.

> As it is, there are many parts, yet one body. The eye cannot say to the hand, "I have no need of you," nor again the head to the feet, "I have no need of you." On the contrary, the parts of the body which seem to be weaker are indispensable… God has so composed the body... that there may be no discord in the body, but that the members may have the same care for one another. [1Cor 12:20-25 RSV]

In one sense, justice is not transcendent, but rather immanent in the actual constitution of material beings; for the way in which agents *ought*[22] to be organised if they are not to come into conflict with each other is entirely a function of their *actual* individual characteristics. In another sense, justice is absolutely transcendent; because the principle itself (that all *ought* to have and enjoy the freedom to be themselves and to become whatever they are capable of) is not subject to negotiation.

---

22 I discuss the significance of the word "ought" at length in Chapter 7.

Justice is a kind of beauty, because it is a harmony, ordering or organization of being of which a rational account can be given; namely that it is how agents can live together in stable fellowship.

> Behold, how good and pleasant it is when brothers dwell in unity! It is like the precious oil upon the head, running down upon the beard, upon the beard of Aaron, running down on the collar of his robes! It is like the dew of Hermon, which falls on the mountains of Zion! For there the Lord has commanded the blessing, life for evermore. [Ps 132:1-3 RSV]

> My soul takes pleasure in three things, and they are beautiful in the sight of the Lord and of men; agreement between brothers, friendship between neighbours, and a wife and a husband who live in harmony. [Sir 25:1 RSV]

We legitimately employ differing means and modes when evaluating order; as determined either by our immediate purpose, or else by that aspect of our own nature involved in the evaluation. Similarly, we use different terms of speech to describe it in different contexts. Beauty and justice are both expressions of order, coherence, harmony or intelligibility. Beauty is the term used in an aesthetic context and justice is the term used in an ethical context.[23]

> Measure and proportion manifest themselves in all areas as beauty and virtue. [Plato "Philebus" (64e)]

---

23 See page 281.

Chapter 4 The Mystery of Life

> What is man, and of what use is he? What is his good and what is his evil? The number of a man's days is great if he reaches a hundred years. Like a drop of water from the sea and a grain of sand so are a few years in the day of eternity. [Sir 18:1-10 RSV]

Motivation

Human beings are mostly concerned about human beings, so if we are going to construct any edifice linking Earth with Heaven which has relevance to human beings, human life must feature significantly in this undertaking. While such a perspective may at first seem unduly anthropocentric and conceited, reflection will show that this is not the case; so long as the notion of what is "human" is generalised. What really matters is life – and sentient (that is, conscious) life, especially. To our present knowledge, only human beings clearly qualify as sentient, and so the present discussion is limited to a consideration of humanity.

What is Life?

Typically, people try to identify what they mean by life by means of some kind of definition. So, when at high school, I was taught that all lifeforms are characterised by: reproduction, respiration, alimentation, excretion, growth and movement. The idea being communicated was that this list of characteristics was definitive of life: that anything which exhibited all these behaviours was alive and anything which did not was not alive. The matter of sterile creatures such as mules was carefully ignored and the singular immobility of lichens likewise glossed-over.

In my view, this taxonomical approach to understanding the nature of life is wrong. Listing all those characteristics which happen to be shared by those things which one usually identifies as being alive is no way to come to understand what it is to be alive. To give a good account of life – one that is based on understanding rather than convention – it is necessary to reflect on what one actually recognises as life in living things. It is not adequate simply to undertake an accountancy exercise. One should ask: "If I encountered an entirely alien phenomenon, how would I decide whether it was alive or not?"

Consider the following questions, then. Could there be a life-form:

1. which was immortal and so had no need to reproduce?
2. which was not based on cellular structure?
3. which was not based on carbon chemistry?
4. which was not based on any kind of chemistry at all; but on something entirely different, such as magnetic fields in plasma?

In the past, life, especially human life, has typically been thought of as a mystical substance, extrinsic or additional to common matter. The scholastics understood the anima or soul of a living creature as its "organizing and motivating[1] principal", and insisted that each living thing had a soul in addition to its material composition. This anima was nevertheless thought to be inherent in and dependent upon the material constitution of the living creature; except in the case of human beings, where it was said to be immaterial: a spirit. From their notion that the human soul was spiritual, the scholastics deduced that it must be immortal. Most of this narrative is, I believe, quite wrong. I think that the answer to the question "What is life?" is quite obvious.

Life as motion

Life is characterized by order and organization; but not all that is ordered is living. Obvious counter examples are a diamond crystal, a silicon integrated circuit, and a virus outside its host cell. These are all static, apart from the tendency of all things to degrade. In particular, the stability of their pattern of existence does not depend on a flux of matter or energy. This is exactly why they are not living.

Living things are constituted with internal processes organised so as to obtain their self-preservation. This is what makes life to be life and distinguishes it from non-life. The soul of a living thing amounts to those very processes by which it establishes, preserves and stabilises its distinctive form against the universal entropic tendency to dissolution. Living things seek to preserve their own form. They strive to be eternal, but within time. Life is sustained order which maintains its identity and pattern by continually jettisoning entropy into a current of matter or energy. Living organisms are characterized by both stability of form and continual motion and change; primarily the flux of matter and energy through them.

---

1 The original idea of "living" was that which was self-moving or automotive, as in the antique name for molten Mercury metal "quick-silver", meaning living or moving silver. "Quick" being, of course, an antique synonym for "living"; as in "the quick and the dead" and "to quicken".

> Hence it is not a bad name for the body to call it a river. Possibly, to be exact, the existing substance does not remain in our body for even two days. And yet Paul, let us say, or Peter, is always the same, and this not only his soul, the substance of which is not with us in a state of flux nor ever has fresh elements introduced: he is the same, however fluid may be the nature of the body, because the form which distinguishes the body is the same. [Origen "Selections from the Psalms"]

Persistence in flux

Life exists simply in order to continue to live. This follows from what life is; which is best expressed as "persistent order arising from within and maintained by a flux".[2] It is no accident that the candle or lamp flame features in the ritual of many religions.[3] Fire is not just a symbol of life, though it is this. Fire is *itself* a simple form of life. The flame fulfils my criterion of life. It has a recognisable persistence which is maintained by a flow of matter, into which flux it disposes entropy.

For a living being to be alive, it must be persistent. Hence, any lifelike phenomena which doesn't persist absolutely is flawed, imperfect and only aspirational or suggestive of what Life truly is. Hence, no mortal creature is fully alive; and even the protracted transience of a species, made up of inter-breeding and reproducing individuals, fails to live up to the core reality of what life properly is. Indeed, the entire biosphere of Earth is doomed to perish and so, even if all "living things" are taken together as a whole, this global composite only represents a semblance or intimation of the true form of Life: which is God – the burning bush which is not consumed by its eternal flame.[4]

God is, of course, not alive according to the account I have given of life within space-time. God is eternal outside of time and does not arise from any flux; though God can be thought of as giving rise to a flux of divine energies by which all things come to exist. It is more accurate to say that God is the fountain of all life than to say that God is alive. Nevertheless the Bible regularly speaks of "the living God".[5]

---

2 E. Schrödinger "What is Life?" (1944)

3 The the seven branched menorah lamp of Judaism; [Ex25:31-38] the sacred flame of Zoroastrianism; the sanctuary lamp and votive candles of Catholic and Orthodox Christianity, and so on.

4 Ex 3:2.

5 Deut 5:26. Jsh 3:10. Ps 41:2; 83:2. Jer 10:10. Hos 1:10. Mat 16:16. Acts 14:15. 2Cor 3:3; 6:16. 1Tim 3:15; 4:10. Heb 3:12; 9:14; 10:31; 12:22.

Life as symmetry

Life is a kind of dynamic symmetry. It is an echo of the fundamental symmetry of time-independence; the idea that a thing should, by default, look the same whenever it is observed, unless it is being affected by some external influence. Life is an intimation of immortality in the midst of universal impermanence, an intrusion of eternity into the temporal.

The Cosmos in which life exists is anything but time-independent. Indeed, it is characterized by a huge temporal asymmetry of order. In the past, the Universe is much more ordered (has a much lower entropy) than it is in the future. Admittedly, the type of order found in the early Universe is uninteresting, akin to that of carbon atoms in a diamond lattice; rather than interesting, akin to that of a book of poetry. Even so, the asymmetry of order is queer; for there is no obvious reason why it should exist.[6] It certainly breaks the most basic symmetry which one might expect the Universe to exhibit.[7] Nevertheless, this is the world as we find it; and it is this mysterious physical asymmetry which makes possible the wonderful symmetry of life. It is because the Cosmos as a whole is considerably more ordered than it has any right to be,[8] and is decaying from a state of regimented low entropy to a state of chaotic uniformity, that living beings are able to persist for a while. Out of the inexorable decline and decay of the Cosmos, springs the transient stability of living beings.

Robustness

A quality-metric for life (the degree to which a particular living being exemplifies, the ideal form of Life) can be established in terms of its robustness: its ability to avoid and withstand those extrinsic forces which tend to its dissolution. Accordingly, squirrels are more alive than slugs. This is because squirrels can perceive some threats and run from them. Similarly, human beings are more alive than either; because they can take the initiative and actively modify their environment so as to preclude the occurrence of many threats.

---

6 H. Price “Time’s Arrow and Archimedes’ Point” (1997)

7 This expectation is so strong that when it was found that the Cosmos was expanding (which fact itself contributes to the temporal increase in Universal entropy) the cosmologist Fred Hoyle suggested that this expansion was compensated for by a continual creation of matter throughout inter-galactic space; such that every Cosmic neighbourhood was maintained as time-independent even as the Universe expanded. This Steady State Theory was later found to be incompatible with any plausible interpretation of the evidence of observational astronomy.

8 On the basis that of all possible arrangements of its constituent particles are accounted as being “equally likely”.

Any living creature has a soul or anima;[9] but by soul I mean nothing other than the set of coordinated and harmonious self-sustaining processes going on throughout a living body. This soul comprises gross movement, such as breathing and playing the guitar; chemical metabolism, the business of the body's individual cells; and electro-chemical neural activity, which is the basis of the mind: of both conscious and unconscious thought. The soul is entirely the activity of matter, and an android (such as Mr Data of Star Trek) could easily have a mental soul and so properly be accounted as alive.

What is the meaning of life?

It may seem that the kind of account I have given of life must inevitably result in the conclusion that it is of no intrinsic value, worth or meaning. In fact I am going to argue precisely the opposite; but first I want to suggest that before tackling the question "What is the meaning of life?" one should reflect on how this question arises in practice. I believe that this elucidates what the question really means and generates the answer almost automatically.

Why then, do human beings ask the question "What is the meaning of life?" I think that it is in response to a dawning awareness of mortality. Death is the antithesis of life and is not a part or aspect of life. It is not just the end or terminus of life, as conception is its start; rather it is life's precise negation. Life's entire actuality is directed towards its own continuance, which is to say towards the avoidance of death. Death is the exact frustration of life, it is the defeat which cannot be mitigated or undone. The fact that a living being dies makes a mockery of its own particular life, though life may continue on through progeny.

Adults and death

Once they realize they are going to die, adults spend a lot of effort trying to avoid the question of the meaning of their lives by immersing themselves in various activities: work, sex, sport, politics, parenting or hobbies. The aim is to distract themselves from the inevitability of their demise; but the spectre of their mortality hovers still in the mid distance and will not be turned back by such amateurish devices.

> Man that is born of a woman is of few days, and full of trouble. He comes forth like a flower, and withers; he flees like a shadow, and continues not… there is hope for a tree, if it be cut down, that it will sprout again, and that its shoots

9 The word "animal" is Latin for "living thing".

> will not cease… But man dies, and is laid low; man breathes his last, and where is he? As waters fail from a lake, and a river wastes away and dries up, so man lies down and rises not again; till the heavens are no more he will not awake, or be roused out of his sleep. [Job 14:1-12 RSV]

Children and life

Well-adjusted children are immersed in their lives. Each happening and discovery is a new joy to them, and their lives are an adequate justification of themselves. This is superficially similar to the adult attachment to distractions; but its rationale is very different. Bluntly, this is because the child has no fear from which it requires distraction: it has not yet noticed its mortality. Moreover, it has confidence that its parents have all the answers and will supply all its needs. Only when this naïve faith is lost can adult trepidation take centre stage.

> Children seldom are able to realize that death will come to them personally. One might define adulthood as the age at which a person learns that he must die.
> [R.A. Heinlein "The Moon is a harsh mistress" (1966, 1969)]

God and life

This account of a child's existence is similar to what might be said about God.[10] Everything that God knows is immediate to God. Whereas it is familiar, it is also novel – and a cause of delight. God is sufficient for God. God simply is, and knows with ecstatic joy that it is simply "good to be." After all, there can be no higher justification of anything than its being what it is.[11]

When people have in the past tried to justify their own lives in terms of the purposes of God, they have sought to give meaning to their mortality in terms of the Immortal: but what is God's purpose except just to be?[12] If this is good enough for God, why not so for human beings? After all, Jesus tells us that we must be re-born[13] as care-free[14] children[15] if we would enter His Kingdom.

---

10 Whether God is real or not is the subject of Chapter 14.

11 "And God saw everything that He had made, and behold, it was very good." [Gen 1:31 RSV]

12 Ex 3:14, quoted at the head of Chapter 14.

13 Jn 3:1-8.

14 Mt 6:24-34.

15 Mt 18:1-4.

The last taboo

After talking with a friend a few years ago, it struck me that some modern adults do not satisfy Heinlein's criteria in any but the most superficial manner. While they acknowledge in a perfunctory way that they are going to die, it does not occur to them to dwell on this fact, so they are in no need of distraction from it. It is as if the the word death has been removed from their vocabularies, as if the subject of death is the last taboo.[16]

This verbal impoverishment renders them unable to think about the subject, in much the same way as the limited lexicon of "Newspeak"[17] stunted the mentalities of the inhabitants of "Airstrip One", preventing them from realising that anything was amiss with their lives. The effective loss of the word "death" means that many adults now never frame the question "What is the meaning of life?" and keeps them very much as children, content to carry on with their lives giving no thought to the futility of all their enterprises – until, that is, they are confronted with the death of a loved one; at which point they have no answers.

Supernatural carelessness

This is not a wholesome condition to be in. The child's state of carelessness is due to ignorance of its certain demise. God's state of carelessness is due to the exact opposite condition: namely, clear and certain knowledge of God's invulnerability. The human being can only gain an adult carelessness by first fully acknowledging the threat to their being and then turning to God as a child and so coming to rely on God as their Saviour – the guarantor of their security.

> Blessed be the God and Father of our Lord Jesus Christ! By His great mercy we have been born anew to a living hope through the resurrection of Jesus Christ from the dead, and to an inheritance which is imperishable, undefiled, and unfading, kept in heaven for you, who by God's power are guarded through faith for a salvation ready to be revealed in the last time… As the outcome of your faith you obtain the salvation of your souls.
> [1Pet 1:3-5,9 RSV]

---

16 H. Feifel "The Meaning of Death" (1959)
17 G. Orwell "1984" (1949)

A romantic response

> It is an interesting idea, that we are motivated in most of our adult undertakings by the desire to distract ourselves from the sight of our own death. I'm not sure how accurate this is, but it probably has some merit. However, I don't feel that I fit into any of your archetypes. I don't consider myself ignorant of it, nor do I ignore it. I do not think I am immortal, and I am not depressed.
>
> I think this is because I frame the question of the meaning of life differently than most people. Either I think it is a meaningless question – if it is searching for some kind of ultimate justification; because such a thing seems innately illogical to me. Or I can frame it in the sense that the answer is something extremely personal and subjective; if it be allowed that meaning can be subjective. This is not at all discouraging to me, because I place subjective meaning and values always as the needed prerequisite to any question of should or ought.
>
> It's hard for me to decide whether death is something I find terrible. Either it is terrible, and is inevitable, so it's pointless to worry about it; or it is something to be neutral towards, so it is not worth any worry at all. All I believe is that I will be gone, and in any scenario I am not shocked or horrified by this. I love life too much to be consumed by living. I am too grateful for the chance to breathe to be hateful that my breath will fade. I love life too much to spoil it by thinking poorly of the inevitable nothingness to come.
>
> [J. Kramer "Private Communication" (2012)]

In response to the idea that one's life can have a "personal and subjective" meaning, I would say that this is true in the sense that one can pursue a particular lifestyle and seek *personal fulfilment* in a wide variety of ways. Indeed, I would insist that it is vital to *know oneself* and to discover one's own natural style and aesthetic and so one's proper means and mode of fulfilment. However, the idea of *personal fulfilment* only makes any sense once one has understood what the "ultimate justification" of life is. Without such an understanding, *personal fulfilment* is no more intelligible than an instinct or feeling. With a well founded understanding of "the meaning of life"[18] one can judge whether one's ideas of *personal fulfilment* are rational or spurious.

---

18 See Chapter 6, where I show that life has a simple and straight-forward "ultimate justification" which is not "innately illogical".

As to the question of value and its necessary objective underpinning, as also the origin and significance of the word "ought";[19] for now I will remark only that if one places "subjective meaning and values always as the needed prerequisite to any question of should or ought" then one cannot explain why one values anything except in terms of whimsy. The only proper answer to the question "why do you value X?" is "because I judge that X is valuable." Now, if this means no more than "because I choose to value X," then the original question has not been answered. This is because no account has been given of how, and on what basis, one comes to first perceive or judge that X is valuable; and without such an explanation how can one reasonably come to choose to value X? The implication is that no account can be given of the choice and that all valuing is arbitrary, irrational and idiosyncratic.

It is not worth worrying about death, whether it is "terrible" or "neutral". Worrying about an inevitable disaster rarely makes it less disastrous and never less inevitable. However, if one truly loves life, the necessary corollary of this is that one must hate death – for death is the loss of the thing which one claims to love.

It is true that if death amounts to one's personal non-reality, then death will leave one in no position to love or hate anything. In fact one will not be at all and have no thoughts or feelings about anything at all. Nevertheless, the prospect of death means that mortal life is absolutely frustrated and futile: simply because it all comes to naught, whereas life's basic business is to persist. This is clearly indicated by the very fact that Kramer says that it would "spoil it to think poorly of the inevitable nothingness to come". This is exactly why one avoids doing just so, by engaging in frivolous distractions.

Eternal Life

A human being asks "What is the meaning of my life?" precisely because they have realized that they are going to die. If they thought they were immortal, the question simply wouldn't arise. If their life had no termination, they could happily spend an infinity of time exploring the Universe; admiring its grandeur and beauty; unravelling its secrets; enjoying the pleasures it has to offer; creating and admiring works of art and so on. There would be no reason for doing so, apart from the intrinsic fun of the activity; but this would suffice.

19 See Chapter 7, in particular pages 133-135, where I show that the ideas behind the words "ought" and "purpose" arises necessarily from the very existence of life.

There would be no purpose, other than the pleasure and achievement themselves; but these would be enough. There would be no imperative, except for the simple and child-like joy of "being and doing".

Of course, a certain quality of life would be necessary to suppress the question. The prospect of spending an eternity feeling hungry, ill, lonely or depressed would raise the question of life's meaning even more strongly. The partial death of significant suffering endured with no prospect of relief and no object in view (that is, with no hope) is just as bad in its own way as death proper – and arguably worse.[20]

Without the prospect of Eternal Life, no adequate answer can be given to the "Question of Life the Universe and Everything".[21] With the prospect of Eternal Life, that question simply does not arise. It follows that the answer to the question "What is the meaning of my life?" is not to be framed in terms of some specific purpose, end or goal, as might seem proper. Instead, it is to be found in the remark of Jesus of Nazareth: "I have come that they may have life, and have it more abundantly."[22] The whole point of the redemption was to ratify and re-establish mankind's immortality. Once this was done, the question of the purpose or meaning of human existence ceased to arise.

Progeny and the immortality of the tribe

Both the Greeks and the ancient Hebrews generally got along well enough on the basis that "three score years and ten" was the allotted span of human life, that one had no basis to protest this fact and that one should look for purpose and meaning in progeny.

> Blessed is every one who fears the Lord, who walks in His ways! You shall eat the fruit of the labour of your hands; you shall be happy, and it shall be well with you. Your wife will be like a fruitful vine within your house; your children will be like olive shoots around your table. Lo, thus shall the man be blessed who fears the Lord. The Lord bless you from Zion! May you see the prosperity of Jerusalem all the days of your life! May you see your children's children! Peace be upon Israel!
> [Ps 127 RSV]

---

20 Job expresses this well: "I loathe my life; I would not live for ever. Let me alone, for my days are a breath." [Job 7:16 RSV]

21 Douglas Adams "The Hitchhiker's Guide to the Galaxy" (1979)

22 Jn 10:10 RSV.

> Mankind is immortal because it always leaves later generations behind to preserve its unity and identity for all time: it gets its share of immortality by means of procreation. It is never a holy thing voluntarily to deny oneself this prize, and he who neglects to take a wife and have children does precisely that.
> [Plato "Laws" (IV 721c)]

The Ancient Egyptians had a different take on such matters. While they were happy to enjoy the pleasures of mortal life, they devoted enormous resources to funeral rites and tombs intended to assist the spirits of the dead in the after-life. Moreover, as time went on, both the Hebrews and Greeks came to the view that looking for personal significance in terms of progeny wasn't an adequate answer to the problem of the meaning of life.

> But he who is joined with all the living has hope, for a living dog is better than a dead lion. For the living know that they will die, but the dead know nothing, and they have no more reward; but the memory of them is lost. Their love and their hate and their envy have already perished, and they have no more for ever any share in all that is done under the sun.
> [Eccl 9:4-6 RSV]

The very form of the last quote from Plato's "Laws" makes it clear that human beings desire immortality. Indeed, any reference to progeny as the purpose or fulfilment of an individual implicitly validates the notion that death is problematic and must be answered in some way or other if life is to make sense.

> What Love wants is not beauty… but reproduction and birth in beauty… because reproduction goes on forever; it is what mortals have in place of immortality.
> [Plato "Symposium" (206e)]

Any attempt to resolve the problem of death at the level of the immortality of the family or the tribe implies that the individual is unimportant and that what matters is the collective. Now this might be an adequate account of the matter where coral polyps, ants or meerkats are concerned; but when it comes to sentient beings it is the individual who matters much more than the collective. The collective only obtains whatever value it has from the value of the subjectively conscious individuals constituting it.

Of course, even were it to be granted that the state or tribe or family mattered more than the individual, any account of life's value erected on such a basis would be flawed; because neither the family, nor the tribe, nor the nation, nor the race, nor the species is any more immortal than the individual. All of these are destined (by the Second Law of Thermodynamics[23]) to come to naught in the end.

Serving and obeying God

Understanding this only too well, the writer of Ecclesiastes concluded that human life (viewed in its own terms) was nothing but vanity and emptiness and so of no real value whatever. He could only find solace in an insistence that mankind's proper business was to live quietly and justly and to adhere devotedly to God's Law. It must be clearly realised, however, that this answer is inadequate. The purpose of human life cannot be simply to serve God; at least not in the sense of doing anything that benefits God. This is because God has no need of such service and, even if the case were somehow different, human beings would be incapable of rendering it. The only forms of service that God requires of us is our worship[24] (which is for our benefit, not God's) and that we act in kindness and justice towards one another.

> But Jesus called them to Him and said, "You know that the rulers of the Gentiles lord it over them, and their great men exercise authority over them. It shall not be so among you; but whoever would be great among you must be your servant, and whoever would be first among you must be your slave; even as the Son of Man came not to be served but to serve, and to give His life as a ransom for many." [Mat 20:25-28 RSV]

Neither is it the purpose of human life to obey God. God's only command is that we value and strive for that what is genuinely of benefit to ourselves. We ought to desire God, as our ultimate good and as the fountain-head of our continued existence. We ought to care for each

---

23 This states that disorder (or entropy) inexorably increases as time proceeds. The fact that *locally* order can increase (as in the conception, birth and maturation of a human being, or the construction of a city) does not contradict this law. Any such *local* increase of order always occurs at the cost of a more than compensating increase of disorder in the neighbourhood. Hence the net effect of every process is to increases disorder. The implication is that eventually there will be no order left at all, and that random chaos will universally prevail.

24 This topic is covered in Chapter 16.

other, as secondary goods; helpmates in achieving the fulfilment of our own plans and aspirations.

> One of the scribes... asked Him, "Which commandment is the first of all?"
> Jesus answered, "The first is, 'Hear, O Israel: The Lord our God, the Lord is one; and you shall love the Lord your God with all your heart, and with all your soul, and with all your mind, and with all your strength.'[25] The second is this, 'You shall love your neighbour as yourself.'[26] There is no other commandment greater than these." [Mk 12:28-34 RSV]

This dual command is nothing more than a recall to our rational self-interest from a God who is only concerned for our well-being and who comes among us as a physician to make us whole.

> What is man and of what use is he…? Therefore the Lord is patient with them and pours out His mercy upon them. He sees and recognizes that their end will be evil; therefore He grants them forgiveness in abundance. The compassion of man is for his neighbour, but the compassion of the Lord is for all living beings. [Sir 18:8-13 RSV]

> And as He sat at table in the house, behold, many tax collectors and sinners came and sat down with Jesus and His disciples. And when the Pharisees saw this, they said to His disciples, "Why does your teacher eat with tax collectors and sinners?"
> But when He heard it, He said, "Those who are well have no need of a physician, but those who are sick. Go and learn what this means, 'I desire mercy, and not sacrifice.' For I came not to call the righteous, but sinners." [Mat 9:10-13 RSV]

Of course, according to both Plato and the Catholic Faith, humankind's immortality *as such* was never in jeopardy: the human spirit is of itself immortal. However, apart from the redemption, its eternal destiny was to be isolated: alienated from God, with no adequate context to explore or in which to do anything. Such a hellish eternity is unthinkably awful. The negative lack of fellowship with God being its most terrible aspect; but the prospect of unremitting self-absorbed introspection which could only result in the degradation and dissolution of the personality truly horrid also.

---

25 Deut 6:5.
26 Lev 19:18, 34.

Chapter 5 Futility, Hope and Glory

And Jesus answered them, "The hour has come for the Son of Man to be glorified.[1] Truly, truly, I say to you, unless a grain of wheat falls into the earth and dies, it remains alone; but if it dies, it bears much fruit. He who loves his life loses it, and he who hates his life in this world will keep it for eternal life. If any one serves Me, he must follow Me; and where I am, there shall My servant be also; if any one serves Me, the Father will honour him. Now is My soul troubled. And what shall I say? 'Father, save me from this hour'? No, for this purpose I have come to this hour… Now is the judgement of this world, now shall the ruler of this world be cast out; and I, when I am lifted up from the earth, will draw all men to Myself."
[Jn 12:23-33 RSV]

Motivation

While I accept that the continuance of existence irrespective of the quality of that existence isn't adequate to meet the question "What is the purpose of life?" I suppose that some of my readers will think that *anything* along these lines is wrong. Some will claim that what matters (and so motivates and gives purpose and direction to our lives) isn't existence itself, but rather happiness; and the most romantic[2] will claim that even a short experience of love, happiness and joy is worth more than an eternity of mere existence. Others of a more theological bent will doubtless point out that if the human spirit is constitutionally immortal, then the desire for eternal life is cannot be an effective ethical motivator; for it is necessarily fulfilled irrespective of whatever the individual does. Yet others will point out that people are sometimes willing to suffer or die for a cause or another person that they value. In such cases, it would seem they are motivated by neither their own life nor their own happiness.

---

1 The Greek is "δοξάςω". The root meaning of this word is "belief" or "opinion". The word later came to mean "reputation", "cudos" or "glory", just as the English word "credibility" gave rise to the phrase "street cred." The text might mean "the time has come for me to be proved right."

2 See page 92 for a discussion of Romanticism.

The importance of being happy

The basic problem here is one of "chicken and egg" circularity. On the one hand, happiness is a symptom of security, fulfilment and health: both psychological and physical. On the other hand, all animals pursue pleasure and eschew pain; and human beings in particular aspire to that state of settled comfort and contentment which is known as happiness. So, is life the purpose of happiness; or is happiness, rather, the purpose of life? Is life valueless in the absence of happiness; or is any happiness that does not tend towards the furtherance of life some kind of sham?[3] Does happiness exist as a kind of bribe, to motivate us to strive to maintain our lives; or is happiness itself the entire basis of life's value?

I contend that in the present case this is a false dichotomy, and that the kind of happiness which *ought*[4] to be pursued by a mortal being is none other than the subjective experience and appreciation of being both psychologically and physically healthy, as also physically, economically and socially secure. Moreover, I contend that this kind of happiness ought to be pursued precisely because its pursuit facilitates survival. After all, if one does survive as a healthy and secure individual, with all of ones needs being met – if one does "live long and prosper" – then one can expect to be happy while doing so.

Therefore, even an individual who makes the mistake of setting up happiness (rather than the preservation of their life) as their basic objective will still of necessity seek after life and prosperity, as being the prime requisites of happiness. Hence, it would seem that there cannot be any conflict between the pursuit of abiding happiness and the pursuit of survival. Where life is insecure or compromised there can be no happiness, but only anxiety and fear. Where life is entirely secure and known to be so, happiness must surely follow.[5] Moreover, for a person's happiness to be *abiding,* rather than ephemeral, it is first necessary for that person to *remain* alive.

---

3 Some forms of happiness are bogus, and it is pretty obvious that they are a sham precisely because they are perverted; by which I mean simply that they are based on short-term pleasures obtained at the expense of the long-term welfare of the agent in question. Fake happiness is most obviously encountered in the context of the use of "recreational drugs" (where pleasure or euphoria is obtained divorced from any substantive benefit) and where sexual promiscuity obtains transient feelings of being desirable and valued at the cost of a permanent loss of self-esteem.

4 This is a crucial word. I have much to say about it in Chapter 7.

5 Liberty is also necessary and I will discuss this in the next section. The role of external threat in eliciting courage and so, paradoxically, enhancing life will be covered in Chapter 11.

The purpose of happiness

In its biological origin, pleasure exists in order to positively motivate behaviours which favour the continuance of life; either the life of the subject experiencing pleasure or the life of their progeny.[6] However, the fact that some aspect of reality has its *evolutionary origin* in a particular biological necessity is no argument at all that its only (or even principal) *present purpose* is to be found in this imperative.

For example, an atheist might argue that what had started off with one role in the scheme of things had evolved in such a manner that this original role was either completely lost or else entirely subsumed in a greater one. So does a fish's fin become a lizard's leg, then a bird's wing and finally a penguin's flipper; so does a leaf become a flower petal, a vine tendril or a cactus spine; so does an ape's grunt become a man's word and then a troubadour's song.

A theist can happily agree with this, adding that there could be a yet deeper purpose for such changes of function within God's providential plan. If so, the bald fact of origin (with its associated biological purpose) might itself stands proxy for a more fundamental reality and a deeper divine intentionality. Hence, whereas pleasure arose biologically as an instrumental motivator for insentient animals, it might always have been providentially envisaged by God as the final purpose of humanity.

Quantity or quality of life

A characteristic dispute within Objectivist[7] circles is the "exist or flourish?" question. In brief, it refers to the difference between quantity of life and quality of life. Is it the case that one ought to pursue the temporal prolongation of existence at all costs; or should one set more store by the overall character of one's life, and not simply those aspects of its character that happen to facilitate its prolongation?

The proponents of quantity argue that any behaviour which does not, either directly or indirectly, tend to the prolongation of life is intrinsically worthless; and that to engage in such behaviour is misguided, irrational and futile. The proponents of quality argue that it is the very excesses and extravagances of life which make living enjoyable and so worth-while. They argue that an architect[8] lives to design and construct buildings, he does not conduct his profession in order to live.

---

6 R. Dawkins "The Selfish Gene" (1976)

7 Objectivists are followers of the American philosopher Ayn Rand.

8 Such as Howard Roark. [A. Rand "The Fountainhead" (1947)]

It seems to me that part of this dispute is ill-founded. Just as with the "life or happiness?" question, a great deal of what might at first sight be thought to be excess, extravagance or frivolous entertainment on close inspection turns out to have considerable value in terms of life prolongation.[9] I think that the rest of the dispute can be resolved by thinking of life not as a straight line (of which the only measure possible is length) but as a set of notable events, experiences and actions. One can then clarify one's life-objective as being not so much "to live as *long* as possible" but "to live as *much* as possible". As I have already noted, Jesus of Nazareth said of himself: "I have come that they may have life, *and have it more abundantly.*"[10]

Clearly, the longer one's life is the more opportunity there is for notable events, experiences and actions to occur; the more opportunity there is for one to participate in various realities; the more opportunity there is for one to explore and fulfil one's potential; the more opportunity there is for one to exist – to live as *much* as possible and to *become as much as one can be*. Just as clearly, opportunity does not imply actuality.[11] It is possible for someone to live a long life without ever doing or experiencing anything very much;[12] the sad case of a human being fixed in a permanent vegetative state being an extreme example, but the tragedy of debilitating depression or anxiety also comes to mind.

---

9 Hence, it is termed "re-creation". So, for example, both the theatre and organised religion can be understood as activities which reinforce social and ethical norms and so contribute to the stability, coherence and health of society – which itself facilitates the survival of the individual. Similarly, sport can be understood as basic military training, intended to maintain the citizenry in a physical and psychological condition fit to respond effectively to an external threat; whether military or the result of natural forces, such as a forest fire, typhoon, tsunami or earthquake. It can also serve the purpose of strengthening feelings of solidarity, corporate identity and patriotism. Moreover an element of frivolity or pleasurable relaxation is helpful in maintaining good mental health, see page 146.

10 Jn 10:10 RSV.

11 Especially for a sentient being. A plant is pre-programmed to take every opportunity for growth which presents itself, in accordance with its fixed pattern of being; animals search out opportunities as best they can; but human beings are capable of first imagining and then realising opportunities where none existed before. Not everyone attempts this, of course, and not all of those who do make the attempt succeed.

12 If this is both habitual and culpable it is the deadly sin of sloth.

Clearly, one person might achieve or experience more in a single week than another will in a year or more. What matters (what drives life) is living; and the "amount of living" is not just its temporal extent, but also its intensity: the width of the life-path which is travelled, as well as its length. A rational person would willingly trade one week of intense intelligible activity and experience for a year of forced inactivity; for the former, although a shorter period, would constitute much more existence[13] and incidentally provide much more opportunity for maturation as a human being.

Liberty and choice

Personal freedom is important for two reasons. First, because without it the individual is not able to respond flexibly and to the very best of their own ability to external threat. Second, because without it the individual is not able to explore all those possibilities and opportunities for living life to the full which would otherwise be open to them. Hence any kind of extraneous constraint, or limit on the ability to learn undermines the security of the individual. While it may seem that some forms of constraint (such as containment within an armoured vehicle or a nuclear bunker) increase the security of the individual (and indeed they may do so for a while, when the environment is hostile to their survival) the survival prospects of an individual prevented from flexibly exploiting all the resources otherwise available to them are severely compromised.

Similarly, whereas the handover of personal autonomy to the arbitrary direction of another agent is harmful; deciding to generally trust and obey the instructions of a wise and benevolent mentor can be a life-enhancing choice. This is because one can then benefit from the knowledge and direction of a just ruler who is competent and willing to lead one out of harm's way.[14] Of course, the difficulty with this is that no human master can be expected to be invariably correct in all their decisions, so one has no option but to reserve to one's own conscience the last judgement as to when to obey and when not to do so.

Constraint tends to result in feelings of boredom, depression and despair. Deprived of opportunities for exploration and self-expression human beings atrophy. They are unable to exercise their talents and abilities and so loose them. They are unable to pursue their interests and so become frustrated. If they do not strive to fulfil their potential, they find that their potential collapses back on itself. Instead of "living abundantly" they merely exist, and so lose much of their intrinsic ability to survive.

---

13 In the sense which I elucidated in Chapter 3.

14 Plato "Republic" (IX 590d) quoted on page 331.

Long-term residents of hospitals or correctional facilities can become institutionalised and their prospects of survival upon release be gravely impaired.[15] Conversely, it is found that the life expectancy of those being cared for in nursing homes can be extended by the simple expedient of giving them choices.[16] Of course, human beings can be extremely ingenious, and even in the most unfavourable of circumstances manage to find means of recreation: ways to exercise their abilities and pursue their interests.

The Prometheus paradox

What then of the case of some immortal being who faced the prospect of being tortured for all eternity; as Prometheus was said to be punished[17] by Zeus for stealing fire from Heaven for mankind's benefit? Might such a one not reasonably desire release from the interminable anguish of their existence? Surely, their life is of no value – and might even be construed as a personal liability. Surely in their case, the ending of intolerable pain (at any cost, not excluding the cost of the annihilation of self) is the paramount good.

The answer to the question as posed is that such a life cannot possibly be its own adequate purpose. It would be entirely rational for Prometheus to desire and accept annihilation, if the only alternative was an eternity of unremitting pain. However, it is far from clear that the question is legitimate. Prometheus is portrayed simultaneously as being immortal and yet subject to harm,[18] and so to suffering. Herein lies a hidden contradiction. Pain always signals a weakness, one way or another. This is, indeed, its defining origin: pain exists to indicate immediate threat and vulnerability. A true immortal cannot be vulnerable and would have no business feeling pain, which serves only to warn of a threat to the continued existence of a mortal being. Hence the Prometheus Paradox is not real. It is a phantasm.

---

15 Such was the fate of Brooks Hatlen. [F. Darabont "The Shawshank Redemption" 1994)

16 E. Langer & I. Rodin "The effects of choice and enhanced personal responsibility for the aged." (1976)

17 In the sense of Zeus exacting vindictive retribution, not with any intention of Prometheus' character being corrected.

18 He was supposed to be a titan (a deity of an age before that of the Greek gods such as Zeus) not a human being – and therefore divine; but was nevertheless said to have a liver which could be eaten by a giant eagle.

A similar situation could only arise if the life of some mortal creature was supernaturally sustained while their being was subjected to assaults and violations which were always carefully calculated never to kill them. This would be the ultimate torture. God has the power to act in such a way, it is true; but divine power would never be so exercised, as to do so could serve no rational purpose and would be unjust, vindictive and wicked. There is, of course, the truly horrible possibility that the violence might be self-inflicted; with God's sole involvement being the sustenance of the dysfunctional life of a creature implacably and remorselessly bent on self-destruction. This is the classical idea of Hell, where sinners face the intrinsic consequences of their sin, without any possibility of repentance or healing, for all eternity.

Depression

A superficially similar situation (and one of profound importance) is that where an individual becomes depressed. This condition can arise either from reasonable grounds, perhaps as a result of some abiding philosophical confusion or a great disappointment or loss; or else on an irrational basis, as a result of some brain dysfunction which does not correspond to any external objective phenomenon.

The first form of depression might be called psychological and the second physiological. In either case it amounts to the loss of hope (the ability to envisage that future circumstances will be better than present ones) and so undermines the ability of the individual to actively engage with present realities. Nothing is perceived as worthwhile, because it is believed that nothing can change the predicament in which the individual finds themselves. In turn, this is because no present action is thought to be capable of improving the subject's future prospects.

A life without hope is a travesty of life. Such an existence cannot possibly be its own purpose; but this fact does not contradict my contention that life is always its own purpose. Depression (whether psychological or physiological) is a disorder or sickness of the soul. It can be debilitating and is always morbid, even when it does not result in suicidal impulses. The extremely depressed individual is unable to effectively participate in events, experiences and actions. While they are biologically alive, as a human being they are inactive and so, in a sense, dead – or at best, dying. An existence devoid of hope is simply unsustainable. It is not really life at all, for it has no prospect of continuity. This is, at base, why it is unhappy and felt to be futile. The profound sadness associated with the loss of hope is a signal of the mental sickness which it represents, and indicates the breakdown of fundamental mental survival mechanisms. Happiness will only be restored when the soul is healed, hope is regained and the life-preserving processes which this virtue motivates are reactivated.

Could the ultimately futile have real value?[19]

Some people insist that personal mortality with no prospect of life after death (and even the fact that all the endeavours of humanity are bound to come to nothing, because of the Second Law of Thermodynamics) does not imply that human life is valueless and they point to experiences of love, beauty, exhilaration in sporting or scientific or artistic achievement, transcendent connectedness with the whole Cosmos… or whatever to justify their contention.

> To see a world in a grain of sand,
> And a heaven in a wild flower,
> Hold infinity in the palm of your hand,
> And eternity in an hour…
> [William Blake "Auguries of Innocence" (1863)]

They argue that these transient experiences – and the joy to which they give rise – have intrinsic value, and make human life worthwhile; even when it is known that it will all come to nothing in the end.

> I hold it true, whate'er befall;
> I feel it, when I sorrow most;
> 'Tis better to have loved and lost
> Than never to have loved at all.
> [Alfred Lord Tennyson "In Memoriam A.H.H." (1850)]

They insist that the fact that an individual human being's life ends in death is no more significant (apart from whatever suffering might be involved in the process of dying) than the fact that it ceases at the surface of their skin or began at their conception. After all, why should a *temporal* limit be seen as more significant than *spatial* ones? Why should the fact that one doesn't live for ever be deemed to be tragic when the fact that one's body does not fill the Universe is not in the slightest bit regrettable?

---

19 I thank H.C. Milton for causing me to explore the topics which make up the rest of this chapter.

From a physicist's perspective, this view can be corroborated by noting that the Block Universe[20] envisaged in Einstein's Theory of Relativity suggests that all events and experiences are eternal; in the sense that every event has its own independent self-sufficient reality and that our impression of passing from a past (which was once real but is no more so) to a future (which is not yet real, but is about to become so) via a moving present (which alone, of all moments, is real) is illusory. Hence whatever was, is still so now, and evermore shall be so; just as the Catholic regularly says of his God. According to this narrative it seems possible to say that all transient experiences of joy, love or beauty have an eternal permanence and solidity, existing forever unchanged in the fleeting moment which sees them flower.

Hope for the future

However, human experience of existence is not obviously of a Block Universe in which time has exactly the same status as space. Instead, we have a clear perception of uniformly directed progression. The human being is born innocent and ignorant, then matures into adulthood (becoming either virtuous or vicious) only to grow old and infirm and then, finally, to die.

At first, much of what the human being does is directed towards their future, and their actions are justified in terms of long-term outcomes. Then, as adulthood is reached, almost all activity is justified in terms of immediate advantage or enjoyment. Finally, as old-age is attained, attention switches to reminiscence of the past; because there is no longer any future to look forward to and the present is, too often, far from satisfactory.

---

20 In a Block Universe, time is nothing other than a fourth dimension like the three spatial dimensions. Just as one does not think of "left" being intrinsically different from "right", but only conventionally so, and just as there is no necessity or natural tendency to continually relocate one's position further and further to the left; so in a Block Universe there is no bias as regards time and no basis on which time could be said to flow.

In a Block Universe, "before" and "after" are interchangeable. While there is a sequence of events, there is no means by which to fundamentally distinguish "has been" from "will be". Moreover, there is no reason why there should be a special moment in time that is somehow "now" and hence more real and actual than any other moment; any more than there is any special place in space which is more real and actual than any other.

Perhaps the best response to human mortality is captured as follows:

> Gather ye rosebuds while ye may,
> Old Time is still a-flying:
> And this same flower that smiles to-day
> To-morrow will be dying.
> [R. Herrick "To the Virgins, to Make Much of Time",
> verse one (c 1650)]

Perhaps life (or youth, at least) is worthwhile of itself, even if it is fleeting. In which case one should try to live life to the maximum, even though though this maximum is finite; but this is of little consolation to the old, who have only memories and regrets.

> That age is best which is the first,
> When youth and blood are warmer;
> But being spent, the worse, and worst
> Times still succeed the former.
> [R. Herrick "To the Virgins, to Make Much of Time",
> verse three (c 1650)]

It is of little consolation to someone suffering from disability, depression, or chronic pain that they were once fit, happy and pain free. What *would* help is hope that in the future they will once again be able to walk and run, or see, or think clearly – or simply be free of pain or anxiety. Hope is what makes suffering endurable and life worthwhile. The problem with hope (like life, from which it springs) is death. Hope looks forward to better times; but (without the prospect of Eternal Life) in the end there is only death: the most undesirable outcome of all.

Why we experience time as directed towards the future is hotly debated.[21] Whatever the cause of this polarity, I think it is foolish to ignore it, and that any account of life which neither values hope nor allows that the future justifies the present is thereby inadequate. It is well and good to say that one should live in and for the present; but to insist on this absolutely, to the point that one discounts the future, is to ignore the reality of physical and psychological pain. To tell someone suffering from chronic depression that they should live in the present moment is cruel. For them the present is intolerable, and it is largely so simply because they have no hope for the future.

21 I suspect that it is attributable to life itself, which is predicated on the existence of a source of low entropy energy. This automatically results in a temporal direction: from low entropy, or "the past", to high entropy, or "the future". [H. Price "Time's Arrow and Archimede's Point" (1996)]

The pain of loss

My own experience is at odds with that of Tennyson.[22] I accept that good experiences do not become bad ones simply because they cease. Moreover, I acknowledge it an unqualified privilege to have even temporary possession of or association with some good; for knowledge of that good can remain even when the immediate association with it has ceased. Nonetheless, I know that the present pain of bereavement, betrayal and loss can be so acute as to make the past joy of possession and fellowship fade into insignificance. Moreover, as life proceeds, it becomes more and more characterized by loss: of physical and mental abilities, of health and of loved ones. In the absence of any belief in personal immortality it takes great strength of character for a human being to respond to this stark reality with quiet resignation rather than increasing sadness and despair.

Vanity and Value

I want to establish that if death is absolute, then life is worthless; and yet I do not wish to argue that transient experiences of love, beauty – or even mere pleasure – are worthless in themselves. To maintain such a position might seem difficult; for as soon as it is admitted that any one single fleeting experience has value, it would seem that the entire mortal existence of which it is a constituent part must gain value from it. In fact this is an easy position to maintain; for I can say that all which is of value in mortal experience is of value solely and precisely because it is a glimpse and presentiment of eternal reality. In which case, every such experience is a cause for hope that death is not the utter extinction of personal life.

The value of any experience does not derive from a source outside the person experiencing it. To this extent the Existentialist is right. Neither does human life take its worth from such experiences; but rather such experiences are of value precisely because they are experienced by a human being with an immortal spirit capable of participating in the Eternal Life of God. Belief in the immortality of the human spirit and the objective reality of Goodness, Beauty and Justice makes it possible to explain how fleeting experiences can have value. Every experience of love, beauty or communion is an intimation and pledge of the glory and rapture that is laid up in Eternity for the souls of God's friends.

22 Quoted above on page 88.

The challenge of Romance

By romance I do not mean erotic attachment; unless one wishes to abstract and generalise this in a way of which Plato might have approved[23] but would be thought decidedly queer today. Romanticism is the conviction that there is much more to the business of living than discovering, accepting and then faithfully reproducing pre-determined norms and pre-existing realities. It is the notion that the individual can truly originate and create something that is specific to and expressive of themselves and not simply derivative of an extrinsic and inevitable givenness.

Romanticism as a rejection of law

For anyone cleaving to this meaning of romanticism, Plato's world of unchanging and objective Ideas or Forms is liable to appear a fearful prospect, for it would seem to rule out any possibility of newness and originality. In contrast, some notion of creative anarchy, or "wildness" will likely appeal; where the absolute potentiality of non-existence and disorder, with its lack of constraint and presumptive bias is valued.

> Ancient poetry and art is rhythmical nomos,[24] a harmonious promulgation of the eternal legislation of a beautifully ordered world mirroring the eternal Ideas of things. Romantic poetry, on the other hand, is the expression of a secret longing for the chaos which is perpetually striving for new and marvellous births, which lies hidden in the very womb of orderly creation… [Greek art] is simpler, cleaner, more like nature in the independent perfection of its separate works; [Romantic art], in spite of its fragmentary appearance is nearer to the mystery of the Universe. [A.W. Schlegel "Vienna Vorlesungen uber dramatische Kunst und Literature" (1809-1811)]

I have already discussed "disorder" and "chaos" in Chapter 3. All I would add here is that neither disorder nor chaos can be associated in any way with a striving after anything. There may be a deep order underlying apparent chaos, and this order may have a teleological character; but the surface-level chaotic appearance itself cannot be the basis of any striving or creativity. Rather, life (and so the genesis of "new and marvellous births") is order within flux. Chaos itself is not alive and has no womb.

23 Plato "Symposium" (201d-212c)
24 This is Greek for "law".

Moreover, it is not true that chaos "lies hidden in the very womb of orderly creation." Rather the opposite is true. Much of physical reality on the human scale of things is characterized by disorder. Consider a scree slope, the weather, an overgrown copse and the Himalayas, for example. Humans are prejudiced in these matters and tend to focus on the order which facilitates their continued existence and the disorder which threatens it. The sub-atomic world is much more regimented, with electrons orbiting nuclei, so to speak, according to the rigid legislation of Quantum Mechanics and so on.

Nevertheless, there is some validity in the idea that chaos is creative. In particular, without random variations evolution would have no resources to work with. However, it is the laws of existence which both give rise to these variations and result in their selection on the basis of fitness for survival. The variations are themselves no more than the raw materials of genesis. Finally (except, perhaps, in the case of basic quantum randomness) every appearance of randomness may be a delusion. If so, every event which seems to be arbitrary and beyond the pale of law is actually intelligible and only appears to be random as a result of the observer's subjective ignorance.

The distinction which Schlegel is trying to establish is between two mentalities rather than two metaphysics. The first expects that simple laws inevitably result in limitation, regimentation and conformity. The second expects the exact opposite. The first seems reasonable, but is in fact false; the second, while seeming absurd, is in fact true. There are many examples in Mathematics and Science where simple non-linear systems manifest exuberant behaviours and give rise to unpredictable outcomes which are often characterized by considerable beauty.

The truth is that it is simple and apparently prescriptive laws which give rise to diversity and make originality possible. Conformity and conventionality have to be imposed extrinsically on a non-linear system in order to make it behave in non-original and non-idiosyncratic ways. In human terms this is done first by proscriptive socialisation and second by education conceived of as indoctrination and conditioning.

Romanticism as a rejection of reason

Romanticism is, secondly, the notion that rationality and logic – that is, "pure reason" – is an inadequate basis on which to establish value and describe reality. I have discussed the need for faith to underpin and justify reason in Chapter 2. Now, I wish to point out that even if reason is accepted as the basis on which we ought to proceed, it requires premises as a substrate to work on. Reason can only take us from a starting point to a finishing place. If one starts from nowhere and with nothing one cannot get to anywhere or obtain anything. Reason serves to disclose the connectedness of ideas and to unfold the implications of deceptively simple axiomatic systems, but reason cannot possibly establish anything if it is given nothing to work with.

Without faith, conviction and passion, reason is nothing. It has no rationale. Reason requires the demands of the appetites and desires, the pull of affection and the light of intuition; else it has no basis on which to act. Before one can decide what is the right course of action, one has to have an idea of one's objective and of the challenges which will have to be overcome if that objective is to be achieved; but neither the objective nor the challenges are determined by reason.

I have suggested[25] that the most basic value for any living being is its own existence; and that its most fundamental, non-negotiable and constitutive necessity, desire and purpose is that it should continue to live.[26] Even so, life understood simply as "persistence within flux" does not represent a necessity of itself. For a candle-flame to be a candle flame, it must indeed continue to burn; but there is no absolute requirement that it do so. Not even the flame itself has any desire in the matter; except in the most reductive sense: namely that it is clearly necessary for the particular flame's existence that it burns.

Romanticism as a rejection of selfishness

Romanticism is, thirdly, the idea that some thing or person or ideal or experience is of such undeniable importance that it trumps the value of the self. It therefore leads to acts which seem to be either selfless and courageous or else very foolish. Patriotism, friendship,[27] spousal and parental love, religious conviction and even intellectual integrity[28] can be at the base of such an upsetting of the hierarchy of values.

If I believe that my own life is finite and that death will inevitably come at some point, then it would seem that the question as to whether I should value a temporary extension of my own days more than the welfare of some other person or group of people whom I love (or more than the upholding of some principle that is dear to me, for that matter)

---

25 See Chapter 4. I shall take up this theme again in Chapter 7.

26 From this, perhaps, all other subsidiary objective might be deducible by reason – but only in principle. The task of doing so is much too large to be seriously undertaken.

27 "Greater love has no man than this, that a man lay down his life for his friends." [Jn 15:13 RSV]

28 The diverse cases of Socrates, Athanasius, Galileo, Joan of Arc, Thomas More and Marcel Lefebvre come to mind.

can be addressed rationally.[29] All that is necessary is that an exchange rate be established, which would make it possible to compare the "worth to me now" of the continuance of my life with the "worth to me now" of the alternative on offer. Sadly, this is doubly problematic.

First, the "worth to me now" (were this quantifiable, which it is not) is an inadequate measure. What is of low "worth to me now" might become of great "worth to me at some future date."[30] There is simply no stable measure of comparative value and neither is there any basis on which to decide what moment in time should serve as a reference point; unless this is the moment at which the commodity in question has its maximum value – but how could one recognise this beforehand?

Second, and more fundamentally, where can the alternative obtain its value if not from my life? For the psychopath this conundrum is of no consequence; as they set no value on anything other than their own immediate interests and the gratification of their own imperative desires. For those of us with consciences, however, this is a real problem. Are we to discount all our romantic impulses as mere animal instincts (forced on us by the evolutionary demands of the selfish gene) and so not value them as being noble and worthy of approval, but rather dismiss them as irrational and sub-human?

The teaching of Jesus of Nazareth is clear on this matter. He says that: "He who finds his life will lose it, and he who loses his life for My sake will save it."[31] Jesus' point is that this present mortal life is not what is fundamentally at issue. Only a few verses further on He says: "And whoever gives to one of these little ones even a cup of cold water because he is a disciple, truly, I say to you, he shall not lose his reward."[32] So Jesus must not be understood as saying that one should not be concerned with what is good for oneself; rather He promises that even altruistic acts will attract a benefit, which fact serves to make them rational. Similarly, when questioned by Peter as to the recompense a disciple might expect for their extravagant and romantic commitment to the Gospel, Jesus says:

> "Truly, I say to you, there is no one who has left house or brothers or sisters or mother or father or children or lands, for My sake and for the Gospel, who will not receive a hundredfold now in this time, houses and brothers and sisters and mothers

29 Note the basic meaning of "rational" as being "in due proportion".

30 So, a friend might counsel a bereft lover: "You'll see things differently in a while. After the rain, the sun will shine again and your life (which now seems empty) will once more be worthwhile."

31 Mat 10:39 RSV.

32 Mat 10:42 RSV.

> and children and lands,[33] with persecutions,[34] and in the age to come eternal life. But many that are first will be last, and the last first." [Mk 10:28-31 RSV]

The existence of romance is a testament to eternity. Without a fundamental conviction that the romantic gesture or principled stand *matters* in some non-negotiable sense, there would be no rational point in making it. Erotic devotion itself cannot *matter* unless at least either the lover or beloved *matters*; because the love which binds them is a property of their relationship and can only have significance, value and meaning relative to their existence and to their shared life.[35]

Moreover, without some belief in a recompense or happy resolution beyond death, what could motivate any extravagant self-sacrificial romantic act? We are not here talking about a trade-off between "length of mortal life" and "intensity of mortal life". The romantic act typically curtails life, or else accepts some great limitation on it. It does so because some other reality is accepted as *mattering* more than the mortal life of the romantic individual. Without such a conviction the romantic act is nothing more than a tragic, futile, despairing and suicidal gesture.

The only thing which could possibly be of more value to me than my mortal life (and the finite opportunity it affords me to explore and realise my potential) is the prospect of an immortal existence; with the possibility of unlimited opportunities to experience and learn of reality, to grow into perfection and to become so much more than I can imagine.

> I think that many have sacrificed themselves for a cause not because it would be truly more horrific for them to have not done so, but because of a deep seducing desire to *have* the desire of an impassioned and romantic soul. The concept of an afterlife certainly does make this rational, however, in these days people tend to not actually believe in Heaven – though they will protest that they do. But if one sincerely believed, they could rationally commit the sacrifice.
> [J. Kramer "Private Communication" (2012)]

---

33 This promise is so direct as to make it seem that no act of "sacrifice" could ever be real, as the good which is "sacrificed" is always returned with a huge return. It also seems unrealistic, and certainly does not chime with the experience of Christians throughout the ages. Jesus may be referring to the undoubted fact that in giving up one's secular connections and wealth one gains access to the fellowship and commonwealth of the Church.

34 Here is the sting in the tail. Only the promise of life eternal can compensate for secular persecution and martyrdom.

35 Unless love is itself the ultimate good, being the very nature of God.

Suicide is not romantic. Suicidal, thoughts, by definition, result from the denial of one's own worth – which itself results from a loss of hope. However this comes about, and whatever the mitigating circumstances, this is a tragic state of affairs for anyone to find themselves in. It has no glory or grandeur. A suicidal person should command sympathy and those who becomes aware of their plight should offer immediate and substantial help.

Jesus' sacrificial death was the ultimate in extravagant and passionate romantic acts. It was no kind of suicide or defeat or tragic gesture. It was motivated by hope and by a belief in life as the ultimate value. Jesus was willing to suffer rejection, indignity, agony and death in order to build a bridge[36] between God's holiness and humanity's disorder and imperfection. Jesus was sure that it was the way in which He could best reconcile God with humanity. He understood His passion as a means to self-fulfilment and self-glorification, not a means to self-destruction.[37] Jesus saw His death as a means of rebirth to eternity, both for Himself and for those who He would draw to himself by it.

> Why, one will hardly die for a righteous man – though perhaps for a good man one will dare even to die. But God shows His love for us in that while we were yet sinners Christ died for us. [Rom 5:7 RSV]

If a human being believes in eternal life after death, where virtue is rewarded, it is easy to understand how they can rationally act contrary to the interest of the preservation of their mortal life. Indeed, it is difficult to understand (apart, of course, from fear of the pain associated with the process of dying; which Jesus knew as keenly as anyone else[38]) why anyone with a belief in eternal life would seek to postpone the commencement of that time of uncompromised bliss. As the Apostle Paul puts it: "My desire is to depart and be with Christ."[39]

---

36 This is the fundamental idea of priesthood. A priest or "pontifex" is one who "builds a bridge"; first between God and humanity, and second between one human being and another.

37 Jn 12:23-33, quoted at the head of this chapter.

38 Mk 14:32-36.

39 Php 1:23 RSV.

Chapter 6 Body, Soul and Spirit

> May the God of peace Himself sanctify you wholly; and may your spirit and soul and body be kept sound and blameless at the coming of our Lord Jesus Christ. [1Th 5:23 RSV]

Motivation

In order to understand how reality and life can have significance, it is necessary to address the question of transcendence and the human spirit. In particular, I have argued that the question "What is the Meaning of Life?" arises when a human being becomes conscious of mortality, or unjustifiable suffering – but what do we mean by *conscious*?[1]

Mind and matter

I have no difficulty in attributing the whole of the mind: memory, reason, appetites, emotions and imagination to the workings of dynamic electrochemical brain processes. On this basis, all creatures with a nervous system must think to some degree; the more complex their nervous system the more complex their thought. This is necessarily true once "thought" is equated with "activity of the nervous system."

A bacterium and a mushroom are both alive, but neither has a nervous system and so can have no mind and cannot think at all. An earthworm and a snail have only minimal nervous systems and so have primitive minds and can barely think. A bear and a wolf have large brains and so have sophisticated minds and are pretty good at thinking; but they are nowhere near as clever or reflective as a chimpanzee or a dolphin.

On the one hand, the mind is a higher form of being than the body; because the material body is commanded by the mind. On the other hand, the biological purpose of the mind is to preserve the body's life; so (as far as Biology is concerned) that which is master (the mind) has mastery only for service of that which it masters, namely the living physical body. From a cosmological perspective the relationship between mind and matter is clearer.

---

1 See S.C. Lovatt "New Skins for Old Wine" Ch 4 for a fuller account of this topic. This book is subsequently referred to as LNS.

> In so far as matter is important to the existence of mind, whereas mind is not important to the existence of matter, in that proportion we are emboldened to say that mind must, in the ultimate constitution of things, have a higher value and importance than matter has. For you can conceive of matter as existing for the sake of mind, whereas you cannot possibly think of mind as existing for the sake of matter.
> [R.A. Knox "In Soft Garments" Ch 2 (1941)]

Awareness, self-awareness and consciousness

Awareness can be used as a synonym for consciousness, and in casual speech these words are interchangeable; but it is important to distinguish between them in technical use. In this chapter I shall use the word "awareness" to indicate of a dynamical system that its internal processes are modulated in some congruent manner by external facts. In other words, a system is aware if there exists within it some kind of model, representation or theory of the reality which lies beyond it; and this model is subject to correction as external events unfold.

To say that a system is self-aware indicates that it has some means of monitoring its own internal states and has generated a mental model of the behaviour of its own mind; treating its internal states as themselves objective facts which have to be accounted for in a manner that is susceptible to analysis and rational discussion. In other words, a self-aware mind thinks about its own thinking.

To say that a being is conscious is entirely different from either of these statements. I find that it is true of myself that I am not simply an *object* of experience (that is, a thing to be aware of or to be known about) but also that I am a *subject* who experiences – and also an *agent* who acts. My subjective experience of being conscious is irreducible to any account of the organisation and movement of the matter which constitutes my nature, and which is all that Science concerns itself with. In other words, there is no way to jump from the idea of "matter in motion" to the idea of "consciousness". Going from "matter in motion" to "mind" and "thought" is easy enough: this is nothing other than mathematics and engineering. It is accounting for *personal subjective experiential consciousness* that is difficult. Indeed it seems to me that this difficulty is an unbridgeable ontological chasm. I cannot see how any degree of recursive self-reference could account for my consciousness; though it plausibly explains the self-object of which I am subjectively conscious.

I have already claimed that Mr Data would be alive[2] and have a soul, if he were ever to be constructed. However, I do not claim to know whether he would be subjectively and experientially conscious; and what is more, I can't rightly say how one could possibly find out. All the obvious experiments would simply confirm that he had a mind and a memory and feelings and emotions, and that he was self-aware; if, that is, these features had either been explicitly incorporated into his programming or else implicitly allowed a means to develop.

I do not even know that you who now read this text are subjectively and experientially conscious. I simply cannot know this, but only presume it on the basis of your similarity with myself, which I suppose to be apparent.[3] Simply observing (or even conversing with) another agent could never give one adequate reason to definitively conclude that they were conscious. It would be easy to conclude that they were intelligent, aware and even self-aware; but none of these properties (nor even their combination) corresponds with *experiential consciousness.* This being so, there is no external test which could possibly establish to my satisfaction that any being other than myself personally experiences reality as a subject and thus is properly conscious.[4] Moreover, I frankly acknowledge that I cannot offer you any solid evidence that I am myself subjectively and experientially conscious.

> Science may be able to explain how my brain works. It may be able to explain my thoughts – why my past history and state of my physical body and brain lead me to think certain things, feel certain emotional states and act in certain ways. I wouldn't be surprised if we are able to eventually construct some robots or other machines that are able to simulate the same thought processes. I wouldn't be surprised if we are eventually able to show how certain individual neurones firing match certain thoughts; but none of that explains why *I am actually aware* of all this. I feel myself, as a single unit… at this very instant. There is something intangible there that is me. Something very personal, which can never be shared with anyone else: my consciousness; and the interesting thing is that this consciousness appears to be totally immune to investigation by scientific methods.
> [S. Robinson "private communication" (2003)]

---

2 So far as his mind was concerned. An android's body is not living, because its ordering is static rather than dynamic.

3 I take my reader to be human. I beg pardon for any presumption.

4 This means that a Logical Positivist (see page 48) will deny that the term "consciousness" (as I use it here) means anything.

I experience everything in the world in more or less the same way: as mental impressions of sense-data, or as abstractions understood in terms of such mental impressions. However, I do not experience or understand my consciousness in this way at all. Rather, it is my consciousness that *does* all the experiencing of things. It is the person or subject which itself *understands;* and so is sometimes called the "hypostasis"; which in Greek means under-standing, foundation, basis, substrate or sediment. Even though the hypostasis is itself fundamentally ineffable, it is the foundation and basis – the sediment – of all knowing. This hypostasis, which I cannot know you possess, is a mystery to me. Indeed, even my own consciousness is a mystery to me. This is because it is entirely unlike anything else. For the understanding to understand itself is as difficult as it is for a mirror to reflect itself.[5]

Two problems

> It is difficult for me to make specific objections when it's hard for me to pin point exactly what I am questioning. Your thesis seems to lie in you saying "My subjective experience of being conscious is irreducible to any account of the organisation and movement of the matter which… is all that Science concerns itself with." Now this is confusing to me. Why can physical processes or "matter in motion" not explain the sensation of consciousness? [J. Kramer "Private Communication" (2012)]

The real question is: how could physical processes explain consciousness? Matter in motion seems to have no relationship or point of contact with consciousness. Matter in motion can certainly explain what we are conscious of: that is, the contents and activity of the mind. However the quality "being conscious of" something is not a fact about the thing, or any kind of data which adds to one's affectedness by the thing: the in-form-ation of one's soul resulting from one's knowledge of the thing. "Being conscious of" something is an entirely subjective, interior and personal phenomenon; and so *spiritual* rather than *material.* It is inaccessible to any possible observer and so entirely disjoint from any account of material existence, or so it seems to me.

> It is common to see a paper on consciousness begin with an invocation of the mystery of consciousness, noting the strange intangibility and ineffability of subjectivity, and worrying that so far we have no theory of the phenomenon. Here, the topic is

5 A. Siddiqui "Private Communication" (2012)

> clearly the hard problem – the problem of experience. In the second half of the paper… the author's own theory… turns out to be… of the more straightforward phenomena… the reader is left feeling like the victim of a bait-and-switch. The hard problem remains untouched… What makes the hard problem hard and almost unique is that it goes beyond… the performance of functions… even when we have explained the performance of all the cognitive and behavioural functions in the vicinity of experience… Why is the performance of these functions accompanied by experience? A simple explanation of the functions leaves this question open. [D. Chalmers "Facing Up to the Problem of Consciousness" (1995)]

The "easy problem" asks the question: "How is it that complex living systems are objectively aware? How is it that they can respond coherently, in a 'meaningful manner' to external stimuli?" This sounds like a deep question; but it pales into insignificance before the "hard problem". This asks the question: "How is it that I come to *subjectively experience* things like pain or pleasure or 'blue' or 'the smell of a rose'? Moreover, what do I mean by 'experience'?" There is a great difference between describing the molecular processes going on in the neurones of a human being's brain and accounting for the subjective feelings and the personal experience of consciousness which is somehow associated with these processes.[6]

The easy problem

It is conceivable that internal states of a sufficiently complicated dynamic material system might map onto – and so represent – aspects of its present and past environment. These states would then be identifiable as impressions or memories and constitute knowledge or ideas: the coinage of consciousness. They would not, however, amount to *subjective experience*. A written diary has such internal states, but it is not thereby conscious; so also does an exposed photographic film, and it has no consciousness either. In both cases, some representation of external reality exists in the internal state of the system, but this fact does not result in personal, subjective, experiential consciousness. Making the persistence of such states dependent on a flux of energy or matter (that is, making them the properties of a living being) doesn't add any mystical substance which would make the system conscious.

---

6 C. Koch "What is Consciousness?" in "Discover" (1992)

It is further conceivable that some dynamic internal states or processes of very complex organisms might serve as analogues of external systems. These would be more than just impressions of observables. They would amount to models of reality and would yield predictions of future phenomena based on present observation. The activities of such model processes would be identified as deliberation. Other higher level processes might modify and adapt these models; in response to experience and according to certain rules, and so be called learning processes. Finally, if such a deliberative system were to become able to monitor its own internal states, it would inevitably develop mental processes to model its own behaviour and so become reflectively self-aware; but still not subjectively and experientially conscious.

This seems to me to be a complete solution in principle of the "easy problem" of consciousness. Macroscopically, a behavioural account is given in terms of meaningful responses made to environmental stimuli. Microscopically, a physiological account is given in terms of potentially observable brain states and processes.

The hard problem

This account of the mind does not, however, even begin to account for my *subjective experiencing* of reality. An electronic personal organizer or programmable calculator has internal states, but I have no basis for thinking that it *understands* what it has been programmed with; still less that it *experiences* being programmed. A computer can be programmed with models of external realities, and interfaced with sensors that enable it to compare the predictions of its models with experimental observations. It could even be allowed to modify its models in response to these comparisons. It may therefore be said to be aware in the merely behavioural sense of this word – defined in terms of a "meaningful" response to stimuli. However, there is no reason for believing that it subjectively *experiences* anything.

The "hard problem" always involves the word "I" or "me", and cannot be formulated without use of one or other of those words. If "you" or "they" – or even "we" is used instead, then the point of the question is lost. This is because I cannot possibly know that anyone other than myself *subjectively experiences* any thing. I can only conjecture that they do and as soon as the problem is expressed in the plural, the point of it is lost.

The human spirit

I can see no way forward without invoking the spiritual. On the one hand, I admit that I hardly know what I mean by consciousness. On the other hand, I am convinced that I am conscious; and that this is the only thing about me which is of ultimate value and really matters to me.

Apart from consciousness, even my mind wouldn't matter: because there would be no experiencing subject to be conscious of it. If I were not experientially conscious, I doubt that mere knowledge of my mortality would cause me to question the purpose of my life; for it is the idea of my consciousness ending which is fearful to me, not that of awareness ceasing – though I admit that consciousness without anything to be conscious of amounts to very little of value. Indeed, if I were not conscious, I wonder whether the notion of "purpose", or the possibility of consciousness itself for that matter, would even occur to me. Perhaps the fact that I do entertain these concepts is some sort of evidence that I am subjectively and experientially conscious.

Plato suggests that the human soul (by which he meant what I would term the mind) was itself tripartite, consisting of: first, appetites, drives and instincts – the "gut"; second, the emotions, passions and feelings – the "heart", the seat of personality and character, virtues and vices; and third, the reason or intellect – the "head".[7] The distinction between the first two parts is not always clear, and neither is that between the last two. Plato did not mean that there were three souls (in my terms three minds) but only that the soul had three levels of sophistication, which a modern mind might identify with three stages of evolution: the reptile, mammal and primate.

The soul of a human being can informally be described as *spiritual*, in that its mental part – and especially the intellect – is somehow intimately associated with, linked to and suffused by the conscious hypostasis. Nevertheless, if soul means life, then the soul of a mortal man is just as physical and mortal as that of a slug; though the soul of man be ever so intellectual and rational. I therefore prefer to reserve the word "spirit" to signify the basis of subjective experiential consciousness present in each personal being: their hypostasis.

> Spirit is a term Scripture sometimes uses for the mind; as when insisting that a virgin should be holy: "in spirit and in body".[8]

---

7 Plato "Republic" (IV 434e-441c) The same division features in Kabbalistic thought, where "nefesh" [נפש] is the gut-soul; "ruach" [רוח] (literally "spirit" – which agrees with Plato's use of this term) the heart-soul; and "neshamah" [נשמה] is the head-soul.

8 1Cor 7:34.

> Sometimes it employs the term for the soul or life, for instance in James: "As the body apart from the spirit is dead";[9] and sometimes for the consciousness which is associated with life, as in the words: "No-one knoweth the things of a man save the spirit that dwelleth in him."[10]
> [Origen "Selections from the Psalms."]

On this basis, each human being is tripartite: having first, a physical body; second, a soul: the life-activity of the body; and third, a spirit: the subjectively conscious person.[11]

> The word of God is living and active, sharper than any two-edged sword, piercing to the division of soul and spirit, of joints and marrow, and discerning the thoughts and intentions of the heart. [Heb 4:12 RSV]

The soul (and the mind, which is an aspect of the soul) is the activity of the body and when this ceases the soul has no other reality by which to continue. Hence the soul is just as mortal as the body, because it is derivative of the body and has no existence apart from the body. I am not here saying that there is nothing in a human being which survives death; but only that the mind or soul is, of itself, not immortal.

Nature and Person

The *nature* of a being is "that by which it acts"; that which connects it with the rest of reality and which allows it to affect and be affected by its environment. The nature of an inanimate being is passive. It does not encompass any principle of self-sustenance. By contrast, the nature of any living being is responsive, self-sustaining and even adaptive.

Any biological nature consists of a body and soul. The body is its physiological and biochemical construction; the soul is its metabolic

---

9 Jas 2:26.

10 1Cor 2:11.

11 1Th 5:23, quoted at the head of this chapter. I am not referring here to the tripartite division of the soul itself, as if the spirit were the same as the reason or intellect. Though many philosophers have assumed that the conscious mind, the intellect, the spirit and the person are identical, I do not. I contend, rather, that the reason or intellect is a part of human being's soul and is neither part of nor else identical with their spirit, hypostasis or person. Moreover, I am not claiming that human beings have two souls, an animal soul and a spiritual soul. Rather, I am contending that the human soul is one thing altogether (a part of human nature: the objective *livingness* of a human being) and that the spirit is of an entirely different order: the subjective *consciousness* or personhood of a human being.

and, in the case of animals, mental processes. The soul is inseparable from and dependent upon the physicality and stability of body, and the body is reliant for its continuance on the motility of the soul.

> Behold how both the soul and the body look and attest to one another: even as the body must have the soul so as to live, so must the soul have the body to see and hear.
> [Ephraim the Syrian "Hymn Eight: On Paradise."]

Since my mind is an aspect of my soul, it is a part of my nature.[13] As such it both mediates the world to my spirit and my spirit to the world. In both directions it imposes its own bias on the impetus it receives. What I perceive is filtered by my expectations and prejudices. When I decide to act, my decisions are flavoured by my personality.[12] This is constituted from my intrinsic talents and deficiencies; and from my acquired habits, virtues and vices – which largely amount to the relative importance and detailed significance which I regularly give to various factors such as my personal security, anticipated pleasure or pain, the long term effect on friendships and so on.

My spirit is not any kind of aspect or part of my nature. Just as my nature is the answer to the question "*What* is acting?" so my spirit, hypostasis or person is the answer to the question "*Who* is acting?" Nature and hypostasis go hand-in-hand and neither is reducible to the other. The question "What?" is equivalent to "which (type of) thing or object?" whereas the question "Who?" is equivalent to "which particular person, subject or agent?"

> The name "man", according to the most truthful and natural expression, applies to neither the soul without [the] body, nor to the body without [the] soul; but to that composition of soul and body made into a unique form of beauty… But though the soul be immortal [by grace] yet it is not the person,[13] and so the Apostle does not consider [death] to differ in any wise from destruction… [Photios of Constantinople "On the Resurrection, against Origen" cap 1 #5]

12 Personality is a different notion from that of person or hypostasis. My personality or character is an aspect of my mind, and so of my nature. It is not at all equivalent to my person or spirit. Similarly, my conscience is arguably a part of my personality rather than an aspect of my consciousness.

13 I think the implication here is that the person is the combination of soul and body, but this is not my contention. This is certainly not the case of the Divine Messiah. His body and soul were both entirely human and yet His person was entirely divine.

Now, the hypostasis, consciousness, person or spirit might have a merely passive role in the composite human reality. However I don't think that this is a sustainable position. The very fact that I am now discoursing about my consciousness implies that my mind must somehow be informed of the existence of my consciousness (else how does it know that there is anything to discuss?) and that my consciousness must be the informant. Hence, my consciousness must have an active role of some sort. The connection between the mind and the consciousness cannot be of any simple form, however. In particular, it cannot consist of some kind of data-transfer. My reasons for saying this are two-fold.

Theoretically, a data-transfer paradigm is liable to limit one's understanding of the spirit-hypostasis to the idea of it being some kind of co-processor. The most that such a bolt-on component could do for the human being is to enhance the natural abilities of their brain; perhaps even to the level of adding certain paranormal or psychic powers, but no more. Now, for the spirit to be conscious of the mind, the mind's activity has to be accessible to the spirit; but this does not mean that the spirit must be conceived of as a separate entity with a data-connection linking it to the mind. Alternately, the spirit could be a transcendent quality of the mind: something added to it holographically at every point; an all-pervasive context for the mind which changed its character without affecting its operation: entirely extrinsic in its ontology, while intrinsic in its association with and penetration of the mind's existence.

The data-transfer paradigm seems to be refuted by the experimental evidence.[14] The two cerebral hemispheres of the brain are normally connected together by a bundle of nerves called the Corpus Callosum. This is severed in human beings who have "split brains", generally as a result of surgery to treat drug resistant epilepsy. Such people exist as two more or less independent personalities;[13] with their right hand not knowing what their left is doing. In such subjects very little information fed to one side of the brain (via one eye, for example) gets transferred to the other side,[15] except in those rare cases where the cerebral cortex regenerates some of the connectivity previously eliminated by surgery.

It follows from this that if there is any two-way data transfer between the mind and the spirit the latter is as strictly segregated according to brain hemisphere as is the former. In other words, either the spirit has no unity in itself; but only as a result of the functioning of the physical Corpus Callosum (which seems absurd) or else there is no data transfer as such from the spirit to the mind.

---

14 J.V. McConnel "Understanding Human Behaviour" (1974)

15 Some connectivity is maintained via the brain-stem.

Two theories of immortality

Two distinct theories of immortality feature in Catholic doctrine. One is Jewish in origin, the other Greek. The Ancient Hebrews, unlike their Egyptian contemporaries, had little interest in the matter and knew nothing of eternal life, beyond the superstition that a ghost might persist in "Sheol" in some kind of half existence after bodily death.

> To Thee, O Lord, I cried; and to the Lord I made supplication: "What profit is there in my death, if I go down to the Pit? Will the dust praise Thee? Will it tell of Thy faithfulness?"
> [Ps 30:8-9 RSV]

> The dead do not praise the Lord, nor do any that go down into silence. [Ps 115:17 RSV]

> The fate of the sons of men and the fate of beasts is the same; as one dies, so dies the other. They all have the same breath, and man has no advantage over the beasts; for all is vanity. All go to one place; all are from the dust, and all turn to dust again. Who knows whether the spirit of man goes upward and the spirit of the beast goes down to the earth?
> [Eccl 3:19-21 RSV]

Many Greeks contemporary with Socrates and Plato also found the idea of life after death difficult, though Pythagoras had taught that souls were immortal and transmigrated from one body, on its death, to another newly born.

> Men find it very hard to believe what you [Socrates] said about the soul. They think that after it has left the body, it no longer exists anywhere; but that it is destroyed and dissolved and... is dispersed like breath or smoke...
> If indeed it gathered itself together and existed by itself and escaped these evils... there would then be much good hope, Socrates, that what you say is true; but to believe this requires a good deal of faith and persuasive argument – to believe that the soul still exists after a man has died and that it still possesses some capability and intelligence.[16]
> [Plato "Phaedo" (70a-b)]

---

16 I, of course, contend that the immortal spirit has no such capability.

Resurrection of the body

Isaiah is the first prophet who offers any hope of life after death:

> Your dead shall live, their corpses shall rise. O dwellers in the dust, awake and sing for joy! For your dew is a radiant dew, and the earth will give birth to those long dead. [Is 26:19 RSV]

However, he may be referring to a political revival of the nation rather than the bodily revival of individual human beings. The book of Job also seems to refer to a resurrection:

> For I know that my Redeemer lives, and at last He will stand upon the earth; and after my skin has been thus destroyed, then from my flesh I shall see God, whom I shall see on my side, and my eyes shall behold, and not another. [Job 19:25-27 RSV]

Sadly, the Hebrew text is corrupt and the Greek[17] and Syriac[18] versions differ in meaning, so it is impossible to reconstruct the original with any degree of certainty.

The first clear promise of personal resurrection is found in Daniel:

> At that time your people shall be delivered, every one whose name shall be found written in the book. And many of those who sleep in the dust of the earth shall awake, some to everlasting life, and some to shame and everlasting contempt. [Dan 12:1-2 RSV]

Belief in the resurrection of the body became commonplace among the Jews after their return from exile in Babylon.[19] It is most poignantly expressed in the following passage.

> They did not know the secret purposes of God, nor hope for the wages of holiness, nor discern the prize for blameless souls; for God created man for incorruption,[20] and made him in the image

17 A translation of the Greek Septuagint: "I know that He who will deliver me is eternal on Earth to restore my skin that suffers this. It is the Lord who has performed for me what I myself know, what my own eye has seen and no other."

18 A translation of the Syriac version: "I know that my redeemer is living and that in the end he will appear on Earth; and these things encompass both my skin and my flesh. If my eyes see God they will see the light."

19 See 2Mac 7:9-23; 14:46.

20 And hence not for bodily dissolution.

> of His own eternity,[21] but through the devil's envy death entered the world, and those who belong to his party experience it.[22]
>
> But the souls of the righteous are in the hand of God, and no torment will ever touch them. In the eyes of the foolish they seemed to have died, and their departure was thought to be an affliction, and their going from us to be their destruction; but they are at peace. For though in the sight of men they were punished, their hope is full of immortality. Having been disciplined a little, they will receive great good, because God tested them and found them worthy of himself; like gold in the furnace He tried them,[23] and like a sacrificial burnt offering He accepted them.[24] In the time of their visitation[25] they will shine forth, and will run like sparks through the stubble. They will govern nations and rule over peoples, and the Lord will reign over them for ever. [Wis 2:21-3:8 RSV]

The problem with the Jewish theory of resurrection is that it makes no provision for continuity. The fact that a new living body comes to exist which has some close similarity to one which previously existed does not mean that the new life is a true continuation of the old one. Every time someone falls asleep and then wakes up again there is a similar discontinuity in existence. The fact that the newly woken being can recollect much of what happened to the being which previously fell asleep does not constitute proof that they are the self-same person. After all, two copies of the same book are not the self-same book.

On a psychological level, what is commonly called "personal identity" amounts to nothing more than a continuity of memory and personality; but this is not what one thinks of, on a deeper level, as true personal identity. If it ever becomes possible to transfer memories and personality traits from one human being to another, I would not account this as an exchange or duplication of spirit or hypostasis; for I am neither my memories nor my personality. Both of these can and do change, while I remain the self-same person.

---

21 Compare Plato "Timaeus" (37d, 39e).

22 See what Saint Paul [Rom 5:12 quoted on page 168] and Saint Peter [2Pet 1:2-4, quoted on page 302] have to say about this.

23 The just are accepted by God as a result of this assay, by which their worthiness is established.

24 That is, as a holocaust is accepted. The primary idea of holocaust here is not of the suffering and destruction of the victim but of divine approval and acceptance, leading to union with God.

25 That is, when the just are raised from the dead.

Survival of the soul

The second theory of immortality claims to be based on secular experience, and does not rely on divine intervention at the end of time. It claims that within each human being there is a "spark of immortality". I would identify this "spark" with the spirit, person or hypostasis, but more typically it has been identified with the soul; on the naïve basis that the consciousness, mind and will were one and the same thing. There is a serious problem with this theory, however. It does not extend its promise of immortality to the body, and so to the brain and mind.

Now, it would seem that without a nature (constituted of a physical body and rational soul) an incorporeal person would be able to do nothing whatsoever. Without a mind the spirit could not even be conscious (as there would exist no thoughts for it to be conscious of) even though it is the spirit that is the foundation of consciousness. I suppose that this most unsatisfactory potential state of being is very close to the form of ghostly survival envisaged by the ancient Hebrews.

Reconciling the two theories

The Jewish idea of physical resurrection complements the Greek idea of spiritual immortality. The prospect of a new and immortal body living on a new Earth beneath a new Heaven is a promise of a nature truly fit for the purposes of an immortal spirit. God, who is just, is obligated to provide for each and every created spirit a nature by which it can experience and act. Any spirit denied such an instrument would have no integrity and such a denial would be a direct affront to divine justice.

The soul and spirit are entirely distinct; the first is a product of the body and the second is independent of all physicality. Nevertheless, each needs the other. Human nature needs the human spirit if it is to have meaning and significance and an identifiable continuity of existence. Conversely, each human person needs a soul and body in order to experience, think and do anything whatever. Together the nature and person form one integral reality: the human being.

The cinema analogy

Consider the following analogy. Let the human spirit be a cinema projector and let the ensouled body be a film. In combination, the projector and film can manifest the story which the film's information constitutes as moving images on a viewing screen. The film without the projector cannot tell its story, the projector without the film has no story to tell. Each exists for the other. Each is pathetic without the other.

What matters to the film (what gives it purpose, its teleos) is that it be projected. What matters to the projector (its teleos) is that it has a film to project. The crucial difference between the two is that whereas the film can incorporate within its own existence pattern and ordering a narrative of its teleos, the projector cannot do so. The film's information could be a story about the wonder of cinematography and about how a film only has a significance if its story is told and about how this requires a projector;[26] whereas the projector cannot refer to its futility in the absence of any film except implicitly, by an absolute mute passivity.

Fulfilment of the film's teleos is contingent on two conditions. First, the information which it carries must be preserved. Second, this information must be made manifest. It is not at all obviously important that the physicality of the film itself is preserved. What is most important about the film (what gives it a teleos[27]) is the information it contains. If the film was transcribed onto a DVD, then played back using laser-beams, electronics and a plasma screen – what would it matter? The original film would thereby become redundant, but its message would be preserved, though transferred from one medium to another.

What matters to the projector, what gives significance to its existential form, is the exercise of its function: that it has something to project. It would be no consolation for any self-respecting cinema projector to be placed on display in a museum alongside cans of film; forever inactive, never again to fulfil its purpose, having been rendered obsolete by electronics. Its teleos would be absolutely frustrated.[28]

Imagine that there were two projectors and two films and that the films were swapped round. Each projector would then have a different story to tell while remaining the same projector it always was. Clearly, the teleos of neither of the films nor either of the projectors would be in any way compromised by this exchange. Now imagine that one of the films were to be copied and run in both projectors. Each would now

---

26 Actually, an audience is needed too; which role God plays in reality. See page 154 for Plato's words on this matter.

27 This isn't strictly true. A blank film also has a teleos: to become the carrier of some information. Every thing has some kind of teleos, vocation or potential. Low level things have multiple potentialities, (in Platonic jargon these are called its "seminal reasons") and their histories of becoming represent the sequential resolution of the ambiguities which characterize their mode of being. Higher order things (such as a hammer, television or giraffe) tend to have more specific and exclusive potentialities. Sapient beings are paradoxical in the sense that they have a wide array of potentiality, a highly ambiguous teleos – and yet beyond this variety of "ways of being" is one single teleos: to be united with God in friendship.

28 Contrary to this analogy, the human spirit is not a mechanism, is very much eternal and is in no way subject to obsolescence. Even so, it requires to be re-united with its "film library"; but if that "library" has been transcribed from fragile cellulose nitrate onto robust polyester, so much the better.

show forth the self-same story, while remaining entirely separate and distinguishable projectors. Once again, the teleos of no being is impeded in this situation and there is no paradox; neither is there any cause for confusion. Only if the second film was either destroyed or permanently archived would its teleos be frustrated and so an injustice be done.[29]

It is very clear to the soul-mind (the film) that what is of paramount importance to itself is the subjective experiential consciousness (the projector) with which it is associated; that is the hypostasis which is the principle of personal continuity and identity. This need of the soul is felt keenly, simply because the spirit is extrinsic to its own existence and beyond its ken.

The second need of my soul (namely that "it will continue to be") is manifestly fulfilled (for now, at least) by the very fact that my mind is now actively considering what matters to it. Hence this vital requirement is not so keenly felt; as its loss does not seem so much of an immediate possibility. Of course, if my mind ceased to be, then nothing could matter to it: because it would no longer be capable of caring.

The idea that many years after I die, some *other* being will arise which has inherited all my memories and experiences and has a similar personality to mine is no real answer to my *own* fear of death. What "the I who am the cinema projector" requires is an assurance that it will be "me, myself, I" that lives again (that is, shows the same film – or at least a similar one) not just some other person (film projector) very much like me: the self-same being[30] not just a precisely similar being.[31]

What is the point of mortality?

If the hope of life after death is what gives meaning to our present mortal life, isn't this life itself redundant? It would seem to be nothing more than a hiatus: an exercise in waiting for the real action to begin. In which case, why does it exist at all and why does it feel so very important? Is this feeling merely a delusion; or is it, rather, a hint of the real significance of mortal existence?

If we are destined to live happily for ever with God then why should I strive to maintain my mortal life or to defend the lives of others? If my spirit is immortal, what care ought I have for the welfare of my mortal nature, which is ephemeral? If my personal survival is assured, it would seem that I am in need of nothing to sustain the integrity of my

29 Justice is that state of harmonious coexistence in which every being is free to conduct its own proper business according to its form; that is to express itself and to fulfil its teleos. See page 65.

30 In Greek: "ὁμοούσιος".

31 In Greek: "ὁμοιούσιος". Note the extra "ι".

being. Hence, there is nothing here which is really good for me;[32] but only things which are attractive in an illusory and distracting way, as tending to the temporary postponement of death. How then can I be motivated in this life by what is good for me, when it seems there is no such thing here? How then can I truly love?

These matters are mysterious. Our present perspective is limited; fixed within the physical world and mortal existence. We are like fish trying to understand the rationale of their lives from within the close confines of an aquarium. Nevertheless, we can observe that our present existence is characterized by doubt, choice and the ability to learn – rather than clear knowledge – and this, I believe, is all the clue we need.

Some have thought that the purpose of this mortal existence is to serve as a time of probation, testing or trial prior to the reception of divine approval and an eternal reward. I think this is mistaken; mainly because it suggests that God is concerned with catching us out.[33] The image of a stern bearded foreman hiding in the sky, watching our every move in order to condemn us for our sins is entirely different from that painted in the Bible, where God explicitly calls, requires and expects His people to aspire to righteousness, to do justice and chose life.

> The Lord said to Cain, "Why are you angry, and why has your countenance fallen? If you do well, will you not be accepted? And if you do not do well, sin is couching at the door; its desire is for you, but you must master it." [Gen 4:6-7 RSV]

> Justice, and only justice, you shall follow, that you may live and inherit the land which the Lord your God gives you.
> [Deut 16:20 RSV]

> Wash yourselves; make yourselves clean; remove the evil of your doings from before my eyes; cease to do evil,[34] learn to do good; seek justice, correct oppression; defend the fatherless, plead for the widow. [Is 1:16-17 RSV]

32 Hence the Gnostics teach that this life is the result of a Cosmic accident or mistake which has resulted in the improper mixing of spirit and matter and the business of life is for the spirit to purify itself of all involvement with matter and so return to "the source".

33 Hence the conventional interpretation of the Adam and Eve story as a test which they failed and in doing so deserved to experience God's retributive wrath. See Chapter 12 for my take on this story.

34 See also Ezk 18:21-23, quoted on page 164.

> The Lord hates all abominations, and they are not loved by those who fear Him. It was He who created man in the beginning, and He left him in the power of his own inclination. If you will, you can keep the commandments, and to act faithfully is a matter of your own choice. He has placed before you fire and water: stretch out your hand for whichever you wish. Before a man are life and death, and whichever he chooses will be given to him.[35]
> [Sir 15:13-17 RSV]

I believe that the purpose of this mortal life is to allow us to grow into an ethical maturity,[36] which is only possible in a context which is defended from God's immediate presence; though not remote from God's protection, support, aid and encouragement.[37]

> But Thou art merciful to all, for Thou canst do all things, and Thou dost overlook men's sins, that they may repent. For Thou lovest all things that exist, and has loathing for none of the things that Thou has made, for Thou wouldst not have made anything if Thou hadst hated it. How would anything have endured if thou hadst not willed it? Or how would anything not called forth by thee have been preserved? Thou sparest all things, for they are Thine, O Lord who lovest the living. For Thy immortal Spirit is in all things. Therefore Thou dost correct little by little those who trespass, and dost remind and warn them of the things wherein they sin, that they may be freed from wickedness, and put their trust in Thee, O Lord.
> [Wis 11:23-12:2 RSV]

> The spirit of those who fear the Lord will live, for their hope is in Him who saves them. He who fears the Lord will not be timid, nor play the coward, for He is his hope. Blessed is the soul of the man who fears the Lord! To whom does he look? And who is his support? The eyes of the Lord are upon those who love Him, a mighty protection and strong support, a shelter from the hot wind and a shade from noonday sun, a guard against stumbling and a defence against falling. He lifts up the soul and gives light to the eyes; He grants healing, life, and blessing. [Sir 34:13-17 RSV]

---

35 Deut 30:19-20, quoted on page 119.

36 See pages 327-331.

37 That is, God's grace. I return to this theme in Chapter 12.

This life is not a test or period of probation but rather an educational opportunity. People talk flippantly of "The University of Life", but I think that this reflects life's true purpose. This mortal life is the beginning of the immortal and forms its template. What is built here as temporary somehow becomes the basis of what continues for ever. St Paul expresses this idea well:

> For no other foundation can any one lay than that which is laid, which is Jesus Christ. Now if any one builds on the foundation with gold, silver, precious stones, wood, hay, straw – each man's work will become manifest; for the Day will disclose it, because it will be revealed with fire, and the fire will test what sort of work each one has done.[38] If the work which any man has built on the foundation survives, he will receive a reward. If any man's work is burned up, he will suffer loss, though he himself will be saved, but only as through fire. [1Cor 3:11-15 RSV]

The same theme is taken up by Origen:

> Whoever is saved is saved by fire, so that the fire may melt and dissolve any admixture the man has of the leaden element, so that all may become good gold... As the furnace tests the gold, so trial tests righteous men.
>
> All then must come to the fire, all must come to the furnace. For the Lord sits and refines and purifies the sons of Judah. And when we come there, if a man bring many good works and some small mixture of wickedness, this small item is dissolved and purged away like lead by the fire, and all that is left is pure gold. The more a man brings there of lead, the more he suffers burning, that the lead may be fully melted, so that even if there be little gold it may still be left in purity.
> [Origen "Sixth Homily on Exodus"]

On this basis, the quality of one's experience of eternity is hugely influenced by the use one makes of the opportunities of mortality; in accordance with Jesus' parable:

> A man going on a journey called his servants and entrusted to them his property... Now after a long time the master of those servants came and settled accounts with them. And he who had received the five talents came forward, bringing five talents more...

---

38 Compare Wis 3:6, quoted on page 111.

> His master said to him, "Well done, good and faithful servant; you have been faithful over a little, I will set you over much; enter into the joy of your master."…
>
> He also who had received the one talent came forward, saying, "Master, I knew you to be a hard man… and I went and hid your talent in the ground. Here you have what is yours."
>
> But his master answered him, "You wicked and slothful servant!… take the talent from him, and give it to him who has the ten talents." [Mat 25:14-28[39] RSV]

"The wages of sin is death"[40] precisely because sin is that which tends to frustrate, compromise and undermine life. I suspect that in God's dealings with humanity there is never any extrinsic penalty for sin, and no rationale for one. As justice is its own reward, because justice is nothing other than that which brings fullness of life; so wickedness wreaks its own vengeance. This is because sin is that which inevitably, in the very order of reality, brings the impoverishment of life and, in the end, death.[41] Hence, God says "Vengeance is mine"[42] because Reality itself faithfully and inexorably yields the dividend of sin and there is no call for any human agency to add to the recompense.

---

39 Compare Lk 19:12-27.

40 Rom 6:23 RSV.

41 So sin brings death while sin itself is made rational by the prospect of death: a truly vicious circle. See Rom 5:12, quoted on page 168.

42 Deut 32:35 RSV.

Chapter 7 Being Good

> I have set before you life and death, blessing and curse; therefore choose life, that you and your descendants may live, loving the Lord your God, obeying His voice, and cleaving to Him; for that means life to you and length of days.
> [Deut 30:19-20 RSV]

The problem of purpose

We now come to the central thesis of this book. In this chapter I shall try to explain how what *is* the case gives rise to what *ought* to be done. This is not a minor issue, as it may seem; rather it is the keystone which will hold together the entire edifice which I am attempting to construct. The basic idea is that "it is good to be" – hence the title of this book.

The immediate problem facing anyone at every moment of their lives is "What ought I to do, and why?" This question can be variously interpreted, as the word "ought" is given a variety of meanings. The word "ought" points to the idea of good, value, use, purpose or objective – in Greek "teleos". As one takes good to mean pleasure, power, knowledge, security, happiness, fame, acceptance, wealth, power or status (or some blend of these) than the question "What *ought* I to do, and why?" takes on entirely different meanings. The advice of Midas, Moses, Mohammed, Machiavelli, Morrison,[1] Marx and Mandleson[2] would be very different, I suppose; and it would be so precisely because their motivation (what they perceive as being desirable) differs.

At the root of the question "What ought I to do, and why?" lies the deeper question "What really matters?" and beneath this the deepest question of all "Why does anything matter at all?" This is the perennial question of adolescence. As I have already pointed out,[3] the child hasn't yet noticed this question and gets on with enjoying existence, taking life as it comes. The typical adult has given up on this question; having adopted some idiosyncratic blend of pleasure, status, fame and wealth as defining their life-goals. It is the adolescent who notices this question, and often becomes obsessed with it – before generally giving up on it and joining the crowd of disillusioned adults.

---

1 Jim Morrison of "The Doors".

2 Lord Peter Mandleson of North Greenwich.

3 See page 72.

The is – ought dichotomy

I have already suggested that the related question "What is the meaning of life?" stands proxy for the adult's intimation of mortality; and cannot be answered in terms of some extrinsic purpose, but only by an assurance of immortality.[4] I shall next argue that Goodness (the foundation of value or worth) is identical with Being; and that these two apparently very different words are synonyms, only distinguished by a conventional segregation of use according to context. The motivation behind this argument is simple. It seems to me that any other attempt to understand value or worth leads directly to what is known as the "is – ought dichotomy". This is the famous difficulty that knowing about whatever is in fact the case gives no obvious indication as to what *ought to be done* about it.

The "is – ought" dichotomy was first noted by the empiricist philosopher David Hume.[5] It arises most starkly, perhaps, in the field of medical ethics[6], where experts in gynaecology or genetic Engineering try to adjudicate moral[6] questions on the basis of their technical expertise – and regularly fail; having instead to fall back on their non-expert philosophical or political beliefs about "the sanctity of life", "the right to chose", "the autonomy of the patient" or whatever. Those aware of this problem often respond to it by postulating the existence of a separate ethical competence over and above any technical understanding; but it is never made clear how such a moral expertise might be constituted.

Want, desire and need

To desire something is to believe that one has a need for a thing; or else to believe that the possession of a thing would make one's life more pleasant in some way. A desire or want can be based on a purely appetitive craving – such as libidinousness, hunger or thirst – and such an instinctive urge can either be for something which is truly good for the agent or else for something harmful, like heroine or gambling, to which the agent has become addicted.

If a want is a desire for some truly beneficial thing, then it is a need. Otherwise it remains merely a want; and if it is a desire for something which is in fact harmful, then this want is immoral. To need something is to have a real want: to lack something which is necessary to sustain ones life. If a need is not supplied then the needy agent will not thrive, will not be happy, and may not even survive.

---

4 See Chapter 4.

5 D. Hume "A Treatise of Human Nature" (1739)

6 I use the words "ethics" and "morals" interchangeably.

People do not always do what they desire to do. One man may go to the dentist in spite of the fact that he is frightened of doing so. Another may go on a diet, in spite of the fact that he wants to eat candy. In such cases an immediate appetitive desire or speculative fear is overcome by a desire for what is believed to be beneficial in the longer-term.

> "I can readily think about my wants, letting the stronger one inform my action. I can have a stronger want for long term health than the immediate joy of candy."
> [J. Kramer "Private Communication" (2012)]

This is the basis of courage and heroism. Sadly, no-one is always heroic: doing what they believe to be right and their innermost soul desires to do. This is because the immediate prospect of pleasure or other obvious benefit sometimes overwhelms their better judgement.[7]

The fact that one desires something does not justify doing what is necessary to obtain it. The statement "I want your possessions so I ought to steal them." is not a well-formed ethical syllogism. The suppressed premise "I ought to do whatever I want." is simply wicked. While it may be the case that "I will in fact do what I want to do." this observation does not make the implied action virtuous.

Virtue, holiness and interior justice (these are equivalent to each other) amount to the alignment of "want" with "need". When we only desire what is good – and all that is good – then we will know peace and joy. In the end, what one wants is what one believes or feels is needful. Virtue resides in true belief about what one really needs, vice resides in false belief about what one really needs.

Relative value

The simple meaning of "value" is that of "utility for a purpose". This kind of value is *relative* value. It is relative in two ways. First, a commodity[8] has value to a moral agent, and so its value is relative to that agent. Second, a commodity can only have value to an agent in as far as they have a purpose or objective (that is, a teleos) which it seems that this commodity can help them attain. Hence, food has value because it enables its consumer to continue to live and because it is pleasurable to eat; money has value because it facilitates trade and economic activity; opium has value because it brings oblivion to a troubled soul.

7 Rom 7:16-25, quoted on page 157.

8 I use this word in its widest sense. The commodity could be "love" or "education" or "happiness": anything which is thought to have value.

The relative value of a commodity derives from the value of the agent who values it and the value of the objective which that agent desires. If the agent were themselves of no value, then nothing which they valued could be accounted valuable on account of their valuing it. Hence rat flees are *valuable* to the plague bacillus in as far as they act as its transmission vector; but this fact does not make rat fleas valuable – unless it be granted that the plague bacillus is itself valuable. Similarly, the drug Ecstasy is *valuable* to its users in as far as it makes them feel at-one with their surroundings; but this fact does not make the drug truly valuable, unless it be admitted that the mere phantasm of a good thing (in this case at-one-ment or peace) is equivalent to that good thing itself.

Even if a commodity is accounted as valuable by one or more human beings, it remains to be shown that it is truly of use; for the purpose in view may itself be spurious,[9] or the commodity may in fact be ineffective in achieving what is a truly desirable goal[10] – and in any case the commodity must derive its value from whatever value its agent has. In other words, relative value is devoid of value unless it references some agent of absolute value. Hence, if human existence is worthless, then even commodities which are of utility to human beings are fundamentally worthless.

Now, I have already argued[11] that the entire Cosmos (and not just humanity) is futile because of the Second Law of Thermodynamics. It would therefore seem that nothing can be of real value. Four responses are possible to this conundrum. These are Nihilism,[12] Hedonism, Existentialism[13] and Realism.

Nihilism

The first response is Nihilism. The Nihilist fully accepts the proposition that no commodity has any kind of identifiable value, because human life is itself futile. They then either advocate suicide or else take a pragmatic attitude and elect to soldier on with life nevertheless. There is no *reason* for the Nihilist to despair and advocate suicide, for that would be to make death desirable and, absurdly, make non-existence a source of value. Similarly, there is no *reason* for them to adopt pragmatism.

---

9 As in the alchemical objective of making “The Philosopher’s Stone”.

10 As smearing goose fat on the chest does not relieve a cough.

11 See Chapters 4 and 5.

12 From the Latin “nihil”, meaning nothing, emptiness or void.

13 From Sartre’s slogan “existence before essence”, asserting that actual human choices do not have to be justified in terms of any prior idea.

The only coherent course open to the Nihilist is entire and exact inaction; for a fundamental lack of value means that there can be no *motive* for any action. However the option of absolute passivity is simply not open to a living being; for a living being is characterized by goal-directed activity: that goal being its own continued existence. Even if the Nihilist decides to refrain from all deliberate action, their heart will continue to beat and their lungs will continue to breath. Of course, if they elect not to eat or drink and to positively oppose their instincts and appetites in these matters, then they will shortly die.

Hedonism

A second response is Hedonism. This accepts the Nihilist analysis but retorts, with reference to the personal experience of appetite and desire, that value is a cypher for what is wanted or desired; and that desire is the basic fact of life and the sole justification of any action. Typically, a hedonist argues that in the absence of any solid basis for value one might as well order one's life so as to satiate desire and avoid what is feared; as this at least minimises pain and maximises pleasure.

> I believe that the source of all value is wanting, in its broadest sense; or, if you prefer, what we like and dislike. I believe value is a purely subjective estimation, and can only logically be so, as it is predicated upon something as subjective as a want. On this account of things life can have value without an afterlife simply because we definitely experience desires when we live and these desires are themselves a sufficient basis for value.
>
> There may well be reasons why we like or dislike things, but these are immaterial when we come to decide what we are going to do. All that we care about then is what we want – not why we want it. If we dig deep enough, every act will be found to stem from a want.
>
> Whether or not the existence of wants evolved as a result of "the survival of the fittest" is unimportant. In the here and now value is not dependent upon survival, but only on subjective wants. Survival may well fall into the category of a subjective want, but value need not only be about survival. Basically, I am proposing that wants and values are near synonymous terms.
> [J. Kramer "Private Communication" (2012)]

Kramer's account serves well enough as a psychological theory. Human beings do generally do what they want to do. Indeed wanting something is pretty much the same thing as willing what is necessary to obtain it, and willing a means is tantamount to action. However, it is worth noting that to "want" something means "to lack" the thing as well as "to value" and "to desire" it. Indeed, I would insist that the subjective desire for or valuation of a thing always arises out of a recognition of personal deficit or need. I would also argue that we "like" what we judge to be beautiful[14] in one way or another.

However, as an ethical theory of value, motivation and desire, Kramer's account is inadequate. To say that the origin of a phenomenon is immaterial when trying to understand it is irrational. I grant readily that an account of the evolutionary or other origin of a phenomenon may not amount to anything like a full explanation of its present reality; but I would expect that an elucidation of its genesis and subsequent reflection upon this narrative would give at least an indication of the phenomenon's significance.

Kramer here allows that there are reasons for our desires, and that survival may be among them; but he does not appreciate that as living organisms our very business is survival: because surviving is what life is all about. He does not recognise that survival is not just a "subjective want" (an arbitrary end, chosen whimsically by a subject) but rather life's basic and constitutive end, if life is to be what life is.[15] Survival is part and parcel of living. Survival is life's characteristic business. Without survival, life does not satisfy the law of self identity and is at odds with itself; hence all living beings need to survive.[16] Previously, Kramer had been more forthcoming:

> I assume that values originated at the same time as desires. Values are real in that we actually value certain things, but not in the sense that what we value is different than what we want. What motivates the convention is surely intermixed with all sorts of things. On the top of the list would be survival and social cohesion. [J. Kramer "Private Communication" (2011)]

I agree that what primarily motivates valuation is indeed "survival" and "social cohesion". This is basic to my case. "Social cohesion" is itself valuable because it facilitates survival. In the end, everything comes back to survival and so to the basic and inalienable nature of life itself. Kramer is right in saying "value need not only be about survival" if he means that values exist which do not have any obvious or direct relationship to survival; but he is wrong if he means that there is any

14 I have discussed beauty at length in Chapter 3.

15 I have discussed the nature and purpose of life in Chapter 4.

16 Not want, see page 120; though this objective need gives rise to much subjective wanting. I take up this argument again on pages 133-135.

rationale for value which, if we dig deep enough, does not stem from the need to survive: for this is the purpose, nature and business of life.

> As we seem to agree, value is dependent on a relative utility; however, I assert that this relativity is no more than a necessary requirement of value. From where does this value and utility originate? From our wants, our instincts and our drives. Our goals stem from our wants, and our wants themselves come from a completely *irrational* process. Not irrational in the sense that our wants are not in accordance with the mathematics and science used to describe them – but that they themselves are not goal oriented. If our wants are irrational then our values and morality are thereby also irrational at their base. Ethics relies upon an initial axiom that cannot itself be justified in the way that all value is justified by it. In response to your question "Why act?" the answer is obvious: "Because I want to!"
> [J. Kramer "Private Communication" (2012)]

Value and utility does not originate in "our wants, our instincts and our drives". Actual utility originates in what is in fact useful, not what we fallibly perceive to be useful.[17] Nevertheless, Kramer is right in identifying "our wants, our instincts and our drives" as the basis for our perception of value and utility. Sometimes we can come to value something independently of such a basis; but even then I'd expect that the basis of such a superficially dispassionate judgement would be the desire to survive.

I concur that "our wants, our instincts, and our drives" are irrational and "not goal oriented", just as Kramer asserts. However, this is where his analysis is flawed. The fact that "our wants, our instincts, and our drives" are irrational and "not goal oriented" (in the sense that they do not require any purpose other than their own satisfaction for them to have the hold on us that they in fact do have) does not mean that they cannot be rationally accounted for within the context where they exist. On the contrary, just as Kramer himself asserts, "every single event happens for a directly physical reason, and thus is rational."[18]

In fact they can be accounted for readily in this way: "our wants, our instincts and our drives" are as they are (either by virtue of evolutionary happenstance or else by divine providence, it matters not a whit) because they regularly facilitate our survival. They are part and parcel of our constitution as living (and successfully surviving) beings.

---

17 Plato, "Theaetetus" (177d) quoted on page 36.

18 See page 49.

The fact that a particular population of mice might systematically favour grass seeds over cheese (when cheese is far more nutritious and so, one might think, more tasty) could not possibly be an irrational or unaccountable fact. It would be accountable in terms of some narrative along the following lines: "Very many mice who had pursued cheese finished up with broken necks, because of a regular association between cheese and mouse-traps; which association can itself be explained in terms of the rational desire of humans not to share their homes (and still less their valuable food supplies) with ravenous, prolific, disease carrying vermin."

Kramer is right when he writes: "Ethics relies upon an initial axiom that cannot itself be justified in the way that all value is justified by it." This is nothing other than an expression of the "is-ought dichotomy"[19] or "Hume's dilemma". Indeed, this is my precise point. What I am specifically arguing is that this initial axiom can be nothing other than "it is good to be." In response to Kramer's assertion that he acts because he wants to, I want to ask: "Why do you want at all? How does it come to be that there such a phenomenon as wanting?"

> I agree that our goals can be explained. However, I do not believe that life in and of itself can have a rational goal, as this would seem to imply that a consciousness already existed to have such a goal. There is nothing more special about evolution happening to be directed towards survival then the fact that a molecule is caused to turn right instead of left. Evolution leaves us with many wants, some of them now redundant, some of them still directed effectively towards survival; but as it stands as a metaphysical issue, we as humans have a starting point of drives, wants, and values not formed perfectly in one direction or towards one goal.
>
> Thus I hardly think there is any reason behind the idea that something is "good", much less joy bringing, simply because it conforms to a purpose which *some of* our desires are in accordance with. It makes much more sense to attempt to fulfil our desires based upon which we want the most after considering each desire's respective consequences.
> [J. Kramer "Private Communication" (2012)]

I agree with Kramer that if there is no basic purpose behind our desires, it follows that nothing is truly good: for the only rational meaning of good is *of having utility for a purpose*. However, I disagree with him that it can make "more sense to attempt to fulfil our desires"

19 See page 120.

if our desires themselves are not rational. How can one make any sense at all out of something that is fundamentally irrational? On what basis do we evaluate our desires to determine which we "want the most"? How would we compare their "respective consequences", even were it possible to clearly identify what these were? What metric would we use? What would motivate us in trading one desire against another? Kramer's system only holds together when underpinned by the unspoken axiom "pleasure is the ultimate good." If this is accepted, then pleasure could – at least in principle – be used as the answer to each of my questions.

> When I say "I value friendship", I mean, friendship is pleasing to me or conducive to future pleasure. I am certain that I would not call it valuable if nothing about friendship pleased me or gave me something else that pleased me indirectly.
> [J. Kramer "Private Communication" (2012)]

I agree with Kramer that evolution, as such, has no extrinsic purpose: it does not occur as a response to some imposed motivation. In particular, it is not a striving after complexity, sophistication, intelligence or consciousness. However, I disagree with him in concluding that evolution has no goal, that evolution is arbitrary or that "there is nothing more special about evolution happening to be directed towards survival then the fact that a molecule is caused to turn right instead of left." Evolution is necessarily about survival, it doesn't just happen to be so. Without the possibility of survival there could be no evolution. No circumstances could arise which would direct evolution towards producing either pink things or intelligent things – unless either pinkness or intelligence was in some way a proxy for survival.

Kramer is wrong to argue that life cannot "have a rational goal, as this would seem to imply that a consciousness already existed." This is because his syllogism implicitly relies on the idea that any goal must be extrinsic to the act or process which has that goal: that the purpose of an act or process is necessarily outside and distinct from the act or process itself. Now while I grant that this is generally true I also insist that life and evolution together form a singular and crucial exception.[20] I shall shortly argue[21] that life is itself the origin, root and fountain-head of value, and hence of purpose.

That which in fact survives shows by its very survival that it is fit to survive. Purpose is nothing other than that which a thing has if it survives as a dynamic entity: that is, if it is alive. Subjectively, purpose

---

20 Evolution is the same phenomenon as life itself, but considered at the level of the species rather than the individual.

21 See pages 133-135.

is the drive to satisfy wants and so to experience pleasure or happiness. Objectively, purpose is the necessity of obtaining what is needed to survive. Purpose is the pattern or form of life itself. When one understands what life is, one understands what purpose is also. Not just the purpose of life, but all purpose; for there is no purpose which is not underpinned by this sole foundation: the purpose of life. It follows from this account of things that one can believe that life has the rational goal of being itself without any need to posit any extrinsic rationale.

Moreover, if life itself (not conscious life, just life) is the basis of purpose, then no kind of consciousness has to be invoked in order to justify the rationality of life's goal. Consciousness only seems to play a part in the argument if one believes that subjective wants and desires (rather than objective needs) are the basis of value: for only a truly conscious subject can experience desire; whereas even an unconscious but living being has objective needs.

Furthermore, even if Kramer's syllogism were valid, this would not warrant rejecting the premise. Rather, if the premise is true, one ought to conclude that there is a pre-existant consciousness: that is, God. One could only reverse the argument so as to invalidate the premise if one already knew for sure that there is no such pre-existant consciousness; and it would seems that this atheistic premise is itself far from certain.

Kramer is right in saying that the legacy of "drives, wants, and values" bequeathed to us by evolution is "not formed perfectly"; but on closer inspection it will be seen that the origin of and rationale for each of our imperfectly formed instincts, appetites and desires is to motivate us to obtain that which we (or else our genes) need for survival. The fact that they are not entirely fit for this purpose is merely an indication of the fact that they have come to be what they are through a complex history of circumstances, rather then as a result of a deliberate design process based on the realisation of a specification. We possess this flawed legacy because it has in fact proved adequate to the task of surviving, in spite of its ramshackle nature.

> Is not the honest answer to the question "why did we develop wants?" simply "breeding"? The ability to breed requires the parents to be alive, but this is only secondary.
> [J. Kramer "Private Communication" (2012)]

One can conceive of a life-form which was not subject to senescence, was able to adapt to changing circumstances (as a chameleon adapts its skin pigmentation to varying environments, but in a more open-ended way) and was entirely unable to reproduce. Such a life-form would still have objective needs, most obviously for sustenance. For it to be motivated to address these needs they must feature in its life-process as wants. Hence, wants are not necessitated by reproduction, but merely by the life of the individual. "Wanting" fits a particular living being for obtaining what it needs for *survival*. A living being which does not "want" things is not motivated to actively obtain them and can only passively take advantage of what it actually needs when and if they happen to become available. Moreover, the selection criterion which favoured the development of "wanting" was the *survival* of the fittest individuals.

While it can be argued that the phenomenon of "wanting" evolved from the process of reproduction, this simply means that "wanting" is founded on whatever a species needs in order to reproduce, adapt to changing circumstances and so *survive*. Reproduction is part of the life of the species. It renews the species as cell division renews the body of a multicellular organism. If a living being lives and has the ability and opportunity to reproduce it will do so, as this is part of the pattern of its life; but this is only secondary. From this perspective, the psychological wants of individuals still have to be understood as the subjective realisation of objective needs; only now the needs relate to the survival of the species rather than to the survival of the individual.

Existentialism

This is a more positive response. While the Existentialist acknowledges the basic problem of value as I have outlined it here, they assert that individuals are capable of creating purpose and value by willing it into existence as a free choice.[22]

> Nietzsche's writing is life-affirming in both style and purpose. His prose is almost entirely a beckoning to go further, a constant sense of revolution and overthrowing. His purpose being to create natural values that accept life and to love life.
> [J. Kramer "Private Communication" (2012)]

This is a noble and romantic notion, but it does not stand up to analysis. Unless human existence actually has some basic value, no amount of impassioned insistence on its value can make it valuable. Saying something three times doesn't make it true.[23] If the Nihilist is right and human beings have no *intrinsic value*, Existentialism is no more than Pragmatism clad in a fig-leaf. If the Nihilist is wrong and

22 See Chapter 2.
23 As the Bellman believed, according to L. Carroll. See "The Hunting of the Snark: Fit the First." (1876)

people are somehow fundamentally worthwhile, then the Existentialist's conviction that human life has value is justified; but their impassioned and well-meant romanticism is redundant.

Kramer asserts that "natural values... accept and love life." This is exactly my point; except that I argue that all true values necessarily do this, because of what value is. There is no need to "create" such values but only to discover them: they are "natural", not "artificial".

> I have a fairly good idea as to why Nietzsche and Heidegger are both loved by a certain group of young males. I think primarily it is that adopting their philosophies tends to free one from responsibility. It is extremely important for a young person to go through such a philosophical step, so that they can start again from the base up; but too many people forget that it is just that – a step. As for me, I find that once I have been freed, I do not simply want to float around in nothingness, but have the desire to create anew; but it is exactly being stuck in that nothingness and not being able to see the next step that creates the sickness of Nihilism and Existentialism.
> [J. Kramer "Private Communication" (2012)]

My only criticism of what Kramer writes here is that one should be ware of trying to "start again from the base up." In fact no-one can do this. We all exist within a cultural context and cannot free ourselves from it. Indeed, if we could do so we would have nowhere to start from in "creating anew", so we should not seek to do so. In order to reach the sky we must stand on the shoulders of giants; but we must take care of which giants we ask a "piggy-back".

> "Every one then who hears these words of mine and does them will be like a wise man who built his house upon the rock; and the rain fell, and the floods came, and the winds blew and beat upon that house, but it did not fall, because it had been founded on the rock. And every one who hears these words of mine and does not do them will be like a foolish man who built his house upon the sand; and the rain fell, and the floods came, and the winds blew and beat against that house, and it fell; and great was the fall of it." [Mat 7:24-27 RSV]

We must each accept personal responsibility for our world-view: our ethic and our aesthetic. We can use the ethic and aesthetic of another as a template; but in the end we are individually accountable for our own decisions and habits of thought and action.

Realism

The prevalence of Nihilist and Existentialist ideas in contemporary discourse amply demonstrates that many people have come to recognise the basic futility of mortal existence, when that existence is evaluated rationally on its own merits. The Realist stands firm against this post-modern consensus; agreeing with the Existentialist's conclusion, but disagreeing with the Nihilist's premise. The Realist rejects the fundamental value problem; on the basis that certain entities (typically human beings) do have intrinsic value and that certain purposes are actually useful to these entities. The fundamental problem for the Realist is that of establishing how any entity can have intrinsic value.

What could intrinsic value be?

Some Realists attempt to establish a meaning for intrinsic value with reference to God. They claim[24] that contingent beings can only have value if they are valued by an Unvalued Valuer – that is, by God.[25] Alternately, one can equate Value with Being. This is consistent with the notion that God's non-contingent reality underpins Value, but it goes much further. Rather than allowing it to seem that God could in principle elect to constitute Value (and hence Justice) arbitrarily, it gives Value a specific and definite meaning: that of Being Itself and, by simple and direct extension, Order and Existence; which, for living beings, is Life.

Equating Value or Goodness with Being may itself seem arbitrary, and no better than the alternate expedient of referring Value back to God directly. In fact this is not so. The point is that Being works as an explicit and definite solution to the problem of Value. It is not subject to arbitrary interpretation,[26] but only contextual application.[27] It has all the characteristics required of the answer; in a way that Pleasure, Money,

---

24 Following a pattern of reasoning very like that of the "Cosmological Argument", see Chapter 14.

25 This is true as far as it goes. Moreover, it forms some kind of argument for God's reality, if only it first be admitted that "there are thing of value." However, this proposition is much more contentious than the related statement "there are things which exist." Furthermore, this approach is problematic, as it tends to empty the idea "value" of any meaning. If intrinsic value is understood simply as value relative to God, then "value" is no less arbitrary than it is real, see page 182.

26 That is, the insistence of someone that the word "value" means whatever they wish, along the lines favoured by Humpty Dumpty. [L. Carroll "Through the Looking Glass and What Alice Found There" (1871)]

27 This is the working out *in practice* (within any particular concrete situation or circumstance) what "value" and "justice" already mean *in principle*.

Fame and so on do not. The only other concepts which come close are Happiness and Love. Being solves the Value problem as follows.

First, for any commodity to be of value to a subject, it is first necessary that the subject be real. Were the subject not real, they would be in no position to value any commodity. The subject needs to be real if it is to value anything; so it is clear that Being is at least an example of a valuable commodity, and also that it is the most necessary and needful commodity. Moreover, it is only with reference to the value of a subject that any commodity can have value. Without Being there can be no valuable valuer and hence no Value at all. So, the first good of any subject is their own reality, and this implies their being.

Second, without Being there can be no commodity. It is necessary for a commodity itself to have Being; for otherwise it is not possible for it to have any attribute, let alone be of any use. Some purely imaginary commodities can be valuable; but even these have a kind of Being: as *real* ideas (of unreal things) in the *real* mind of a *real* subject. Being objectively *real* is the most complete and perfect mode of Being. An *imaginary* being only participates vicariously in the reality of the subject imagining it. Without Being, a commodity has no reality; it is impossible to conceive of a commodity entirely lacking in Being.

Therefore, on a second count, wherever there is Value there is also Being. Just as it is impossible for any other commodity (such as Love or Happiness) to be possessed if the subject has no Being; so also a commodity cannot be possessed if it has no reality itself. Hence all other commodities (even those which might seriously be proposed as alternate foundations of Value) are dependent upon Being for their value in a way that Being is not reciprocally dependent on them.

Third, identifying Being with Value is coherent. If Value is equated with Being the question "Why is Being valuable?" does not arise; because it reduces to "Why does Being share in the quality of Being?" which answers itself.

A superficially similar result follows from equating Value with any other commodity; but equating Value with Prestige, say, is not so satisfactory. This is because the question: "What, then, is Prestige?" arises, and this has to be answered in psychological and sociological terms – which tends to relativize Value to humans and so to their existence, life and… Being. A similar weakness underlies any other supposed base value. Only Being itself escapes this problem; because the question "What is Being?" cannot sensibly be answered with reference to any concept other than Being itself. Being is at once mysterious and ubiquitous. One has to either accept Being for what it is, everywhere; or else deny everything – including that denial itself.

Fourth, some commodities can be identified with Being. For example, if Beauty and Justice are kinds of Order, and if Order is the basis of Existence; then the value of Beauty and Justice can be traced back to the fact that they are instances of Existence, and so of Being.

Moreover, many other commodities are valued because they facilitate survival: which is the continuance of a thing's existence. Human beings value food and drink, shelter, warmth and so on because they are necessary for life – or else make it more secure. Other commodities, such as music, drama and sport are valued because they inspire, entertain and recreate. They contribute to psychological and physical health and also to community cohesion; and hence to the survival of the state, clan, family and individual.

Fifth, identifying Being and Value does not devalue other goods. On the contrary, it explains how other things which do in fact have real value come to acquire it. Happiness, Love, Beauty, Art, Religion and Justice are all readily accounted for in terms of Being and the health and the survival of sentient life. Crucially, identifying Being as Value does not detract from the centrality of God. On the contrary, God is then identifiable as the Good, the Ground of all Being, and Being Absolute. God is God precisely because God is entirely ordered, stable and coherent. God is characterized by Justice, Peace, Love and Joy.

Sixth, ethics now becomes rational. If what is right (what a sapient being ought to do) is identified with that which facilitates and promotes survival (primarily the continued existence of the individual, but also of the family and society – because these themselves favour the survival of the individual) then it becomes proportionate, coherent and reasonable to do what is right; for else one will soon finish up doing nothing at all.

Ought is the present imperative of the verb "to be"

Taking the existence of a thing (for a living being, this is its life) to be exactly the same thing as its value heals the "is – ought" fracture. It means that at any moment in time, every thing ought to be exactly what it is – trivially, and by definition. Looking forward in time, any deliberative agent therefore ought to do whatever is going to preserve their own existence; for just as "it is good to be" so also "it is good to strive to continue to be", or else nothing whatever is good.

> Only a living entity can have goals or can originate them. And it is only a living organism that has the capacity for self-generated, goal-directed action. On the physical level, the functions of all living organisms... are actions... directed to a single goal: the maintenance of the organism's life.
> [A. Rand "The Objectivist Ethics"]

It is only because of life that there are ends. Inanimate objects do not have objectives or purposes – except in relation to other living agents that may employ them as tools. The very idea of an end, purpose, objective or goal implies the existence of some living agent to have that end, purpose, objective or goal. Without life there would be no such thing as purpose. Hence, life is the source of value because only life is end-directed and the end to which life is directed is itself.

> We agree much of the way, but then there is a sharp breaking point. I hear you say that we should do what is of value, and I agree. I hear you say that value arises in relation to utility towards achieving some particular goal, and I agree. When, however, you refer to intrinsic utility, intrinsic value, intrinsic good – that is where I part company with you. It is a word game to define value as being; primarily because being is a function and goal of value. The fact that value would not exist without a goal oriented being is no more to the point than the fact that human language would not exist without humans. Does this then make language synonymous with humans?
> [J. Kramer "Private Communication" (2012)]

Being is not "a function and goal of value" it is the sole foundation of value. Without life, the concept of value could not arise and value can only be understood in terms of its origin, which is life. Kramer admits This when he says that is a "fact that value would not exist without a goal oriented being". Life is all about survival. "Survive" is what life does: intrinsically, not coincidentally. The constitutional business of life is survival: the self-maintenance of its own existence.

The form of life is identical with its survival processes. Hence, the fact of existence (which is a term applicable to non-living objects as well as living things) underpins survival, and so existence is an even deeper foundation of value than survival or life. Life is a form of existence: the form which maintains its own pattern by process, organisation, information and effort. More generally, the concept of "being" underpins that of "existence" and so being itself is the fountain-head of value.

> There is implanted in the soul by nature a faculty of desiring that which is in harmony with its nature, and of maintaining in close union all that belongs essentially to its nature: and this power is called will. For the essence both of existence and of living yearns after activity… and in this it merely longs to realise its own natural and perfect being. [John of Damascus "An exact exposition of the orthodox faith" lib 2 cap 22]

Language could exist without humans, but not without intelligence. The fact that language cannot exist without intelligence[28] does not make language identical with intelligence. However, it is difficult to see how intelligence could be itself without language. My experience of my own intelligence is all about an interior dialogue: a speaking to and with myself. Hence it may be that language itself is the basis of intelligence; just as life is the basis of value.

To take Kramer's rhetorical point further. The fact that the highest (or most valuable) kind of value would not exist without humans (or other similar beings) suggests that the highest form of value is more or less identical with being human: that is with impersonated or inspirited being. This is indicated in Genesis, where God sets about making the first Earthlings in the Divine Image.

I have already argued[29] that life is a form of symmetry, an echo of eternity in temporal existence. On this view of things, "ought to do" is the present imperative tense of the verb "to be", along the lines of "I ought to do whatever I expect will result in me continuing to be."[30] Hence, on a naïve view, change is always and absolutely bad (because it entails some thing ceasing to be what it is) and constancy is always and absolutely good; just as Plato has his mysterious *Athenian* caution:

> "Change… except in something evil, is extremely dangerous."
> [Plato "Laws" (VII 797d)]

Continuity and change

Of course, reality isn't as simple as this. In Plato's world of the Ideals,[31] perfect being is absolutely stable; but in the material world continuance isn't quite the same thing as static permanence. A thing can maintain or disclose its self-identity through a process of *development* – as an acorn grows into a tree, or a caterpillar becomes a moth; or through a process

28 Not the subjective consciousness of a person, however. Two computers exchanging information according to some protocol share a language: one that was devised for them by an intelligent third party.

29 See page 70.

30 The answer to the question "Why ought I to want to continue to be?" is that the choice "not to be" eliminates the possibility of any further oughts. Life is contradicted by and inconsistent with death. One can either be alive and choosing to live, or be dead and unable to make any choices. [Deut 30:19-20, quoted on page 119 and Sir 15:17, quoted on page 116] The consequence of opting for non-existence is, of course, non-existence; which is self-consistent but nothing more.

31 LNS Ch 1.

of *evolution* – as humankind arose from more primitive hominids; or through a process of *education* – as a student becomes a professor. In each case, some realities remain fixed while others change. Indeed, the genius of life is to adapt itself to new contexts (and so preserve its identity) by these three kinds of self-modification.

> In a higher world it is otherwise, but here below to live is to change, and to be perfect is to have changed often.
> [J.H. Newman "An Essay on the Development of Christian Doctrine" Ch 1 (1845)]

In the case of *development*, the interior form or defining information of a thing is fixed; while the outward manifestation of that form may change out of all recognition, in accordance with a process which itself is set by the form. In the case of *evolution*, the defining information of a species changes slightly and the outward appearance or behaviour is only modified a little; but the impact of the external changes on the survival prospects of the species may be dramatic. In the case of *education*, additional information is mostly layered on top of what was known before. Education, then, is a kind of growth.

Mind and matter

As long as beings are considered solely as objects, this analysis leaves a lot to be desired. In particular, it is cold and mechanistic. Whereas it solves the "is – ought" problem it seems to do so in a solipsistical way: defining it out of existence, as it were. The "value" that it gives to everything by identifying Good with Being seems itself to be valueless. Something is surely missing.

This is not a fair criticism, however; for if all beings were purely physical objects there wouldn't be any issue about value or purpose beyond a cold technicality of utility. However, each human being is more than just a physical object. Every one, I have argued, is a spiritual person with a material nature.[32] It is precisely because human beings are personal subjects and agents as well as physical objects that the issue of significance is so emotive – significant, one might even say.

> Can a thing matter in itself… can anything matter, unless there is somebody who minds?
> [R.A. Knox "In Soft Garments" Ch 2 (1941)]

32 See Chapter 6.

The force behind the need for meaning – the desperate cry: "What's the *use* of it all?" – arises individually from the human person, not generally from human nature. To this extent, Sartre is correct: the experience of existence is more fundamental and urgent than any knowledge of essences. It is because human beings are in part spiritual that what happens to them *matters* in an unconditional sense. Spirit *matters* in a way that matter itself does not *matter.* It is difficult to say why this is so; but that is because everything relating to the human person is difficult to say.

Power or being?

Nietzsche remarks that life looks to express itself in power and that this is its defining characteristic

> The living thing did I follow… to learn its nature… Wherever I found a living thing, there found I the Will to Power; and even in the will of the servant found I the will to be master.
> [F. Nietzsche "Thus Spoke Zarathustra" cap 34 (1887)]

> Psychologists should bethink themselves before putting down the instinct of self-preservation as the cardinal instinct of an organic being. A living thing seeks above all to DISCHARGE its strength – life is WILL TO POWER; self preservation is only one of the indirect and most frequent RESULTS thereof.
> [F. Nietzsche "Beyond Good and Evil" cap 1 #13 (1886)]

However, he is mistaken in erecting this "The Will to Power" as fundamental in opposition to "being itself". Some living beings are of a most gentle and unobtrusive nature. They can nonetheless be successful in Darwinian terms: phytoplankton and earthworms spectacularly so.

Nietzsche admits himself that self preservation is one of the "most frequent results" of his supposed "Will to Power" and singularly fails to give any justification for his postulate of "Will to Power" as an additional and more basic rationale for life. He simply asserts that "life is Will to Power" rather than "Continuity in Flux".

Jesus of Nazareth explicitly contradicts Nietzsche's teaching when He says "All who take the sword will perish by the sword."[33]

33 Mat 26:52 RSV.

The value of existence

My identification of the value of a thing with its own being might be taken to make humanity sufficient for itself and remove the need to rely on God to provide meaning in human life. On the one hand, this is true; for the identification of Good with Being means that every thing has its own value in and of itself and does not require any extrinsic validation. On the other hand, such an identification is the core of traditional Theism. In any orthodox analysis of the "Problem of Purpose", the role of God is that of ultimate guarantor of value and expert *testator* as to what is just rather than that of *proscriber* of what is righteous. What is good is entirely so because it is wholesome and beneficial to life, as a matter of objective fact. What is good is not at all so because God decides as a matter of whim that it should be said to be so.

Kindness

Kindness and generosity are not incompatible with an ethic of rational self-interest.[34] In brief, it is sensible for anyone and everyone to treat those in need in the way which they would like to be treated should they themselves ever be in need. This is because by so doing they will tend to educate their fellows into realising that it is better for everyone to live in a compassionate and caring society; where those who find themselves incapable of sustaining their own lives are provided for until the emergency they find themselves in has abated: if, indeed, it ever can abate. The short term premium of caring for the sick, destitute and aged when one is young, affluent and healthy is a much smaller loss than the gain represented by a long term assurance of support should one ever oneself become vulnerable.

Conflict

An immediate problem which arises is that of conflict. It is not obvious that what is good for one moral agent is always good for everyone else. Hence, achieving one's own good might seem to involve frustrating that of others in a "dog eat dog" manner. In which case, a concern for ones own interest is no basis for social justice and equity.

Now, in the sub-human world, value conflict is ubiquitous. It is, after all, hardly good for a rabbit to be eaten by a fox. The prophet Isaiah is very conscious of this general problem and, as we have already seen,

---

34 LNS Ch 8.

answers it[35] with a promise that it will be solved in a future reality fully characterized by justice and peace, where all creatures are given reformed natures which can be harmoniously expressed and fulfilled without conflict. The related question: "Why, then, is it necessary for the present reality to be characterized by conflict and suffering?" is so important that I postpone it for consideration in Chapter 11.

Generally, in the human world conflict should not be accepted as being normal and inevitable. Except in the case of some absolute and immovable constraint which leads to a "win-lose" situation, it is better for people to trade, cooperate, negotiate and pool their knowledge and resources than to engage in confrontation, violence and war. Moreover, often what at first seems like a simple "zero-sum game" can, with good-will and ingenuity, be subverted and a "win-win" outcome be obtained.

Most resources are not limited in any sense that matters; but only relatively so, because of the expense involved in increasing their availability. It is characteristic of human ingenuity that all resources become more and more available as technology advances. It is therefore generally more efficient, cost effective and rational to work on increasing the availability of any resource which seems liable to become rare and expensive rather than to get into destructive conflict over the limited pool of that resource which is currently available.

The fact that sometimes one party must loose and another win doesn't mean that there is a rational basis for confrontation. Competition should not be viewed as necessitating confrontation; but rather as being an incentive to personal excellence and individual achievement. The systematic existence of such competition (so long as it is fair and well judged) benefits everyone, including even those individuals who happen to lose out on particular occasions. It means that those who are most fitted for a role get to fill it, which is of general benefit; often much more so to the community at large than to the successful individual. It is the mark of a moderate and rational but unsuccessful competitor to shake hands with the victor and congratulate them. It is the mark of a vicious man to storm off and harbour a grudge.

Ayn Rand insisted that "there are no conflicts of interests among rational men"[36] and I think she was right. Were two virtuous people to be faced with a life and death choice, which they must take together, and as a result of which only one will live, they would accept the reality of the situation and agree to some amicable means of deciding their individual fates. Conflict could only take place if and when one or both ceased to be rational. In the case of the sharing of a limited resource,

---

35 Is 11:1-9, quoted on p 65.

36 A. Rand "The 'Conflicts' of Men's Interests."

this might result in them electing to maximise their time of companionship and so choosing to die together. Otherwise it would result in one choosing to die so that the other might live, because that is what the person electing to die themselves wanted. This act of seeming "self-sacrifice" could in fact be the largest life act that the person who elected to die might ever make. Their way of living life to the maximum could be to die so that the other person might live and thereby achieve some goal which the person dying greatly desired to have achieved.

The fact that a person can have values which are more important to them than the simple prolongation of their own *mortal* life does not mean that these are founded on any value other than life itself; but only that this *mortal* life is not the fundamental value.[37] Of course, if death is not the terminus and extinction of life but rather the portal to eternal fellowship with God, then neither it (nor any finite quantity of suffering) is of much account and no reasonable person would countenance confrontation simply to avoid death. What would be the use of it?

Self-affirmation or self-sacrifice?

It is typical in popular Christianity to emphasise the idea of altruism, of self-giving disinterested love or self-sacrifice. Jesus' passion and death is presented as the pre-eminent example of this, and any man who wishes to follow Jesus is expected to imitate Jesus' example and "deny himself".[38] Such a view is in conflict with the ethical system which I am developing here, so how can I claim that my system is Christian?

The first thing to be said is that Jesus' testimony is not so straightforward as it might seem. We have already seen that He is unequivocal in affirming the injunction of the Torah "You shall love your neighbour *as yourself*."[39] This predicates the whole of ethics on self-esteem: for if you do not respect and value your self, you do not have to respect and value your neighbour. Furthermore, just after the verse at issue, Jesus sets out man's legitimate objective as being to save his own life,[40] even as He says that the only way of doing so is by temporarily losing it in pursuance of gospel values.

Moreover, the terms self-giving[41] and self-sacrificial never occur in the Revised Standard Version of the Bible; while the term self-denial

37 This should not be surprising as mortal life has death mixed in with it, and so is compromised and imperfect. See page 94.

38 Mk 8:34, quoted on page 144.

39 Lev 19:18.

40 Mk 8:35-37, quoted on page 144.

41 This phrase is a great favourite of recent popes.

only occurs once[42] and then with only equivocal approval. The term self-control (which has a different meaning) is more common; with seven occurrences in the New Testament[43] and two in the Old[44]. The term self-abasement also occurs twice, in a passage which merits quoting.

> Let no one disqualify you, insisting on self-abasement[45] and worship of angels, taking his stand on visions, puffed up without reason by his sensuous mind… Why do you submit to regulations… according to human precepts and doctrines? These have indeed an appearance of wisdom in promoting rigour of devotion and self-abasement[45] and severity to the body, but they are of no value in checking the indulgence of the flesh.
> [Col 2:18-23 RSV]

It would seem that the Apostle Paul associated devotional rigour and personal humiliation with sensuality and irrationality, judging them to be more a form of twisted and dishonest spiritual masochism rather than any kind of effective asceticism.

Elsewhere, the Apostle seems to explicitly command altruism when he writes "Let no one seek his own good, but the good of his neighbour."[46] Nonetheless, the Apostle cannot mean to teach that one should always pursue the good of one's neighbour in antagonism to one's own. To do so would overturn both the Torah and rationality. In fact the original Greek of this verse does not obviously recommend altruism. Transliterated, it reads: "Seek no man seek himself, rather everyone the other."[47] Moreover, the context of the verse[48] does not enforce the RSV interpretation. Taking into account this context, the most plausible meaning of the verse is that we should take care not to harm our neighbour's virtue by acts which we know to be moral but which they may not yet understand to be so.

---

42 Sir 11:18. There is, of course Mk 8:34, quoted on page 144; however, the Greek word used there means "forget oneself" more than "deny oneself".

43 Acts 24:25. 1Cor 7:5&9; 9:26. Gal 5:23. 2Tim 1:7. 2Pet 1:6.

44 Prov 25:28. Wis 8:7. There is also a reference in 2 Esd and eight in 4 Mac.

45 The Greek is "ταπεινοφροσύνη": humility or humiliation.

46 1Cor 10:24 RSV.

47 The double "seek" correctly represents the original text.

48 This is a discussion of the advisability of eating meat consecrated to idols. Paul observes that although eating such meat is objectively moral, to eat it might easily scandalize someone of a naïve and delicate faith. He therefore rules that one should forego the benefit of eating the meat out of an obligation of care towards one's theologically unsophisticated neighbour. In the long run this will be to one's own benefit, as it will strengthen the bonds of mutual respect within the Church community.

The meaning of sacrifice

The English word "sacrifice" has three different and conflicting meanings. The first is well described in the following passage:

> "Sacrifice" is the surrender of a greater value for the sake of a lesser one or of a non-value. Thus, altruism gauges a man's virtue by the degree to which he surrenders, renounces or betrays his values (since help to a stranger or an enemy is regarded as more virtuous, less "selfish," than help to those one loves). The rational principle of conduct is the exact opposite: always act in accordance with the hierarchy of your values, and never sacrifice a greater value to a lesser one.
> [A. Rand "The Ethics of Emergencies"]

It is this understanding of sacrifice which underpins much popular preaching; with its cry to give up that which is precious to oneself on the basis that it is somehow good to do oneself harm. It is associated with the idea of mortification, in which death of the self is seen as the path to salvation[49] – though what is saved if the self is destroyed is unclear.

The second meaning is more scriptural. In the Hebrew Bible a sacrifice sometimes involves the surrender of a thing of limited value – such as a lamb or bullock – in exchange for a thing of *much greater* worth – such as victory in battle or a good harvest. This notion makes out that sacrifice as constituting a form of exploitative trade; but one in which it is God who is exploited, not the person making the sacrifice. This idea is common in pagan religions, of course. Plato expresses the state of play starkly, in terms of a trio of questions:

> What benefit do the gods derive from the gifts they receive from us? What they give us is obvious to all… but how are they benefited by what they receive from us? Or do we have such an advantage in trade that we receive all our blessings from them and they receive nothing from us?
> [Plato "Euthyphro" (15a)]

The third meaning is also scriptural. The Bible often represents sacrifice as no kind of surrender at all, but a form of celebration, sharing or bonding: a means of friendly table fellowship with God.[50] In the

---

49 St Paul tells us that is to be put to death is not the self, but rather bad practices and habits. [Rom 8:13. Col 3:5] See page 162.

50 Hence the Mosaic Communion Sacrifice [Lev 3,7 & 22] and the Catholic Mass. See Chapter 16.

holocaust or worship sacrifice, the offering was entirely destroyed: not to punish it, nor to show that it was unworthy of God, nor to inconvenience the person making the offering; but to symbolically unite the victim, understood as being worthy – and so the worshipper – with God.[51]

Rational Worship

The life of each believer should be a "rational sacrifice" for three reasons. First, because each human being is a rational agent and can only offer their lives to God as the outcome of a rational decision. Second, because the only proportionate offering that anyone can make to God in return for God's deliverance of their entire life from futility is their whole selves. Third, because once one's life has been renewed by God's grace it has become a faithful image of the divine nature and so is worthy of God. In this idea of self-sacrifice there is no hint of self-deprecation or self-destruction or of giving up one's identity or denying one's own value. Rather, there is an expectation of fellowship with God, which is our ultimate fulfilment.

> Present your bodies[52] as a living sacrifice,[53] holy and acceptable to God, which is your spiritual[54] worship[55]. Do not be conformed to this world but be transformed by the renewal of your mind, that you may prove[56] what is the will of God, what is good and acceptable and perfect. [Rom 12:1-2 RSV]

Paul enjoins us to present ourselves as worthy *living* victims in a *rational* oblation by coming to *understand* what justice is and then making that idea our own. It is in this way that we are called to forget ourselves. The "self" to be forgotten is not the true self but only that which the Apostle Paul sometimes calls "the flesh"[57] the lower or animal nature of mankind.[58]

---

51 Wis 2:21-3:8, quoted on page 111.

52 The Greek is "σώματα".

53 The Greek is "θυσιαν": a sacrificial victim. Compare Wis 3:6, quoted on page 111.

54 The Greek is "λογικὴν": logical, reasonable or rational.

55 The Greek is "λατρειαν": the sacred service of the Temple.

56 The Greek is "δοκιμάζειν": to assess, test, appraise, approve, verify and recognise as genuine – a very important idea.

57 The Greek is "σαρκι". [Gal 5:13-24. Rom 7:18; 8:5-13. 1Cor 3:3. Eph 2:3]

58 The terms "lower" and "animal" are not necessarily pejorative. Paul treats of the appetites as he finds them within himself: namely, out of control and so disordered and immoderate. [Rom 7:15-23]

Giving up one's imperfections and vices in exchange for internal harmony and the prospect of fellowship with God is a very attractive and one-sided deal. In fact, Jesus says that it is the privilege of the disciple to follow in the path which He trod in pursuance of the mission that was the consuming passion of His earthly life. This is the only path which leads to fulfilment and a life that is fully human.

> If any man would come after Me, let him deny[59] himself[60] and take up his cross and follow Me. For whoever would save his life[61] will lose[62] it; and whoever loses[62] his life[61] for My sake and the Gospel's will save it. For what does it profit a man, to gain the whole world and forfeit[63] his life?[61] For what can a man give in return for his life?[61] [Mk 8:34-37 RSV]

59 The Greek is "ἀπαρνησάσθω": to be forgetful; to loose sight of; to be detached or disconnected from.

60 The Greek is "ἑαυτὸν".

61 The Greek is "ψυχὴν": breath, life or soul.

62 The Greek is "ἀπολέσει": to end, destroy, abolish or ruin.

63 The Greek is "ζημιωθῆναι": to damage, harm or injure.

Chapter 8 Love

> He who has My commandments and keeps them, he it is who loves Me; and he who loves Me will be loved by My Father, and I will love him and manifest Myself to him... If a man loves Me, he will keep My word, and My Father will love him, and We will come to him and make Our home with him.
> [Jn 14:21-23 RSV]

Motivation

I have already used the word love on quite a few occasions, so it is about time that I gave some account of what this word means. Clearly, love is a topic of great interest to human beings. Just as clearly, it is a word that is at the heart of the message of Jesus of Nazareth; at least according to the tradition which claims the Apostle John as its authority.

Three kind of love

In trying to understand love, it is unwise to begin with love as a human emotion elicited by another human being. This is a bad place to start because it is too charged and too full of subjectivity. One should rather start with the kind of love exemplified in statements such as "Helen loves chocolate" or "cows love grass" and only when one has some clarity about this kind of proposition raise the stakes to statements such as "David loves Jonathan" or "Abraham loves God."

Rational love

There are three uses of the word "love". They are all related, but cannot quite be reduced to the same idea. The first and most common use of the word is to identify the attraction, impulse or movement of an agent towards what it perceives to be its own proper good, benefit and advantage. Love, in this sense, is a response of the (non-sexual) appetites. It can be said to be rational because it is based on self interest and is proportionate to that self interest.[1]

---

1 Proportion and ratio are pretty much synonyms, hence proportionate and rational have the same base meaning.

> Love, yearning for the object beloved, is desire; having and enjoying it, is joy. [Augustine "City of God" XIV #7]

> Love is something pertaining to the appetite... Now in each of the appetites, the name "love" is given to the principle movement towards the end loved... the aptitude of the sensitive appetite... to some good... is called sensitive love.
> [Thomas Aquinas "Summa Theologica" II(1) Q26 #1]

There can never be love without desire, but there are many kinds of desire. The lover desires who or what they love because they believe, or instinctively feel, that possession of or association with the object of their love will benefit them.[2] However, if an artist knew that their work of art could only become what they wished it to be in isolation from themselves; then their desire for it to become what they envisaged would make them desire to free it, so that it could fulfil their purpose for it, its teleos.[3] Examples of rational love are: "mould loves damp," "dahlias love sunshine," "squirrels love acorns," "Paul loves exercise," and "Andrew loves arguing."

A reason for frivolity

Sometimes, an apparently irrational desire can actually be rational, because it provides a joy which benefits our psychological state. The benefit to one's psychological health accruing from otherwise worthless, frivolous, or even risky activities (such as solving crosswords, playing "snap", watching a TV "sit-com", sky-diving, betting on the outcome of sports events, falling in love, eating ice-cream, non-procreative coitus, or going shoe-shopping) can be considerable.

> A desire for chocolate appears to be irrational, as it increases the likelihood that one will become obese and die young; but it could be argued that the pleasure of eating chocolate is itself valuable[4] and more than compensates for the potential harm.
> [J. Kramer "Private Communication" (2012)]

---

2 Of course, the lover may only feel an instinctive desire and be unable to give any rationale for it. People mostly love food because of the pleasure of eating, not because eating it keeps them alive. Nevertheless, at root the love of such objects is rational, as it is underpinned by their benefit to the lover.

3 This is the significance of the exile of Adam and Eve from God's presence in the Garden of Eden. [Gen 3:20-24] See Chapter 12.

4 Plato "Protagoras" (351e-358c)

This benefit can partly be explained in terms of the release of endorphins in the brain. Such releases are functionally associated with events which are beneficial to the agent – or to their genes, in the case of sexual infatuation or orgasm. They have the effect of extending the immediate pleasure experienced as a result of some achievement into a longer-term mood, experienced as a feeling of well-being. Their objective role is to subjectively motivate the individual to seek to replicate advantageous occurrences and so reinforce and extend the mood; but sometimes they are triggered by extraneous circumstances which the brain mistakes for such beneficial events.

The value of entertainment and of frivolous activities is based on the fact that such mistakes are regularly and sometimes systematically made. Without the regular release of endorphins, a human being can become depressed:[5] convinced that there is nothing they can do to obtain happiness. This can make them stop striving to attain any end and can even make them suicidal. Hence, for any-one who is depressed (or might become so – which is most of us) indulging in frivolity of one kind or another, from time to time, can be very beneficial.[6]

Pleasure is not a good in itself, but it is a quasi-good in two ways. First, because it generally motivates people to seek what is actually good for them. This is its teleos. Without pleasure we would simply not be motivated to do anything. Second, pleasure (even pleasure obtained from entirely frivolous activities, such as blowing soap bubble from hoops or non-procreative coitus) helps our brains to function better because it produces endorphins. Although the Hedonist is wrong to pursue pleasure as the basic good, the Puritan is wrong to disdain pleasure and insist that there is no value associated with it.

The rational love of persons

What, then, is it for one person to desire someone else? One kind of desire is a wish to associate with and to enjoy the fellowship of the beloved. This is the response of a friend. Friendship is the highest form of rational love. It is based on the rational appreciation of mutual value, leading to sincere and abiding reciprocal benevolence and cooperation. Friends love each other because each offers the other an abiding commitment to mutual assistance in time of need and a competence which will help them to become a better person, day by day.

---

5 See page 87.

6 Plato “Laws” (IV 803c-804b), quoted on page 154.

> As the Father has loved Me, so have I loved you; abide in My love. If you keep My commandments, you will abide in My love, just as I have kept My Father's commandments and abide in His love... This is My commandment, that you love one another as I have loved you. Greater love has no man than this, that a man lay down his life for his friends. You are My friends if you do what I command you… I have called you friends, for all that I have heard from My Father I have made known to you… This I command you, to love one another.
> [Jn 15:9-17 RSV]

Friendship is a kind of trade. At its most basic level it is seen at work in apes who pair off to groom each other on an "I'll scratch your back if you'll scratch mine" basis. At its highest level it is witnessed to by the words John Henry Newman wrote of Ambrose StJohn:

> From the first he loved me with an intensity of love, which was unaccountable… As far as this world was concerned I was his first and last.
> [J.H. Newman "Letter to Lord Blachford" (May 31, 1875)[7]]

Love motivates friends to care for each other's good as if it were their own; because the good of the lover becomes entangled with the good of the beloved, so that neither can stand confidently alone. The true friend seeks association with and benefit from their beloved. They do not seek to possess or dominate or control. The friend always sees their beloved as an autonomous person and an ally; never as a resource, or as an object, or a slave. When someone's enthusiasm for their friend becomes very great – because they come to believe that their friend is able to supply very many of their needs and wants and is able to rectify or compensate for their deficiencies – then friendship merges seamlessly into what is commonly called love.[8]

Irrational love or romance

The second use of the word "love" is to identify the attraction or movement of a living agent towards what it instinctively identifies as being in the interest of its genes or of its species. This is the biological basis of all familial and romantic affection. This type of love is irrational, because it is not directed towards the self-interest of the lover. Indeed, it is often perceived (both by the lover and

7 W. Ward ed. "The Life of Cardinal Newman, Volume II" (1912)
8 Plato "Laws" (VIII 837a)

by impartial observers) as a malady or madness.[9] Although romantic love is related to the sexual appetite, its ambit is wider than this; as it also has something in common with the more general instinct to value and support family members who share much of one's own genetic inheritance.[10]

Beauty

The appreciation of beauty is closely related to romantic love. Often the first motion of the lover towards the beloved arises from a perception of beauty[11] (which is not *quite* the same as sex appeal) in the body or soul of the beloved. More generally, beauty is attractive because it is an intimation of wholesomeness, health and order. It suggests that the object or person perceived as beautiful is reliable and worth-while; either as a source of good genes for breeding purposes or else as an effective provider of sustenance, protection, council or direction. Hence, beauty (whether of body or soul) can be used as a criterion for choosing either a breeding partner or a friend. In the first case it is related to irrational love, in the second case it guides rational love.

Joy or Bliss

The third use of the word "love" is as a synonym for "joy" or "bliss" which is, more properly, love fulfilled.[12] Joy arises from the attainment of some object which is truly desirable. In the material world, no good is ever entirely attained by any agent, hence no love is ever completely transformed into joy.

> Joy… doth not want heirs, it doth not want children[13] – joy wanteth itself, it wanteth eternity, it wanteth recurrence, it wanteth everything eternally-like-itself.
> [F. Nietzsche "Also Sprach Zarathustra" (1885) Ch 79 #9]

---

9 See for, example, Plato "Republic" (X 572-575) "Phaedrus" (231, 244-245, 249-252, 256) "Symposium" (212-222)

10 R. Dawkins "The Selfish Gene" (1976)

11 Plato "Phaedrus" (232e, 249-250)

12 See quote from Augustine "The City of God" on page 146.

13 In "Symposium" (206e) Plato considers love as an aspect of eternity active within temporal existence. Here, Nietzsche considers joy as itself eternal, transcendent and divine.

The love of pets

How does the love of a pet owner for their pet fit into this scheme? Clearly, the returned affection is rational. The owner provides for the needs of the pet, so it is rational for the pet to love their owner. It is less clear what motivates the benevolence of a pet owner towards their pet.

One possibility is that it results from the owner subconsciously mistaking their pet for offspring, in which case the love of an owner for their pet is quasi-parental and hence fundamentally irrational. Sometimes owners do treat their pets like substitute children; but I think that this is not a good general account of the phenomena of pet ownership or of the love of owners for their pets. After all, children themselves often very much like having pets, and it does not seem to me plausible to explain this fact in terms of some supposed prepubescent parenting instinct. Moreover, children generally talk of and treat their pets as if they were friends and play-mates, not offspring.

I suppose that the first pets were working animals, like horses, dogs and hawks. These were tamed and used for particular purposes. They certainly benefited their owners and had definite utility. Hence it was rational for their owners to value them, to be sad when they became sick or old, and to suffer their loss when they died.[14] Nowadays, most pets are not kept for the sake of their being any practical use. Many offer the possibility of a kind of companionship and even real affection, and all have a kind of beauty which can be appreciated by their owners.

Crucially, the relationship of owner and pet is unstable. It is difficult not to develop a definite sympathy for and affection towards any living creature with which one regularly associates; even if one is a farmer rearing the animal for slaughter. One gains a respect for the creature's abilities and a sympathy for its deficiencies, and even without engaging in anthropomorphic self-delusion one discovers a connection between its existence and one's own: a fundamental commonality of being.

The love that a pet owner has for their pet therefore has two components. Its lower part is based on an appreciation of the beauty and abilities of the pet. This aspect is dominant in the relationship between an aquarist and their fish. The higher part is a peculiar kind of friendship; where the pet is valued either for its utility (this is rare) or else for its companionship alone.[15]

---

14 Similarly, we are told of a Centurion who had a servant who was so "dear to him" [Lk 7:2 RSV] that the Roman officer "earnestly besought" [Lk 7:4, Mat 8:5 RSV] Jesus to heal him.

15 According to the Torah the animals were created by God so that Adam might not be lonely. [Gen 2:18-19]

Disordered love

Rational love is well-ordered or moderate when the perception of benefit is in proportion[16] with the real benefit. It becomes immoderate when the perception of benefit is out of proportion with the real benefit, or where some disadvantage is overlooked or deliberately ignored. In such a case, what is objectively a less valuable good might be preferred to what is objectively more valuable. Immoderate love results from sinfulness,[17] which is an underlying confusion about what is really advantageous to the agent. Any deviation from moderation degrades a love which could be rational into one that is irrational, at least to a degree.

Romantic love is always disordered in a superficial sense; because it is directed towards a person who is not desired out of any appreciation of an objective benefit to the lover – except in so far as the lover is doomed by their genes to be disconsolate in the absence of a breeding partner. On a deeper level, any love which is associated with the appreciation of beauty has the potential of being well-ordered and moderate; as long as that beauty is understood to be an intimation of Divine Beauty. Even so, it can only become properly ordered, and so have any chance of lasting, if it is transformed into (or at least is supplemented with) friendship.

Infatuation

The first way in which romantic love goes wrong is when the love for a human being gets in the way of the love of God. Love of the mortal beloved should always lead on towards love of all else that is beautiful and beneficial – and in the end to the Divine.[18] If any love (whether it be romantic, familial or rational) does not do this, but fixates the lover on the mortal beloved themselves so that the lover is distracted from God, than that love is disordered and is bound to be harmful to the lover.

> To another [Jesus] said, "Follow Me." But he said, "Lord, let me first go and bury my father." But He said to him, "Leave the dead to bury their own dead; but as for you, go and proclaim the Kingdom of God." Another said, "I will follow you, Lord; but let me first say farewell to those at my home." Jesus said to him, "No one who puts his hand to the plough and looks back is fit for the Kingdom of God." [Lk 9:59-62 RSV]

---

16 Or ratio, hence rational rational.

17 Or concupiscence, see page 162.

18 Plato "Symposium" (210-212)

> [Jesus] said… "A man once gave a great banquet, and invited many... but… the first said to him, 'I have bought a field... I pray you, have me excused…' And another said, 'I have married a wife, and therefore I cannot come…' And the master said to the servant, 'Go out to the highways and hedges, and compel people to come in… I tell you, none of those men who were invited shall taste my banquet.'... If any one comes to Me and does not hate[19] his own father and mother and wife and children and brothers and sisters, yes, and even his own life, he cannot be My disciple." [Lk 14:16-26 RSV]

Lust

Lust is the second way in which romantic love goes wrong. Lust is a desire to possess, control and use another person who is viewed as no more than a resource to be exploited.[20] It is wrong for anyone to own or exploit anyone else in this way. It degrades the object of such "love" and is incompatible with the benevolence which both romantic love and friendship claim to represent. Much bad eroticism is about possession and domination. The willingness or desire of the lust object to be exploited doesn't make such a relationship any less abusive.[21]

God is Love

The most fundamental precept of Catholicism is that God is Love; from which it follows that Love itself is of ultimate value. This is a mystery. After all, how can Love itself be the object of Love? Nevertheless, this is what the Doctrine of the Trinity amounts to.

> Beloved, let us love one another; for love is of God, and he who loves is born of God and knows God. He who does not love does not know God; for God is love. In this the love of God was made manifest among us, that God sent His only Son into the world, so that we might live through Him. In this is love, not that we loved God but that He loved us and sent His Son to be

---

19 This is a colloquial use. It means "discount the love of".

20 Lust is usually motivated by the sexual appetite, but not always.

21 I am not here asserting that all eroticism featuring submissive and dominant roles is perverse. It might sometimes be wholesome for one person to take charge for the sake of the person who is taken in hand. An analogy might be made with the relationship between a spiritual director and their directee, where submission and obedience in all matters not pertaining to sin is vital. [Plato "Republic" (IX 590d), quoted on page 331]

> the expiation for our sins. Beloved, if God so loved us, we also ought to love one another. No man has ever seen God; if we love one another, God abides in us and His love is perfected in us… So we know and believe the love God has for us. **God is love**, and he who abides in love abides in God, and God abides in him. [1Jn 4:7-12,16 RSV]

The Father loves the Son and the Spirit.[22] The Spirit and Son return that love. Moreover, it is the eternal love which the Father and Son have for each other which brings the Spirit into being – and it is the Spirit who binds the Father and Son together in their eternal embrace of love. So the three persons of God love each other into being, and the only being that they have (what other being could they desire?) is the love which they have for each other. The three persons give rise to the one love which binds them; yet without the love they share, the persons would not be at all. So which comes first? The community of Lovers who together *are* God, or the single act of Love which *is* God? The only orthodox answer is "neither." Love without lovers is just as impossible as Lovers who do not love.

> The Spirit of the supreme Logos is a kind of ineffable yet intense longing or "eros" experienced by the Begetter for the Logos born ineffably from Him, a longing experienced also by the beloved Logos and Son of the Father for His Begetter; but the Logos possesses this love by virtue of the fact that it comes from the Father in the very act through which He comes from the Father, and it resides co-naturally in Him… Yet the Spirit belongs also to the Son, who receives Him from the Father as the Spirit of Truth, Wisdom and Logos. For Truth and Wisdom constitute a Logos that befits His Begetter, a Logos that rejoices with the Father as the Father rejoices in Him… This pre-eternal rejoicing of the Father and the Son is the Holy Spirit who… is common to both… Yet the Spirit has His existence from the Father alone, and hence He proceeds as regards His existence only from the Father. Our intellect, because created in God's image, possesses likewise the image of this sublime Eros or intense longing – an image expressed in the love experienced by the intellect for the spiritual knowledge that originates from it and continually abides in it. [Gregory Palamas "Topics of Natural and Theological Science" #36]

---

22 The love that is spoken of in connection with God is not the love of desire or aspiration, but rather the love of union, fulfilment or attainment; that is, more properly, ecstatic joy.

The love of mankind for God

The greatest good for any human being is that they should live for ever in friendship with God. Hence the desire which should consume ones heart and excite ones appetites and motivate ones whole life (if only one was entirely clear-sighted and rational) is the love of God; for God is all that truly matters. God is the fountain-head of all being and the source of Eternal Life. This love is the most self-interested of all loves, as well as the most spiritual. It is the love that gives hope and meaning to ones life and it is the only basis on which a rational respect for oneself and ones neighbour can be constructed.

The love of God for mankind

One problem remains. How can God love mankind, either as a whole or as a set of individual human beings? It would seem that this is impossible; because God is self-adequate and in need of no external good – not even that of companionship: for the interior communion of Father, Son and Spirit is entirely adequate on that count. The idea that God has an irrational love for human kind as some kind of progeny is impious. As Plato reminds us procreation is what mortal humanity has, in the natural order, *instead* of immortality.[23] How then could such an irrational appetite possibly arise within the Immortal Godhead?

God loves mankind in a manner analogous to that in which an artist loves his masterpiece; as a reflection of himself and an expression of his abilities. This is quasi-parental and hence irrational, in as far as the object of the love is of no use to the lover; but it is rational in as far as the object of the love is a manifestation of the life of the lover, and so participates in their own form. To the extent that the creature participates in the form of the Creator, to that extent the love of the Creator for the creature is rational; because it is self love by proxy.

God's love for human beings is also similar to that of a pet owner for their pets. Rather than being a demeaning idea, this is ennobling; for the vocation of "entertaining" God, as Plato puts it is a high one.

> Man… has been created as a toy for God… this is the great point in his favour. So every man and woman should play this part and order their whole life accordingly… A man should spend his whole life at play – sacrificing, singing, dancing… Our species is not worthless, but something rather important! [Plato "Laws" (IV 803c-804b)]

23 Plato "Laws" (IV 721c) & "Symposium" (206e) see page 77.

Though we are far beneath the competence and puissance of God, still God has a real sympathy and compassion towards us.[24] God loves each individual human being because God knows what they are capable of becoming – with divine help, encouragement and guidance. God offers to each and every man and woman the prospect of an elevation of dignity and power, so that they might become truly worthy of divine love[25] by coming to share in the divine nature.[26]

> But what… if man had eyes to see true beauty – divine beauty, I mean, pure and clear and unalloyed… in that communion only, beholding beauty with the eye of the soul, he will be enabled to bring forth, not images of beauty, but realities (for he has hold not of an image but of a reality), and bringing forth and nourishing true virtue to become the friend of God[27] and be immortal, if mortal man may.
> [Plato "Symposium" (211e-212a)][28]

It is according to this foreknowledge that, amazingly, God offers the hand of friendship to sinners.[29]

> To believe in God as love means to believe that in pure personal relationship we encounter, not merely what ought to be, but what is, the deepest, veriest truth about the structure of reality... belief in God is the trust, the well-nigh incredible trust, that to give ourselves to the uttermost in love is not to be confounded but to be "accepted", that Love is the ground of our being, to which ultimately we "come home"... the specifically Christian view of the world is asserting that the final definition of this reality, from which "nothing can separate us", since it is the very ground of our being, is "the love of God in Christ Jesus our Lord".[30] [J.A.T. Robinson "Honest to God" (1963)]

---

24 Sir 18:8-13, quoted on page 79.
25 Wis 3:5, quoted on page 111.
26 1Thes 4:3. 2Pet 1:4, quoted on page 302.
27 Greek: "θεοφιλεῖ γενέσθαι", " become the God-friend".
28 I have used the Jowett translation here, as more faithful to the Greek.
29 Ex 33:11. Job 29:4. Ps 25:14. Is 41:8. Wis 7:14,27. Jn 15:14-15. Jas 2:23.
30 Rom 8:39.

Chapter 9 Sin and Wickedness

> I do not understand my own actions. For I do not do what I want, but I do the very thing I hate. Now if I do what I do not want, I agree that the law is good. So then it is no longer I that do it, but sin which dwells within me. For I know that nothing good dwells within me, that is, in my flesh. I can will what is right, but I cannot do it. For I do not do the good I want, but the evil I do not want is what I do. Now if I do what I do not want, it is no longer I that do it, but sin which dwells within me.
>
> So I find it to be a law that when I want to do right, evil lies close at hand. For I delight in the law of God, in my inmost self, but I see in my members another law at war with the law of my mind and making me captive to the law of sin which dwells in my members. Wretched man that I am! Who will deliver me from this body of death? [Rom 7:16-24 RSV]

Motivation

In the next few chapters I shall develop an account of the relationship between humanity and God. My main purpose is to attempt to make some sense of the unsatisfactory predicament that we presently find ourselves in. I shall attempt to offer some insight as to why this mortal life, which is often a "vale of tears", is necessary for our own good; and also why God often seems so distant and unconcerned with human woes. I am not interested in an explanation along the lines of "Human beings deserve to suffer because they are sinners," as this begs the two questions "What is sin and why is God so bothered about it?" and "If sin is so bad, why does God allow human beings to sin?" Nevertheless, those subsidiary questions are valid in themselves and require some kind of answer.

The will

The will is an agent's faculty for determining what action is to be taken by them in response to experience or given data. The reason plays a part in this determination, by elucidating the implications of the known facts based on a logical application of the subject's established beliefs, values and expectations.

The business of the will is complicated by the fact that the issues involved vary widely in character. Before it can be decided "what is best", these diverse considerations must somehow be merged into a single measure. This requires a metrical formula which makes it possible to trade each off against the others; in the way that a table of exchange rates enables one to trade currencies. This metric is unavoidably subjective and personal, as there can be no single proper and correct way to combine such disparate factors.

The basic automaton

Consider some automaton having a small number of simple senses, each characterized by a few variables; and whose only objective is to continually maximize one of these variables by changing its location on a rail track. To be specific, imagine that it has a photocell and that its objective is to maximise the exposure of this photocell to light as its environment changes in various ways. In any given situation it is faced with the choice of moving forward or backward along its rails. It has to process its various inputs in some way in order to decide which way to move. This processing is the exercise of its will.

At any moment, the automaton will have some metrical formula for processing all the available data (past and present) so as to generate an output which drives its servo-motor and moves it to or fro along the track. Ideally, the automaton should have the ability to evolve this metrical formula, according to some definite scheme, in response to its experience. If the automaton is able to evaluate successive versions of its metrical formula and so choose to rely on whichever version of its formula it identifies as superior, then one might expect that over time it will evolve a metrical formula which is generally successful at keeping its photocell well illumined.

Conscience

The formula which the automaton uses to translate its past and present experience into decisions about what it ought to do for the best can be identified as its conscience. If its conscience is well-formed, it will systematically obtain good outcomes for the automaton. If it is malformed, it will be unsuccessful and often result in actions contrary to the automaton's defining objective.

Mice and Men

When it comes to making decisions, human beings, mice and automata are in the same boat and act in the same way. This is because: first, they *have* to make decisions – choosing not making a decision is itself a decision[1] and will have consequences; and second, no amount of empirical evidence can possibly constitute a definitive reason for making any decision.

When it comes to deciding what to eat for breakfast; who to take as a friend or spouse; or what philosophy, lifestyle or career to adopt, it is impossible to know for certain what is "for the best". In particular, this can be affected by subsequent decisions made by other people, of which one can have no present knowledge or even reasonable expectation. The best one can do is adopt some pragmatic process which accepts as input the information which is in fact available and produces as its output a decision. However, adopting such a process is itself problematic; for this itself is a decision, and before this decision is made there is no process available for making decisions.

Given that mice and men both do in fact make decisions, it is apparent that they must have an initial decision making process built into their brains. If there was no such instinctive process they would be permanently paralysed, unable ever to act in any way. This initial process is like the "boot sector" of a computer's system disk (the absolutely basic and necessary programme upon which all subsequent meaningful activity is based) but from whence could such a biological boot sector come?

The answer to this is pretty obvious. It comes from the evolutionary heritage of the experience of one's ancestors. In the last analysis, life is all about survival. The decisions which a living organism makes are validated by the fact that it survives and has progeny. This kind of validation is not rigorous, of course. The fact that some theory *works up to a point* does not mean it is true; but only that... it *works up to a point*.

Human beings adopt ideas which enable them to attribute sense to the Universe because decisions made on the basis of the understanding which such ideas promise have consistently resulted in survival. If what seems to be reality were in fact a delusion, there would be no accounting for the fact that treating it as objective results in so much technological success. The fact that Objective Realism and Monotheism are useful, in that they motivate and enable Science and Technology – and so happiness and survival – is the basic justification for adopting these beliefs.

---

1 Rush song "Freewill" (1980)

Wishful thinking

It is always open to the moral agent to choose to ignore the most plausible conclusion as to which course of action ought to be followed in favour of another one which is somehow more desirable. So, a husband faced by a midwife with the dilemma "Shall I save the mother or the unborn child?" might personally desire one objective above the other and so be prejudicially motivated to favour this conclusion, whatever the dictates of reason told him was the prudent choice.

This freedom to chose the desirable over the reasonable arises from a lack of clear knowledge of what is actually good. When evaluating what action is for the best, in accordance with the dictates of conscience, one would like to be able to start from basic values and somehow compute from these a relative assessment of the benefit which one might expect to obtain as a result of choosing each alternate option available. This would entail estimating various partial advantages and disadvantages and then merging these estimates together into one single overall measure of nett benefit. Once this was done, the option associated with the most beneficial outcome would be the one which ought to be adopted. To act in this way is to act in accordance with the fundamental virtue of sobriety or prudence.[2]

Sadly, the integrity of this process is vulnerable to attack. Whatever the most plausible view of a question might be, there are always alternative possibilities which simply cannot be excluded, given the partial and ambiguous nature of human knowledge. Often it is clear that some greatly desirable advantage is unobtainable only because it is associated with some greater disadvantage. Now, because the estimates of advantage and disadvantage are necessarily subjective and uncertain, it is always open to the moral agent to adjust them in order to make it appear that the benefit is worth the risk. To act in this way is to violate one's conscience, and to act in accordance with the fundamental vice of recklessness. It amounts to lying to oneself or *wishful thinking*, to put a more palatable gloss on the matter.[3]

A second vulnerability is the temptation to ignore the dictates of reason. Rather than deceiving oneself about the significance of the conclusions which result from the processing of raw data, one can

---

2 This would be a formidable and perhaps imponderable task to execute formally; but it is one which each human being perforce does instinctively, informally or intuitively many times in their lives. My business here is not to elucidate the technicalities and fallibilities of this process but to describe an altogether different deficit.

3 Dishonesty is the root of all wickedness. Jesus of Nazareth calls Satan "The Father of Lies". [Jn 8:44 RSV]

deceive oneself about how the raw data should be processed. This second vulnerability can be treated as an aspect of the former; for if only one knew clearly that some process of deduction was reasonable and that none other was allowable, then one could not be tempted to ignore the dictate of reason any more than one is ever tempted to believe that one plus one is three. One might earnestly wish that some other way of looking at the facts was possible but, given that one knew clearly that it wasn't, one would necessarily have to accept the unpalatable conclusion and get on with making the best of the situation.

A third vulnerability is, of course, simple fallibility. With the best of intentions, human beings make mistakes. Where these are truly accidental – the result of some frailty, such as tiredness – and not the result of carelessness then they have no subjective ethical significance.[4] Such mistakes still indicate a defect of nature; but they are symptomatic more of limitation than of disorder and immoderation.

Intrinsic evil

It is important to note that the most important aspect of moral dilemmas is not the immediate, particular and practical outcomes associated with choices but rather the long-term, global, cultural and sociological outcomes. It may be that some choice, viewed in isolation, might be clearly to the advantage of all those parties concerned; however this is not enough to make it a good option. Indeed, it could be a very bad option if it involved breaching a general rule of conduct which it is highly advantageous to maintain. This is because once such a rule is infringed, even subtly, it will inevitably be breached over and over again – each time more easily and overtly than the last – until in the end the general rule will become defunct and the great advantage which resulted from its maintenance will be lost. This is what people mean when they refer to "the thin end of the wedge" or "a slippery slope" in debates regarding ethical questions.

An example will best serve to elucidate what I mean. It is a general principle of ethics that the intentional taking of innocent life is always reprehensible. I think that the rationale for maintaining this principle is obvious. Imagine the kind of "wild-west", "gangster" or "police state" society which would result if it were negated. Now consider an emergency situation in which very many human lives can somehow only be saved by the assassination of one innocent individual. If this "sacrifice" is made it will establish a precedent and lead, by incremental extension, to great injustices; for example the "sacrifice" of many

4 I consider the question of culpability and blame on page 164.

innocent individuals in order to save the life of some dignitary such as a head of state. Hence, the long-term and global effects of breaking such a rule are very severe, and this fact ought generally to outweigh all other considerations.

These kinds of acts are sometimes described as "intrinsically evil", meaning that the wider effects of approving them would be so serious as to make doing so generally unthinkable.[5] Of course, in extreme situations it might be imperative to act in exactly such a way as would generally be judged to be reprehensible. For example, if the only way to save the entire human race was to intentionally kill a number of innocent individuals it might become proper, though most regrettable, to do so. Sometimes the ends do justify even the most unpalatable means.

Concupiscence

There is a conflict between our sapient rationality and our animal instincts, drives or appetites. There is nothing wrong or evil, as such, with animal instincts. Animals, after all, get along well enough with their powerful instincts and limited ability to reason. Nevertheless, instinct can only be valid "on the whole". In particular cases it can easily fail. The example of the hedgehog curled-up in the headlight beams of an oncoming car makes this clear. Human instincts such as: to eat food when it is available, so as to survive the next shortage; to mate with every willing and available sex-partner, so as to maximise the number of one's progeny; to brag and boast and show-off before others and to antagonise rivals, so as to gain social status, all have associated disadvantages which only the reason can evaluate.

Typically, instinctive drives are focussed on short-term and immediate benefit. The role of the reason is to moderate these impulses and to bring them into harmony, ordering them towards the end of personal survival and fulfilment; and this often involves deciding to resist the impulse of instinct. Once one starts to habitually make choices recommended by instinct (because they are expected to lead to outcomes which are more immediately desirable) rather than because one honestly and reasonably believes they are prudent, one has adopted a false measure or account of what is right.

This state of internal disorder (which is a lack of correspondence between what is really beneficial and what is perceived to be so) is called concupiscence or immoderation. It can be identified with what the

5 For example: homosexuality is often condemned as liable to undermine marriage, contradict an understanding of sex as primarily procreative, devalue family life in general; and so be contrary to the common good of society and the survival both of the State and the human race.

Apostle Paul refers to as the "sin which dwells within me",[6] as also the "law at war with the law of my mind… the law of sin which dwells in my members"[7] and "the flesh"[8] with which "I serve the law of sin."[9] Most people would acknowledge some sympathy with the Apostle's heart-felt description of his personal experience of concupiscence. We feel that though we often know well enough the right thing to do, this doesn't mean that we do it. Frequently, our judgement is clouded by the immediate instinctive attraction of some other imprudent choice.

Short-term or long-term benefit?

Faced with a choice between one option with a large and obvious immediate advantage, but which seems liable to lead to disaster in the long term, and an alternative which promises long-term success, but offers no immediate gratification, most people find it difficult to act in accordance with what they honestly believe to be in their long term interest. In effect, they gamble on something unexpected turning up which will make it possible to avoid the ruin of the second option, once its benefit has been obtained. It isn't so much that they "cannot do" what is right,[10] but more that they habitually prefer short-term benefits to long-term ones.

The rational basis of such wishful thinking is obvious. Our ability to predict outcomes declines rapidly as the more and more remote future is considered. Hence, if one action is projected to produce an immediate benefit and a remote disaster, while another is foreseen to produce immediate suffering and an eventual triumph; it is not obvious that the second action is the better choice. After all, the immediate benefit of the first option is pretty certain and it might lead to other unpredictable opportunities which make it possible to avoid the expected disaster.

There is always a judgement call to be made, as to how prospective outcomes should be discounted. This is certain to result in disagreement among persons of good will who are posed the same dilemma. Even were they to agree about both the immediate and long-term consequences of every choice, they will hardly agree about the likelihood to be associated with each.

---

6 Rom 7:20 RSV, quoted at the head of this chapter.

7 Rom 7:22 RSV, quoted at the head of this chapter.

8 Rom 7:18 RSV, quoted at the head of this chapter.

9 Rom 7:25 RSV.

10 The Apostle's language is confused. For example, he says: "I do not do what I want", "the evil I do not want is what I do" and "I can will what is right, but I cannot do it". Taken at face value, these statements are absurd for in normal speech "to will" some act is the same as "to do" it.

Culpability

From one point of view, the notion of blame or culpability can be identified with the objective fact of an ill-formed conscience or disordered will. Somehow, a person has come to adopt an improper settled view of what is right and wrong. Their wickedness is identifiable with this malformation of their will. From this viewpoint, personal evil is always a species of sickness.

> Wickedness is discord and sickness of the soul… No soul is willingly ignorant of anything… ignorance occurs precisely when a soul tries for the truth, but swerves aside from understanding… There are, it appears, these two kinds of badness in the soul. Most people call one of them "wickedness", but it's obviously a disease of the soul… They call the other one ignorance… but they aren't willing to agree that it's a form of badness. [Plato "Sophist" (228b-d)]

When a human being habitually ignores long-term or global consequences in deciding what is right, it is their bad conscience which is the immediate cause of the evil acts they commit. It is therefore appropriate for them to be punished so as to induce them to adopt a more prudent and responsible measure of what is right. Were their concupiscence ever to be rectified, the fact that they used to be wicked would cease to be of importance. Their sin would lie in the past: in the evil will or imprudence which they have lost. Their virtue exists in the present: in the good will which they have gained.

> But if a wicked man turns away from all his sins which he has committed and keeps all My statutes and does what is lawful and right, he shall surely live; he shall not die. None of the transgressions which he has committed shall be remembered against him; for the righteousness which he has done he shall live. Have I any pleasure in the death of the wicked, says the Lord God, and not rather that he should turn from his way and live? [Ezk 18:21-23 RSV]

However, it is also true to say that once a specific pattern or habit of thought has been established, a person cannot act differently. They have become habituated in wrong action. They are a hostage to "the law of sin"[11] established in their soul. In this sense it is no longer their fault when they do wrong, as they cannot help themselves.

11 Rom 7:23 RSV, quoted at the head of this chapter.

Corruption of the soul

Every imprudent (or sinful) act which is executed on the basis of a malformed will (though objectively wrong, and a serious matter on that account) is only marginally corrupting. The fact that the will is already malformed mitigates what is called the *culpability* of the act. The sinner is only doing what has become natural to them, and are not thereby making themselves any worse. When Paul writes of the conflict between what he knows to be right and "wills to do" and what he finds himself actually doing, he is referring to the incremental degeneration of the conscience. Each small blameworthy decision is so easy. The reason for making it is always clear and present, the reason for not doing so is often obscure and remote; yet on each occasion one is conscious of fiddling the books, even as one convinces oneself that the dishonesty is justified.

Sadly, each dishonest tweak of the conscience has an effect on the agent's moral perspective. They become desensitised to some issues, such as damage done to social relationships or the long-term profitability of the company for which they work, and fixated on others; such as the gaining of the approval of their immediate superior or maximising this year's performance bonus.

> Nor is there any reason why it is made difficult for us to do good other than that long habit of doing wrong which has infected us from childhood and corrupted us little by little over many years and ever after holds us in bondage and slavery to itself, so that it seems somehow to have acquired the force of nature.
> [Pelagius "Letter to Demetrias" (8:3)]

On this perspective, while it is the disinformation of the will which is truly sinful; this generally accumulates as the sediment and legacy of repeated bad decisions and the words and actions that flowed from them. Hence, it is individual sinful actions which are crucial; not so much because they have bad external effects, but because it is these which establish and reinforce bad habits, or as Jesus says "defiles a man".

> And he called the people to him again, and said to them, "Hear me, all of you, and understand: there is nothing outside a man which by going into him can defile him; but the things which come out of a man are what defile him... Do you not see that whatever goes into a man from outside cannot defile him, since it enters, not his heart but his stomach, and so passes on?... What comes out of a man is what defiles a man. For from within, out of the heart of man, come evil

> thoughts, fornication, theft, murder, adultery, coveting, wickedness, deceit, licentiousness, envy, slander, pride, foolishness. All these evil things come from within, and they defile a man." [Mk 7:14-23 RSV]

One encounters a certain circularity here. Individual wicked acts are subjectively *culpable* only in so far as they further deform the conscience or defile the heart; but the fact that the conscience is deformed is only important because this leads to further wrongdoing: individual wicked acts, sins, which are wrong because they are objectively *harmful*.

Education in virtue

The answer to sin is moral formation, which is an important aspect of education. It is notoriously difficult, however, to reliably educate people into being habitually courageous, kind and just. This is because knowledge is not always attainable by a steady process of incremental learning in which one idea is calmly established on foundations laid down by earlier study. Rather, it is sometimes necessary to challenge and revise – or even reject – cherished beliefs and attitudes. The situation is aggravated when it comes to ethical questions. In such matters the evidence is necessarily equivocal, the arguments contentious, and the level of personal commitment to favoured hypotheses often high. Persuading someone to change their mind about an ethical matter is therefore a difficult task. People often resist such an educational process, regarding it as a form of indoctrination.

Culpable acts are worthy of punishment precisely because they exist on the periphery of the will. They are acts which required the conscience to be modulated before they could be performed. Hence, there is a good hope that punishing these acts will reform the conscience, as the correctional pain endured will tend to condition the culprit into not repeating the vicious act. There is little point in punishing bad habits, because they are deeply ingrained and not susceptible to easy modification. Any attempt to correct such vices after the event is more liable to produce resentment of and alienation from the teacher. The culprit will feel that they are unable to act differently and that it is unfair to punish them for something that seems beyond their control. Bad habits can best be broken by providing a sufficient positive incentive to act differently or, failing this, an automatic deterrent which it is certain will take immediate effect should the unwholesome act be committed or, even better, contemplated.

Sin and death

An awareness of inevitable mortality tends to undermine the rational basis of virtue; for why should any moral agent care about what happens after they cease to exist? When "ought" is understood in terms of facilitating the survival of the self and when there is no prospect of the self surviving, then "ought" ceases to have any intelligibility. This is, perhaps, an over-statement. What is certainly needed as a foundation for justice is that there is some kind of "eternal dimension" to human existence; but this does not have to be personal immortality. So, if a person believed that they might achieve something of eternal significance[12] then they might value this possibility and be willing to strive to achieve it. Sadly, the Second Law of Thermodynamics falsifies all such beliefs, so far as this world in concerned; for no matter what the individual achieves, it is bound to come to nothing in the end. Moreover, may people have no reasonable expectation of achieving anything remarkable. Finally, the prospect of some kind of impersonal eternity cannot motivate a person to behave virtuously as death approaches. When an individual has achieved all that they are going to achieve there is no point in them trying to do anything else worthwhile.

Given the prospect of approaching death, a rational agent should become progressively less responsible and increasingly concerned only with cramming as much experience into the last few hours of their life as possible for it is only in this way that they can add to their life: by intensifying and deepening it, rather than extending its duration. They should enter a second childhood, where the hazard to their own life associated with risky actions is discounted; not out of ignorance or a clouding of their reason, but because the threat is subsumed in the steadily increasing danger of death associated with simply existing for another moment.

Hence, once a person is diagnosed with some terminal disease, they might as well drink as much alcohol, smoke as much tobacco and eat as much rich food as they care to – as well as engage in whatever dangerous but gratifying activities they were previously too timid to experience. As the Apostle Paul remarks "If the dead are not raised, 'let us eat and drink, for tomorrow we die.'"[13] Hence, the fact of death tends to encourage the reflective person towards wickedness.

---

12 Such as a scientific breakthrough or work of art, or even just the passing on of their genes to the next generation: so that they could understand their own mortal life as a link in an immortal chain of life.

13 1Cor 15:32 RSV, quoting Is 22:13.

> Everything before them is vanity, since one fate comes to all… This is an evil in all that is done under the sun, that one fate comes to all; also the hearts of men are full of evil, and madness is in their hearts while they live, and after that they go to the dead. [Eccl 9:2-3 RSV]

> Sin entered the world through one man, and through sin death, and thus death has spread through the whole human race, by reason of which everyone has sinned.[14]
> [Rom 5:12.[15] Jerusalem Bible Standard Edition (1966)]

Before all other reasons, we tend to sin simply because of our mortality, not because of some other flaw in our nature. The prospect of the (apparent) extinction of our being alone is enough to account for human wickedness. After all, what greater perversion of being could there be than for it to not be?

Justice and Life

Turning the argument of the last few paragraphs on its head, it follows that for there to be any rational basis for the mortal individual to live justly, death must be something other than the final extinction of being. The choice before the rational person is either to believe that death is absolute and that the idea of justice a delusion, or else to accept that the claims of justice are real and that they imply a continuation of life beyond death.

Existentialism

Existentialists seeks to avoid this dichotomy by claiming to be the origin of their own ethics. Laudably, they refuse to accept that value is extrinsic to those things which are themselves valuable (that is, they reject the idea that they are are only valuable because God, or some other authority, asserts them to be so) but then, either due to an exaggerated humanism or a stark atheism, wrongly insist that things must somehow obtain their value entirely and solely from and within this world of suffering, impermanence and uncertainty.

This is a noble idea. It springs from a conviction that human beings really do matter; even though they are finite and frail and subject to

14 See parallel accounts, quoted on pages 111 and 302.

15 This is the alternate translation given at the end of footnote "j". The Greek should be transliterated "to all men mortality did pass through for that [ἐφ' ᾧ] all did sin." I thank M.P. Cullinan for bringing this to my attention.

ultimate frustration. It is a well-motivated attempt to deny the soul-destroying nihilism which forever batters at the door of the post-modernist heart. However, it is fundamentally irrational, and therefore covertly yields the field of battle to the forces of despair.

The facts are: first, a thing which is itself worthless cannot supply worthiness to another thing; and second, all material things are subject to a physical law of futility and so the whole Cosmos is doomed to finish up in a state of random uniformity. Hence, this world cannot, of itself, accommodate the idea of value; nor can it support the idea of justice as a firm foundation for the modern notion of "universal human rights".

Those who stand firm for the rights and dignity of the human individual while denying any reality beyond their present physicality exhibit a fundamental inconsistency. Unknowingly, they inherit their conviction that the human being is significant from a philosophical tradition which they otherwise repudiate.[16] Their repudiation of this tradition means that they have no rationale for asserting that human beings are worthwhile beyond an irrational prejudice or conviction.

Original Sin

Original sin is the idea that human beings have no rights enforcible upon God; that the individual is autonomous from the very first moment of their existence and must answer for their own actions, making their own way in the world without any intrinsic right to expect or demand divine help or assistance. This state is described as one of sin for three reasons.

First, because it describes a state of separation from God, which is the basic meaning of the word sin. Ironically, the converse idea (that God is separated from mankind) is described by saying that God is "holy"; the base meaning of the word "holy" also being "separate". Hence, holiness and sinfulness are the same reality seen from two different perspectives.

Second, because this state has commonly been understood[17] to have resulted from a rebellion of humanity (in the persons of Adam and Eve) from God's domination, divine anger has been thought to be directed towards the entire human race on account of this supposed sin.

---

16 This Objective Realist tradition acknowledges the stark dichotomy I have set out, and resolves it by cleaving to the ideas of "justice" and "value". In doing so, Objective Realists are driven to conclude that human beings must have within them at least the possibility of immortality and that it is this potential which renders them significant and intrinsically worthwhile.

17 Arguably by St. Paul [Rom 5:12, quoted on page 168] and definitely St. Augustine in his famous dispute with Pelagius.

> This evil influence… comes from a source… innate in mankind as a result of crimes of long ago that remain unexpiated… you should take precautions against it… seek the rites that free a man from guilt… seek the company of men who [are] virtuous… run from the company of the wicked… if by doing so, you find that your disease abates somewhat, well and good; if not then you should look on death as the preferable alternative. [Plato "Laws" (IX 854b)]

Third, because it is supposed that the guilt of the original offence (not simply its consequences) is somehow transmitted to subsequent generations and therefore that all human beings are conceived and born in a state which is worthy only of divine disapproval and punishment.

The Eastern Church fathers are much less keen on this last idea. They teach that though we inherit the effects of the disobedience of the first humans, which is primarily death; we do not inherit any guilt and deserve no punishment on account of original sin. The Western tradition, following Augustine, speaks of Adam's *guilt* being inherited by his descendants, even though Adam's own sin was forgiven, and his personal guilt absolved.[18] Catholicism understands this inherited *guilt* to be no more than a lack of grace;[19] which deprivation makes human beings intrinsically unworthy of God, but is not itself deserving of any punishment.[20] This interpretation aligns Catholic doctrine with the Eastern tradition. Protestantism, however, tends to take Augustine's language at face value and entertains the idea that the *guilt* of original sin itself invites retributive punishment.

I write more about this in Chapter 12. For now, all I wish to assert is that there is no need to postulate a historical offence (and certainly not continuing racial guilt) in order to account for the condition in which humanity presently finds itself. The fact that our knowledge of what is objectively good for us is always imperfect, coupled with the certainty of death and the uncertainty of there being any worthwhile personal survival beyond it is more than enough to account for human sinfulness.

From this perspective, the narrative of the first two human beings found at the beginning of Genesis can best be understood as a parable of ethical autonomy and mortality. To what extent it is rooted in historical events I cannot personally determine; neither do I have any intention of pronouncing on this matter of fact.[21]

---

18 Canon five of the Fifth Session of the Council of Trent refers, in passing, to "the guilt of original sin".

19 See the first two canons of the Fifth Session of the Council of Trent.

20 See footnote 45 on page 211.

21 See page 203.

Chapter 10 Clearing the Decks

Those who pay regard to vain idols forsake their true loyalty. [Jonah 2:8 RSV]

Motivation

Much of the previous discussion has been predicated upon the reality of God. It is now time to investigate the validity of this idea. Arguably, this task should have been tackled right at the beginning of the discussion, but I have postponed it in order to first establish the proper context. Now that we have discussed being, existence and knowledge; have related reason to faith and reality; and have developed theories of beauty, justice, truth and value; we are ready to proceed. All of these ideas will feature in the discussion which follows, and without the work we have done this discussion would be pretty much incomprehensible.

Before looking at the positive arguments for the reality of God, some further preparatory work is still necessary. This is connected with clearing away various common prejudices and presuppositions and is the business of the present chapter.

What is God?

The discussion of this and the next few chapters is not going to be about getting to the God of any particular religion. Rather, we will be dealing with the God of Natural Theology or Metaphysics. Although, as a Catholic I believe in a personal God, I shall endeavour not to involve any such notion in what follows.

The concept of God which I shall have in mind throughout is that of some objective source of being or basis of reality and value which is distinct from the Cosmos; a basis of reality that is itself not dependent for its being or rationale on any thing that we could experience. Of course, the "gods" of many religions don't qualify as candidates for such a God. Indeed, the kind of "God" that many Christians informally profess belief in doesn't either.

Some believers are happy to attribute to God a dependence upon the Cosmos which make the "divinity" nothing more than the most elevated of all things; not absolutely distinct from everything else, but only the greatest thing of all.[1] There are understandable motives for holding such a view of God, as I shall describe in Chapter 11. It is normally adopted with the intent of portraying God as compassionate, loving and caring; all of which I believe God to be, in a fundamentally important but not simple sense. However, good motives do not excuse the simple and stark metaphysical mistake. If God is not absolutely independent of the Cosmos, totally invulnerable to harm and discomfort, utterly other and entirely sovereign; then God isn't God and can't serve the role which God must serve if reality is to make sense.

Does God exist?

I have already commented on the word "existence". Things that exist are disturbances in some matrix and *stand out* as deviations from the norm. That norm may itself be composed of other smaller things, in a hierarchy of being, on many scales of time and space. In this strict sense of existence, the question "Does God exist?" has a trivial answer: **"No, God does not exist!"** God isn't a thing like this at all. God is not a part of or even surrounded by some greater whole. God is utterly other.[2] God cannot be associated with anything. God doesn't inhabit some environment of things (even Heaven) which can form a backdrop against which God *stands out*. God is without any context. God is not an actor on a stage: **"God is no thing at all!"** A better question to ask is simply: "Is God?" but this sounds contrived and affected in English, so I tend to ask: "Is God real?" which gets to the nub of the question well enough.

Reductionist explanations for Theism

Before presenting any sensible reasons for believing that God is real, it is expedient to present a number of bad reasons which often form the basis of arguments used by atheists in attempts to "explain away" theism in reductive terms.

---

1 Such a "divinity" is simply not divine. At best it is the daemonic Demiurge of Gnosticism; an agency that God might use to do the "dirty work" of creation. Plato's use of the word Demiurge (the Creator) is altogether different. He conceives of the Creator as perfectly good and absolutely divine. The word "Demiurge" (in Greek "Δημιουργός") originally meant "worker on behalf of the populace". It became idiomatic for "Master Craftsman" and was used to mean "The Creator of All". It never meant anything remotely like "half-god".

2 In particular, God is not at all like an invisible pink unicorn. [R. Dawkin "The God Delusion" (2008)]

An emotional crutch

It is manifest that certain people choose to profess belief in some kind of divinity in an attempt to make sense of their lives. Perhaps they feel unloved, or that their life can have no meaning without some great figurehead "up there". Perhaps they feel overwhelmed by their troubles or just by the size of the Universe. Whatever the occasion, a desire for something to be so does not obviate reality to conform to that need.

Of course, the fact that some people may entertain the notion that "God is real" from personal inadequacy does not even remotely imply that "God is not real". In any case, it is equally obvious to me that certain people profess disbelief or disinterest in God for similar reasons. For them, the idea of God is in some way incompatible with them maintaining respect for themselves,[3] or else conflicts with their understanding of what is right,[4] or else is too much of a psychological hazard;[5] hence they conclude that the idea of God's reality cannot be countenanced: the cost is simply too high. On the contrary, the fact that many people experience within themselves a sense of radical personal inadequacy is some sort of an argument for God being real; but not a particularly good one.

A support for sanity

This is a more sophisticated and significant version of my first bad rationale for theism. The idea is that as humanity evolved self-consciousness, and as individuals grew aware of their mortality, the thought that their lives were futile would have driven them mad if another idea hadn't developed in parallel. This was the comforting hypothesis that there was an ultimate purpose in life; beyond, above and

---

3 Many homosexuals are atheists because they think that belief in God is incompatible with them having any self-esteem. Those who feel themselves to be failures are atheists because they cannot stand the thought of absolute failure, condemnation and damnation.

4 Many feminists are atheists because they think that God is a patriarchal archetype. Marxists are atheists because they think that God is a capitalist archetype. Many scientists are atheists because they can only conceive of God as a false explanation for phenomena which are not yet understood but which they expect will be accounted for scientifically in the future. They think that to believe in God is to undermine the basis of science.

5 Those who has experienced much rejection or disappointment in human relationships may become depressed and not dare to countenance the possibility of being absolutely let down by discovering for sure that God is not real. They may feel that it is better to leave the issue unresolved and live a life not relying explicitly on God.

apart from their doomed mortality. This transcendent significance was labelled “God”. So “God”, on this account of the matter, is an expedient developed for us by Nature to stop us going mad. “God” is an indispensable component of the mental framework of any self-conscious rational being: a conceptual antidepressant, if you like.[6]

This is plausible, apart from the fact that there are very many people who profess to be agnostic or atheist, have no notion that their lives have any lasting or objective significance and yet maintain their sanity well enough. Now, I’m not sure that I could do this if I somehow became unconvinced of God’s reality after forty years of theism; but the fact that they can and do so tends to invalidate this argument.

Moreover, I think that belief in God doesn’t really answer this purpose. The futility of final personal extinction is no more mitigated by the fact that “God is real” than by the fact that friends and family may survive one’s death – for a while. The horror implicit in the idea that my particularity will be terminated can only be mitigated by a belief in some kind of continuity of my own life, my own experience and my own activity after death; or so it seems to me.

Now, this has most definitely not been a core feature of all religions. Whereas the Ancient Egyptians had a sophisticated doctrine of life after death, at least for their royalty; the Hebrews and Greeks both got by with no belief in any kind of worthwhile afterlife.[7] Even in Jesus’ day, the elitist and traditionalist Sadducees rejected the novel doctrine of the populist and progressivist Pharisee party in this regard.[8] For the Sadducees it was enough to be faithful to God. This service was its own reward.[9] It was sufficient to do what was right simply because it was right; and to expect no reward or recompense except, hopefully, some tranquillity and prosperity in this short life.[10]

An externalization of parenthood

This is the first of two related psychological theories of theism. It is the idea that the manifestly unsafe dependency of the infant upon its fallible parents is transformed into a supposedly safe dependency upon a fictional infallible parent figure: God. This gives security just as

---

6 Adopting this explanation involves admitting, of course, that it is at least plausible that mortality is pretty much equivalent to futility and that one must either admit that human existence is senseless – and risk insanity – or else identify some hope for human existence beyond its all too apparent mortality.

7 See page 109.

8 Mat 22:23.

9 Ps 1 & 118.

10 Job 1:8-11; 42:10.

it dawns upon the child that its parents cannot be relied upon for truth, or even sustenance and shelter.[11]

This is yet another version of the first two explanations for theism. It has the advantage of not claiming that it is *necessary* to externalize parenthood to maintain sanity, but only that it is a strategy commonly employed to do so.[12] Moreover, there is some truth in it. The Apostle Paul himself affirms the relationship between parenthood and God when he writes: "I bow my knees before the Father, from whom every family in heaven and on earth is named."[13] However, this analysis tells us nothing whatsoever about whether God is or is not in fact real; but only about what our response might be if God were not real.

A projection of the Super-Ego

This is a more abstract variation of the last hypothesis. Rather than identifying the origin of the notion of God as "The Parent", God is said to buttress "conscience". Whatever the origin of our interior moral sense we bolster it by externalizing it and giving it the status of the decrees of an infallible sovereign. We can then use this fabrication as either an emotional crutch – or as a stick to beat our back with, as the mood takes us. Now, I am sure that this process takes place. In fact, I think it is often manifest in fundamentalist forms of religion. However, the fact that this happens does not constitute any kind of disproof of God's reality; it only tells us something of human brokenness.

The "opium of the people"[14]

The political theorist gives yet another explanation for theism; namely, that it is a scheme hatched by secular authorities to enslave the people whom they rule. On the one hand, "God" conveniently serves as a source of ultimate authority; which can be used to keep the populace in awe of their rulers, and so subjugated. On the other hand, "God" can offer the prospect of "Sugarcandy Mountain",[15] "Cloudcuckooland"[16]

---

11 An individual who has had problems with their parents tends to have a negative attitude towards God: especially when God is presented to them as a parent, whom they cannot choose and who did not choose them; rather than as a friend, whom they can choose and who has chosen them with full knowledge of who and what they are.

12 Hence it cannot be falsified and so is not, strictly speaking, scientific.

13 Eph 3:14-15 RSV.

14 K. Marx "Contribution to Critique of Hegel's Philosophy of Right" (1843)

15 G. Orwell "Animal Farm" (1945)

16 Aristophanes "The Birds" (434 BC)

and "pie in the sky when you die"[17] and so calm discontent among the downtrodden and disadvantaged. It is certain that the idea of God has too often been used in this way. Indeed, leaders of the Catholic Church have done so in the past and continue to do so in the present. However, the fact that something has been misused and exploited for ill does not mean that it is itself wrong or evil; but only that some human beings are wicked.

A conceptual virus

It has been proposed that there is an evolution of ideas parallel to the evolution of biological species.[18] Those hypotheses and beliefs survive which are most "fit" to do so. They can prosper in two ways:

> **symbiotically**, by helping their holders to survive and prosper, but not especially procreate – ideas are passed on by conversation not by copulation;
> **parasitically**, by diverting much of the energy of those who hold them into popularising and propagating them, perhaps contrary to their own self-interest.

Some forms of religion (especially those which make much use of guilt and threats of damnation) match up well with the model of a contagious "social disease". Moreover, the Evangelical preoccupation with proselytism conforms closely to this paradigm, as does Richard Dawkin's militant atheism. However, this theory hardly explains the success of more gentle religions like Buddhism, Jainism or Judaism.[19]

Of course, Christianity claims to be "good news" and to have a message that is the key to the living of a fulfilling life.[20] The Gospel therefore presents itself as a symbiotic idea. The simple pleasure and satisfaction of seeing others discover the same truth and delight that oneself has benefited from is a first motive for "passing it on". A second motive for evangelism is the prospect of recruiting friends with whom one can cooperate and work towards establishing a community of shared values: the Kingdom of God.

---

17 J. Hill "The Preacher and the Slave" (1911)

18 R. Dawkins "The Selfish Gene" (1976)

19 Judaism has never developed any strategy to spread beyond the boundaries of the Jewish race – except in its derivative forms, Christianity and Islam. In Buddhism and Jainism, there is no real tradition of proselytism.

20 Similar claims are made by other religions, notably Judaism.

The Force of Convention

> You talk about how belief in God can come about through *non-logical* means. I would recommend discussing the influence of tradition and society insofar as the idea of God may be too difficult to dismiss without violating social norms. Also, another influence stems from morality. Many young people are "forced" to go to church[21] because their parents are convinced that the only way they will not turn into immoral beasts is through God and religion. Lastly, belief in God can stem from a certain sense of expediency. For those not concerned with the "examined life", God (as they view Him) is a nicer, less worrisome, and easier way to explain away the troubles and vicissitudes of life.
> [J. Kramer "Private Communication" (2012)]

Kramer's first possibility is a powerful factor. Many people in the past have "gone along with the crowd" in accepting the reality of God for fear of disapprobation and social exclusion,[22] just as many now eschew religion for fear of seeming weird in post-Christian secularist societies.[23] It is fashionable among passably well educated youths to read and quote Nietzsche, Hitchens or Dawkins, and it helps one's social status to do so. It is nowhere fashionable to read and quote Plato, Origen, Aquinas or Newman; and if one does so one must be prepared to be dismissed as a freak. Moreover, this "conformist explanation" for belief (or disbelief) in God only explains how it might be sustained once it has become popular. It does not explain how it first became popular, which is the more important question.

Kramer's second point is related to the externalisation of parenthood, as it is parents who force their children to attend Church in this way. While I do not think that ethics is based on religion, I do think that a major (and perhaps the only) task of religious practice is to educate and seduce human beings into living in accordance with the principles of justice; so while the parents who Kramer refers to are mistaken on one level, on another they may be right. However, forcing someone to do something against their will is hardly compatible with educating them to act justly themselves. Once more, this "explanation" for belief in God only explains how it can be passed on from parent to child once it has arisen. It does not explain how it first arises.

---

21 Kramer speaks from his experience in the U.S.A.

22 This is still the case in large parts of the U.S.A. where atheism can seem to be a heroic enterprise, and theism a symptom of a dull mind.

23 As exists in almost all of Western Europe and the Old Commonwealth.

The last possibility Kramer mentions is close to my "emotional crutch" option, but it is also related to a desire to avoid personal moral responsibility. First, one doesn't need to struggle with ethical problems if one thinks that all the answers are readily available, courtesy of God. Second, God can be a convenient culprit to blame for one's own failings.

Three wrong ideas of God

I shall now discuss three wrong ideas of God. My motivation is toestablish a context in which a better view of God can be obtained.

Deism

One response to the problem of evil and suffering (addressed at length in my next chapter) is to distance God from any responsibility for and involvement with the Cosmos. Such a deity is a remote being who is at best "watching us from a distance",[24] with no particular interest in and certainly no commitment to "the world that He created".[25] Deism is, I think, a logical possibility, and I will not attempt to refute it here beyond remarking that it is difficult to see why God would go to the bother of creating a whole Cosmos and then neglect its upkeep. Deism is, of course, entirely foreign to the Judaeo-Christian tradition and incompatible with the idea that God is either loving or just.

Dualism

Another response to the presence of evil in the world is to hypothesize that it has a primary source other than God, such as "Arhiman" of the Zoroastrian religion or "Lord Foul" of Stephen Donaldson's fictional Land.[26] Supposing that such an agent of evil exists makes it possible to insulate God from all possibility of moral blame.

The Judaeo-Christian tradition has always rejected this solution.[27] While Satan is a feature of their theologies, he and his demons are only bit players. Although they are denizens of a spiritual realm, they are no more than wrongdoers, in the same way that human beings are. Such is Tolkein's vision of Sauron in "The Lord of the Rings". While Sauron may be responsible for tempting many humans to sin,[28] his role is not different in kind from the responsibility which a lesser being (for example the wizard Saruman) can have in leading others down the wide road to wickedness, failure and despair.

---

24 J. Gold "From a Distance" (1985)

25 F. Mercury "Is this the world we created?" (1984)

26 The Land features in "The Chronicles of Thomas Covenant, the Unbeliever" series of fantasy books.

27 It was, however, espoused by the Gnostics, Manichees and the Cathars.

28 Gen 3:1. Job 1:6.

According to the Christian tradition, evil is not a "thing in itself", a substance which can subvert other things – as vividly portrayed in the form of a smoking coal[29] or the glowing and steaming green "Illearth Stone".[30] Rather, evil is no more than a defect in reality, a distortion of the truth; a disordering of things which are in themselves entirely good.

It is not true to say that "good and evil are two sides of the same coin", or that "good requires evil in order to exist". Good is harmony, wholesomeness, health, order, justice and peace. Good has no need for conflict, discord or disease in order to be real. The ultimate good of any thing is for it simply to exist. The purpose of life is to live. God, while no thing, is Being Absolute, is Good, is Love.[31] On the contrary, even in the greatest evil there is necessarily a core of good. The most perverted act is a misguided attempt to obtain what is (wrongly) perceived to be of benefit. Evil wishes for its own good, and is (sadly) reinforced in its wickedness by its inevitable failure to achieve this desired end. Manifestly, the idea that Evil has no reality independent of Good implies that there is no need to hypothesize a source for it.

This analysis contrasts with that of Buddhism, which identifies existence with striving, suffering and pain (and so concludes that existence is itself evil, rather than good) and prescribes the pursuit of "Nirvana" (which is non-existence; a blending back into the background as a water drop merges with the ocean and loses its identity in doing so) as the practical answer to the problem of evil and suffering.

The source of order and meaning

It may seem odd that I give "the source of order and meaning" as an example of a mistaken idea of God. My point is that the problem of evil can be dealt with by redefining what is "good", "noble", "just" or "loving" as simply being whatever God says they are. Over two millennia ago, Socrates asked the question: "Is piety that of which the gods approve, or rather do the gods approve of piety?"[32] He meant: "Is that which is *good* in fact *good* only because of some arbitrary heavenly diktat; or is it rather the case that heaven recognizes what is *good* as an objective and impartial observer and then recommends it to us as a friend would, so as to benefit us?"

If one says that the purpose of everything: all goodness and beauty; justice, the standard of what is right and wrong – the meaning of it all – are derivative of the Will of God, one makes God into a despot. This is because God is then freed of all responsibility to explain the Divine

29 T. Gillian & M. Palin "Time Bandits" (1981)
30 S. Donaldson "The Illearth War" (1978)
31 Ex 3:14. Mk 10:18. 1Jn 4:8.
32 Plato "Euthyphro" (15a).

Economy to us; to set us any kind of example of morality in His dealings with us; or to abide any challenge from us. The problem of evil and suffering simply does not then arise. God is *loving* and *just* only insofar as our own invented concepts happen to match up with God's inscrutable nature; and what seems to us to be harsh and wicked is in fact kind and noble – merely because God specifies that it is so.

Perhaps the most extreme version of this error was identified by William Blake; who parodied the "God" of the establishment of his day as the great rule-maker or remorseless engineer in the sky. For Blake, this "God" (whom he named "Urizon") was a source of constraint, guilt and misery; an oppressor rather than a saviour, a proponent of fear and hatred rather than of delight and love. He saw Newton's Physics as implicated in all this; but at that time there was no idea that "to determine" and "to cause" were in any way different.[33] Blake proposed that the popular idea of Satan was a happier notion than Urizon; for the "vice" which he promoted was more wholesome and life-affirming than the "virtue" promoted by the Church.[34]

God's choice and responsibility

If God is the basis and creative source of the Cosmos, it is God who must have determined (within the limits set by logical necessity) the specifics of its constitution. Therefore, God must have inevitably decided "what was good" in as far as God gave reality to one rather than another of a set of possible Universes. So, for example, in a Universe where sapient beings could easily re-attach any protuberance which was severed from their body, it would not be grievously wrong to cut off an innocent person's head. Similarly, in a Universe where sapient beings found sexual intercourse to be an effective means of cementing social bonds, the use of contraceptives might be beneficial and moral.

To this extent, God does rule the Cosmos by diktat; for God decided how in fact to constitute this Universe: to make it this way and not some other. God is sovereign and answerable to no-one else so far as the Act of Creation is concerned;[35] though in that Act, God accepted a moral responsibility for the created Universe. The fact that God made a world in which we human beings consider that a maker has a responsibility of care towards what they make itself tells us a great deal about the character of God.[36]

33 See page 274.
34 W. Blake "The Marriage of Heaven and Hell" (1790-1793) & "Songs of Experience" (1794)
35 Rom 9:1-21.
36 Wis 11:23-12:2, quoted on page 116.

Nevertheless, it is good simply to be. God cannot possibly vary or modulate this. In this regard, God has no choice in setting up the ethics of the Cosmos. The foundational principle of ethics is the goodness of being. All detailed morality flows from this immovable axiom, once the specific characteristics of the ethical agents and objects which populate the world are determined.

The Natural Law

The Catholic Church is committed to the idea of the Natural Law. This amounts to the simple notion that human reason can discover how they ought to act by examining their own constitution and needs.[37] It implies an understanding of law as intrinsic to those agents which it governs, and as arising from values which are objectively beneficial to them. Every human being has an in-built notion of what is good for them. So we know that when we are thirsty we should drink; when we are at a cliff edge we should not jump; and when we are dealing with others we should respect them and treat them fairly. These things are true because they tend to benefit us. We know this instinctively.

The Natural Law is not imposed upon humanity by some external deviser of game rules; rather it arises as an inevitable expression of what it is to be human. It is more akin to the operating instructions and maintenance handbook which ought to accompany any piece of equipment purchased from a reputable manufacturer than to "English Grammar", "The Data Protection Act", or "The Queensbury Rules of boxing" – all of which are arbitrary and conventional.

To maintain a commitment to Natural Law ethics implies holding fast to the belief that one is not to do something simply because God commands it, and rejecting the idea that what is right is right simply because God has specified it to be right. Rather, it implies believing that God made us precisely in order that we should achieve our own fulfilment, and so live happily for ever; and that God's business with us is directed to this end.

> I have seen the business that God has given to the sons of men to be busy with. He has made everything beautiful in its time; also He has put eternity into man's mind, yet so that he cannot find out what God has done from the beginning to the end. I know that there is nothing better for them than to be happy and enjoy themselves as long as they live; also that it is God's gift to man that every one should eat and drink and take pleasure in all his toil. [Eccl 3:10-13 RSV]

---

37 Hence the importance of the oracular instruction "Know thyself."

We can play our part in achieving this goal only by acting in accordance with our own constitution, which itself is an image of the Divine Nature.[38] Every morally defective act impedes the agent's own fulfilment, and is wrong solely because of this fact; for "God is not offended by us except by what we do against our own good."[39]

God is good

What then is meant by saying "God is good" or "God is just"? If one is going to maintain a Natural Law perspective, one must avoid making this mean that "God is the prescriber of what is good." There is, however, another error equally to be avoided. This is the idea that there is some external standard which constrains God to act in a way foreign to God's nature. If such a standard did exist, then God wouldn't be God and the external standard would be a better candidate for true divinity.

Fortunately, our analysis of "what is good" enables us to avoid both mistakes. We have seen that the fundamental good of any thing is its own existence and the continuance and fulfilment of that existence.[40] This is its definitive purpose. We have seen, similarly, that the sole good of God is God's own being. The purpose, objective and business of God is simply to be God.[41] These observations are not subject to negotiation or debate. The only issue subject to discussion is what specific means and acts tend to the good of an agent: how, that is, an agent ought best or most usefully conduct their affairs.

Now, human beings can at best have correct belief about such matters. More generally, they are mistaken to various degrees. By contrast, God has a clear understanding of the human condition in general and of the circumstances facing each individual human being in particular.[42] God therefore knows exactly, unfailingly, and without any cloud of uncertainty, what course of action is in the best interest of every human being; both as a matter of general rule and in each specific instance. God is therefore the pre-eminent ethical expert. At one level, this is what is meant by saying that God is good or just;[43] namely that God knows – and seeks to show us – what is in fact beneficial for us, so as to induce us to act accordingly.

---

38 "Then God said, 'Let us make man in our image…' So God created man in His own image, in the image of God He created him; male and female He created them." [Gen 1:26-27 RSV] "God created man for incorruption, and made him in the image of His own eternity." [Wis 2:23 RSV]

39 Thomas Aquinas "Summa Contra Gentiles." lib 3 cap 122

40 See pages 71 and 133.

41 See pages 64 and 72.

42 Ps 138:1-16.

43 Ps 144:7-17.

God is impassible

It is important to note that God cannot be hurt (or be in any way affected or inconvenienced for that matter) by anything we do, whether we act virtuously or viciously. God has nothing to loose or gain so far as the divine contentment and joy in being is concerned. God is far above and beyond our puny affairs.

> What is man, that Thou dost make so much of him, and that Thou dost set Thy mind upon him, dost visit him every morning, and test him every moment? How long wilt Thou not look away from me, nor let me alone till I swallow my spittle? If I sin, what do I do to Thee, Thou watcher of men? Why hast Thou made me Thy mark? Why have I become a burden to Thee?[44]
> [Job 7:17-20 RSV]

> If you have sinned, what do you accomplish against Him? And if your transgressions are multiplied, what do you do to Him? If you are righteous, what do you give to Him; or what does He receive from your hand?[45]
> [Job 35:6-7 RSV]

While this may seem disappointing and a basis for a fundamental dissociation from God, in fact it is a basis for hope. It means that God has no motive to exact retribution for the wrong we do and also that God is well able to afford to forgive us gratuitously. It means that God's commands are authoritative *not* because they are determinative of what is right (as the prescriptions of a petulant Emperor ought to be obeyed by his servants if they wish to keep him placated and avoid his retribution) but because they are trustworthy – in the way that the instructions of a wise teacher should be obeyed. God's commands show us what is right, they do not set and fix what is right.

> He has showed you, O man, what is good; and what does the Lord require of you but to do justice, and to love kindness, and to walk humbly with your God?
> [Mic 6:8 RSV]

---

44 These are the words of Job, rather than his any of his "comforters", and I think they are meant to be taken seriously.

45 These are the words of Elihu (rather than one of Job's three so-called "friends", who manifestly do not know what they are talking about) and I think that they are to be taken as true.

God is bound by Justice

This means that the principles of justice which are apparent to human reason bind God as strongly as they bind us – more strongly, in fact;[46] because we obtain a certain latitude of application by virtue of our ignorance.

> Of a truth, God will not do wickedly, and the Almighty will not pervert justice.[45] [Job 34:12 RSV]

Nevertheless, the rationale for God's action (and inaction) is often mysterious to us, due to our restricted view of reality, and often God's apparent attitude can seem obtuse. On the one hand, our ignorance of the whole picture means that we should exercise restraint before complaining about God's mode of dealing with ignorance, injustice and suffering in the world. On the other hand, the fact that we do have a pretty good idea of the nature and demands of justice means that it sometimes behoves us to remonstrate with God.[47] It was on this basis that Abraham demanded, holding God to strict account before the destruction of Sodom and Gomorrah: "Shall not the Judge of all the earth do right?"[48] Such a question would not make any sense if justice were no more than whatever God decreed it to be.

How then does this position not amount to justice being an external constraint on God's actions, extrinsic and foreign to the Divine Being? This is an important question, but one that is easily answered. God's justice arises on the one hand from the necessary harmony, coherence and integrity of God's nature and interior life, and on the other hand from God's omniscience and exterior benevolence.[49] All of these characteristics are necessarily constitutive of God's own nature and are in no way external to God. Hence justice is intrinsic to God, not extrinsic: native, not foreign. It is no kind of constraint on God, but is rather God's most basic characteristic. It is not even right to say that God is inclined, of God's own initiative, to be just; rather, one should say that God is entirely obsessed with justice and that the nature of God is Justice itself.

---

46 Plato was sure that "It's vital that somehow or other we should make out a plausible case for supposing that gods do exist, that they are good, and that they respect justice more than men do." ["Laws" (X 887b)]

47 The hero of the film "Priest" [J. McGovern & A. Bird (1994)] does exactly this; and his impassioned prayer is answered; though in a manner which means that he would never know that his righteous complaint was heard.

48 Gen 18:25 RSV.

49 See pages 154 and 182.

Chapter 11 Evil and Suffering

> Thou hast turned cruel to me; with the might of Thy hand Thou dost persecute me… Yea, I know that Thou wilt bring me to death, and to the house appointed for all living. Surely one does not turn against the needy, when in disaster they cry for help. Did not I weep for him whose day was hard? Was not my soul grieved for the poor? But when I looked for good, evil came; and when I waited for light, darkness came. My heart is in turmoil, and is never still; days of affliction come to meet me.
> [Job 30:21-27 RSV (verse 24 NRSV)]

Motivation

It is with trepidation that I attempt an explanation of the presence of evil and suffering in the world. I consider this to be the central problem of religion; or at least of Theodicy, the justification of God's ways to human judgement.[1] The problem is familiar to any but the most callous soul. It is this: "How can a God that is both benevolent and omnipotent tolerate death, sickness, suffering, injustice and pain? It would seem that either God doesn't take any account of such matters, in which case God isn't benevolent; or else God is unable to do anything about them, in which case God isn't omnipotent."

It is possible to avoid this difficulty by taking one of the two gambits offered, namely: "God is not omnipotent" or "God is not benevolent". Now, it may be possible to make some sort of a case for either a just but impotent God, or for an omnipotent but disinterested God; however I have no interest in doing so. My conviction, fostered by the Judaeo-Christian tradition, is that God is both benevolent and omnipotent. I wish now to explore how this can be, given our experience of sorrow and death. To this end, I shall first review the three standard defences of God's supposed purpose in allowing, tolerating or even employing evil.

---

1 Some say that it is not for human beings to question, contend and dispute with God. I strongly disagree. I think that I am in good company here, namely Abraham [Gen 18:23-33] and Moses, [Ex 32:9-14] the two men singled out by the Bible as "friends of God".

Evil is a necessary means to an ultimately good end

It can be argued that evil is a necessary means to a desirable end. In its most extreme form this notion can be expressed as "everything has a meaning and happens for a good purpose: no matter how bad something seems to be, in fact it is good; or at least will necessarily lead to a good result which could not be obtained otherwise." An analogy can be drawn between how a surgeon might amputate the leg of a patient so as to stop them dying of gangrene and God's supposed toleration or use of evil. The final end of the surgery is good even though the particular act is formally harmful.

However, this analogy is false. Whereas a human surgeon cannot work miracles God is not so limited, and it would seem that God should never have to use evil means to attain good ends. God should be able to avoid the necessity of any evil act by employing miraculous means.[2] Moreover, it is difficult to see how any good results from many natural disasters and personal tragedies, so this defence is unconvincing.

Furthermore this defence seems to imply that God has to allow or incite some people to become moral monsters in order to achieve certain ends; and in particular that God had to allow or incite the immense personal tragedies represented by the wickedness of Pharaoh, Hitler, Stalin and Pol-Pot in order to create the the Plagues of Egypt,[3] Nazi Gas Chambers, the Soviet Gulags and the Cambodian killing-fields; though it is not apparent what good these horrors represent, or consequentially produced. Most terribly, it seems to mean that God had to allow or incite Lucifer to fall and Judas to become embittered and betray Jesus.[4]

> "Truly, I say to you, one of you will betray me… The Son of Man goes as it is written of him, but woe to that man by whom the Son of Man is betrayed! It would have been better for that man if he had not been born." [Mat 26:21-24 RSV]

This seems particularly cruel and unfair. If pursued rigorously it leads to Calvin's horrible idea that God purposefully employs Satan to incite people to sin so that they will deserve punishment and allow the divine disapproval of injustice to be manifested.[5] Nevertheless, it can be argued with some sense that God's theoretical omnipotence is often limited in practice by the just requirement that God ought not to force the divine will upon us, which leads to the next defence.

---

2 M. Knight, J. Herrick eds "Humanist Anthology" (2000) p132-133.

3 Ex 9:12; 10:1,20; 11:10; 14:8.

4 "Priest" [J. McGovern & A. Bird (1994)]

5 J. Calvin "Christianae Religionis Institutio" lib 2 cap 6 (1536)

Moral evil is an inevitable consequence of freewill

It can be argued that for God to regularly act so at to prevent suffering would involve interfering with human autonomy, to the point where it was entirely undermined. A loving God, intent on allowing humanity to grow into ethical maturity in an environment one stage removed from the divine presence must accept and work through such suffering in the Cosmos, rather than preventing it. Such a God has to respond to evil as an independent agent: that is by specific miraculous intervention, where and when God judges it to be appropriate. The only alternative would have been to refrain from creating at all. Hence, it can be argued that moral evil is an inevitable consequence of God granting sentient[6] beings (mankind, angels and the like) autonomy and so making them sapient[7].

However, while this might explain God's toleration of moral evils (that is, those perpetrated by human beings) it does not explain the existence of physical evils such as earthquakes, plagues and droughts; unless these are supposed to result from the malignity of fallen angels. Moreover, it can be objected that this argument cannot even explain moral evil. After all, how can a just and omnipotent God have let human beings acquire a predisposition towards doing evil? Couldn't God have created us with freewill but also with a strong predisposition towards doing good? If not, how can God be said to be omnipotent?[8] In any case, how can it be right for God to allow the innocent to suffer, sometimes terribly, at the hands of the wicked? The attempted extermination of Jews and other "undesirables" by the Nazis is only the greatest example of a series of moral outrages which, it would seem, God ought to have prevented either by subtle providence or miraculous intervention.

This argument is not valid, however. According to Catholic theology the human predisposition to evil (technically, concupiscence) is neither a positive force nor a radical defect in our nature. It is not some extrinsic characteristic which God either imposed on humanity or else allowed us to acquire; rather it is the basic condition of any finite moral agent left to its own devices – that is, apart from God's systematic help. At base, concupiscence is an expression of the Second Law of Thermodynamics, according to which any isolated system tends to become disordered. A living body continually fights this tendency by means of elaborate repair mechanisms, but no such system can be perfect and eventually the accumulation of partial repairs results in death. This is analogous with what happens to a moral agent. Even a perfectly just finite moral agent would eventually become disordered, confused and corrupt if left to

---

6 Sentience is "personal subjective experiential consciousness" [LNS Ch 4]

7 Sapience is sentience together with the knowledge of good and evil.

8 See "The Encyclopedia of Unbelief" ed. G. Stein (1985)

itself; merely as a result of the basic instability inherent in perfection. Sadly, there are very many more ways of being wicked than of being virtuous; and once one has become unjust there is no easy way back.[9]

> The good is susceptible to becoming bad... but the bad is not susceptible to becoming; it must always be… It is impossible to be a good man and continue to be good, but possible for one and the same person to become good and also bad; and those are best for the longest time whom the gods love.
> [Plato "Protagoras" (344d-345c)]

God couldn't have created humanity with an independent will and yet with a "strong predisposition to doing good." This is a contradiction in terms. No such strong predisposition could ever be strong enough. Moreover, if God were to systematically and effectively protect the "innocent" from the "wicked" this would become very obvious very rapidly; and would have seriously deleterious side effects.[10]

Physical evil is a means to increase moral urgency

It can plausibly be argued that the existence of physical evil is necessary in order to create "moral urgency", so as to elicit heroism and virtue.

> Physical evil has been the goad which has impelled men to most of the achievements which made the history of man so wonderful. Hardship is a stern but fecund parent of invention. Where life is easy because physicals ills are at a minimum we find man degenerating in body, mind and character… Which is preferable – a grim fight with the possibility of splendid triumph; or no battle at all?
> [W.D. Niven "Good and Evil" (1913)]

So, war nurtures the heroic nature of warriors, and natural disasters bring out the charitable nature of those humanitarians who strive to bring relief to their victims. Implicit in this argument is the idea that the suffering inherent in these calamities is somehow outweighed by the virtue inculcated by them.[11] There are, however, three defects in this argument.

---

9 This argument does not apply to God. First, because God is infinite rather than finite and so can be perfectly robust and second, because God is outside time and is therefore not susceptible to change.

10 I take this point up again on page 192.

11 O.S. Card "The Worthing Saga" (1992) p227-230

First, would it not be better for such evils to be eradicated, rather than that their victims be offered respite and recompense? Surely, the elimination of physical evil would make the world a better place. If, on the contrary, the presence of physical evil somehow makes the world a better place then the elimination of smallpox, the creation of the polio vaccine and the discovery of antibiotics must have been three of the most calamitous events of recent time; but this seems ridiculous.

Second, human responses to physical evils are not always virtuous. For example, the formulation of anti-retroviral AIDS drugs had very little to do with any heroic struggle to do good. It was driven more by the profit motive of pharmaceutical companies than any concern for the main beneficiaries: promiscuous homosexuals.

Third, some physical evils are so radical that they cannot plausibly be justified in terms of the way in which they are supposed to promote a virtuous response. The ravages of Ebola haemorrhagic fever are a case in point. This disease kills within a couple of weeks, with horrible effect and without any possibility of cure. Earthquakes, volcanic eruptions, meteorite impacts and floods can kill many thousands more or less instantly. What good can possibly result from these tragedies?

In response to these objections, it can be said that the "world being a better place" is not a clear criterion. It must be asked: "Better for what?"[12] In particular, the world would not be a better place for evoking heroic virtue if there were no opportunities for heroic virtue to be exercised. The world was a better place after the eradication of Smallpox partly because of the heroic virtues inculcated in those people who fought hard and long to eradicate the disease, quite apart from the fact that the disease no longer existed. Moreover, the second point is true, but of little significance. The fact that evil can be responded to apart from the exercise of heroic virtue does not mean that it was not apt for the evocation of heroic virtue. All that it means is that an opportunity for ethical growth was missed. Finally, if there is some point in the development of heroic virtue, there must be a range of challenges facing humanity; from those which are simple to address to others which require more sophistication. Perhaps a cure will eventually be found for Ebola haemorrhagic fever, as a result of much dedication and heroism on the part of those researchers who discover it. Nevertheless, I think that the third point is largely true and tends to show that this defence, at least as proposed here, is fundamentally inadequate.

---

12 I suspect that the questioner actually means "happier" rather than "better" and tacitly assumes that happiness is the be all and end all: the purpose and object of life. I have already argued that this is a basic and serious (though understandable) mistake; see page 82.

Suffering gives us a claim on God

This is the answer given to the problem of suffering by C.S. Lewis in his novel "Till We Have Faces", and also by C. Williams in his book "Descent Into Hell". The idea is that our suffering gives us a claim on God's justice, and gives us the right to request from God good things for our loved ones on Earth once we have attained Heaven.

> The main character in Lewis' book was emotionally tormented her whole life by the loss of her sister. She writes a compelling indictment of the gods for their injustice; but, on her deathbed, she is granted a vision that on account of her suffering her sister was spared many worse things. In an instant her lifetime of suffering became for her not an insane tragedy but instead her most precious possession. Perhaps if we are all granted similar merit on account of our trials, we will indeed come in the end to judge them our dearest moments from life. Those who die too young may have a full experience of heaven, but arriving there empty-handed they have no merit with which to bestow gifts on those below.
> [G. Bodeen "Private Communication" (2012)]

At one level this theory is attractive, but underneath it lie two less congenial ideas. First, that a human being can have a greater concern for the good of another human being whom they love than God has. Second, that God will only be beneficent towards human beings as a reward for suffering endured. Although both of these ideas are impious, the idea that suffering can be meritorious is plausible; as is the idea that one person might be able to accept hardship so that another less courageous individual may avoid suffering.

In the first case, a good response to suffering can improve a person's character and make them more holy and wise,[13] so that they gain a better view as to what is truly good and what is truly evil.[14] This will then enable them to better cooperate with God as intercessors,[15] rulers[16] and co-creators[17] of the world. In the second case, a strong person can bear a burden for a weaker person[18] so that both can be saved; but this is not to be construed as the stronger offering to suffer so that the weaker can

13 Rom 5:3. Heb 2:10; 12:6. 1Pet 2:19; 5:6-10.
14 Rom 12:1-2, quoted on page 143.
15 2Cor 1:11. Phil 1:19. Apoc 5:8; 8:3-4.
16 Gen 1:26-28; 2:15. Mk 5:5. 1Cor 6:2-3. Apoc 3:21; 4:4.
17 Gen 1:5,8,10; 2:19-20.
18 Gal 6:1-7. Col 1:24.

escape what would otherwise be their lot. That would put the strong person in the position of bargaining with God; but this is absurd, as they have no commodity to offer in exchange for divine favour. When a stronger soul suffers so that a weaker one can escape suffering, the ordering of events lies within the realm of grace, not human initiative.

> We know that in everything God works for good with those who love him, who are called according to his purpose.
> [Rom 8:28 RSV]

However, this response is not an adequate account of suffering. Some examples of suffering seem to be merely calamitous and not at all educational or improving, while other instances seems to be inevitable and not the kind of thing that could be allocated to one person or another or transferred between individuals. The suffering resulting from an earthquake or plague would seem to be both inevitable and calamitous. These thoughts lead on to the next response.

Suffering is intrinsic to the idea of life

This is a refinement of the first defence. The physics complexities which are necessary if any kind of life at all is to exist unavoidably have instabilities and other negative consequences, such as supernovae, earthquakes, tornadoes, cancer and cholera; and these are experienced by living beings as "natural disasters". In other words, any system which is sufficiently non-linear[19] to support life is bound to exhibit occasional extreme behaviours which are catastrophic so far as life is concerned. It is therefore pretty much inconceivable for life to exist in a perfectly idyllic situation, where all its needs are reliably supplied and its continuance is never threatened: the self-same non-linearities which allow and support life necessarily threaten to subvert it.

Moreover, some forms of pain are inescapable aspects of life. The very concept of animal life implies the destruction of other life in order to construct and preserve itself. Even plant life is competitive and strives against other plant life to obtain resources. Nature is "red in tooth and claw"[20] not because Nature wants to be so, nor because God arbitrarily chose for Nature to be so; but because there is no other way for Nature to give rise to life.

---

19 See footnotes on page 275.
20 Alfred Lord Tennyson "In Memoriam A.H.H." (1850)

Suffering as a necessary part of education

According to St Paul, the present state of affairs is to be seen as provisional. It is a temporary subjection of created being to the process of evolution, with the purpose of bringing sapient life to birth. The painful process of struggle is justified by the end in view, its teleological hope. The temporary distancing of the human soul from God which is characteristic of mortal life on Earth has a similar justification. It too is painful, it too has a resolution: in the Beatific Vision.

> For the creation waits with eager longing for the revealing of the children of God. For the creation was subjected to futility,[21] not of its own will[22] but by the will of the one who subjected it,[23] in hope[24] that the creation itself will be set free from its bondage to decay[21] and will obtain the freedom of the glory of the children of God.[24] We know that the whole creation has been groaning in labour pains until now;[25] and not only the creation, but we ourselves, who have the first fruits of the Spirit,[26] groan inwardly while we wait for adoption, the redemption[27] of our bodies. [Rom 8 19-23 RSV]

Still, it can be objected: "This is all well and good; but surely, a beneficent God would either intervene or else providentially arrange things so that they worked out well for His creatures.[28] The fact that things are not ordered so that suffering is avoided, or at least minimised, shows that God is not real or else is either callous or impotent. There is no conceivable divine purpose which could justify the sufferings of so many people as it is well known have suffered; some due to human wickedness and others as a result of natural disaster."

---

21 That is, the Second Law of Thermodynamics.

22 Not out of some internal characteristic or necessity of the Cosmos.

23 God made the Cosmos the way that it is, for a good reason.

24 That is the prospect of the Cosmos being able to give rise to forms of sapient life which would be apt for redemption and capable of being united in fellowship with God.

25 The process of evolution; in which nature has been struggling with and against itself, with the teleos of bringing forth sapient life.

26 That is grace: God's friendship and the promise of Eternal Life.

27 That is renewal, transformation and resurrection. It is also the job of humanity to mitigate the pain [Gen 1:15] and to work towards turning the Darwinian Jungle into the Garden of Paradise; where all creatures have their rightful place and needful resources, and can prosper together in harmony.

28 Rom 8:28, quoted on page 191.

The only adequate rebuttal of this objection is that it be somehow shown to be incoherent. No other response could do justice to its gravity and significance. Showing that it makes no sense would not lessen the moral force that lies behind the objection: for I take it to be patently obvious that the suffering – as also the wickedness – of humanity is of an abominable character. The only basis on which such horror could be tolerated by a benevolent and omnipotent God is that there is absolutely no alternative to it other than the entire frustration of a central purpose of Creation itself, which would then necessitate its non-existence.

Must God's reality be obscure?

To this end, I first observe that if God acted to systematically prevent all natural disasters, their absence would eventually be noticed and become overwhelming evidence of continual and direct divine intervention. This is unacceptable if it is important that the evidence for the reality of God's being be morally avoidable.[29] The occasional (or even frequent) miracle does not have this effect; for any finite number of miracles can be accounted for as delusional episodes, mass hysteria, freak events or simple good luck.[30]

However, it is not at all vital that the evidence for the reality of God's being should be insufficient to deserve assent. While it can be argued with some sense[31] that it is necessary for God's precise business, will and purpose to be somewhat obscure, the same cannot be said for God's basic reality. In fact, the Bible is quite clear that the reality of God is pretty much obvious,[32] and that it is hardly less apparent that God is good and just.[33] Indeed, I shall propose in Chapter 14 that all of this is subject to some sort of proof, so it would be inconsistent for me to argue here that it is necessary that God's reality should be obscure.

Providential Imprudence

Next, I concede that it is possible to conceive of a world that is pretty much like our own, except for the fact that God regularly intervenes in it to prevent anything from going seriously wrong. This world would be replete with miracles, of course, and none of its sentient inhabitants would be able to doubt that God was both real and beneficent: the empirical evidence would be overwhelming.

---

29 See the discussion of the Babel Fish in Douglas Adam's "The Hitch-hiker's Guide to the Galaxy" (1979)

30 Lk 16:31, quoted on page 231.

31 See Chapter 12.

32 Ps 18:1-4. Rom 1:19-20.

33 Ps 18:7-10. Job 34:12. Mic 6:8.

This knowledge, however, wouldn't force anyone to love or respect God. In fact it might cause some people to resent the divine nannying they were subject to; and with justification, as it would have the effect of making it impossible for humanity to come to "know good and evil." It would have this effect because, no matter what anyone did, things would work out well for them; as a result of God's all-enveloping providence[11] underwriting all their choices so as to prevent any negative outcome. It would therefore be impossible to do wrong; because all acts would have good outcomes, and so no act could possibly be construed as wicked. Hence, no human being would ever be able to realise that some acts were prudent and others reckless. In fact there would be no difference between prudent and reckless acts. The idea of "personal responsibility" and the notion that "actions have consequences" – and that some of these are wholesome and supportive of life while others are perverse and morbid – would be rendered meaningless.

Although good does not require evil in order to exist; nevertheless for a moral agent to come to understand for themselves (rather than to be pre-programmed with the fact) that there are good actions and evil ones (and to become able to personally distinguish between these, and to grow more competent at evaluating and judging such matters) the real prospect of failure, bad outcome and suffering is necessary. Without the real possibility of failure, there is no way to learn from one's mistakes and so to come to know the difference between good and evil.

The mitigation of evil

Now it can be argued that God might still act so as to mitigate the harm resulting from human actions. God could have intervened to prevent quite so many Jews from being humiliated, from suffering, and from being killed by the Nazis, for example. However, while it may seem obvious that God could have done more to ameliorate the extreme suffering of the Jewish people (as also the terrible plight of many other individuals and groups) we should not be entirely confident of this, because we do not know the side-effects which would have resulted from further intervention.

Moreover, we do not know that God does not do a great deal to mitigate suffering. In particular, we do not have knowledge of a world in which God definitely did not intervene to mitigate the harm worked by the Nazis. We only have experience of this world as it is, which incorporates whatever level of divine providence is in fact actual. For all we know, without God's intervention the entire Jewish race might have been killed; in which case the extent of God's action to help the Jews was considerable, if to our eyes entirely obscure.

Furthermore, if God acted to "cap" the negative consequences of human acts (not bothering to mitigate minor bad consequences, so as to allow humanity to learn about good and evil in small matters, while preventing seriously malign effects) it would make minor acts of imprudence or hatred little different from heinous offences, as measured by the severity of their consequence. This would entirely distort the human perception of the relative seriousness of various vicious acts.

Therefore, if an accurate perception of what evil means is to be obtained, it is necessary for God to allow human wickedness to have indefinitely bad consequences in this world; though I suppose that God might screen us from the worst we might wreak by establishing a logarithmic relationship[34] between the severity of the unmitigated consequences of every act and the severity of the actual consequences which providence allowed. For all that we know, of course, this is exactly what God has done. Perhaps this is why the invention of the atom bomb has not, as yet, let to the utter annihilation of humanity.

A disincentive to learning

In a world where everything is down to God's will, there is neither any possibility for human ethical maturity nor any motive for human initiative or effort; for everything is God's act, and negative consequences are of whatever magnitude God allows – according to whatever criteria God might elect to apply. Moreover, in a world where God routinely protected the innocent and ignorant from the consequences of their imprudent actions there would be a serious disincentive against getting involved in any ethical dilemmas – and also against learning anything whatsoever.

In such a world, as long as one didn't know of the peril of living on the slope of a volcano, God would stop the volcano erupting – so as to protect the naïve and innocent; whereas if one did come to understand the threat and imprudently persisted in abiding in that danger, God would not intervene to quiet the volcano – so as to enforce moral responsibility. In such a world, as soon as one had a glimmer of this implication of knowledge, it would make sense to avoid learning anything about the workings of nature and to eschew all scientific and philosophical inquiry; as each and every advancement of knowledge would result in a proportionate withdrawal of divine protection.

34 A logarithmic relationship is one in which a resulting effect increases smoothly with the cause giving rise to it, but according to a law of diminishing returns. So, to take a juridical example, the stealing of £1 might be punished by one week of incarceration, the stealing of £10 by two weeks, the stealing of £100 by three weeks and so on.

The subjunctive mode

For an understanding of "good and evil" it is necessary to have an idea of the subjunctive mode: the notion of "might have been, if only." This allows the idea that I am responsible for what happens; that my will is contributory to reality and that what I do matters, has significance and makes history.[35] This isn't the same as believing that "things could actually have worked out differently," but is the state of mind which understands that outcomes are attributable to actions, that effects have causes, and that my will is one such cause.

If God were to act so as to prevent all evil and unhappiness the subjunctive would be a nonsense. Every event and outcome would then be God's sole responsibility. We would be no more than characters in a novel, and impotent characters at that: plaster saints with sterile virtues who do no wrong – not because they know what wickedness is and seek to avoid it, but because they have no idea of what good and evil are and in their naïvety do all manner of what ought to be foolish and reckless things; but with never an ill outcome, because God prevents them even from "dashing their foot against a stone."[36]

Final considerations

It is important to note also that in the context of eternal life, suffering can always be compensated for.

> For behold, I create new heavens and a new earth; and the former things shall not be remembered or come into mind. But be glad and rejoice for ever in that which I create; for behold, I create Jerusalem a rejoicing, and her people a joy. I will rejoice in Jerusalem, and be glad in My people; no more shall be heard in it the sound of weeping and the cry of distress…
>
> They shall not labour in vain, or bear children for calamity; for they shall be the offspring of the blessed of the Lord, and their children with them. Before they call I will answer, while they are yet speaking I will hear.
>
> The wolf and the lamb shall feed together, the lion shall eat straw like the ox; and dust shall be the serpent's food. They shall not hurt or destroy in all My holy mountain, says the Lord. [Isa 65:17-25 RSV]

35 A. Bennett "The History Boys" (2004, 2006)

36 Ps 90:12.

St John the Divine sees this prophecy fulfilled at the end of time:

> Behold, the dwelling of God is with men. He will dwell with them, and they shall be His people, and God himself will be with them; He will wipe away every tear from their eyes, and death shall be no more, neither shall there be mourning nor crying nor pain any more, for the former things have passed away. [Apoc 21:3-4 RSV]

So the "Problem of Evil and Suffering" is not as important as it at first seems. No-one will have anything to complain about in the long-term, as all will be abundantly compensated for what they have endured. From God's eternal perspective (which we shall ourselves come to share, eventually) what matters about any conceivable Universe is the eventual state of affairs to which it leads. If the means to that end are painful, then this does not matter in any fundamental sense. As long as everything works out well in the end,[37] all that matters is how well they work out: how glorious, wonderful and joyous is the final condition of the saved and justified company of Heaven.

> I consider that the sufferings of the present time are not worth comparing with the glory about to be revealed to us.
> [Rom 8:18 RSV]

Moreover, it doesn't matter how long it takes to reach this end state; for once achieved it will persist for eternity and its positive value overwhelm all temporal disvalue.

Furthermore, much pain can be transformed into a positive experience, if only a suitable attitude is adopted towards it.

> I rejoice in my sufferings… in my flesh I complete what is lacking in Christ's afflictions for the sake of... the Church. [Col 1:24 RSV]

However, this partial truth does no justice to the stark reality of human suffering. It is callous to tell someone who is starving to death as a result of a famine that their suffering is all a matter of perspective, and that they should exercise themselves in adopting a "positive attitude" to their hunger. The Gospel enjoins us to actively alleviate suffering rather than passively accepting it as part and parcel of reality.[38]

---

37 Rom 8:28, quoted on page 191.
38 Mat 25:32-46.

Contrariwise, for even transitory suffering to be justified it must either have a definite purpose, or else at least be unavoidably necessary.

> No appeal to an afterlife can actually eradicate the problem of evil. An injustice always remains an injustice, regardless of any subsequent effort to comfort the victim. If a father, after beating his child unmercifully, later gives him a lollipop as compensation, this does not eradicate the original act or its evil nature. Nor would we praise the father as just and loving. [G.H. Smith "Atheism: The case against God" (1980)]

However, God does not purposefully inflict suffering on any creature. Neither does God stand by as an impassive onlooker. Jesus tells us that not even a sparrow dies alone, but rather that each one dies in the company of our Heavenly Father.

> Are not two sparrows sold for a farthing? And one of them shall not fall on the ground without your Father. But the very hairs of your head are all numbered. Fear ye not therefore, ye are of more value than many sparrows. [Mat 10:29-31[39] KJV[40]]

Moreover, in the person of Jesus, God elected to experience physical, intellectual and emotional pain.[41] Whoever or whatever is to blame for suffering, God chose to become human so as to bear the whole of the pain of physicality, finitude and futility in Jesus' own human Heart.

The best of all possible worlds

It can be hoped that God has created "The *best* of all possible worlds",[42] no matter how unconvincing this seems just now. However, we cannot judge this definitively. We don't know the alternatives open to God apart from "this world as we presently experience it" and "no world at all". Moreover, we can't know for sure what God's purpose is in creating the Cosmos; though I happen to think that it is to provide sentient beings with an environment suitable for them to come to understand for themselves the meaning of justice, and so to become sapient.

---

39 Compare Lk 12:6-7.

40 I have used the KJV here as it renders the Greek better than the RSV, which interpolates "the will of" between "without" and "your Father." I thank A. Siddiqui for bringing the RSV's mistranslation to my attention.

41 Mat 27:46.

42 G. Leibnitz "Essays on Theodicy, concerning the goodness of God, the freedom of man, and the origin of evil." (1710)

Given our ignorance of the exact purpose of Creation, we cannot judge what kind of world is *best* fit to fulfil that purpose. We can't even justify any measure of what *best* might be. Even if it was clear that this measure was "the overall sum of all joy, pleasure, happiness and fun, minus all sorrow, suffering, pain and misery" how could such a utilitarian formula be evaluated?

The Multiverse revisited

Another possibility is that the universe which we inhabit is simply one of many logically possible worlds. After all, it would seem that an infinite God must at least conceive of every possible universe which is coherent; for what could constrain God from doing so? Now, it may be that there is no difference between God conceiving of a universe as possible and God creating that same universe as actual. For a thing to be real may well be identical with it existing within God's mind.[43] After all, what could one think of that would add to the significance, substance or power of divine thought?

If this is the case, the problem of evil is somewhat mitigated. The suffering of this world necessarily arises from the fact that it is possible but not absolutely ideal – if, indeed, an ideal world is possible. The world exists in the way that it does simply because it is possible for it to do so. However, the following objection then arises:

> If God is perfect, how could He create anything which would lead to imperfection?[44] In other words, how can a being who is perfect in his ethical maturity create beings who are not so?
> [J. Kramer "Private Communication" (2012)]

The imperfection (and so sin and injustice) to be found in contingent being is associated with its finitude and temporality. The fact that something is conceivable does not mean that it has to be entirely perfect. While at root it must be harmonious, or else it would tear itself apart in its conception; on a macroscopic or behavioural level it may be chaotic and exhibit conflict.[45] The character of the Cosmos which we actually inhabit exemplifies this. The laws of Physics are coherent and yet give rise to higher-level phenomena which are at odds with each other.

---

43 Hence, the distinction I have made between "real" and "imaginary" is now a distinction between "being conceived directly by God, in the Divine Mind" and "being conceived indirectly by God, in the mind of some creature; that mind itself being an idea in God's mind".

44 Plato Timaeus (30b) quoted on page 320.

45 I have argued that this must be the case in any Cosmos capable of supporting life, see page 191.

An infinite God is not blameworthy for conceiving of everything that is conceivable. It is simply inevitable that such a God would do so. However, it is impossible for a God whose nature is Justice itself to conceive of something that is in any way disharmonious without and apart from a means of perfecting it; a process by which it can be justified, its infirmity healed and its pain wiped away as it is gathered into peaceful and harmonious communion with divinity. This is because divine Justice could not conceive of standing by and tolerating injustice; especially an injustice which only exists because it has been conceived of as possible by divine Justice. Hence the theological version of the Multiverse hypothesis leads directly to the notion that God must get involved in the suffering of creation and take personal responsibility for the mess of this world and work to bring together all things in a final harmony.[46]

> [God] made known to us the mystery of His will… to be put into effect when the times will have reached their fulfilment – to bring all things in heaven and on earth together under one head, even Christ. [Eph 1:10 NIV[47]]

This is what the Catholic doctrines of the Incarnation, Redemption, Sacraments and Messianic Return are all about. They indicate how God's creative act returns whence it came and how all which God has created is to be healed, harmonised and divinized:[48] that is, finally caught up into the divine perfection. The first move in creation is the separation of being from God, so that the creature can be different from its Creator. this is followed by the educative process of sanctification, through which the creature becomes like its Creator, and culminates in atonement: the attainment of full communion between the creature (now both fully autonomous and intrinsically holy) and its Creator.[49]

> We think, indeed, that the goodness of God, through His Christ, may recall all His creatures to one end, even His enemies being conquered and subdued. For thus says holy Scripture, "The Lord said to My Lord, Sit Thou at My right hand, until I make Thine enemies Thy footstool."[50] And if the meaning of the prophet's language here be less clear, we may ascertain it from the Apostle Paul, who speaks more openly, thus: "For Christ must reign until

46 Is 11:9; 56:7; 65:25. Apoc 21:1-5, quoted on page 317.

47 The NIV here better represents the original Greek than does the RSV.

48 2Pet 1:3-4.

49 Origen "De Principiis" lib 1 cap 6 #2, quoted on page 280.

50 Ps 109:1

> He has put all enemies under His feet."[51] But if even that unreserved declaration of the apostle do not sufficiently inform us... listen to what he says in the following words, "For all things must be put under Him."[52] What, then, is this "putting under" by which all things must be made subject to Christ? I am of opinion that it is this very subjection by which we also wish to be subject to Him, by which the apostles also were subject, and all the saints who have been followers of Christ. For the name "subjection", by which we are subject to Christ, indicates that the salvation which proceeds from Him belongs to His subjects, agreeably to the declaration of David, "Shall not my soul be subject unto God? From Him cometh my salvation."[53] [Origen "De Principiis" lib 1 cap 6 #1]

The role of faith

In the end, this is a matter of faith. Once one comes to believe that God is just, then one has no choice but to trust God; even when it seems nonsensical to do so. One believes, in spite of the immediate evidence;[54] because of previous personal experience, intellectual conviction and the testimony of the Church.

Personally, I find the remarks contained in this chapter sufficient to answer the questions which trouble me. However, I accept that the answers I have given are neither complete nor even adequate. I think that a little reflection tells one that no better kind of answer is possible; because we are on the inside of the problem and so cannot possibly be objective. I know that the cry of my heart "Dear God, why did you make, us when our lives are so full of tears?" is adequately answered, for me, by the promise of God: "Behold, I make all things new!"[55] and this I choose to believe.

There is an alternative stance, of course. This is to hold firmly to the conviction that the suffering of the world is too grievous to be accounted for and justified in any way, and simply cannot be allowed to be necessary if God is omnipotent. This belief definitely implies that God is either imaginary or else unjust or impotent; but as there is no reason to chose this belief over any other, and given that it leads to a world-view in which value is impossible and hope, love, justice and mercy are irrational, I see no merit in clinging to it.

---

51 1Cor 15:25.

52 I take this to be a reference to Eph 1:10, quoted on page 200.

53 Ps 61:1.

54 By virtue of intellectual hysteresis, see page 15.

55 Apoc 21:5 RSV, quoted on page 317.

Chapter 12 The Fall

It is not good that the man should be alone.
[Gen 2:18 RSV]

The man has become like one of us, knowing good and evil.
[Gen 3:22 RSV]

And Jacob was left alone; and a man wrestled with him until the breaking of the day. [Gen 32:24 RSV]

Motivation

In this chapter I shall develop the argument that for human beings to attain ethical maturity, there is a need for them to enjoy a certain distance from God; so that they can make their own mistakes and learn from them. This notion is crucial if any explanation is to be given for God's apparent reticence to intervene regularly within the creation.

Adam and Eve

Traditionally, Catholics have understood Adam and Eve to be historic figures. In reaction to the doctrine of polygenism (the idea that human beings derive from a set of disparate ancestral strains) pope Pius XII decreed that it seemed impossible to affirm the integrity of the human race and to account for its uniform ethical status before God without positing a common ancestral pair.[1]

While seeming to assert the historicity of the Adam and Eve narrative, the actual effect of this decree is to relativize it. The pope implied that if it ever proved possible to give a coherent account of the unity of the human race and of the reality of original sin in such a way that did not require Adam and Eve to be actual persons, then the historicity of their narrative (while still possible) would be shown not to be a tenet of the Catholic Faith. A major problem with the Adam and Eve story (which suggests that it should not be taken at face value) is that it implies that their descendants interbred with other beings who had come to exist quite independently of Adam and Eve, while giving no account of the origin of these other beings.[2]

---

1 Pius XII Humani Generis (1950) but see page 170.
2 Gen 4:17,26; 6:1-4.

There is, in fact, a limited amount of genetic evidence in favour of the existence of Eve.[3] This points to her living in Africa, between 50,000 and 500,000 years ago.[4] Similar genetic evidence favours the existence of Adam[5] and points to him living in Africa, between 50,000[6] and 150,000[7] years ago. It is important to note that this evidence for Adam and Eve is not remotely conclusive, but only suggestive.

Grace and graces

The Catechism of the Catholic Church tells us that God created mankind to be His friends.[8] Not out of any need for friendship, but out of overflowing generosity. When someone is in a state of friendship with God, they are said to have "sanctifying grace", which is the indwelling of Holy Spirit, an intimate participation in the Trinitarian life of God.[9]

> If you love Me, you will keep My commandments. And I will pray the Father, and He will give you another Counsellor, to be with you for ever, even the Spirit of Truth, whom the world cannot receive, because it neither sees Him nor knows Him; you know Him, for He dwells with you, and will be in you.
> [Jn 14:15-17 RSV]

The Catechism is very mistaken in stating that friendship with God consists in "free submission" to God[10] and it is only as a result of this misunderstanding that it is able to say that the first humans were God's friends from the beginning. In truth, such a statement is no more than hyperbole. An understanding of "friendship with God" in terms of submission is characteristic of Islam not Christianity. Thomas Aquinas

---

3 R.L. Cann et al "Mitochondrial DNA and human evolution" (1987)

4 R. Groleau "Tracing Ancestry with MtDNA" (2002)

5 G. Weiss "Estimating the Age of the Common Ancestor of Men from the ZFY Intron" (1996)

6 R. Thomson et al "Recent common ancestry of human Y chromosomes: Evidence from DNA sequence data" (2000)

7 F. Cruciani et al "A Revised Root for the Human Y Chromosomal Phylogenetic Tree: The Origin of Patrilineal Diversity in Africa" (2011)

8 CCC #374.

9 CCC #375. This text, refers to "Lumen Gentium", (1964) and implies that the first humans had an intimate communion with God from the very start. The conciliar text does not say this, however. This is a legitimately disputed doctrine. [FCD II sec 2 cap 2 #18.1] The Thomists argue the position adopted by the Catechism while the Franciscans support mine.

10 CCC #396.

teaches that there has to be a two-way traffic or communication in friendship; that is a trade, both give and take.

> Yet neither does well-wishing suffice for friendship, for a certain mutual love is requisite, since friendship is between friend and friend: and this well-wishing is founded on some kind of communication. Accordingly, since there is a communication between man and God, inasmuch as He communicates His happiness to us, some kind of friendship must needs be based on this same communication, of which it is written: "God is faithful, by whom you were called into the fellowship of His Son."[11] The love which is based on this communication, is charity: wherefore it is evident that charity is the friendship of man for God.
> [Thomas Aquinas "Summa Theologica" II(2) Q23 #1]

As I have already pointed out, the only two Biblical figures favoured with the appellation "Friend of God" had particularly tempestuous and argumentative relationships with God.[12] Moreover, Jesus' service is perfect freedom and the *submission* that He requires of the soul consists of the taking up of a very gentle yolk; which gives only rest, not trouble, and demands no hard labour at all.[13]

> O God, who art the light of the minds that know Thee,
> the life of the souls that love Thee,
> the strength of the thoughts that seek Thee;
> help us so to know Thee that we may truly love Thee,
> so to love Thee that we may fully serve Thee,
> whose service is perfect freedom.
> [Gelasian Sacramentory C5/6th]

Original justice

The Catechism also tells us that mankind was originally innocent of any wrong-doing or wicked intent and that our first parents, though primitive in culture and general development, were harmonious of soul and whole-hearted.[14] In my view of the matter, this did not make them friends of God as such; but only children of God. They were morally flawless in the way that an unwritten page is blank, rather than in the

---

11 1Cor. 1:9 RSV.
12 See footnote #1 on page 185.
13 Mt 11:28-30. Jn 8:31-36. 2Cor 3:17. Gal 5:13.
14 CCC #376.

way that a page full of beautiful poetry or a masterful mathematical derivation might be flawless. The moral rectitude of the first humans lay in the fact that they naïvely obeyed God, whom they trusted and accepted automatically and uncritically as a benign authority. This state is called "original justice".[15]

Friendship requires a deeper level of dialogue, with a degree of equality. It is the achievement of the possibility of friendship between God and human beings which motivates the Biblical narrative of the Fall and makes it intelligible. It is only when we realise that this is what the Fall is all about that we can make sense of this important story. Indeed, it is only when we realise what the Fall is all about that we can make sense of our lives and of the human predicament.

The first choice

According to Genesis, God told our first ancestors of the existence of the Tree of Knowledge of Good and Evil, and warned them that if they ate its fruit they would die.[16]

> Now the serpent was more subtle[17] than any other wild creature that the Lord God had made. He said to the woman, "Did God say, 'You shall not eat of any tree of the garden'?"
>
> And the woman said to the serpent, "We may eat of the fruit of the trees of the garden; but God said, 'You shall not eat of the fruit of the tree which is in the midst of the garden, neither shall you touch it, lest you die.'"
>
> But the serpent said to the woman, "You will not die. For God knows that when you eat of it your eyes will be opened, and you will be like God, knowing good and evil.[18]"
>
> So when the woman saw that the tree was good for food, and that it was a delight to the eyes, and that the tree was to be

15 Canon One of the Fifth Session of the Council of Trent.

16 Gen 2:9,16-17; 3:3. Note that God neither revealed the existence of the Tree of Life nor forbade the eating of its fruit.

17 The Hebrew "aruwm"; means "sensible, shrewd, prudent, crafty or subtle". This is a positive connotation, akin to "wise", though wisdom is generally denoted by another Hebrew word, "sakal". There is no reason to think at this point of the story that the serpent was intent on mischief, or was acting contrary to God's will. Compare how Jesus speaks of serpents. [Mat 10:16]

18 This is what happened. The serpent did not lie, except in its assertion that God had mislead them as to the fatal effect of easting the fruit. Even here, it could be said that the serpent meant only "You will not die *immediately*."

> desired to make one wise,[19] she took of its fruit and ate; and she also gave some to her husband, and he ate. [Gen 3:1-6 RSV]

A superficial reading of the text suggests that God intended to keep mankind ethically incompetent and that the reward for moral elevation was toil, pain, suffering and death; but this is absurd. Why should God set out to deny humanity ethical understanding and why should its attainment have such dire consequences?[20] Another reading is needed.

A change in perspective

The intrinsic effect of eating the forbidden fruit is unclear. The serpent is presented as saying that it would "open the eyes" and give wisdom, and indeed it does seem to have had some direct effect;[21] but whether the fruit itself had an innate power or whether it was rather the act of disobedience to God's injunction which had the effect of changing our ancestors' outlook on life is not clear from the story itself. Perhaps eating the forbidden fruit should be understood as standing for whatever was in fact the first improperly ordered act of the human race.

Certainly, the attitude of our progenitors towards each other is presented as changed by eating of the Tree of Knowledge.[22] Why they should feel shame due to their nakedness is obscure.[23] However the idea that they should have progeny only occurs after they have eaten the forbidden fruit[24] and they are only said to have coitus after being excluded from Eden.[25] The implication is that sexual differentiation, desire,[26] procreation and the associated taboos only became an issue once mankind had forfeited the right to eat of the Tree of Life.

---

19 The Hebrew "sakal" means wise, cautious or prudent. Note the woman's motive for eating the fruit: to become wise. It will later be written that one becomes God's friend by gaining wisdom [Wis 7:14,27-28] and also that Adam was saved by wisdom. [Wis 10:1]

20 Gen 3:16-19.

21 Giving birth is painful because a human infant's head is large. Perhaps the consequence of eating the forbidden fruit was an increase in brain volume.

22 Gen 3:7-11.

23 Taboos connected with nakedness arguably arise from a concern that signals of sexual interest should not be given when these are inappropriate, given the social arrangements for the engendering and upbringing of children. In other words taboos against nakedness exist in order to discourage promiscuity and, in particular, adultery.

24 Gen 3:16,20.

25 Gen 4:1.

26 Gen 3:16.

God's purpose in the Fall

Genesis seems to portray God as having presented our first ancestors with an arbitrary temptation, more or less provoking them to disobedience. Is it possible to imagine any scenario more liable to produce disobedience than that God allow everything except one specific action – which action God highlights with a most dire warning?[27] This state of affairs was inevitably going to result in trouble, especially as God did not have the Tree of Knowledge of Good and Evil guarded (in contrast to the formidable guard which God subsequently set on the Tree of Life[28]) quite apart from the intervention of the serpent.[29]

Now, it is absurd that a benevolent God would set up the first humans to fail. Hence, this cannot be the significance of the story; even if that is what it seems to mean on a first reading. Moreover, it could not be an arbitrary act that God warned against. There are plenty of objectively harmful acts which could have been explicitly forbidden, if God had wanted to make a point about the importance of obeying divine decrees. In any case, what reason is there for obeying God's edicts apart from that it is sensible to do so because God only commands what is actually good for us and only forbids what is actually harmful?

No, it was not disobedience as such that was the issue; leastwise not a disobedience to be punished. Rather, God was concerned to inform the first human beings about a particular possibility which was to be desired; though it came with a definite cost: namely, mortality. This desirable object was autonomy (that is: personal moral responsibility and the development of an ethical sense of right and wrong) with the consequent possibility that human beings would become able to attain God's friendship on a basis of quasi-equality. Autonomy (and a moral sense, or conscience) were to be obtained through and by an act of disobedience; although this disobedience was as much the symptom of their attainment as the means by which they were obtained.

---

27 Gen 2:17. It is unclear whether God's warning that death would result from the eating of the forbidden fruit was a threat of retribution (as suggested by Canon One of the Fifth Session of the Council of Trent) or else a caution regarding its inevitable consequences.

28 Courtesy of the Archangel Jophiel, Gen 3:24 RSV.

29 Compare the effect of my command to you now, dear reader: "Don't you *dare* to think about a purple elephant with green spots!"

The Ascent of Man

Human nature was changed absolutely, irreformably and for the better[30] when the forbidden fruit was eaten. Before the Fall, our first parents were innocent, naïve, simple, sinless, pure and amoral souls; with no knowledge of good and evil: not able to conceive of ethical issues, and still less of disobeying God. In a sense they was perfect; though the perfection which they had was nothing like the excellence which it was God's business that they should attain. Their conscience and moral intuition only came to them as a result of eating the fruit of the Tree of Knowledge; by which act humanity became "like God, knowing good and evil".[31] The first humans thereby developed the ability to discern what was good for them autonomously, quite apart from simply being told by God what was good for them. They demonstrated this by going against a direct command of God, the very purpose of which edict was that it should be broken and not obeyed.

God employs a plural pronoun in recognising the change which has taken place.[32] This does not imply that God is talking to any other spiritual beings – though God might well be addressing the angelic host. The point is that whereas before the Fall humanity was of an entirely different category from God, being amoral; as a result of the Fall humanity ascended to a higher level, no longer just being *conscious* but having become moral, gaining a *conscience* and so a real capability for good and evil.[33] After the Fall, God and humanity can be classed together in God's estimation as an "us", because humanity has become like God; whereas before the Fall there was no commensurability, but only a subservient human "we" and a commanding divine "I".

Mankind was first created sentient[34] and with freewill. God then initiated the process which resulted in humanity developing into fully sapient[35] beings, by offering us the prize of "moral awareness" and – after warning what the cost would be – stepping back to let events take their inevitable, tragic[36] but necessary, desirable and glorious course.

---

30 In a sense different from that condemned by Canon One of the Fifth Session of the Council of Trent.

31 Gen 3:5 RSV.

32 Gen 3:22, quoted at the head of this chapter.

33 It is in this sense that human nature was changed for the worse, as is insisted by Canon One of the Fifth Session of the Council of Trent.

34 Sentience is "personal subjective experiential consciousness" [LNS Ch 4]

35 Sapience is sentience together with the knowledge of good and evil.

36 Hence God's poignant act of providing a first set of clothes for His wayward children. [Gen 3:21] This is reminiscent of the act of a tearful mother who knits scarves and jumpers for her children when they leave home to make their own way in the world as adults.

The exclusion from Eden was not so much an act of retribution (or even of corrective punishment for disobedience) as an act supportive (and indeed constitutive) of mankind's transition from being sentient to being sapient. It was the beginning of the greatest romance of all history, in fact the romance which underlies and motivates all of salvation history.

Innocence and experience

It is only relative ignorance and the prospect of death which makes wickedness and hence autonomous virtue possible;[37] so it should not be surprising that mortality and exclusion from the immediate divine presence[38] were the two necessary concomitants of the original choice to become moral beings. Indeed, these are precisely the two changes in human circumstance which constitute that choice. While human beings existed in a state of innocence, they could eat of the Tree of Life. Once they gained a conscience they could not continue in the world-order which had been crafted to give rise to their being. They had to move on from that nursery to greater things.

The Fathers, following the scriptures,[39] teach that the sin of disobedience as such was repented and that God forgave it; but that the consequences (primarily, mortality) remained.[40] The question then arises: "Why, when God granted forgiveness and friendship (that is 'sanctifying grace') to fallen humanity, was the resulting condition (that of 'restored justice') not inheritable?[41] Instead, the unlooked for birthright of every human infant is 'original sin'. Why is this so?"

---

37 A person given knowledge of reality "on a plate" would be virtuous in only a shallow sense. They would not have gained this knowledge as a result of their own effort, experience and initiative. They would never have known "hunger and thirst for righteousness". [Mat 5:6 RSV] See page 22.

38 But not all communication, see Gen 4:6-7, 9-15, 26.

39 "Wisdom protected the first-formed father of the world, when he alone had been created; she delivered him from his transgression, and gave him strength to rule all things." [Wis 10:1-2 RSV]

40 It is the teaching of most Catholic theologians that human nature was vitiated by the Fall only to the extent that the freedom from concupiscence were lost. [FCD II sec 2 cap 2 #24.2]

41 CCC #404. It is defined [Council of Trent. Session V. Canon Two] that "original justice" would have been inheritable but that the restored "state of grace" is not so. However no account is given of why this is is the case.

The new prospect of friendship with God

Before the Fall, humans were amoral, ethically naïve beings. They had no sense of moral responsibility, or of justice, beyond the idea that they should do as they were told by God; that is live in "free submission"[42] to the Divine Will. This state of "original justice" was a negative condition which could readily have been inherited. These first humans were little more than hard-wired automata and their progeny would have been of like nature. They were entirely the responsibility of God, having no capability for any independence of action, able only to live in placid and submissive obedience to God. Hence God had an unlimited duty of care towards them – as of a maker to what he has made – and the first humans had certain rights over (that is, reasonable expectations of) God, as long as they did not separate themselves from God.

After the Fall, humans are no longer hard-programmed automata and neither can their children be so.[43] Every fallen human being is personally autonomous,[44] complete with their own conscience, and is responsible for their own well-being. In place of a naïve innocence and intimacy with God, sapient humanity now has an ethical competence and exists at a certain distance from God. On the one hand, this represents a lamentable estrangement from God[45] – who is now perceived as separate and holy; yet on the other, it represents the acquisition of an invaluable independence from God. Our souls can only be saved[46] or enlightened[47] (that is, fitted for Eternal Life with God) precisely through the exercise

---

42 CCC #396.

43 See Canon Two of the Fifth Session of the Council of Trent.

44 Note that an automaton is autonomous in an entirely different sense from the sense in which a free agent is autonomous. The former is determinately programmed with definite behaviours, whereas for the latter, autonomy means that they have the ability to develop their own style of life.

45 It is this which canon five of the fifth session of the Council of Trent refers to when it speaks of the "guilt of original sin" which is "remitted by baptism". This "guilt" is not of such a character as to deserve vengeful retribution. It is the teaching of both the eastern Fathers and most western theologians that infants who die unbaptized do not go to Hell, properly so called; but only that they cannot be known to attain Heaven. [FCD II sec 2 cap 2 #25] In 2007, pope Benedict XVI called the doctrine of "the Limbo of the Infants" into question by approving the report "The Hope of Salvation for Infants Who Die Without Being Baptized."

46 Mat 10:22; 19:25; 24:13. Mk 16:16. Jn 3:17; 5:34; 10:9. Acts 2:21, 47; 4:12; 16:30-31. Rom 5:9-10; 10:9-13. 1Cor 3:15. 2Cor 2:15. Eph 2:8. 2Thes 2:10-13. 1Tim 2:4. 2Tim 1:9.

47 Mat 6:22-23. Lk 11:33-36. Jn 1:1-9; 8:12; 12:35-36, 46. Acts 26:18. 2Cor 4:6. Eph 5:8. 1Jn 1:7; 2:8-10.

of our freewill; and in particular, by faith. Without autonomy we cannot become God's friends.

This is why God connived to bring about the Fall: so that humanity could become worthy of God. After the Fall, God is not so much the creator and father of humanity, as our potential friend and saviour. Fallen humanity is become sapient and is characterized by the possibility of ethical sophistication and so the prospect of grace: of divine friendship. However, such a positive prospect cannot simply be inherited. Unlike the parent-child relationship, friendship is never a question of rights or obligations. It has to be freely chosen, freely granted and freely received. Hence, a human child cannot possibly inherit "sanctifying grace" from its parents, no matter how holy they are. This is because the child must themselves become a friend of God, on their own account and by God's gracious invitation and initiative.

It should now be clear that original sin is necessarily inherited (or, better, that sanctifying grace cannot be inherited) simply because the nature which we now have is different from that which characterized humanity in its beginnings. The state of "restored justice" enjoyed by the first true sapient humans, was not (and could not possibly have been) the same as the state of "original justice" in which they had been created as merely sentient beings.

The need for subjectivity

It is in order to give us the space to make mistakes and so to learn and to grow that God places us in an environment that is not entirely friendly, with limited intellectual faculties and only subjective opinion to live by. Although autonomy is not a value in itself, it is the only means of attaining wisdom and a personal apprehension of justice.[48] It is the only way to come to understand how to "walk in the truth."[49]

> I will give them one heart, and put a new spirit within them; I will take the stony heart out of their flesh and give them a heart of flesh, that they may walk in My statutes and keep My ordinances and obey them; and they shall be My people, and I will be their God. [Ezk 11:19-20 RSV]

> I will put My law within them, and I will write it upon their hearts; and I will be their God, and they shall be My people. And no longer shall each man teach his neighbour and each his

48 Rom 12:2, quoted on page 143.
49 1Jn 1:6.

> brother, saying, "Know the Lord," for they shall all know Me, from the least of them to the greatest, says the Lord; for I will forgive their iniquity, and I will remember their sin no more. [Jer 31:33-34 RSV]

> For it is not the hearers of the law who are righteous before God, but the doers of the law who will be justified. When Gentiles who have not the law do by nature what the law requires, they are a law to themselves, even though they do not have the law. [Rom 2:13-14 RSV]

Note the contrast between "doing the law"[50] which justifies and carrying out "works of the law" by which "no human being will be justified".[51] "Carrying out "works of the law" is an exterior obedience, and an unthinking conformance with rules. "Doing the law" involves an interior apprehension of justice, by which a human being becomes like God " knowing good and evil." This is what it is to be God's friend.

> This makes sense to me, as it seems easy to imagine we might be overwhelmed by God's influence, and, which is more, I am able to understand the idea of God intending us to be autonomous friends or lovers of His, and in order to develop our independence, we might need to learn to live without God. As Bonhoeffer suggests "only a suffering God can help". Only a God who allows Himself to be ignored in the world is able to help us…
>
> It seems easy to understand this notion of God leaving us if God is a Being, able to intervene and to stand back, but if God is the ground of our Being, it is impossible for Him ever to not be with us, and the only sense in which He could not be with us, that I am able to see, is for us to voluntarily ignore the depth of our lives, and, in an almost paradox, to use Tillich's definition,[52] to ignore *that which we take seriously* in our lives.
>
> Now, I say almost paradox because we are able to ignore *that which we take seriously*, in an example of self-denial, to use that word in an unusual way. In Tillich's terms, this would be living without God, but it is hard to imagine how this would help us to learn to be autonomous. It seems simply that it would be a bad thing.
>
> [H.C. Milton "Private Communication" (2009)]

---

50 Deut 4:1; 8:1, 12:1. Mk 10:17-22. Lk 10:25-28. Jas 1:21-27; 2:20-26.

51 Rom 3:20 RSV.

52 P. Tillich "The Shaking of the Foundations" (1949)

The glory of ignorance

Certain knowledge is pretty much unobtainable in this life. All mortal knowledge is unavoidably filtered by the working hypotheses, presumptions, prejudices and expectations which motivate, guide and enable us – and yet also limit and impoverish our interaction with and investigation of the world. No matter how dispassionate we try to be, we cannot possibly attain to pure knowledge and absolute truth by any purely rational means. On one level this is regrettable, as it is a limitation of our state of being. On another it is wonderful, because it makes autonomy possible and allows learning to occur. Only where there is uncertainty and subjectivity is there room for opinion, courage and discretion; in fact for the exercise of any of the virtues.

Of course, none of this is true of God. God cannot have freewill in this sense. God is omniscient and the only objective observer. God has a perfect and complete understanding of the whole Cosmos. God has no opinions, views or policies. God has all the facts, just as they are, with total clarity of vision. Moreover, God has no need to be rational. All things are equally and immediately present and obvious to God. Though God is well aware of the inter-relatedness and inter-dependence of everything, God does not have to rely on any understanding of contingency and causality to deduce conclusions from premises. There is no possibility of uncertainty or weakness in God.[53]

It is plausible that the ability for the soul to exercise freewill when it has sight of the Being of God will be limited and even entirely subverted. Even if it is excessive to presume that the saints have an abiding and immediate knowledge of everything, it would nevertheless seem that the correct answer to any doubt or question will be readily available to them. This will mean that there is no room for any divergent views in Heaven; not because a party line is imposed, but because the impartial truth is freely available.

What God wants of us in the mean-time is that we try to understand what is right and that we struggle and fight with our own ignorance and imperfections. It is this process that is important. God's purpose is for us to be morally perfected through this struggle; with God's unfailing help and encouragement: that is, by God's grace. What matters is that we learn to "hunger and thirst for righteousness."[54] It doesn't matter nearly as much that we get all the answers right. The desired outcome is that we gain self-knowledge through struggle, as did Jacob[55]; not that we simply accumulate moral truths.

---

53 Jas 1:17.

54 Mat 5:6 RSV, see also Is 56:1.

55 Gen 32:24, quoted at the head of this chapter.

The Ascent of Christ

For many years I have been bothered by the question: "Why did Jesus ascend to heaven[56] after His resurrection, so leaving the Apostles and all those who came to believe through their testimony without the consolation of His physical presence?" I have only recently come to realise what the answer to this question is[57] and that it is intimately related to the issues which we have been considering here. The answer is that Jesus left the world of human affairs for the same reason that God sent the first fallen human beings away from the Garden of Eden. In both cases the rationale was to give humanity some ethical space, so as not to "cramp our style."[58]

Until His resurrection Jesus' physical presence was harmless. Even His closest disciples were more mystified by His teachings than forced to accept any definite conclusions about His nature.[59] They treated Him with respect as a wise rabbi who spoke "words of life",[60] perhaps even as the Messiah;[61] but certainly not as God Incarnate.[62] After Jesus' resurrection the case was entirely changed. Even the hard-headed and rightly sceptical Thomas, when confronted by his Risen Lord, fell to his knees in adoration and acknowledged Jesus as the Divine Messiah.[63]

Theocratic dehumanisation

There is a great tendency, even within a fallible Church, to overstate the trustworthiness of human authorities and to rely on them for everything. The net effect of this attitude is to reject human imagination, active questioning and inquiry in favour of a passive waiting for official pronouncements; to replace original thinking and the quest to obtain a true understanding with the empty repetition of slogans and to substitute an uncritical "holy obedience" for personal moral responsibility. In other words, the effect is to dehumanise humanity.

---

56 Acts 1:1-11.

57 D.J. Goodrum, private communication.

58 There is a second reason for Jesus' Ascension. It shows that His work on Earth was acceptable to God. Jesus' show of entering into Heaven in glory represents the final seal of divine approval on His life, death and resurrection. The Ascension was how Jesus fulfilled the Aaronic Holocaust or Worship Sacrifice; in which the victim was entirely consumed and so removed from the human sphere.

59 Mk 6:52; 8:32. Lk 9:45. Jn 8:27; 10:6; 12:16.

60 Jn 6:68.

61 Mat 16:15-16. Mk:8:29. Lk 9:20.

62 Jn 14:9-10.

63 Jn 20:19-31.

Now, if we knew for certain that some statement or decree came directly from a benign and omniscient source, we wouldn't dream of questioning it – beyond inquiries intended to clarify its meaning. The danger is, in fact, that one wouldn't even do this, but simply treat it as a slogan. Consider how things would have developed if Jesus had remained at the centre of the Church on Earth after His resurrection. Instead of a pope sat in Rome, claiming to speak infallibly from time to time, the All-Wise God Incarnate would be sat in Jerusalem. This would have resulted in every human being seeking out the advice of that Divine Oracle; eschewing any reliance on their own judgement and conscience in the process.[64]

A first intimation of this problem is recorded in the Torah, where Moses' face is transformed by exposure to the divine presence; first on Mount Sinai when he received the Decalogue from God, and then from time to time in the Tabernacle. Moses' response to this is to cover his face with a veil, so as to reduce the impact of his vicarious authority on the Israelites.[65] Similarly, the Holy of Holies in both the Tabernacle and Temple was separated from the rest of the construction by a veil which indicated the need to separate the divine realm from the mundane. This veil was torn in two when Jesus died,[66] showing that the New Covenant would be characterized by a much greater intimacy than the Old; even though it would still be mediated by physicality.

It was precisely in order to avoid this pathological state of affairs (which would have directly contradicted God's business in creating mankind) that Jesus ceased to dwell in the physical world. Instead, He established the Church at the first Christian Pentecost – under the guidance and protection (rather than the control) of Holy Spirit – as His more gentle means of remaining engaged in human affairs. Within the Church, as within the world as a whole, humanity can experience communion with God at one stage removed. God's advice and encouragement is always available: in the words of the Scriptures, the teachings of the Fathers and Saints, the decrees of the Magisterium and the quiet voice of conscience; but God never compels our assent. The ritual sacraments of the Church, as also the "quasi-sacraments" of Nature's beauty and the works of human artistic imagination,[67] mediate God to the human heart without ever forcing the will.

---

64 This would have a debilitating effect on humanity, similar to the culture shock which would affect our society, were we ever to encounter an advanced race of benign aliens. [M.A.G. Michaud "Contact with Alien Civilizations" (2007)]

65 Ex 34:29-35.

66 Mat 27:51. Mk 15:38. Lk 23:45.

67 Plato "Symposium" (201-212).

Chapter 13 The Obscurity of God

> Why dost Thou stand afar off, O Lord? Why dost Thou hide Thyself in times of trouble? [Psalm 10:1 RSV]

Motivation

As a final preparation for the business of presenting various arguments for the reality of God, I shall now address a series of objections taken from an article by Richard Carrier.[1] I have re-ordered his argument and generally speaking summarised his words while preserving his original intent. Whereas Carrier is intent on attacking what he understands Christianity to be, I have have replied with a defence of Monotheism: the belief in an omnipotent, omniscient and omnibenevolent God.

God should be obvious and certain

Carrier argues that if God wished to communicate with humanity, God would do so in an *obvious* way, so that we could tell that it was God; and in a *clear* way, so that would know exactly what God's business with us was. We would then be able to respond to God's intervention in a rational manner. He claims that:

> We would all hear him out and shout "Eureka!" So obvious and well demonstrated would His message be. It would be spoken to each of us in exactly those terms we would understand. And we would all agree on what that message was. Even if we rejected it, we would all at least admit to each other, "Yes, that's what this God fellow told me." Excuses don't fly. The Christian proposes that a supremely powerful being exists who wants us to set things right, and therefore doesn't want us to get things even more wrong. This is an intelligible hypothesis, which predicts there should be no more confusion about which religion or doctrine is true than there is about the fundamentals of Medicine, Engineering, Physics, Chemistry, or even Meteorology.

---

1 R. Carrier "Why I am not a Christian" (2006)

I reply that it is not always proper for God to do everything that God is able to do by virtue of Divine potency: might is not right.

Carrier's first mistake is to conceive of God as "a supremely powerful being." This error compromises his entire argument. It makes him view God as akin to other agencies with which he is familiar, and in particular human beings. This error leads him to believe that it would be possible to reject the obvious and clear message of God. In fact this is not true. No sane person would be able to dissent, were God to intervene in human affairs as Carrier demands that God should.[2]

Moreover, God can't possibly want to "set things right" in the way that Carrier envisages; for if God is God (and not simply the most powerful being that exists) then things must be exactly how God wants them to be and there cannot be any question of setting anything right.[3] Nor can there be any question of God wanting to stop us getting "things even more wrong". This is not God's business at all. The way that things are "wrong" now is itself part of the Creative Act.[4] It is a mistake to think that it ought to be God's purpose *presently* to sort out the mess that humanity is undoubtedly making of its existence. God is not the manager of a holiday resort set with the task of keeping a horde of lager louts in some kind of order.

Rather than stating confidently what God ought to do if God was real and then concluding that God is not real because these things are apparently not being done; Carrier ought to investigate whether there is any way in which the idea of a benevolent and omnipotent God can be reconciled with the Universe as we find it. If he were able to show that no such reconciliation is possible, he would thereby prove that God cannot be both beneficent and omnipotent; however, if he is not able to demonstrate this, then all he can say is that it is not clear how God can be both beneficent and omnipotent: which is not at all the same thing.

In point of fact Carrier does not justify his conclusion. Moreover, I believe that – for those with the right outlook and who are at the right point on their spiritual journey – God's reality is sufficiently obvious to produce exactly the exclamation of "Eureka!" which Carrier says should be forthcoming. I shall take up this point in the next chapter of this book.

Carrier's second basic mistake is to assume that God is in the business of communicating a message. Now at one level Carrier is right. The prophets were very keen to preach the "Word of God" and Jesus went about "proclaiming the Kingdom", His Apostles following close

2 This inconsistency later emerges in his own words. See page 228.

3 God's business is to "set things right" eschatologically, not within the normal course of history. God's Kingdom will only be properly manifested after the return of the Messiah. See pages 199-200 and Chapter 17.

4 See page 191.

in His footsteps. However, at a deeper level this idea is wrong and misleading. “Communicating a message” can mean a number of things:

1. Indoctrination; as in techniques of manipulative political, religious or corporate attitude formation.
2. Spinning a believable lie; as is typical of the public relations business or legal advocacy.
3. Presenting a sales-pitch; as in an advertisement.
4. Telling a story as fiction, for the purpose of entertainment.
5. Imparting information; as in the words of a platform announcer at a railway station.
6. Drilling; as in the memorization of a set of required responses, so that they can be performed automatically in reaction to certain questions or commands.
7. Coaching; as a sports instructor might seek to improve the performance of an athlete.
8. Training; as in those techniques used by military authorities to enhance the character, morale and resolve of soldiers.
9. Education, in which the interior life of the student is changed by a process of engagement with a teacher.

Carrier conceives of God as at best a coach or drill sergeant, and as at worst an indoctrinator. What his argument succeeds in refuting is only his own assumption; namely that God is in the business of “imparting information” to humanity. This should not be surprising. I have already indicated what a terrible effect would follow, were God to communicate with humanity along the lines which Carrier demands.[5]

In fact, God is in the business of coaching, training and most especially of education; but not indoctrination, advertising, public relations or entertainment. God’s purpose is to seduce us gently into friendship; not to train us into dutiful passive servitude, and certainly not to coerce or spiritually rape us.

The idea of freewill is ad hoc

Carrier argues that for a human to have freewill, either their will must be “more powerful than the will of God, and therefore can actually block His words from being heard despite all His best and mighty efforts,” or else it must be that God somehow cares more about preserving our right “not to hear Him than about saving our souls, and so God himself ‘chooses’ to be silent.”

---

5 See page 216.

Carrier then says:

> There is no independent evidence of either this remarkable human power to thwart God, or this peculiar desire in God, and so this is a completely "ad hoc" theory: something just "made up" out of thin air in order to rescue the actual theory.

I reply that the idea of human freewill somehow being "more powerful than the will of God" is certainly absurd; whatever one means by "will", human or divine. I therefore gladly accept his second alternative, namely that God *generally*[6] chooses to *moderate* the impact of divine communication with humanity for the sake of preserving our freewill. Carrier is, however, wrong to set up a dichotomy between God's concern to maintain humanity's autonomy and God's concern to save our souls. First, it is not true that God "chooses to be silent", as Carrier puts it; and second, it is *precisely* through God's gentleness, reticence and reserve that our souls are saved. I shall take up this point once more in a little while.

If the idea that God generally speaks quietly precisely so that it is possible to ignore or mistake the Divine Word was not a core part of the Judaeo-Christian tradition then his critique of the "freewill defence" would have some weight. However, Carrier is not right in saying that this is so.

> And behold, the Lord passed by, and a great and strong wind rent the mountains, and broke in pieces the rocks before the Lord, but the Lord was not in the wind; and after the wind an earthquake, but the Lord was not in the earthquake; and after the earthquake a fire, but the Lord was not in the fire; and after the fire a still small voice. [1 Kings 19:11-12 RSV]

Quite apart from Elijah's particular experience, the prophets generally heard God's word in private and then proclaimed to the people in their own human voice what they had received. Isaiah declares that the Saviour of Israel is a "hidden God".[7]

> Truly, Thou art a God who hidest Thyself, O God of Israel, the Saviour. [Is 45:15 RSV]

---

6 Generally, but not always, see page 224.

7 Only a few verses later, however, the prophet insists that God speaks publicly not "in secret, in a land of darkness"; referring to the events surrounding the promulgation of the Mosaic Covenant.

Moreover Jesus specifically thanks His Father for hiding the core message of the Gospel from "the wise and prudent"[8] and Jesus' practice of teaching via parables was specifically intended to bury the truth so that it took some effort to unearth and was not on show for all to see.[9]

> The kingdom of heaven is like treasure hidden in a field, which a man found and covered up; then in his joy he goes and sells all that he has and buys that field.
>
> Again, the kingdom of heaven is like a merchant in search of fine pearls, who, on finding one pearl of great value, went and sold all that he had and bought it. [Mat 13:44-46 RSV]

In all this, God's purpose is to direct divine revelation to where it will do good and away from where it would do harm: away from those who would treat it as a scientific or political resource, or would wish to debate it and towards those who are ready to engage and wrestle with it,[10] to dialogue with it and to be moulded by the encounter.

> Do not give dogs what is holy; and do not throw your pearls before swine, lest they trample them under foot and turn to attack you. [Mat 7:6 RSV]

In any case, no believer can legitimately claim that Monotheism is anything other than a reasonable hypothesis or rational account: a rather good theory, in other words. While it is backed up by evidence, this evidence no more confirms it beyond all dispute than does the evidence which can be presented in favour of various scientific theories[11] definitively confirms them. It is true that the evidence in favour of God's reality is more indirect, abstract and experiential than the evidence in favour of the typical theory of classical Physics; but the way that modern Physics is going the difference between it and Theology is becoming less and less clear.[12] In the end, all Science is based on faith;[13] and even our acceptance of logic as the basis of dialogue is a matter of conviction.[14]

---

8 Mat 11:25 RSV. St. Paul takes up this theme in 1Cor 2:1-8 and Eph 3:7-10.

9 Mk 4:10-12, quoted on page 230.

10 Gen 32:24, quoted at the head of Chapter 12.

11 Such as Darwinian Evolution, Copenhaganist Quantum Mechanics and Einsteinian General Relativity.

12 The evidence for "Dark Energy", "Dark Matter" and "Cosmic Inflation" is all indirect and circumstantial and there is no clear evidence for "Super Symmetry", "String Theory" or "Multiverses".

13 See page 17.

14 See page 43.

Disagreements among monotheists

Carrier argues that even if the "freewill defence" is valid, there remains the problem of significant disagreements among religious authorities. Even among Catholics, all of whom claim to accept the teaching authority of the Roman Church, there are disagreements.

> These people have chosen to hear God, and not only to hear Him, but to accept Jesus Christ as the shepherd of their very soul. So no one can claim these people chose not to hear God. Therefore, either God is telling them different things, or there is no God.

Carrier argues that if God had a definite message for us, it would have been communicated indifferently to all peoples and nations across the Globe, and all cultures would agree as to the basic business of salvation. Some might reject this message and others might distort it for their own ends; but if God cared to enable mankind to make an informed decision about spiritual matters God would have ensured that every human being had adequate access to the relevant facts.

> Everyone today, everywhere on Earth, would be hearing it, and their records would show everyone else in history had heard it, too. Sure, maybe some of us would still baulk at or reject that message. But we would still have the information. Because the only way to make an informed choice is to have the required information.

Carrier admits that people will disagree about anything, given half a chance, and that "there are always people who don't follow what they are told or what they know to be true." However, he points out that chemists agree on the principles of Chemistry; physicians agree on the basic facts of Medicine and engineers agree on the fundamentals of Engineering. So he asks, why can't theologians agree on the core doctrines of religion?

It would seem, therefore, either that God has no business with humanity; or that God's business is incoherent or mischievous; or that God is ineffective in communicating what God's business is. Now, none of these three options is attractive. It would therefore seem sensible to conclude from the discord among religions that God is no more than the construct (or, rather, a set of disparate constructs) of the human imagination.

I reply that human beings certainly do suffer from conceit and don't like to have their favourite (but mistaken) ideas corrected. Even those who on one level sincerely want to understand the things of God can be loathe to give up cherished ideas which they honestly think are good and wholesome; but which are in fact anything but this.

I think that these considerations are sufficient to account for the observed disagreements among believers, even among those who claim to respect the same earthly authority; however, there is an additional consideration. This is that different personalities, perspectives and histories can easily give rise to diverse narratives or accounts of reality which superficially conflict while being, at a deeper level, entirely compatible and mutually supportive.[15]

What, in any case, would count as "the *core doctrines* of religion"? Perhaps people do agree well enough about these. The Apostle Paul insists that God has adequately and effectively communicated with all peoples,[16] and Catholics believe that every soul (even that of a pagan who has never heard of Jesus) receives sufficient grace to become God's friend. The argument that there is insufficient agreement about "the *core doctrines* of religion" should be reversed. It should in fact be argued that what it is necessary to believe in order to be on the path of salvation is quite simple and straight-forward; indeed that it is pretty much common knowledge, so there is no excuse.[17]

> He that cometh to God must believe that He is, and that He is a rewarder of them that diligently seek Him. [Heb 11:6 KJV[18]]

The Jewish tradition also takes this line;[19] with the idea that for a gentile to please God, they must simply live a moral life according to the Natural Law, as summarised by the Seven Commandments supposedly given to Noah.[20] In the end, it doesn't really matter

15 For example, "Matrix Mechanics" and "Wave Mechanics" were originally proposed (by Heisenberg and Schrödinger, respectively) as antagonistic accounts of Quantum Mechanics. Subsequently, it was shown that they were alternative and equivalent treatments of exactly the same (pretty much incomprehensible) reality. More recently, Feynman developed yet a third account, the "Path Integral Formulation of Quantum Mechanics."

16 Acts 14:16-17. Rom 1:19-20. In fact there is a considerable uniformity in fundamental ethics from one culture to another.

17 Rom 1:20; 2:1.

18 The KJV avoids the RSV's unfortunate statement that "God exists".

19 Jewfacts "Gentiles".

20 (1) To set up courts of justice. (2) To respect property rights. To refrain from: (3) eating meat cut from living animals; (4) incest and adultery; (5) homicide; (6) blasphemy and (7) idolatry. [Gen 8:20-9:17. Rom 2:14-16]

whether each of us has the right beliefs about anything; beyond the basic ideas that decency, integrity and kindness are good things whereas dishonesty, duplicity and cruelty are bad ones. What matters is our sincerity of heart and desire for justice. "Be excellent to one another"[21] pretty much sums it up.

God would be more humanitarian

Carrier argues that if God were definitely benevolent, loved justice and hated evil, God wouldn't give up trying to help, cure or educate someone until their resistance to divine intervention became truly extreme. Any one who is really benevolent readily forces another person to act against their own immediate desires, over-riding their freewill in the matter, if that is necessary in order to rescue them from calamity.

> Such people don't give up on someone until their resistance becomes intolerable – until then, they will readily violate someone's free will to save them, because they know darned well it is the right thing to do. God would do the same. He would not let the choice of a fallible, imperfect being thwart His own good will.

I reply that it is absolutely evil for someone to be spiritually raped. This can never be "for their own good". A one-off human coercive intervention can be benevolent, as it has no implication for the way in which the coerced person lives their life once the coercion ends. This is because the human coercer is finite and escapable. Contrariwise, even a single dramatic divine intervention would have profound implications for the remainder of the life of those affected; because it sets a precedent of indefinitely large significance and wide-ranging application.

Now this isn't to say that such interventions don't take place. Typically, God acts in a dramatic and public manner when there is a pressing need to establish the credibility of some authority which will then abide for a long time afterwards.[22] The two prime examples are the establishment of the Mosaic[23] and Messianic[24] Covenants, each of which

---

21 "Bill and Ted's Excellent Adventure" dir. S. Herek (1989)

22 A possible contemporary exception to this general rule is "The Miracle of the Sun" which is recorded as having taken place at Fatima in 1917 [J. de Marchi "Fatima: The Facts" (1950)] Even more dramatic exceptions are envisaged in the prophecies of "The Warning" and "The Miracle" supposedly communicated to the Garabandal visionaries by the Blessed Virgin Mary. [F.S.V.Y. Pascual "The Apparitions of Garabandal" (1966)]

23 Ex 13-14; 33:9-10. Num 12:5; 14:14. Deut 31:15.

24 Mat 17:1-9; 28. Mk 9:2-10. Lk 24:1-9; 33-53. Jn 20-21. Acts 1:1-3.

is supposed to have been associated with dramatic historic events. In neither case, however, was the divine intervention so dramatic that it forced all those who witnessed it or had proximate knowledge of it to accept that it definitely meant what it appeared to mean; leastwise not once the passage of time had erased its immediacy from their minds.

Various Old Testament figures (especially, but not only various prophets) are presented as having had direct encounters with God. Some of these interactions were pretty coercive. Jonah is the most obvious example of "divine bullying", but the experiences of Elijah and Jeremiah were similar.[25] However, these were all events in the lives of individuals who had specific tasks to perform. God's intervention in their lives set no precedent and was private, not public;[26] though the effects – as evinced in the subsequent lives of the prophets – were public, of course.

God deals with each of us as individuals, in accordance with our own peculiar needs. God knew that Jonah would not be harmed by being "bullied." Jonah certainly wasn't going to be convinced that God was real as a result of it. He already believed that much quite definitely. No, the main risk was that Jonah wouldn't be able to accept the reality of God's benevolence towards sinners and so would turn his back on God's justice, preferring his own retributive notion of "justice". In the cases of Elijah and Jeremiah, God's intervention was in the lives of men who were already intimate with the Divine. Although God certainly bullied or cajoled them into doing things, these things were actions which flowed from a faith which already existed. The basic orientation of their lives was not affected, but only affirmed.

The analogy of a father or friend

Carrier argues that just as his father or a friend doesn't violate his free will when they advise or admonish him, and still less when they answer his questions clearly, neither would God do so by acting similarly. A good God must be motivated to act towards each of us with at least as much benevolence as a friend or father, and yet Carrier claims that:

> God doesn't do anything at all. He doesn't talk to, teach, help, or comfort us, unlike my real father and my real friends. God doesn't tell us when we hold a mistaken belief that shall hurt us. But my father does, and my friends do. Therefore, no God exists who is even remotely like my father or my friends.

---

25 1Kings 19:1-18. Jer 1:4-10; 15:10-18; 20; 38.

26 Elijah's miracle of fire [1Kings 18:20-39] being a notable exception.

I reply that it is wrong to argue from what it is right and proper for a human being to do to what it is right and proper for God to do. Human beings are not God and are not infallible. Their answers, admonitions, and advice are never ultimately authoritative and unquestionable, and we always know this to be the case. Hence, we always subject them to our own scrutiny and evaluation, except in the case of a truly urgent emergency.

God is not anything like a human being. Every one of God's actions is necessarily indefinitely puissant and, if not moderated, forces the outcome. This is why God regularly acts through intermediaries. Even when God came into this world in the person of Jesus, He chose to do so in an obscure way and to teach in parables. Jesus was careful to talk-down the idea that He was the Messiah. Even when He rose from the dead, Jesus chose to reveal Himself informally and only to a select group[27] rather than to appear publicly in glory.

In any case, God does do all the things that a good God should do; if only you look in the right places.[28] God simply doesn't do these things in the dramatic way that one might naïvely desire. Instead, God generally acts gently in our lives, so as to foster our autonomy.

The analogy of a physician

Carrier argues that a physician is not vague when he counsels a patient as to how they can get well. On the contrary, he speaks clearly and in terms his patient can readily comprehend. He answers the patient's questions, and is ready and willing to present the evidence on which he is basing his treatment recommendation.

> He won't hold anything back and declare, "I'm not going to tell you, because that would violate your free will!" Nor would any patient accept such an excuse – to the contrary, he would respond, "But I choose to hear you," leaving the doctor no such excuse.

I reply by pointing out that the relationship we each have with God is not comparable to the physician-patient relationship (where it is the business of the physician to actively cure the patient who is passive in the physician's care) but rather the teacher-student relationship (which is predicated on a certain equality, and on friendship) with the prospect of this developing into the lover-beloved relationship.

27 Quite a few, actually, but still select. [Acts 13: 30-31. 1Cor 15:2-8]

28 The Bible, Church teachings and the Sacraments. Also the witness, advice and ministry of friends. [Lk 16:29-31, quoted on page 231]

The teacher's best tactic at all times is to ask questions and to challenge and to critique their student, not simply to drill them. Even if the student demands to be given the right answers (perhaps so that they can be memorized for an exam) it is wrong for the educator to accede to this request. Indeed, one of the first things which the student must learn, if they are ever to understand anything at all, is that they must not make such demands; or at least never expect them to be satisfied. Moreover, the student who truly pleases his teacher is the one who challenges and even contradicts his words. This is because they thereby shows that they have started to think for themselves and have accepted from the hand of their teacher the flame of sceptical inquiry[29] and desire for knowledge of good and evil; which is the one gift he truly wishes to impart.

Carrier's problem here is that he doesn't recognise how high the vocation which human beings have received from God is. He presumes a much lower vocation; one that seems more reasonable. Once he finds that this doesn't fit in with the facts he then claims that Monotheism is false, whereas what he should do is go back and check his premises.

The example of Christ and His Apostles

Carrier argues that the autonomy of the Apostles was not compromised by their spending three years in the society of Jesus, being instructed by Him; or by their witnessing His resurrection. Not even the autonomy of Thomas, who had the chance to place his hands in Jesus' wounds, was harmed.[30] Neither was the freewill of Saul of Tarsus violated by his dramatic conversion experience,[31] or by the fact that he claimed to have received a direct revelation of the Gospel from Jesus.[32] Carrier then agues that if Christianity were true the Gospel would be presented to each and every one of us immediately by God, in much the way that God dealt with Thomas or Saul of Tarsus. He asks:

> Was their free will violated? Of course not. Nor would ours be. Thus, if Christianity were really true, there would be no dispute as to what the Gospel is. There would only be our free and informed choice to accept or reject it. At the same time, all our sincere questions would be answered by God, kindly and clearly, and when we compared notes, we would find that the Voice of God gave consistent answers and messages to everyone all over the world, all the time.

---

29 "Pass it on, boys, pass it on!" [A. Bennett "The History Boys" (2004, 2006)]
30 Jn 20:24-29.
31 Acts 9:1-20.
32 1Cor 11:23. Gal 1:12. Eph 3:3.

I reply that for the Apostles to accept what Jesus said as authentic required a step of faith; one which many of their contemporaries didn't make. It was not obvious to them that Jesus was the Messiah,[33] let alone that He was God. After all, both the religious and secular authorities rejected Him and many of His disciples forsook Him when He spoke words which they couldn't accept.[34]

Our present circumstances are not so far removed from those of the Apostles. They existed within a religious tradition with its authoritative texts. They had met a teacher who seemed able to expound those texts and represent and develop that tradition in ways that rang true to them. He worked miracles and claimed peculiar authority, but seemed every bit as human and frail as they. Then He died, ignominiously executed as a political agitator by the Roman authorities. Then they became convinced that He was really alive again in their midst, and that He actually spoke to them and ate physical food with them.

We exist in exactly the same tradition. Nowadays it has a few more texts; some telling the story of the life, death and resurrection of that Teacher whom the Apostles met and others presenting His teachings as understood by them. His followers claim that miracles are still worked in His name, from time to time; and His chief follower claims to be able to speak with a peculiar authority when this is needful.

The main difference between us and the Apostles is that we haven't had material contact with Jesus. This is not necessary for us, whereas it was very necessary for the Apostles; for they were being constituted as prime witnesses to the resurrection and the authoritative exponents of the New Covenant. It was their role to testify personally to the historic reality of the Incarnation and to establish it as a matter of record.

Carrier continues:

> God would make sure He told everyone, directly, what His message was. Everyone would then know what God had told them. They can still reject it all they want, and God can leave them alone. But there would never be, in any possible Christian Universe, any confusion or doubt as to what God's message was. And if we had questions, God himself would answer them… Indeed, the very fact that God gave the same message and answers to everyone would be nearly insurmountable proof that Christianity was true. Provided we had no reason to suspect God of lying to all of us, Christianity would be as certain as the law of gravity or the colour of the sky.

---

33 Mat 8:24-27; 11:2-3. Mk 4:437-41; 6:2; 8:27-30. Lk 8:22-25. Jn 12:34.

34 Jn 6:60-66.

This pretty much makes the points that I have been arguing. If God did communicate with humanity as Carrier demands, then "there would never be... any confusion or doubt as to what God's message was... Christianity would be as certain as the law of gravity or the colour of the sky." This is, of course, contradictory to the statement: "They can still reject it all they want."

So, what we do not have is an infallible divine oracle. As I have already argued,[35] the existence of such an oracle would undermine human autonomy. Knowing *clearly* what God's message was and knowing that the message was *definitely* from God would make that message as impossible to reject as the fact that the cloudless sky is blue. Carrier continues:

> If Christianity were true, there would be no point in "choosing" whether God exists any more than there is a choice whether gravity exists or whether all those other people exist whom we love or hate or help or hurt. We would not face any choice to believe on insufficient and ambiguous evidence, but would know the facts, and face only the choice whether to love and accept the God that does exist.

Carrier is crucially mistaken here. Not even this choice would be open to us. This is because God is not anything like a human being. God isn't any thing that one can chose to adopt an attitude towards. Once one knew clearly that the omnipotent and benevolent God, the source of all beauty and life, the very ground of all being, was real; then it would make no sense to do anything other than adore this God: because this God would necessarily be the most adorable object of love.

God does not respect agnostics

Carrier claims that many unbelievers are reasonable and open minded. He asserts that:

> I and countless others have chosen to give God a fair hearing – if only He would speak. I would listen to Him even now, at this very moment.

Carrier claims that the problem that he and others have is that God remains silent; the evidence in favour of God's reality remains sparse and the arguments put forward by monotheists remain weak.

---

35 See page 215.

I reply that God speaks everywhere. The danger is that while on one level a person can be willing to hear God's voice, on another they can be hostile. They can insist that the answer be given in their own terms, even when those terms exclude the very answer that is supposedly being sought. It behoves each of us to examine our heart, to make sure that we are not imposing preconditions on God which make it impossible for us to hear God's voice and recognise the everyday evidence of God's reality. Jesus puts the matter before us in stark semitic style.

> When He was alone, those who were about Him with the twelve asked Him concerning the parables. And He said to them, "To you has been given the secret of the kingdom of God, but for those outside everything is in parables; so that they may indeed see but not perceive, and may indeed hear but not understand;[36] lest they should turn again, and be forgiven. [Mk 4:10-12 RSV]

Jesus means that He uses parables in order to get people to ponder on His preaching, so that they might come to a personal understanding of it and so enter the Kingdom. This process is necessarily open to the possibility that an individual will fail to perceive Jesus' intent and remain outside. The last phrase means only that those who do come to understand and accept Jesus' message will be forgiven and that those who do not, and chose to remain outside the Kingdom, will not be.[37]

Moreover, I suspect that Jesus is also exasperated with the behaviour of those who should know better. Elsewhere He chides the Pharisees:

> You search the scriptures, because you think that in them you have eternal life; and it is they that bear witness to Me; yet you refuse to come to Me that you may have life… If you believed Moses, you would believe Me, for he wrote of Me. But if you do not believe his writings, how will you believe My words? [Jn 5:39-47 RSV]

---

36 More accurately: "so that in seeing they see without perceiving; in hearing here without understanding".

37 He does not mean, as it might seem from this translation, that God disguises and hides from full-view the divine message precisely so as to ensure that most people will not understand it and so be condemned because of their incomprehension. After all, not all those who were "outside" the inner circle with "the twelve" were somehow destined to be lost, which is what the text might otherwise seem to mean. The New Testament includes a number of statements conveying the universal vocation of salvation. [Mat 11:21. Jn 7:37; 12:32. 1Cor 10:32-33. 1Tim 2:1-4.]

Jesus puts the onus firmly on those who refuse to see what is in front of their noses. As Jesus elsewhere has Abraham remark:

> If they do not hear Moses and the prophets, neither will they be convinced if someone should rise from the dead.
> [Lk16:31 RSV]

I shall next present the evidence and arguments in support of the reality of God. I only beg my reader to take note of Jesus' warnings and give God a fair hearing on God's terms, not just their own.

Chapter 14 The Reality of God

> Do I not fill heaven and earth? says the Lord. [Jer 23:24 RSV]

> From the greatness and beauty of created things comes a corresponding perception of their Creator. [Wis 13:5 RSV]

> Do you know the ordinances of the heavens? Can you establish their rule on the earth? [Job 38:33 RSV]

> God said to Moses, "I Am who I Am." And He said, "Say this to the people of Israel, 'I Am has sent me to you.'" [Ex 3:14 RSV]

> Whatever my eyes desired I did not keep from them; I kept my heart from no pleasure, for my heart found pleasure in all my toil, and this was my reward for all my toil. Then I considered all that my hands had done and the toil I had spent in doing it, and behold, all was vanity and a striving after wind, and there was nothing to be gained under the sun. [Eccl 2:1-11 RSV]

In this chapter I shall present four arguments for the reality of God. They call upon ideas which I have developed earlier in this book and form the final justification and resolution of these ideas.

The Argument from Design

The first of the arguments for the reality of God proposes that God must be the Creator of the world, because the world is so beautiful. Finding a watch on the beach is tantamount to knowing that somewhere there is, or was, a watchmaker.[1] Similarly, the world (and in particular life) is too wonderful and complex to have come about of itself. The Argument from Design is not so much about demonstrating the mere reality of God, as about establishing God's character as an intentional originator: a Master Craftsman with specific business to conduct. Before it became clear that Darwinian natural selection might effectively favour the growth of complexity and diversity over geological time, this argument seemed a powerful one. Latterly, it fell out of favour; though in a more abstract form it is has re-emerged as the Strong Anthropic Principle.

---

1 W. Paley "Natural Theology" (1802)

The uncertainties in Darwinism

The mere fact that natural selection could in principle drive evolution, does not mean that in practice it has done so. Darwinism is constituted of two independent elements. These are: first, "mutagenesis", the fact that occasional mistakes in a cell's copying of its genes can give rise to variations which significantly affect the character of its offspring; and second, "natural selection", which prospers favourable genetic variations in accordance with the principle of "the survival of the fittest". Both of these elements have to be up to the task for Darwinian evolutionary theory to be in fact the explanation of the origin of species.[2]

The background rate of mutation

I take it for granted that evolution happened as a matter of historical fact; but this is not to say that Darwinism is the complete explanation as to how or why evolution happened. Evolution as such is a "Natural History" account of what did in fact happen, rather than a scientific theory. For Darwinism to be established as a complete explanation for evolution, it would first have to be shown that the historic rate at which random mutations appeared was large enough to provide a sufficiently diverse gene pool for natural selection to work on.

The main evidence in favour of this hypothesis is the fact that evolution has taken place; but this observation simply begs the question. It supports nothing beyond a viciously circular argument. Accepting that evolution has occurred does not force one to grant that any particular mechanism is responsible for it, and so does not establish that the historic mutation rate is large enough to account for evolution.[3] Moreover, the question at hand is complicated by two other linked considerations.

The first of these is that throughout geological time a sequence of catastrophic events has influenced the path of evolution in dramatic ways. To what extant these events impeded or provoked the diversification of life and its general increase in complexity is unclear; as is whether they can properly be described as random, rather than disastrous – or providential.

---

2 Surprisingly, Charles Darwin [1809-1882] knew nothing of genetics or mutagenesis. In particular, he was unaware of the pioneering work of the Augustinian monk, Gregor Mendel [1822-1884]. Darwin's original theory proposed no mechanism for the inheritance of characteristics; though it was based on the postulate that they are handed on.

3 The overwhelming preponderance of mutations are either harmful or else neutral in character. Only a tiny minority are at all beneficial.

The second complication is that the fossil record makes it clear that the rate of evolution is not at all steady. In particular, there was a tremendously long period (between about four thousand million years ago and about one thousand million years ago) when life on earth was confined to the oceans as single-celled organisms. Only when life colonised the land did it become diverse.[4] Hence we know that for a very long time the rate of mutagenesis was insufficient to allow evolution to produce the level of species diversity which we now observe.

It might seem that the way to decide whether the background rate of mutation is enough to explain the more recently observed facts of evolution would be to set up an experiment in which it was certain that there were no extraneous influences and to observe the rate of evolutionary change. Unfortunately, this is fraught with difficulty.

First, it would be entirely impracticable. This is because the kind of evolutionary change one is concerned with is only known to occur on a time-scale of tens of thousands of years or more. Any attempt to extrapolate from smaller changes would be crucially dependent on so many assumptions as to make it worthless. A recent experiment in which mutagenesis of the bacterium Escherichia Coli was observed in the laboratory over twenty thousand generations proved to be problematic.[5]

Second, we already know that there is no such unique number as "the rate of evolutionary change." The slow rate of change before one thousand million years ago conflicts with the fast rate characteristic of more recent times; so we know before we start that it will not be possible to obtain a single base-line rate. Either the rate of mutagenesis is itself unstable, or else the potential for mutagenesis to notably change the observable character of a living organism changes because of changing circumstances. Perhaps both of these factors are subject to significant variation, it is impossible to say.

Third, even if it were somehow shown that the rate of mutagenesis was sufficient to support the generality of evolutionary change, this would not prove that it was sufficient to give rise to every aspect of what has in fact happened. In particular, human intelligence seems to be a unique phenomenon and is therefore difficult to account for in terms of any general theory.

---

4 This aboriginal step-change in the rate of evolution may have been caused by some catastrophic event, such as a nearby super-nova bathing Earth in mutagenic radiation. Alternately, it may have been caused by the "seeding" of the biosphere with extra-terrestrial viruses as a result of comet impacts; or even by the intervention of some extra-terrestrial civilisation.

5 J.E. Barrick et al "Genome evolution and adaptation in a long-term experiment with Escherichia Coli." (2009)

Fourth, it would be impossible to be sure that one had excluded all extraneous influences. After all, if one is trying to show that "providence isn't involved in evolution" one would have to exclude providence from the experiment, which is something of a tall order. As an alternative, it may eventually become possible to model the process theoretically; but the complexity of ecological systems makes this a daunting prospect. Pending the success of either of these investigations, one must conclude that whether or not the background rate of mutagenesis is sufficient to explain evolution is an open question.

Consistency of progression

It is uncertain that, left to itself, natural selection could ever produce the wide range of highly distinctive creatures which are now found to exist. It might do so in theory; but whether it did do so in practice one simply cannot say, except as a matter of faith. It may be that the cumulative effect of random changes can only be slight, no matter what the rate of background mutagenesis; in which case Darwinism cannot account for the observed emergence of dramatic difference.

There is neither evidence nor any rationale for believing that evolution is directed towards any particular kind of outcome. Its only teleos is that of life itself: namely survival. There is no reason to believe that evolution is about the production of more sophisticated or intelligent creatures from ones that are less so. In fact, evolution sometimes produces creatures which are degenerate compared to their precursors. A well-known example of this is the existence of blind cave fish.

Evolution, as we know it, is profligate and wasteful; featuring mass extinctions and many singularly peculiar creatures. The fact that many dead-ends and catastrophic events feature in the evolutionary story makes it clear that if the process is in any way directed by an extrinsic teleos, it is not directed as the human mind generally conceives of direction. Indeed, the fact that evolution is profligate and wasteful can be used to argue that it cannot be organised by a benevolent God: for what kind of benevolent Creator would employ such a messy and ramshackle means to achieve their purpose?

This rhetorical question can be answered, however. The kind of Creator who might be at work would be less of an engineer or architect, who seeks to impose an extrinsic blue-print on the raw material of the physical world and more of an artist or poet, who makes use of pre-existent random things by incorporating them into their work in accordance with an emerging idea; a teacher or coach, who incites the innate creativity out of a student; or a lover, who elicits the intrinsic fecundity of the object of their love.

The Anthropic Principle

Given that I exist, I must of necessity do so in a Cosmos which is suitable for my existence. This observation is called the Weak Anthropic Principle. It follows from this truism that I must observe that the Cosmos is suitable for my survival. Those aspects of cosmic order which appear tuned to allow for our specific kind of life require no additional rationale. Values for the constants of Physics incompatible with the formation of carbon based macro-molecules would only rule out our own type of life, not life in general. Even if the laws of Physics were very different, then although I would not exist, some other form of life might well do so and be asking questions like "why is the Cosmos just right for me?" in my stead.

However, I shall next argue that if any of the laws of Physics were to be changed even slightly, then no life of any kind could have come into being. This contention is called the Strong Anthropic Principle. If it is true it is indisputably queer that the Cosmos is suitable for my existence in such a singular manner, and it would seem that the Universe had to be carefully engineered in order to allow for the emergence of life. Professor Paul Miller puts the case as follows:

> Although the specifics of carbon Chemistry… may not be necessary for life… a living being must contain organized complexity, or information… [which] requires… a local decrease in entropy.
>
> Entropy is… the disorder in a system, and… entropy always increases… cups fall and shatter, they do not coalesce and jump back onto their saucers. More importantly, without sustenance and breath, bodies die and decay, while corpses do not come back to life.
>
> A living being with the ability to ask the question "why am I here?" must contain an incredible amount of order to be able to frame such a deep, information filled thought, whatever kind of Chemistry or Physics underlies the being.
>
> So the question is, "what kinds of Universe could allow such order to arise?" If the answer is "just about any" then we should not be so surprised about our Universe – the right, well suited type of order would arise to fit the environment in any Universe. However, if the answer is "almost none", then we do need to question why the Universe is so special.[6]

6 P. Miller "The Anthropic Principle"

Of course, if there are an infinite number of Universes, each with its own distinctive Physics, then there is nothing to explain. No matter how unusual it is for a Universe to be "life friendly", those few which are so will give rise to life, and whenever life achieves consciousness it will start writing books like this one.

This possibility is known as the Multiverse Hypothesis. It conflicts with the hope of many theoreticians that only one Physics is coherent. If its laws featured no arbitrary parameters, then everything would be explained – except for the fundamental question: "Why is there anything at all?" It would, however, be truly remarkable if the only possible set of laws and fundamental constants is exactly the one which we know gives rise to life in such a precarious manner.[7]

On the Multiverse account of reality, one avoids invoking an infinite Creator as the designer of the Cosmos at the expense of postulating an infinite (or extremely large) set of worlds.[8] It is, however, possible to make the Multiverse hypothesis more palatable, as Miller describes:

> Many cosmologists are attempting to find what explanation they can within Science, in preference to invoking a Creator… the ripples left on the cosmic background radiation… provide strong evidence for a period of… exponential expansion… in the first 10-33 seconds of the Universe's existence. If such an era existed… There could be a plethora of… sub-Universes, that are completely unobservable to us… it is not so surprising that one of a multitude of sub-Universes happens to have the right conditions for life.

As someone suspicious of the application of probability theory to reality, I cannot resist pointing out that this argument is all about how likely it is that the Cosmos is exactly how it is. Given that the Cosmos is in fact what it is; we know the probability (in one sense of the word) that it is so; namely unity. Only if one can legitimately conceive of a set of equally likely alternatives[9] (and this necessitates knowledge of a symmetry of some unknown system which is supposed to underlie all possible Universes) can one start to ask questions such as: "What proportion of all possible Universes are compatible with life?"

---

7 This would mean that logic itself necessitates life. Of course, the prologue of John's Gospel, [Jn 1:1-4, quoted on page 49] with its statement that the Logos is both the principle of creation and the basis of life can be construed as presenting exactly this doctrine.

8 Arguably, this set constitutes "the mind of God" under another name.

9 There is a fundamental problems with probability, see page 282.

String theory is typically put forward to serve as the underlying system. This unsubstantiated theory has the property of being compatible with a large number of highly diverse types of space-time. Hence, if every possible variant of space-time is arbitrarily taken to have the same basic probability and to have somehow occurred,[9] then "it is not so surprising that one of a multitude of sub-Universes happens to have the right conditions for life." However, what is being done here is to explain a finitely surprising particular (that is, the existence of sentient life) in terms of an infinity of unsurprising particulars. It is not at all clear to me that this is a worthwhile enterprise.

Miller continues:

> It is well known that all life on Earth (barring the strange sulphurous life arising around deep-sea volcanic vents) is ultimately dependent on the inflowing energy from the sun. The sun is an average star, and, like all stars, can provide the power for life, by providing vast amounts of energy (as heat and light) at very low entropy (from a small region much hotter than the rest of the Universe).
>
> Hot spots, such as stars, are necessary to allow any form of organized complexity to arise. Living things must all take in low entropy (hot or organized) energy and release it at high entropy (useless waste heat) in order to increase or at least maintain their internal information. The "hot spots" which allow any living being to survive, must also be there for it to evolve, so must remain stable over a large period of time, compared to typical physical processes in the life cycle of the being.
>
> Now, in our Universe there is a specific resonance in the nuclear reaction process, which enables stars to burn at all, and endure for the billions of years that have been necessary for life to develop. In a Universe almost the same as ours, but perhaps with a slightly different electron mass, the resonance would not occur, stars would not shine, and the Universe would be dark, dead and dull.[10]
>
> There is a multitude of similarly finely tuned properties of our Universe... The delicate balance between the original expansion of the Universe and the gravitational attraction, which tends to pull everything back together, ensures that the explosive debris from one star can arrive in the vicinity of another star which forms separately. All life on Earth is made from atoms of debris from the first star, and relies on heat and light from the

---

10 Sir. Fred Hoyle was the astrophysicist who discovered this fact. He was an atheist at the time, but subsequently became a convinced theist.

> second star, namely our sun. In a gravitationally stronger Universe, the first star would swallow the second, while in a… more spread-out Universe, the debris would never reach another star.

This is a telling argument. Darwinism can't help here. Even if the laws of Physics could mutate, it is difficult to see how natural selection could operate. Of course, it might just be that the Cosmos is a self-consistent solution. The idea being that the Cosmos was created (or the laws of Physics at least massaged) by gods who evolve within the Cosmos and then travel back to the beginning of time to ensure that the Cosmos starts off just right. Miller expresses a related idea, more prosaically:

> A similarly untestable possibility put forth by scientific skeptics is that the Universe is really infinite in time, and just bounces in and out of big crunches[11] and big bangs. There is supposedly a new set of laws of Physics each time round (though, this is rather implausible in my view, as the new mashed-up fundamental laws must always lead to another bouncing Universe, without being specifically tuned!)

Miller concludes as follows:

> While scientific skeptics deny the Strong Anthropic Principle, many theologians and religious scientists embrace it, as it points to a Creator who stimulates life and enables us to flourish. The uncovering of such a fertile Universe, which is so clearly conducive to beauty, encourages process theologians, as it appears that the Universe follows a very thin line between rigid order and incoherent chaos. Other religious thinkers remain wary of the whole argument, and… are loathe to incorporate any scientific evidence, which may be later reinterpreted, in their vision of God. As the "many Universe" theories are not completely outside the realms of falsifiable evidence, it is perhaps right to be patient before hailing the fine-tuning as proof of God. Nevertheless, I for one do not cease to be amazed by the transcendent beauty inherent within the Laws of Nature. These will always speak to me of the nature of God.

---

11 More recent observations indicate that the expansion of the Cosmos is accelerating rather than slowing down, so it will never reverse and the Cosmos will not end in a "Big Crunch".

Probabilities and Necessities

> The argument from design strikes me as particularly weak. I will propose a counter to it in the form of a conversation between two schoolboys.
>
> The first says: "It's going to be a one!" before he roles a hundred sided die and it comes up as a one.
>
> Now the other says: "There's no way it just landed on the one by chance! A ghost must have caused it to do that."
>
> Then the first boy cooks up an uncharacteristically adult response: "Sure, my chance was one in a hundred; but what is the chance of there being a ghost?"
>
> The other boy, confused, says: "I have no idea..." The first then asks: "In which case, how can you unfavourably compare the chance of the die-roll being a 'one' all by itself to the chance of something of which we have no idea of the likelihood?"
>
> The first boy is saying that the fact that something has only a small chance of occurring *naturally*, is not a good enough reason to postulate something like a ghost; because we have no idea as to whether there is a greater chance of there being a ghost than this event occurring *naturally*. Hence, to postulate God in the view of great natural improbability is unjustified, because one is not comparing two probabilities; but rather one probability with an unknown and assuming that the unknown is larger.
>
> [J. Kramer "Private Communication" (2012)]

On a superficial level this is no counter to the argument from design. According to the notion of what a hundred sided dice is, there is a one percent chance of it doing exactly what it did and the fact that it did do what it did is no more than slightly surprising. It is not at all unaccountable – beyond the absolute unaccountability of all supposedly random events. There is no need to invoke any extrinsic cause to explain the phenomenon, once randomness is allowed to serve as an explanation for anything.

On a slightly deeper level, the parable amounts to the assertion that "When a thing happens, it has happened; and it is immaterial to argue about how 'improbable' it was. If we truly understood what was going on we might comprehend that what seemed surprising and unusual was in fact inevitable, unavoidable and certain." Now this is a true statement. It amounts to the idea that there is no such thing as truly unaccountable phenomena, no *natural* randomness. However, this is no counter to the Argument from Design, which then becomes: "The fact that what is inevitable, unavoidable and certain involves intelligent conscious life tells us that the origin of the Cosmos definitely implies life, intelligence and consciousness.[8] It is therefore reasonable to suppose that this origin also somehow encompasses these three phenomena."

There are two ways in which it would seem this is possible. The obvious way is that the origin of the Cosmos itself is in some significant sense "alive, intelligent and conscious". This is the "Personal God" hypothesis. The second is that although the origin of the Cosmos is not in any significant way itself "alive, intelligent and conscious", yet it has these three characteristics as potentialities. Similarly, the rules of chess do not constitute a game of chess but they nevertheless give rise to every game of chess that could ever be played. Similarly, the laws of Quantum Mechanics do not constitute chemical reactions but they nevertheless give rise to every chemical reaction that could ever occur. This is the "Impersonal Force of Nature" hypothesis.

The problem with the second hypothesis is that while it can serve as an explanation for life and intelligence it cannot do so for consciousness. Consciousness constitutes an aspect of reality which is entirely different from any other, and seems to be nothing like anything that could be explained in terms of the potential for abstract laws or axioms to unfold in concrete existence.[12] Hence it seems most reasonable to conclude that the origin of the Cosmos is in some significant sense conscious and so personal or hypostatic. This does nothing to explain what person, consciousness or hypostasis is; but it does account for this existential phenomenon as being derivative from an original fountainhead.

The fact that someone draws a picture of a murder, does not imply that they are themselves a murderer, or even that they approve of murder; but it does imply, among other things, that they have an idea:

1. of what life is.
2. of what death is.
3. of cause and effect.
4. that people are agents.
5. as to how one might go about killing.
6. that some people believe that killing can be justified.

The fact that someone attempts to talk about their being conscious doesn't prove that they are conscious; though it is suggestive they are so. The actual existence of consciousness within the Cosmos does, however, imply that the origin of the Cosmos is conscious or personal in some way or other.

---

12 As I have argued at length in Ch 6.

Kramer is being to unkind to his second school-boy. This young man is not asserting that one (unknown) probability is greater than another (known) one. Rather he is asserting that a particular improbability is simply too much for him to personally accept. I grant that in the particular case Kramer which dramatises his judgement is foolish; but in general such judgements are not foolish. We make them all the time and on this basis it is said "there's no such thing as a coincidence."

I further grant that such judgements are always based on common-sense and emotion, and I concede that I do not like this fact. I suppose this is why I am personally suspicious of "the Argument from Design" and find the arguments presented later in this chapter more satisfactory. Nevertheless, many Atheists use similar common-sense and emotion based judgements in rejecting the idea of God, when they claim that any explanation for the Cosmos which avoids the idea of divinity (no matter how otherwise extravagant it might be) is preferable to an explanation in terms of God. Hoyle has a point when he writes:

> Would you not say to yourself, "Some super-calculating intellect must have designed the properties of the carbon atom, otherwise the chance of my finding such an atom through the blind forces of Nature would be utterly minuscule." Of course you would... A common sense interpretation of the facts suggests that a superintellect has monkeyed with Physics, as well as with Chemistry and Biology, and that there are no blind forces worth speaking about in Nature. The numbers one calculates from the facts seem to me so overwhelming as to put this conclusion almost beyond question. [F. Hoyle "The Universe Past and Present Reflections." (1981)]

Subsequent to Hoyle's discovery, other instances of the fine tuning of Physics have come to light.[13] Perhaps the most significant of these is that relating to the "zero-point energy" of the vacuum.

Any simple quantum mechanical theory of the vacuum tends to the strange conclusion that empty space has a extremely large "zero-point energy" density; whereas common experience tells us that the vacuum has, in fact, a density pretty close to zero. Now, for a long while it was thought that the density of the vacuum was precisely zero, and once it was realised that quantum mechanics did not allow this to be true it was taken for granted that some fundamental symmetry of Physics would eventually be found which forced some other antagonistic phenomenon into exactly cancelling out the huge "zero-point energy" of the vacuum.

---

13 P. Davies "The Goldilocks Enigma" (2006) Chapters 7 & 8.

This was a plausible hope, though it was highly unsatisfactory that no definite way of effecting such a cancellation was forthcoming.

More recently, it has become accepted that the best way of accounting for certain astronomical observations is to hypothesise that the Cosmos is pervaded by "dark energy" which tends to cause it to expand at an ever increasing rate. The simplest way to account for this dark energy is to identify it with the zero-point energy of the vacuum. Unfortunately, the vacuum density compatible with the astronomical observations is about 10^{120} times smaller than the simplest finite estimate of the vacuum's zero-point energy. This huge discrepancy has been called "the worst theoretical prediction in the history of Physics!"[14]

A number like $1/10^{120}$ is difficult to stomach. It represents neither an exact cancellation, which might have a basis in some mathematical symmetry; nor an accidental cancellation. The idea that two independent contrary effects might cancel to this degree of precision is unbelievable: the ratio $1/10^{120}$ has the appearance of a contrivance or purposeful choice, in the same way as Hoyle's nuclear resonance does. Hence, it can be taken as evidence in favour of the Cosmos having an Intelligent Designer.

On the other hand, this ratio can also be taken as evidence in favour of the Multiverse hypothesis; for if this hypothesis is true, then most Universes with intelligent life can be expected to be only marginally suitable for the evolution of such life – simply because there must be many more ways of arranging things so that they are "barely adequate" than so that they are "exactly right". Now, it is presently thought that galaxy formation would be impossible if the dark energy density was as little as ten times larger than in fact it is. Hence, the level of supposed cancellation is close to the worst level acceptable; just as would be expected if the Multiverse hypothesis were true.

However, this argument is not altogether convincing; as our theories of galaxy formation may themselves be too dependent upon our specific experience. If we lived in a Universe with a dark energy density ten times larger than in fact it is, we would know that it was possible to discover a theory of galaxy formation which allowed our Galaxy to have been formed in the presence of this higher level of dark energy density. This very fact would make us persist in our theoretical endeavours until we had found such a theory. Contrariwise, because we don't live in such a universe, we have no motive to set about discovering this theory, if it exists; so we are liable never to find it and instead presume – out of conceit – that it doesn't exist.

---

14 P. Hobson et al "General Relativity: an introduction for Physicists" (2007)

The Cosmological Argument

The next argument for the reality of God is more abstract. Instead of considering the details of the material world, it treats of only the general characteristics of things. It synthesises five arguments for the reality of God which were developed by Plato and Aristotle, subsequently popularised by Thomas Aquinas and which to modern ears sound like variations on a theme. The single summary argument is called the Cosmological Argument.

All things are contingent

It is a fundamental expectation of Physics, based on a uniform experience of the material world, that every thing which one encounters will be *contingent*. Simply put, this means that it always makes sense to ask about any thing, event, process or phenomenon: "Why is this what it is?" or: "How did (or does) this come to be what it is?" or: "What gave (or gives) rise to this?" In other words, the physicist presumes that everything which they experience or observe requires explanation. It is never acceptable to say merely: "This is exactly what it is simply because it is so. It just has to be that way. There is no need to inquire further. You can and must simply accept it for what it is." Physics does not deal in "Just So Stories."

What is contingency?

It may be worthwhile to dwell a little on what contingency is. Consider a simple universe which only contains electrons. Each electron is exactly alike every other one. It has exactly the same mass and electric charge, intrinsic angular-momentum (imagine each electron to be a small spinning top) and magnetic moment. Now the properties that identify an electron as being an electron to no degree determine either its position in space or its velocity. The trajectory of each electron is, in fact, partly determined by the trajectories of every other electron; but not even an exact knowledge of the positions and velocities of every other electron would be sufficient to fix the trajectory of any one electron on which we might focus our attention.

Hence, the electron is a contingent object. A full knowledge of "what it is to be an electron" does not make it inevitable that "there is an electron" anywhere in particular – or that it must be doing anything specific wherever it might happen to be. Only when one combines a knowledge of the location and velocity of any particular electron with the fact that it is an electron, does it become definite that there is an electron doing such and such, at such a time and in such a place. However this kind of definition is not one of necessity, but only a determination by assertion or by empirical observation. Now, one might hypothesis that it is inevitable that "this electron must in fact be doing what it is in fact doing", but if one does so, every scientific aspiration is renounced; for then each empirical fact is raised to the rank of necessity and every "Why?" is deemed to be answered by "Just because it's so!"

In fact, the laws of Physics can be applied to our electron-only universe and would in principle fix the motion of every electron; if only the position and velocity of each was known at some moment in time – I leave aside the relativistic problem of "simultaneity". The laws of Physics have the function of taking one set of facts (namely the positions and velocities of all the electrons at one instant) and predicting or explaining other sets of facts (namely the subsequent trajectories of all the electrons) in terms of this first set.

The significance of contingency

Now any attempt to explain some thing or event by referring it to other things and events is unsatisfactory. First, because such explanations always refer to general laws as well as to particular things, and these laws are themselves facts, with no trace of self evidence or necessity about them; so the question always arises: "Why are these laws what they are?" Second, the other things and events require explaining just as much as does the thing or event which they are supposed to explain.

No extension of this kind of explanation can remove this basic defect and once this is clearly understood, it would seem to follow that the whole Cosmos must itself be contingent. After all, it is entirely constituted of objects and laws which each require explaining. How then could the Cosmos as a whole have a different character? It would therefore seem that the Cosmos itself requires an explanation, and that this explanation must be external to itself.

For a Physicist, the Cosmos certainly requires an explanation. The Physicist wants to have answers to the following questions. How did the Cosmos come to be what in fact is? Why does space-time happen to have the dimensionality which in fact it does have?[15] Why is the Cosmos in the low entropy state which we find it to be in, when this would seem to be so very unlikely? Why is it governed by those laws of Physics by which in actual fact it is governed, rather than by some other set of laws? Why do the fundamental constants which feature in these laws have the values which in fact they do have?

---

15 That is, three space dimensions and one time dimension.

Even if the laws of Physics are eventually shown to be necessary (in the sense that if there are to be any such laws, then they must be the very ones that they are) the question "Why are there any laws at all?" will still require an answer. This is a query about being and not-being, not about any particular way of being and, as such, it seems to be unavoidable. One can label the required explanation for the very being of all things: "God: the Uncaused Cause; the Ungoverned Governor, the Unmoving Mover and so on."

> When we find one thing producing a change in another... will there ever be in such a sequence, an original cause of change? How could anything whose motion is transmitted to it from something else be the first thing to effect an alteration?... the entire sequence of their movements must surely spring from some initial principle. [Plato "Laws" (X 895a)]

God is no thing

The riposte "All you've done is to replace the problem: 'What made the World?' with the problem: 'What caused God?'" is easily answered. The expectation of Physics that reality is contingent only relates to that category of being called "things". Things are those beings with which a material observer can interact (directly or indirectly) by an exchange of energy and momentum. Regarding beings other than "things" (if indeed there are such) Physics has no expertise whatever.

If God is real, then God is outside space-time, is not part of the Cosmos and does not interact with physical reality in the sense of exchanging energy and momentum with any thing. Although God is the foundation of all physicality God has no physicality at all. God does not exist in the way that any physical thing exists. God upholds the laws of Physics but is not governed by them. God is "no thing" and these laws simply do not apply to God as such; though they may constrain God's actions in the physical world. We can have no legitimate prior expectations of God, beyond God's reality.

We are therefore free to postulate (being motivated to do so by the pressing need to solve the contingency problem) that God is non-contingent; which means that God is necessary or absolute being. In other words, God is what God is because God is unavoidably so. God (who is "no thing") is real in a manner that no other being is real.

It would therefore seem that:

1. There is a first cause, which can be labelled God.
2. God is extra-cosmic; that is, God is neither a part of the Universe nor identical with the Universe as a whole.
3. God is Necessary Being and the Uncaused Cause.
4. God brings all Cosmic things and events into being via a metaphysical dependence which is entirely different from the physical causation of one event by another.

Some alternatives to Monotheism

There are a three alternatives to this conclusion. They are:

1. **Pantheism:** the Cosmos as a whole is not contingent.
2. **Polytheism:** the basic presumption of Physics is wrong.
3. **Solipsism:** the Cosmos is itself imaginary.

Pantheism

The theory that the Cosmos as a whole is not contingent, even though its parts are, isn't as ridiculous as it may at first seem. It might just be that everything has a variable *degree of reality* and the larger something is, the more fully real it is and the less extrinsic explanation it requires. If this were so, on the microscopic scale of Quantum Mechanics existence would be fragile – hence all the problems that physicists have with "the collapse of the wave packet" and "wave-particle duality"; on the macroscopic scale of everyday life existence would be experienced as robust but contingent; and on the cosmic scale existence would be necessary. This amounts to Pantheism: the idea that the Universe is divine and so absolutely necessary. While it sounds like a nice idea, this account strikes me as more poetic than metaphysical.

Alternately, some physicists conceive of a plurality of parallel universes, each existing with its own peculiar set of laws.[16] They then insist that although each *particular* universe has only a *possibility* of existence, the totality of all these alternate universes can be taken as absolutely inevitable. This idea can be taken still further, with each universe being pictured as fracturing into a set of sub-universes at every instant in time; so that all possible outcomes occur for every interaction which takes place within it. This is the Many World Interpretation of

16 As previously discussed, see page 238.

Quantum Mechanics.[17] In such a schizophrenic Cosmos, everything is certain and nothing unlikely, let alone impossible. It seems to me that this way lies madness; for once this outlook is adopted everything must be understood to be what and how it is merely because it is so.

Of course, this narrative doesn't account for the reality of the entire Multiverse; it simply assumes that the Multiverse as a whole is necessarily real, without admitting that this assumption is being made. While on the one hand it describes the Multiverse in the same manner as everything else (and so tacitly places it in the category of "contingent thing") on the other hand it raises the status of the Multiverse to that of being absolutely necessary. It thereby equates the Multiverse with "God" and amounts to Pantheism; because it construes the totality of physical reality (the Multiverse) as itself being non-contingent and hence divine.[18]

Polytheism

The theory that the fundamental assumption of Physics is wrong and that in fact there are a number of non-contingent things within the Cosmos amounts to Polytheism. Rather than conceiving of one transcendent God external to the Cosmos, a number of local deities are postulated. These are sources of being (space-time itself and the physical laws which go with it) and are the uncaused causes of every other thing.

This is less tidy, economical and generally satisfactory than Monotheism. In particular, it is important to appreciate that Polytheism with one god is not at all the same as Monotheism; as this single god would exist as a thing within the Cosmos and so would certainly violate the laws of Physics.

Moreover, pantheism is incoherent. If there was a thing which was necessary then it would of necessity be ubiquitous, because it would be just as true that it was necessary at every place and every time; so there would have to be an infinity of gods, divinity entirely filling up the cosmos. Now this is either absurd, as entirely at odds with the empirical evidence, or else equivalent to Pantheism or Monotheism – depending on how one envisaged this filling up. Any attempt to avoid this conclusion by conceiving of the gods as non-necessary channels of necessity, can best be understood as a return to Monotheism; with the complication that creation is understood as being mediated by contingent beings – which one might justifiably call angels rather than gods.

---

17 M. Tegmark "The Interpretation of Quantum Mechanics: Many Worlds or Many Words?" (1998) and D. Dutch "David Deutsch's Many Worlds." (1998)

18 See page 251 for a monotheistic, version of the Multiverse hypothesis.

Solipsism

The theory that the Cosmos is imaginary and that the only thing which exists is my mind amounts to the idea that I am myself God. This is "Solipsism" – an extreme form of the philosophical system called "Idealism". Although this position is formally irrefutable, the fact that it entails the idea that I can imagine geniuses such as Bach, Rembrant and Einstein – who are all capable of work which is utterly beyond my own competence – renders it implausible.

A critique of the Cosmological Argument

The only kind of explanation which completely satisfies the intellect is one which follows logically from premises that are themselves accepted as true. This kind of certainty is only available in Mathematics. The laws of Physics cannot be expected to account for things in the way that a proof in Mathematics does. Now, it can be argued[19] that:

1. The Cosmological Argument relies on the unspoken premise that "the Universe is such that a rigorous account can be given of phenomena", but there is no reason to believe this is so.
2. There cannot be a necessary axiomatic basis for the Universe; because all axiom systems are arbitrary, only being true in as far as they are coherent.
3. All consequences of necessary axioms are necessary. Hence, if there is a necessary axiomatic basis for the Cosmos, there is no place for freewill; for all events would be necessary.
4. Any necessary cause must be unchanging and could only give rise to timeless consequences. Hence, if the Cosmological Argument were true, the Cosmos ought itself to be static and eternal: but it isn't so.

Science or superstition

I reply that the Cosmological Argument is not about completely satisfying the intellect; but rather concerns itself with addressing the deficit in all contingent being. It asserts that this deficit must be supplied unless one accepts that in at least one case "Why?" is not a legitimate question; which, it must be granted, is an option. Of course, as soon as one allows that "Why?" is not *always* a legitimate question regarding any material phenomenon, one reneges on any firm commitment to Science and accepts the superiority of superstition.

19 C.D. Broad "Religion, Philosophy and Psychical Research" (1953)

God is not a set of axioms

The fact that all axiomatic systems are arbitrary does not relate to God, because there is no reason to believe that God's nature is basically that of a set of axioms. Even if some axiomatic system does fully represent God, this system would not be identical with God's being: it would only correspond to it and describe it. The necessity of God's being would lie in the divine reality itself, not in the axioms which described it.

Moreover, perhaps the unique set of axioms which corresponds to God's reality (if, indeed, there be such a set) itself has the singular property of being necessary. Given that we have no explicit knowledge of this set of axioms, it is extravagant to make definite claims about its basic nature. It is certainly unreasonable to insist that God must be of such a character which renders it impossible for God to be at all.

Necessity and freedom

The Monotheist does not concede that the Act of Creation is necessary. The Cosmos is only necessarily possible, not necessarily actual. Every mathematical theorem is necessary before it is discovered; but this doesn't mean that human mathematicians have always known about it. All that it means is that there always was (and always will be) the potential for it to be discovered.

Similarly, although the Uncaused Cause eternally implies the possibility of the Cosmos in which we live, it does not necessitate the Divine Act by which it was created. Indeed, it is not clear that the world which we inhabit is other than the imaginings of God.[20] If the Cosmos we live in exists solely within the Divine Mind, then it is liable to be one of many possible alternate universes being contemplated by God[21] and nothing of its particular form or composition will be fixed of necessity. All that would be necessary is that God should contemplate every possibility, of which our particular reality is merely one.

---

20 The alternate possibility (which seems implicit in the Genesis creation narrative) is that God *gratuitously* gave an independent reality to the idea of the Cosmos which already existed eternally in the Divine Mind; and that it is this establishment of the Universe as somewhat independent of God and at a certain distance from God's influence which constituted the Act of Creation. There was no necessity for God to do this – and if God has so acted, this divine act is, perhaps, the greatest mystery of all.

21 This is a monotheistic version of the Multiverse hypothesis.

Neither should it be maintained that every detail of the Cosmos is predetermined in the Act of Creation. It may be that every moment in time is characterized by contingency. If so, even though all events are caused (that is, they obey the laws of Physics and "one thing leads to another") some, perhaps many, event sequences could arise from instances of spontaneous symmetry breaking or singular instabilities.[22] In which case the reason why one such sequence arose rather than another would have to be looked for either in its future (and so it be allowed that causality runs backwards in time as well as forwards) or outside time altogether – either in God, or in the exercise of freewill by some sapient being.

The emergence of space and time

The question: "How can temporal facts arise from a time-independent cause?" is of the same form as: "How can spatial facts arise from a non-spatial cause?" Pleasingly, the Cosmos is of such a character as to answer this conundrum. Explicitly, there is in its existence one point (the singularity which we conventionally think of as the beginning of the Universe) where and when all of its matter and energy is collected together. Space and time only emerged from the formlessness of the original singularity once the Big Bang occurred. "Before" the Cosmos began to expand, space and time were only theoretical possibilities. Once the expansion started they became practical realities. This is exactly what one might expect, if a non-spatial and non-temporal cause gave rise to space-time.

God is not atemporal in the sense of being fixed at one moment in time. God is atemporal in the sense of not being within time at all. This fact no more prevents God from conceiving of time and making it a reality than the fact that God is not orange prevents God from making oranges.

---

22 Such singularities do not have to be of a dramatic character. The toppling of a perfect pin which was at first balanced precisely on its point springs to mind as a simple example of such an instability. The fact that in reality any such singularity would be destabilised by extraneous "random" influences does not lessen their fundamental significance.

The Ontological Argument

The next argument for the reality of God is even more abstract. It is called the Ontological Argument. It is the Philosopher's argument, whereas the Argument from Contingency is the Physicist's and the Argument from Design that of the Biologist.

> Even the fool is convinced that something exists in the understanding, at least, than which nothing greater can be conceived. For when he hears of this, he understands it, and whatever is understood exists in the understanding; and assuredly that "than which nothing greater can be conceived" cannot exist in the understanding alone. For suppose it exists in the understanding alone; then it can be conceived to exist in reality, which is greater.
>
> Therefore, if that "than which nothing greater can be conceived" exists in the understanding alone, the very being "than which nothing greater can be conceived" is one than which a greater can be conceived; but obviously this is impossible. Hence, there is no doubt that there exists a being "than which nothing greater can be conceived" and it exists both in the understanding and in reality.
>
> [Anselm, Archbishop of Canterbury[23]]

A first view

The Ontological Argument uses the idea of perfection, greatness or superiority to show that the Greatest Conceivable Being[24] is necessarily real. It can be parodied as follows: "Because it is possible to conceive of 'the best possible thing' and it is better to be real than not, then the best possible thing must be real." In this presentation the Ontological Argument is clearly flawed, because at most it only proves that one must *conceive* of the best possible thing as being real – which is no great surprise.

Similarly, it might be argued that it is possible to imagine "the Best Tooth-pick", which would not be the best if it did not exist – therefore it must be *imagined* as existing. However, to infer that this means that the Best Possible Toothpick actually exists is faulty logic. At most, all we have shown is that the "Best Possible Toothpick" must be *imagined* as existing, not that it must actually exist.

---

23 Who lived from 1033–1109.

24 The GCB is not the greatest being that some specified conceiver can conceive, but the greatest being that any possible conceiver could conceive.

> Even if it is granted that a supremely perfect being brings existence with Him because of His very title, it still doesn't follow that the existence in question is anything actual in the real world, all that follows is that the concept of existence is inseparably linked to the concept of a supreme being. So you can't infer that the existence of God is something actual (unless you help yourself to the premise that the supreme being actually exists, in which case He will actually contain all perfections, including the perfection of real existence!)
> [R. Descartes "Objections and Replies" (1641)]

The fact that we can frame a concept which can only be coherently conceived as corresponding to an existent being, does not itself mean that this being actually exists. However, as we shall see, the Ontological Argument has much greater force than this when properly presented.

Major Premise: Let it be supposed that the Greatest Conceivable Being (hereafter known as the GCB) is a thing like other things, and so is contingent. It follows that this *supposed* GCB is not necessarily real. Hence, it must be possible to conceive of this *supposed* GCB as not being real, but only imaginary; for all states of affairs which could in fact be true (in this case: "The *supposed* GCB is not real, but only imaginary.") must, at least in principle, be conceivable.

Now, it is certainly possible to conceive of this *supposed* GCB as being real; because the fact that the *supposed* GCB is *conceivable* means that there is nothing intrinsic to its constitution which stops it from being real. The only possible reason for it not being real is that either some extrinsic circumstance prevents it from so being; or else some extrinsic precondition which is required for it to be real does not prevail, which amounts to more or less the same thing.

Minor Premise: It is better to be real than to be imaginary. Hence, the *supposed* GCB, conceived of as real is better than the *supposed* GCB, conceived of as unreal. Therefore, the *supposed* GCB conceived of as unreal is not in fact the GCB. It is simply not possible for the *supposed* GCB to be conceived as imaginary, because as soon as an attempt is made to do this the being so conceived ceases to be the GCB.

Conclusion: The major premise necessarily implies that it is possible for the *supposed* GCB to be conceived as imaginary – but this has been shown to be absurd, because the GCB *must* be conceived of as being real. Therefore, the negation of the major premise must be true. Hence, the GCB is not a contingent thing like other contingent things, but is real of necessity. This Being is generally called God.

It can be objected that the two propositions "it is better to be real than to be imaginary" and "it is better to be conceived of as real than to be conceived of as imaginary" are not equivalent.[25] This is true; but the Ontological Argument doesn't rely on the idea that they are equivalent. The second proposition means that somehow it enhances a thing which is not real to be thought of as being real; but this is absurd. If a thing is in fact not real it makes no difference to its unreality that some conceiver happens to conceive of it as real. Hence, if the Ontological Argument relied on the second proposition, it would itself also be absurd.

What the Ontological Argument in fact relies on is the following argument. If "it is better to be real than to be imaginary", then "an object of thought which is conceived of as being real is a better object of thought than one otherwise identical but conceived of as only imaginary." This is not at all the same as the second proposition.

> If you attend carefully to this difference between the idea of God and every other idea, you'll undoubtedly see that, even though our understanding of other things always involves thinking of them as if they existed, it doesn't follow that they do exist but only that they could. Our understanding doesn't show us that actual existence must be conjoined with their other properties, but from our understanding that actual existence is conjoined, necessarily and always with God's other attributes, it certainly does follow that God exists.
> [R. Descartes "Objections and Replies" (1641)]

Something is not quite right

Now, in the Ontological Argument, the phrase "Greatest Conceivable Being" can be replaced everywhere by "Greatest Conceivable Toothpick" (or GCT) without changing the structure of the syllogism. The extravagant conclusion follows that the GCT is real. Recognising this difficulty, skeptics generally assert that what I have designated as the minor premise is flawed.

> The most definitive refutations of the Ontological Argument are usually attributed to the philosophers David Hume and Immanuel Kant. Kant identified the trick card up Anselm's sleeve as his slippery assumption that existence is more perfect than non-existence. The American philosopher Norman Malcolm put it like this: "The doctrine that existence is a perfection is remarkably queer. It makes sense and is true

25 G. Bodeen "Private Communication" (2012)

> to say that my future house will be a better one if it is insulated than if it is not insulated; but what could it mean to say that it will be a better house if it exists than if it does not?"[26]
> [R. Dawkin "The God Delusion" (2006)]

Kant believed that the argument is flawed because it treats existence as a descriptor which adds something to the nature of a thing. On the contrary, he asserted that a thing's nature is not enhanced by it existing; and that whether a thing exists or not is incidental to its perfection.

> Being is evidently not a real predicate, that is, a conception of something which is added to the conception of some other thing. It is merely the positing of a thing, or of certain determinations in it… The proposition "God is omnipotent" contains two conceptions, which have a certain object or content; the word "is" is no additional predicate – it merely indicates the relation of the predicate to the subject.
>
> Now, if I take the subject (God) with all its predicates (omnipotence being one), and say "God is" or "There is a God" I add no new predicate to the conception of God, I merely posit or affirm the existence of the subject with all its predicates – I posit the object in relation to my conception. The content of both is the same; and there is no addition made to the conception (which expresses merely the possibility of the object) by my cogitating the object – in the expression "it is" – as absolutely given or existing. Thus the real contains no more than the possible. [I. Kant "Critique of Pure Reason" IV (1791)]

From this it would seem to follow that a GCB conceived of as imaginary is no less than a GCB conceived of as real.

> "God is omnipotent" – that is a necessary judgement. His omnipotence cannot be denied, if the existence of a Deity is posited… But when you say "God does not exist" neither omnipotence nor any other predicate is affirmed; they must all disappear with the subject, and in this judgement there cannot exist the least self-contradiction… I find myself unable to form the slightest conception of a thing which when annihilated in thought with all its predicates, leaves behind a contradiction; and contradiction is the only criterion of impossibility in the sphere of pure a priori conceptions.
> [I. Kant "Critique of Pure Reason" IV (1791)]

---

26 N. Malcolm "Anselm's Ontological Argument." (1960)

Being real is better than being imaginary

I do not believe that Hume, Kant and Malcolm are correct. I think that it is obvious that a real house is to be preferred over an imaginary one. After all, what does "better" mean? It means something like: "provides greater advantage to its possessor in regard to those matters in which it might be expected to be advantageous," or else: "serves its purpose more adequately." In fact, "better" is a teleological term.

Now a house existing only as a set of plans provides no advantage – as a house – to its possessor whatsoever. A house that is real (even if it is far from the ideal house) is indefinitely better (that is, more effective) than one which exists only in concept or, in other words, is imaginary.[27] Similarly, an imaginary "God" is of no utility whatsoever to its own unreality, and of little use to whatever being happened to conceive of it. It is indefinitely better for God that God is real, and it is pretty obvious that this is better for humanity too – given the advantage that might be hoped to accrue from an association with the real God.

However, it can be objected that having reality does not always make a thing greater.

> Take, for example, possible worlds including or not including persons suffering everlasting torment. Many people, apparently including Christ, suppose that it would be a greater possible world where such a person was imaginary rather than real. "Better for that man if he had never been born!"[28] Since it appears false that being real is always greater than being unreal, that thing which nothing greater is conceivable may be unreal. [G. Bodeen "Private Communication" (2012)]

---

27 However, the plans for a mansion (together with the funds adequate to construct it) might be preferable to an actually existing log cabin. This is indicative of the fact that a unique metric for "better" cannot be established when more than a single criterion (such as total floor area, resilience to earthquake damage, level of thermal insulation) is involved. Which is better: a glorious palace made of glass, which is impossible to keep warm and which would collapse as a result of the slightest earth-tremor; or a small but cosy cottage with thick stone walls and a thatched roof supported on strong oak beams? In truth, it is impossible to identify one thing as greater than another thing unless the former excels (or at least equals) the latter in every regard. In connexion with God, the matter is simple: the divine nature must be conceived of as sufficiently multi-dimensional so as to be able to harmoniously accommodate and encompass every possible excellence.

28 Mat 26:24, Mk 14:21. Compare Mat 18:6, Mk 9:42, Lk 17:2.

Jesus' exclamation is only an expression of emotion. If what He said were really to be taken at face value, then it undermines the whole of the rest of His Gospel. Moreover, it is incoherent: for if the man had not been born nothing could be either good or bad (let alone better) for him. However, Jesus' statement ought not be taken in this way. It is not meant to be understood as referring to the relative value of reality and unreality, but rather as a poignant evaluation of Judas' act of betrayal.

If the Ontological Argument is valid, it has implications for how we must view "The Problem of Evil." However, the Ontological Argument should be judged on its own merits and "The Problem of Evil" then looked at in the light that it sheds. Any attempt to deal with them together is liable to produce much confusion. As to whether "someone suffering everlasting torment" is, properly speaking, conceivable; of that we cannot be sure. It may be that this is a contradiction in terms. God's mercy and justice may make it entirely impossible. One cannot use specific examples which are only *supposed* to be conceivable and only *supposed* to be intrinsically evil to refute the Ontological Argument.

The absurdity of necessary existence

Hume attacks the Ontological Argument by asserting that as anything which can be conceived of as existing can just as well be conceived of as not existing, the very idea of "the necessary existent being" is absurd.

> I shall begin with observing, that there is an evident absurdity in pretending to demonstrate a matter of fact, or to prove it by any arguments a priori. Nothing is demonstrable unless the contrary implies a contradiction. Whatever we conceive as existent, we can also conceive as non-existent. There is no being, therefore, whose non-existence implies a contradiction. Consequently there is no being, whose existence is demonstrable. I propose this argument as entirely decisive, and am willing to rest the whole controversy upon it.
>
> It is pretended, that the deity is a necessarily existent being, and this necessity of His existence is attempted to be explained by asserting, that, if we knew His whole essence or nature, we should perceive it to be as impossible for Him not to exist as for twice two not to be four. But it is evident, that this can never happen, while our faculties remain the same as at present... The words, therefore, "necessary existence" have no meaning; or which is the same thing, none that is consistent.
>
> [D. Hume "Dialogues Concerning Natural Religion" (1779)]

In my view, Hume is largely correct in the assertions he makes here; but is nevertheless mistaken in the conclusion which he draws.

First, I agree that any attempt to argue the reality of God out of nothing is doomed to failure. How could it possibly be valid to establish such a momentous result without reference to anything at all? However, the Ontological Argument in fact rests on a number of background premises, many of which are in principle disputable. They might be enumerated as follows:

1. Thought can and ought to be rational and the rules of classical logic are a good representation of rationality.
2. It is correct to speak of beings and it is correct to make a distinction between "real" and "imaginary" beings.
3. It is correct to speak of "value" and of "greater" and "lesser".
4. It is possible, in principle, to attribute relative value to beings according to various criteria.
5. It is better for a being to be real than to be imaginary, every other aspect of its constitution being unchanged.

Now, denying any of these basic premises has a much wider impact on one's world-view than making one an Atheist rather than a Monotheist. It is therefore not true that the Ontological Argument produces God out of a hat or defines God into existence. Rather, what it shows is that it not possible to be a rational Objective Realist without being a Monotheist too. In other words, the Ontological Argument shows that the structure of the Cosmos as we experience and understand it is indicative of it being derivative of Absolute Being.

Second. I agree that nothing is demonstrated conclusively unless its converse is shown to be absurd. However, this is exactly what the Ontological Argument, as presented here, claims to do.

Third, I agree that any thing which exists might just as well not do so. However, the Ontological Argument as presented here does not deal with physical existence but rather with reality; and it is not at all clear that every being which is real might not be so. *This is in fact exactly the point at issue.* To simply presume that all of reality is contingent is to fatally prejudice the question. A second unwarranted assumption: that the only way in which a being can have reality is by it having material existence is equally prejudicial.

Finally, I concede that it is ludicrous to suggest that the human mind could comprehend the Divine Nature, should there be such. However, it turns out that it is not necessary to do this in order to understand how it is that God is necessary being.

The incompatibility objection

It can be argued that the GCB is a contradiction in terms as some perfections are incompatible, not just incommensurate. Hence, whereas it is possible for a being to be both perfectly square and perfectly circular if its reality is at least three-dimensional;[29] it is not possible for a judge to be both perfectly just and perfectly merciful. This is, supposedly, because justice amounts to "giving to each subject exactly what they deserve" and mercy amounts to being more generous than this, at least in some cases. Hence justice and mercy are in conflict and it is impossible to be perfectly just and perfectly merciful. Multiplying dimensions simply doesn't help here.

To this objection I reply by questioning the basic assumption that any perfections can be absolutely contradictory. In particular, I reject the definitions of mercy and justice that the example entails. So far as God is concerned, no created being actually deserves anything of its own right; so all of God's actions towards creatures are essentially those of mercy[30] not justice. However, it is only proportionate, right and proper that God does act towards creatures with mercy; for else they could not exist and the very act of creation would be made into an absurdity. So, in God justice and mercy do not conflict but are corroborative aspects of the same reality.

Moreover, it is also just of God to be merciful to the sinner in view of the fact that God foresees that in the future they will be a saint, if only God is presently merciful. Arguably, the same is true in the human context also. It is just to be merciful; where mercy means giving a culprit a chance to repent and change their ways. It is merciful to be just; where justice means imposing a penalty which is crafted to bring about penitence and reformation in the heart of the wrongdoer.

I maintain that any other supposed examples of incompatible perfections could be dealt with either by postulating a sufficient dimensionality for God or else by elucidating the true nature of the perfections involved and in doing so establishing that their apparent incompatibility is illusory.

---

29 This is a cylinder with a length equal to its diameter.

30 The word mercy does not simply mean "letting someone off a punishment which they deserve as a result of misbehaviour". It also means kindness, generosity and benevolence. The "Good Samaritan" was, in this sense, merciful to the man who had been set upon by thieves and left for dead when he came to his aid. [Lk 10:37] When the eastern liturgies cry out over and over "Lord, have mercy!" they are not asking for forgiveness, but rather for divine assistance.

> Your choice of a Toothpick was much too trivial. The standard counterargument replaces theism with maltheism: the greatest possible malevolent being; when such a solution is plugged into the Ontological Argument, it has all the same greatnesses of the GCB including necessary non-physical reality except that instead of loving humanity it hates humanity.
> [G. Bodeen "Private Communication" (2012)]

Such an argument confuses evil for a form of being. It is closely connected with Bodeen's previous objection.[31] I would contend that evil is always a deficit of being, so that which is evil is always less than that which is good. In any case, this objection would not invalidate the Ontological Argument. As Bodeen admits, if one ignores the idea that "evil is a deficit of being" the Ontological Argument still works: only it would not be clear whether the GCB was good or evil or some hybrid of both. The question of the moral character of the GCB is independent of whether the GCB is real or not.

> Consider an analogy with numbers. Whether you pick a finite number or a transfinite number, there is always a greater conceivable number. Similarly, if the greatness of a being is evaluated by its possession of properties, then there is always a greater conceivable being with either a greater number of properties or a greater degree of those properties. In that case that thing which nothing greater is conceivable is not well-defined: it seems to refer to a possible entity but does not.
> [G. Bodeen "Private Communication" (2012)]

God is absolutely infinite: neither finite nor transfinite. I have already explained that the divine nature must be conceived of as multidimensional so as to accommodate an absolute infinity of excellences. Moreover, God is not a number and Bodeen's argument relies on an analogy. In the same way, God is not a thing, but a "being" – and a being which is as unlike any thing as absolute infinity is unlike any number. Analogies do not constitute any kind of argument as they are only as valid as they happen to be valid, and no more so; and to determine the scope of their validity requires a fundamental understanding of the state of affairs, which cannot itself be based on the analogy.

---

31 See page 257.

The real difficulty

The real difficulty with the Ontological Argument – the feature that invalidates the extravagant conclusion that "the Greatest Conceivable Toothpick exists" – is quite different from what Hume, Kant and Malcolm envisage. It is that in conceiving of the GCT as existing one is forced to derogate from its perfection.

No physical toothpick could be perfectly sharp or perfectly rigid or perfectly resistant to corrosion. Hence when one tries to compare the imaginary GCT with its best possible material realisation, one cannot unequivocally say which is "greater"; for though any physical toothpick has indefinitely greater practical utility, the ideal toothpick is in every theoretical way indefinitely better. Hence one cannot conclude that the GCT conceived of as existing is in fact a greater object of thought that the GCT conceived of as only imaginary, and so one cannot infer that the GCT necessarily exists.

A similar argument will apply to any other "Greatest Conceivable Thing". The granular and quantum-mechanical nature of matter will always prevent its exact physical realization. Hence, there is always at least one "extrinsic circumstance" which necessarily prevents us conceiving of any "Greatest Conceivable Thing" as actually existing. This circumstance is simply "materiality" or "existence" itself; which limitation happily prevents the Ontological Argument from generating a multitude of spurious "Greatest Conceivable Things".

> The only existence that is at issue here is necessary existence, which gives the thing that has it the power to create itself or to keep itself in existence, and when I examine the idea of a body[32] I perceive that no body has such a power as that. From this I infer that necessary existence doesn't belong to the nature of a body – however perfect it may be – any more than being without lowlands belongs to the nature of highlands[33] or having angles summing to more than 180° belongs to the nature of a triangle![34]
> [R. Descartes "Objections and Replies" (1641)]

However, this circumstance fails to apply as soon as one abstracts one's thought beyond material things to consider beings in general

32 The word "body" is here used in the way that I use the word "thing".

33 Descartes seems to mean that a highland region might contain some lowlands without ceasing to be a highland region: no existent thing has to be entirely perfect, let alone self-existent.

34 Descartes takes this to be absurd – though, of course, it is not; if the triangle is drawn on the surface of a sphere.

which do not obviously have to be part of the physical contingent order. Hence, the "flaw" that we have identified in the Ontological Argument does not hinder its application to the GCB, which is not supposed to *physically exist*, but rather to *be real*.

> Now let us turn from body and consider the idea of a thing[35] – whatever it turns out to be – that has all the perfections that can exist together. Is existence[36] one of these perfections? We will be in some doubt about this at first, because our finite mind is accustomed to thinking of these perfections only separately, so that it may not immediately notice the necessity of their being joined together. But if we address ourselves attentively to the questions: "Does existence[37] belong to a supremely powerful being?" and – if it does – "What sort of existence[37] is it?" we'll be able to perceive clearly and distinctly the following facts.
> (1) Possible existence,[37] at the very least, belongs to such a being, just as it belongs to everything else of which we have a distinct idea, even if it's an idea put together through a fiction of the intellect.
> (2) When we attend to the immense power of this supremely powerful being we shan't be able to think of its existence[37] as possible without also recognising that the being can exist by its own power, from which we'll infer that it really does exist and has existed from eternity.[37]
> [R. Descartes "Objections and Replies" (1641)]

The Forms

Interestingly, the Ontological Argument is applicable to any simple concept such as "triangle" or "the solution of this algebraic equation" and arguably to ideas such as "justice", "beauty" and "friendship". The only qualification required of such a concept is that all of its excellences are independent – that is every one of them can simultaneously be optimized without conflict.

---

35 In this translation, Descartes uses "thing" in the way that I use "being". Note that the rest of this extract employs the word "being".

36 In this translation, Descartes uses "existence" here in the way which I use "reality".

37 The final step in Descartes' argument is mistaken, as it is presented here. The fact that some particular being, if real, would be capable of sustaining itself does not entail that this being is in fact real and does sustain itself; but only that if it were real, it would not be dependent for its sustenance on any extrinsic circumstance.

The perfect horse (the Lowest Common Denominator of horses, if you like) cannot be real; for the excellence of a carthorse excludes that of a racehorse. However, when one eliminates from the idea of horse all those characteristics which differentiate types of horses, one arrives at an idea of what a horse necessarily is. This is the Ideal or Formal Horse: the Highest Common Factor of all horses. This isn't itself a horse, as it lacks many attributes (such as any particular level of strength or ability to gallop) which are basic to any horse. Even so, the Ontological Argument can be applied to this pared down Ideal Horse to show that it is necessarily real even though it doesn't exist. Similarly, it seems plausible that the Greatest Conceivable Toothpick is also real, though it does not exist. The reality of the Forms can be understood as them either all being "ideas in the mind of God" or else constitutive aspects of the divine nature, which amounts to much the same thing.

Pascal's Wager

Pascal pointed out that the arguments for and against the reality of God – or, more fundamentally, whether that there was any point to "life the Universe and Everything" – were not fairly balanced, even in the absence of any evidence one way or the other. Following Plato's account of Socrates' argument,[38] Pascal observed that either there was a purpose to life or there wasn't. Moreover, one could either live one's life as if there was a point to it all or as if there was no such point. Now, if there is in fact no point to life it doesn't matter at all how one lives – because there is no significance in anything whatever. On the contrary, if there is in fact a point to life it behoves us to attempt to discover it, and to do our best to live according to our best appreciation of whatever the significance and purpose of life might be.[39]

---

38 Plato reports Socrates arguing that it makes sense to believe that there is a good life after bodily death. He observes that either this hope is true, in which case one should live one's mortal life preparing for the blessed eternity which follows; or else it is false, and one might as well act according to the same (misguided) hope: because at least then one will live without fear and be of good cheer. See "Phaedo" (91a-b), quoted in the dedication of this book, on page 3.

39 Pensées (1670). Pascal actually worded his argument in terms of the existence of God and of personal benefit and happiness. His version of the argument can, therefore, be construed as recommending the abandonment of personal integrity for the sake of selfish gratification; but I do not believe this to have been Pascal's fundamental intent. Of course, I have argued in Chapter 4, that the purpose of life is manifest.

Hence, whether or not life has any value or rationale it makes sense to act as if it does. This is because if life has no purpose one has nothing to lose by living as if it did have one, even though one is wrong; whereas if it does have a rationale one has very much to gain: in potential, the attainment of that value and the fulfilment of the purpose of life. Hence the rational person is compelled by their rationality to act as if life has value and is purposeful, and to seek to discover – as well they may – what that value and purpose might be. There is no possible motive for acting otherwise and to do so would be irrational and imprudent.[40]

Moreover, there cannot exist any valid argument or evidence against the proposition that existence is significant. This is because if there were such a valid argument or evidence then that argument or evidence at least would have significance, meaning and some kind of value; but this possibility is excluded by the supposed conclusion of the argument itself, namely: "Life the Universe and Everything are devoid of value and significance."[41] Furthermore, this statement is itself incoherent, for if it were true it would be of significance and so contradict itself. So if one is going to be rational one must adopt its negation; which amounts to the statement: "there is, of necessity, some significance to be found in Life the Universe and Everything." The astute reader will recognise here a version of the Ontological Argument; where rationality itself here gives rise to the necessity of value and significance rather than to "The Greatest Conceivable Being" as such.

Of course, neither Pascal's Wager nor the version of the Ontological Argument which I have suggested that it implies directly addresses the reality of God. However, once one recognises that God is identical with the basis of value ("The Good", as Plato names this) then there is little to be chosen between the statements "God is real" and "Being has significance."

---

40 This purpose might be no more than hedonistic pleasure; in which case the fact that it is rational to live life as if it had significance would not force any-one to behave in a prudent or sober manner. However, people typically find that the pursuit of pleasure or fun or excitement as goals in their own right is ultimately unsatisfying. This is because these good things are in fact not the ultimate good, but at best contributors to and indicators of that good.

41 It could be argued that if everything is pointless, then even this proposition is pointless and while it seems to have a significance this is no more than a delusion. However, if this is the case, how does it come to be the case that the contention is being pressed that "life is devoid of significance"? It would seem that the idea that anyone would bother to argue this case is incompatible with the case which they are supposed to be arguing for.

The Argument from Justice

For ethics to be possible, it would seem that two elements are necessary: first, the continual threat of harm – up to that of avoidable death;[42] and second, the continual hope of safety. What results from the interplay of these two elements is a game where the achievable objective is to "live for ever" and the winning strategy is "wholesome and just living".

Human mortality is incompatible with justice

According to the account of the basis of ethics given in Chapter 7, it would seem that ethics is impossible within the world as we find it. This is because the ongoing threat to life is of a much higher calibre than is compatible with ethics. It encompasses not only the possibility of injury and of avoidable death, but also the certainty of mortality. This renders all attempts to survive futile.

If the individual is doomed to die someday, then what exactly is the point of somewhat postponing that day? How can there be a rational motivation to do what is necessary to preserve life? After all, no act or policy can obtain this goal. Moreover, if life itself is the basic value for a living being and yet life is not a sound currency (being debased by the certainty of death) nothing can have any stable value, because the foundation of value is itself not firm.

Justice is concerned with the wide-range and long-term implications of acts, as opposed to their immediate impact; but if "in the long run we are all dead"[43] such concerns are irrational. To be concerned with what would good for us when we no longer exist and are therefore incapable of benefiting from anything is incoherent. Hence, mortality makes injustice and irresponsibility entirely reasonable.[44] Indeed, the long-term perspective which is necessary to motivate a prudent attitude is precluded by the inevitability of death. Hence it would seem that any rational mortal should ruthlessly pursue immediate gratification. They should "seize the day", reckless of possible harm and remorseless when confronted with actual negative consequences.[45]

It can be argued that a concern for justice can be rationalised in terms of the benevolence of parents for their children and for future generations beyond them. Now it is true that parents have an instinctive

42 See page 192.

43 J.M. Keynes "A Tract on Monetary Reform" (1923)

44 As I have already argued, see page 167.

45 I do not mean to imply that the motto "seize the day" is immoral, but only that it is inadequate. Ruthlessness, recklessness and remorselessness are the basis of wickedness. [LNS Ch 8]

concern for their children and even grandchildren – if only they meet them – but this is no sound rationale for justice. First, because familial bonds are always partisan and are often inimical to justice. Second, because this kind of concern for progeny is itself irrational, being based on the exigencies of the "selfish gene". Third, because it does not extend to the indefinite future, but only to those generations which can be clearly envisaged and empathised with; whereas a true concern for justice might be more focussed on those individuals with whom one has no personal connection whatsoever.

Human immortality is incompatible with justice

The human spirit's supposed immortality doesn't make ethics, as I have accounted for it, any more rational. The problem we here encounter is the opposite of what I have just previously described. Instead of all effort to survive being futile, now it would seem that no effort whatsoever has to be made; because survival is guaranteed whatever the individual does. Hence, immortality makes irresponsibility and injustice every bit as reasonable as does mortality.

Heaven and Hell

The standard way out of this conundrum is to adopt the idea of extrinsic post-mortem reward and retribution; but this doctrine does not make any sense. It depends on two strange ideas. First, that God freezes the ethical character of every soul at the moment of death, such that from this moment they are incapable of moral improvement; and, second, that God punishes wrongdoers in a manner which is additional to the inevitable outworking of their wrongdoing.

This doctrine combines the promise of eternity with the threat of indefinitely severe retributive punishment, and so transforms the most desirable prize of all – eternity life – into a highly undesirable penalty – eternal damnation. It also implies that justice is defined relative to God: that what is wrong is wrong fundamentally because God punishes it, and what is right is right fundamentally because God rewards it; but in that case, why should God bother with vice and virtue at all?[46] After all, none of the actions of humanity can possibly harm God, so why should God bother to punish any of them? Contrariwise, the idea of objective justice only makes sense if virtue brings its own prize, and vice its own penalty; just as the Apostle Paul suggests, when he writes "The wages[47] of sin are death."[48]

46 Job 7:17-20, quoted on page 183.
47 The Greek is "όψώνιον": a soldier's rations or allowance. [cf Lk 3:14]
48 Rom 6:23 RSV.

Moreover, God takes no delight in punishing anyone, and as soon as anyone repents, God is ready to forgive.[49] This being so, what could motivate God to heap extra punishment onto the head of a sinner above the suffering that inevitably results from their sin, especially if it is entirely ineffective at evoking repentance?

I suppose that God could have a just concern to deter wrongdoing by imposing a penalty on the perpetrator in addition to the harm which they would suffer as a result of the act – perhaps to reflect back on the wrongdoer the harm that their actions would have on others.[50] So, it could be to the great advantage of a person contemplating murder to be deterred from committing murder by dint of a fear of retribution in addition to the simple fact that the act of murder will traumatise and dehumanise them. However, there would be no need to make the deterrent infinitely severe in order for it to be effective. In fact to do so would be a bad juridical strategy; because it would mean that once anyone has committed one murder they might as well commit others, as they can expect to be punished with infinite severity in any case.

Soul and Spirit

The answer to our conundrum "How can Justice be justified within human existence?" is to be found in the distinction I have proposed between soul and spirit. It is the human spirit which is immortal, but the human soul which is either moral or immoral.

The immortality of the spirit gives some intrinsic basis for hope; but the quality of such immortality, divorced from a soul and body (and so unable to experience and effect reality) would be minimal. Arguably it would be entirely unconscious and therefore subjectively indistinguishable from non-existence. Only the extrinsic divine promise of a bodily resurrection (and so the post-mortem survival of the soul as well as the spirit) can give hope of a worthwhile life after death. It does so on the basis that this eternal life will be enjoyable and engaging; the soul being occupied with the contemplation of God's beauty and in convivial conversation with the angels and saints.

Mortal life is the preparation for this communion. Virtuous habits must be established in the soul before it can be commenced, and a personal understanding of justice must be attained. Only then can the soul aspire to friendship with God as some kind of equal; being able

---

49 Wis 11:23-12:2 and Ezk 18:21-23, quoted on pages 116 and 164.

50 This is the first rationale for the Catholic doctrine of Purgatory: that even when one has been forgiven by God there is still a need to do penance and make restitution for the harm that one's sin has done to others. Technically, this equitable debt is called "the temporal punishment due to sin".

to enjoy harmonious and rational intercourse with God based on this shared knowledge. Once divine communion is achieved, justice as I have accounted it (the habitual character of soul which fits and enables an agent to do what promotes their continuing life) becomes superfluous. What remains relevant is the harmonious, peaceful and coordinated quality of soul which this practical pursuit of justice has achieved and which is altogether necessary for association with God.

A soul which has become entirely virtuous by the moment of bodily death, has no need for any improvement pending the resurrection; but a soul which has not achieved this goal and is still disordered by bad habits, is in need of further sanctification. The requisite post-mortem process of purification is liable to involve suffering;[51] just as does the moral struggle we experience between birth and death. It is partly the prospect of the pain associated with this purgation which should deter the soul from wrongdoing in this life; for it is particular acts which establish unwholesome habits that must be overcome before the soul can enjoy eternal life with God.

A soul which has become irredeemably vicious[52] before death is incapable of improvement pending the resurrection and will be unable to sustain itself afterwards. Hence, the soul of the altogether wicked individual is doomed even as their body is raised[53]. Although their spirit is immortal, their body and soul will shrivel, decay and dissipate; not as a result of any divine intervention to harm them, but as a direct result of their own unwholesomeness and internal disunity, the terminal illness of their way of being. For the irredeemably wicked, the resurrection is not to eternal life, therefore, but to eternal death.

> They shall suffer the punishment of eternal destruction and exclusion from the presence of the Lord and from the glory of his might, when he comes on that day to be glorified in his saints. [2Thes 1:9-10 RSV][54]

Jesus compares this with being cast into Jerusalem's smouldering rubbish dump Gehenna, mistranslated by the RSV as "the hell of fire":

> "Whoever says, 'You fool!' shall be liable to the hell of fire." [Mat 5:22 RSV][55]

---

51 This process is often described as a purifying fire. It is a second basis of the Catholic doctrine of Purgatory. See page 117.

52 See page 290.

53 Acts 24:15.

54 Also: 2Mac 7:14. Jas 5:20. Mat 7:13; 10:28. Apoc 20:6.

55 Also: Mat 7:19; 18:9. Mk 9:43. Jn 15:6.

or as being cast into "outer darkness":

> "Truly, I say to you, not even in Israel have I found such faith. I tell you, many will come from east and west and sit at table with Abraham, Isaac, and Jacob in the kingdom of heaven, while the sons of the kingdom will be thrown into the outer darkness." [Mat 8:10-12 RSV][56]

or a "furnace of fire":

> "The angels will... separate the evil... and throw them into the furnace[57] of fire." [Mat 13:49-50 RSV][58]

or eternal flames:

> "If your hand or your foot causes you to sin, cut it off... it is better for you to enter life maimed or lame than… to be thrown into the eternal fire." [Mat 18:8 RSV][59]

or else eternal punishment:

> "Then they also will answer, 'Lord, when did we… not minister to thee?' Then he will answer them, 'Truly, I say to you, as you did it not to one of the least of these, you did it not to me.' And they will go away into eternal[60] punishment,[61] but the righteous into eternal[61] life." [Mat 25:44-46 RSV]

I suggest that this diversity of expression arises from the fact that Jesus is referring sometimes to the reformatory sufferings of Purgatory and sometimes to the terrible possibility of "final damnation" which consists of the self-destruction of the soul combined with the pathetic persistence of the spirit in Sheol.[62]

---

56 Also: Mat 22:13; 25:30.

57 The Greek is "κάμινος": an oven used for refining metal, baking bread or firing pottery. In all applications, the fire is transforming not destructive.

58 Also: Mk 9:43,48. Lk 16:24.

59 Also: Mat 25:41. Mk 9:43, 48.

60 The Greek is "αιωνιος": eternal, endless or everlasting.

61 The Greek is "κόλασις": to correct; from "κόλος": a dwarf. Hence to prune or cut down to size.

62 See page 109.

A life motivated by a "hunger and thirst for righteousness"[63] ends in the stable possession of God; because the person who lives such a life is thereby "transformed by the renewal"[64] of their soul so that they are "conformed to the image"[65] of the divine Logos until they "have put off the old nature with its practices and have put on the new nature, which is being renewed in knowledge after the image of its creator."[66]

Recapitulation of the argument

Premise one: Justice is of definite value, and is rational.
Premise two: Death makes justice irrational.
Conclusion one: Death cannot be the absolute termination of life.

Premise three: The certain prolongation life after death also makes justice irrational.
Conclusion two: Life after death must have a different quality than life before death. It must be sufficiently similar to it as to make mortal life a suitable prologue for immortality, but sufficiently different from it so as not to subvert the nature of Justice.

Solution: The Justice which we aspire to in this mortal life is the projection onto temporal affairs of an eternal stability. As Life is an echo of eternal stability, so is Justice also a participation in that stability. Personal or internal justice is its psychological image. Social or external justice is its sociological and political image, which is the proper way for individuals to communicate in society.[67]

The purpose of mortal life is first to maximise its own mortal existence, this is the very nature of life; but second, and more significantly, to attain immortality by coming to share in the eternal stability which is the basis of both Life and Justice. Both of these goals motivate virtue; because within the human soul virtue is identical with peaceful and harmonious order. The eternal stability to which mortal life aspires is what we otherwise name God.

---

63 Mat 5:6 RSV, see also Is 56:1.
64 Rom 12:2 RSV, quoted in full on page 143.
65 Rom 8:29 RSV.
66 Col 3:9-10 RSV.
67 The correlation of personal and social justice is masterfully explored by Plato in "Republic".

Chapter 15 Will and Grace

> Now the Lord is the Spirit, and where the Spirit of the Lord is, there is freedom. [2Cor 3:17 RSV]

Motivation

Much of this book is about process, education and becoming. In particular, I have argued that God steps back from centre stage in the human drama in order to give us the autonomy, space and freedom to learn, grow and mature. Now this all presumes that the idea of freedom makes sense; but this is not obviously the case.

Most religions are split into two camps. One faction claims that human beings are free agents, able to determine their own actions, as self-moving movers[1] independently of external control. They claim that the future is ours to create. The second faction claims that God's decree (or karma or fate) determines every event and that human autonomy is no more than a mirage. The existence of this disagreement is no kind of argument against the validity of a religious outlook on life. Indeed, it does not originate from any properly theological problem; rather, it is a manifestation of a deep philosophical problem.

The problem of freewill

In the absence of autonomy, a human being seems to be no different in principle from an animal or mechanism and it is difficult to see on what basis one might argue that human beings have a special dignity and inalienable rights. Hence, it seems to be necessary to insist on the existence of human freewill and self-determination if one is to uphold any idea of justice; yet, as we shall see, it is difficult to explain what might be meant by freewill or to account for how it comes about.

The classical problem of freewill[2] can be posed in the following psychological terms. It would seem that freewill cannot possibly exist: for either everything that I do is either determined by my past and present experience; or else it is not. If it is so determined, I have no

---

1 This self-mover is also the source and spring of motion in everything else that moves; and a source has no beginning... since we have found that a self-mover is immortal, we should have no qualms about declaring that this is the very essence and principle of a soul. [Plato "Phaedrus" (245c-e)]

2 D.J. O'Conner "Freewill." (1971)

freewill: for my actions are fixed by external factors. Contrariwise, if it is not so determined, then any "freewill" I have is indistinguishable from random behaviour, can have no ethical significance, and is not at all what one naïvely means by freewill.

A second version of the problem is the Metaphysicist's difficulty. Every action has a cause and, on a naïve account of Newtonian Mechanics, causes determine act, effects and events. Hence, freewill is incompatible with Newtonian determinism. If an escape from this conclusion is attempted by recourse to a dualistic particle-wave interpretation of Quantum Mechanics (where causes do not determine effects, but only the probabilities of events) one finishes up with the prospect of a universe of individual events all of which are absolutely arbitrary (which means that no account can be give of them) and so are devoid of any possible ethical significance.

Causality and determinism

While these two versions of the problem are not identical, I think they are equivalent. I shall next argue that both syllogisms are invalid. In order to do so, I shall distinguish clearly between the verbs *cause* and *determine*. In common use these are synonyms; but in philosophic use, Popper has shown[3] that a valid distinction can be drawn.

To physically *determine* something is to fix it either beforehand in time or remotely in space, with full knowledge of what one is achieving and with whatever degree of precision is desired. This involves the idea that there exists some formula or set of formulae which can be used to calculate the outcome of some circumstance more quickly than it comes to be physically realised. Quite apart from the complications introduced by Quantum Mechanics, the laws of Physics do not generally allow this. Ironically, it can sometimes be calculated that to calculate the response of a system more quickly than in fact it responds would require a computer larger than the observable universe.

To metaphysically *cause* something is a weaker (but much more important) concept. To be the cause of some effect is to be that which it depends upon; such that the existence of the effect can be traced back to the cause. A cause is that reality apart from which the thing in question would not be what in fact it is. There is no need that any degree of knowledge (not even exact precision) of the cause(s) of an effect should predictably determine it in any sense beyond the obvious fact that if one follows the subsequent sequence of events one will always discover what actually happens.

3 K.R. Popper "Indeterminism in Quantum Physics and in Classical Physics" (1951-2)

The Butterfly Effect

It is characteristic of linear Newtonian Mechanics[4] that all causes are deterministic. This means that it is a relatively simple matter to extrapolate from what one knows about the here and now to temporally or spatially distant events and results.[5] As soon as non-linearity is envisaged, however, this characteristic fails.[6] The remote result (in space or time) of any cause becomes highly unpredictable, no matter how accurately the cause is initially specified. This characteristic is commonly known as "The Butterfly Effect"; with reference to the idea that the fluttering of the wings of a butterfly in a Hampshire garden might give rise to a hurricane over Miami.[7]

The magnetic pendulum

A simple example is the magnetic pendulum. Consider a standard pendulum, free to swing in any direction, whose bob is a lump of soft iron. Place beneath it a horse-shoe magnet, such that the two poles lie in a horizontal plane just below the lowest point which the bob can reach, with the body of the magnet symmetrical about the vertical dropped from the point of support of the pendulum. Obviously, the bob has two symmetrical possible points of lowest potential energy. Each is close to one or other of the magnetic poles. These two points of static equilibrium can be labelled "Green" and "Purple".

Now consider the following thought experiment. Keeping the line which supports the bob tense, deviate it from the vertical by an angle θ

---

4 Linear mechanics is defined by the characteristic that the response of a linear system to the simultaneous application of any two stimuli, inputs or disturbances is given by the arithmetic sum of its separate responses to each individual stimulus. Linear mechanics governs only the simplest of things, for example the swinging of a pendulum – as long as the angle of swing is small. Linear mechanics is beloved by physicists because it is possible to predict the behaviour of any system so governed with great exactitude. In other words, linear mechanics is deterministic.

5 This is related to a result in Physics called Liouville's Theorem, [Symon "Mechanics" Ch 9 (1971)] which states that the degree of indeterminacy of a system's configuration remains the same (rather than increasing, as one might have expected) as time proceeds.

6 The response of a non-linear systems to two simultaneous stimuli is not given by the arithmetic sum of its separate responses to each independent stimulus, but is instead something else entirely. No real system is perfectly linear; and all complex systems (such as any that involve the flow of gas or liquid, see page 61) are highly non-linear.

7 This idea is explored in the film "The Butterfly Effect", written and directed by E. Bress & J.M. Gruber (New Line Cinema, 2004).

along the compass direction specified by an azimuthal angle φ measured clockwise from the line joining the centres of the two magnetic poles. Hold the bob at rest in this position, then let it go without imposing any initial velocity.

The bob will start to fall under the influence of gravity, and in response to the magnetic attraction of the poles of the horse-shoe magnet. It will begin to swing about in some complex pattern of movement. As the bob picks up speed, it will start to loose energy to atmospheric drag; so it will slow down and eventually come to rest near one or other of the two magnetic poles. The outcome of the experiment can therefore be identified as either "Green" or "Purple", in accordance with which of the two alternative final states is in fact attained.

This experiment can be repeated over and over again, for different initial positions; that is, different values of θ and φ. A graph can then be compiled of all the results obtained. Plotting θ on the horizontal or x-axis and φ on the vertical or y-axis, each trial can be represented as a single green or purple dot, depending on the bob's final position of rest.

If the bob is released close to either pole, it will come to rest quickly enough. There will be a compact region of green dots surrounding and close to "$\theta=\theta_0$" and "$\varphi=0$", which represents the "Green" point of minimum potential energy. Similarly, there will be a compact region of purple dots surrounding and close to "$\theta=\theta_0$" and "$\varphi=180^\circ$", which represents the "Purple" point of minimum potential energy.

The common sense expectation would be for the rest of the graph to be symmetrical and divided up into compact clusters of green and purple dots, which could be merged into simply shaped blotches. In fact, while the graph is symmetrical, it features areas where regions of green dots are penetrated by smaller regions of purple dots which are penetrated in turn by even smaller regions of green dots and so on, indefinitely. This is an example of fractal Physics[8] and such phenomena are common to all non-linear systems – that is, all real one.

Although the simple equations of Newtonian Physics govern the trajectory[9] of the bob at every instant, the end result is very often not

8 See pages 52 to 61.

9 In Mathematical Physics, the trajectory of a point object consists of a parametrical time-plot of its three-dimensional position and three-dimensional velocity taken together in a six-dimensional mathematical vector space called "phase space". This can be generalized to a system consisting of N particles, by extending the dimensionality of phase space to "6N". Liouville's Theorem can then be stated as follows: "The uncertainty in the configuration of any system, measured as a 6N hyper-volume in phase space is constant in time." In principle, the system considered could be the whole Cosmos, in which case N would be exceedingly large.

determined by any level of accuracy to which the initial conditions $[\theta,\varphi]$ are specified.[10] This is nothing to do with random air movements, Brownian Motion, the microscopic variability of viscosity or Quantum Mechanics. All these would confuse the situation in practice; but even when the pure Newtonian system is modelled with ultimate numerical accuracy, the type of behaviour I have described inevitably results.

Ubiquitous radical indeterminacy

At first, when the magnetic pendulum is released, its trajectory is predictable. Tiny changes in its initial conditions produce only tiny changes in its subsequent motion. However, as it is a non-linear system, this behaviour cannot continue. At some point, its trajectory ceases to be well defined by the initial conditions; the precision with which these have to be applied in order to have an accurate idea of what the system's motion will be falls indefinitely close to zero – that is, ultimate and unattainable accuracy.

What at first had seemed to be a single trajectory is revealed to have been, all along, an indefinitely tight bundle of alternate trajectories. Eventually, this bundle unravels and its constituent trajectories (which had at first kept close formation) diverge rapidly – so rapidly, in fact, that they soon lose any semblance of similarity.[11]

The result of this unravelling of trajectory bundles is that two indefinitely similar starting positions can result in two radically different outcomes. So, if the initial position $[\theta_1,\varphi_1]$ results in the final outcome "Green" it is entirely possible that the initial position $[\theta_1+\varepsilon,\varphi_1+\eta]$ will result in the final outcome "Purple" for very many combinations of *indefinitely* small values of ε and η.[12]

10 The presence of non-linearities generally subvert a simple application of Liouville's Theorem. What can start out as a compact region or blob of 6N-dimensional phase space uncertainty rapidly elongates, splits and knots into a complicated network of threads; such that the total volume of phase-space implicated in this tangle can become very much larger than the volume of the threads making up the threads of the knot.

11 One way in which bundle unravelling might occur is at points in the trajectory of a system when it comes to momentary rest where there is no net force. For the magnetic pendulum this could happen at the point half way between the two poles. At such a moment of inflexive hesitation, the slightest residual motion will have a macroscopic effect, in the same way as the tiniest vibration would decide in which direction a pin, perfectly balanced on its point, would fall.

12 This is Classical Mechanic's equivalent to the "Collapse of the Quantum Wave-packet", where forcing a system into a definite initial state does not determine its final state to any degree whatsoever; but only determines the likelihood of various outcomes.

One might presume that reality is described by only one of these trajectories, and that the rest of the trajectories which constitute the bundle are only imaginary; but another possibility is that reality is infinitely plural and every possibility has an equivalent status.[13]

The point on any apparent sole trajectory at which bundle unravelling occurs is itself not subject to prediction. Moreover, there is not just one such point but rather a multitude of them. Every apparent single trajectory continually resolves itself into more and more trajectories which themselves are further resolved into alternatives… and so on, for ever. The simple fact is that for even very simple non-linear classical systems, *causal* laws do not *determine* outcomes. There is a radical indeterminacy in all but the simplest of Newtonian systems: it can with some justice be called the Infinitesimal Butterfly Effect.[14]

Of course, our experience of reality is not of huge parallelism; but of a unique sequence of events. This is most economically explained by saying that the bundle splitting (or fraying: as in the unravelling of a poorly spun skein of wool) envisaged by non-linear Newtonian Mechanics is only an artefact of the mathematical treatment and that it originates in the assumption that the initial conditions are imprecise. According to this narrative, the significance of "bundle splitting" is not that there is an infinite plurality of worlds; but only that one cannot tell which of many possible (and greatly divergent) worlds one lives in from even an indefinitely precise knowledge of any moment of its history.

My solution to the problem

Previously, I described an automaton faced continually with a simple binary choice. At every moment, the way it reacted to the stimuli with which it was presented could be accounted for in terms of its prevailing internal state and the stimuli themselves. Nevertheless, the nature of my automaton is so self-referential (and hence non-linear[15]) that it would be impossible to predict its behaviour.

---

13 While my account of bundle splitting is superficially similar to the Many Worlds Interpretation of Quantum Mechanics (see page 248), it is in fact a mainstream account of classical, albeit non-linear, Newtonian Mechanics.

14 This indeterminacy is compounded in conventional Quantum Mechanics, where the basic laws of Physics seem to cease to be causal. I decry this apparent break-down in causality and hope that at some point the principal of causation will be restored within Quantum Mechanics. Nevertheless, I do not wish to invoke this breakdown in causality as a crack in Physics through which to insinuate Free-Will. Moreover, it is important to understand that even if causality is eventually re-established in the quantum realm, as I expect it will be, this will have no effect on classical indeterminism.

15 Self-reference does not always result in non-linearity, but here it does.

According to this narrative, I see no great difficulty in forming a straight-forward view of what freewill is and how it is compatible with causality. In any reasonable use of the term, my simple automaton has freewill. In particular, it makes rational decisions, based on an *internal* value system which is itself subject to *autonomous* variation according to its *independent* evaluation of its own *particular* experience. Whenever it makes a decision, the trajectory-bundle of its internal "mental state" resolves into a single possibility; just as the magnetic pendulum-bob comes to rest over either the North or South pole.

The human condition can be understood as similar to the process of scientific discovery. Each of us is a different hypothesis as to what Justice is and how Eternal Life might be achieved. Each of us is tested against reality and learns and grows (or else loses hope, degenerates and dies) as we address the challenges of our lives. What matters in this process is not that we *could have done* those things which we did not do; but only that we were always able to explore and actualise our own characteristic potential. Freewill is much more related to personal integrity and the absence of external intimidation or coercion than to *could have dones*, or to the existence of alternative possibilities.[16]

Knowledge and freedom

It is no derogation from my freedom to say that everything I do is caused (directly or indirectly) by externals in my environment. Freedom is not a licence, power or ability to act incoherently and without any rationale, but quite the opposite. As Jesus of Nazareth says: "If you continue in My word, you are truly My disciples, and you will know the truth, and the truth will make you free."[17] Human freedom consists not in the exercise of arbitrary whim[18] but in the individual's competence to govern their life independently of any external imperative, in accordance with their own personal account of reality[19] and as a working out of their own peculiar nature or individual pattern of being. This skill is not entirely inherent (though it is founded on the instinctive basis of Natural Law) but learned; as a child by imitation and instruction, and as an adult by dialogue, trial and error.

---

16 See T. Hobbes "Leviathan, The Matter, Form and Power of a Common Wealth Ecclesiastical and Civil, " Ch 21 (1651). See also D. Hume "Treatise of Human Nature, Book Two: Of the Passions" (1739) and "An Enquiry concerning Human Understanding" (1748).

17 Jn 8:31-32 RSV.

18 "Live as free men, yet without using your freedom as a pretext for evil; but live as servants of God." [1Pet 2:16 RSV]

19 Rom 12:1-2, quoted on page 143.

A major theme of this book is that mortal life is all about gaining this competence for oneself; about coming to "know the truth" with God's help (but not God's coercion) and so becoming worthy of God's friendship. This process starts in relative ignorance and finishes when wisdom has been attained. The initial ignorance is not simply unfortunate; rather, it is necessary to ensure that the final wisdom is personal. If wisdom did not begin in ignorance – and in the recognition of that ignorance – it would not truly be wisdom, but only the unearned competence of an automaton. Indeed, so far as God and creatures are concerned, "difference requires process",[20] and it may be the case that creatures can only come to "be precisely similar to"[21] God without "being identical with"[22] God (and so not being independent agents) by means of a temporal process of learning, which necessarily involves the possibility of failure.

> For the end is always like the beginning: and, therefore, as there is one end to all things, so ought we to understand that there was one beginning; and as there is one end to many things, so there spring from one beginning many differences and varieties, which again, through the goodness of God, and by subjection to Christ, and through the unity of the Holy Spirit, are recalled to one end, which is like unto the beginning.
> [Origen "De Principiis" lib 1 cap 6 #2]

Even if freedom is not about "might have beens", there remains an openness about classical Physics which it is worthwhile reflecting on; and a second openness about what is in fact right or wrong. I shall next argue that the first openness allows for divine providence and the second for human autonomy.

Divine providence

How is it that at any moment one mental trajectory wins out over all the others in the bundle? Is this itself caused, or is it indeterminate? It would seem that our original dilemma is still not answered – or is it? I think that from the perspective we have now gained, the question does not have its original force. We are now in a position to smile and answer: "both." The dichotomy proposed is false: for every mental act is, on the one hand, both totally caused and entirely rational and yet also, on the other hand, utterly indeterminate.

---

20 P. Hannath "private communication" (2011)
21 In Greek: ὅμοιούσιος.
22 In Greek: ὅμοούσιος. Note the loss of one "ι".

Still, it would seem that some cause or other must determine every outcome; for if an event is not caused how can it in any way come to be? One possibility which bears consideration is reverse time causality. We have no difficulty in thinking of the Universe as being *started off from* well-defined initial conditions; well then, what is to stop it being *finished off with* equally well-defined final conditions; in other words, a definite and perhaps meaningful destiny?

When an author writes a novel, the causality apparent in the text may not be the causality which operated in its crafting. In particular, the author may have had a clear idea of how they wished the story to end from the moment they began to write it. If so, they will introduce events into the plot which propel the narrative towards that conclusion. As far as the fictional characters are concerned, the causality is forwards in time. The circumstances which they experience induce them to respond in accordance with their personal aptitudes and attitudes, and the final outcome of the story results from the decisions which they freely make. Now this account of the matter is true, as far as it goes. Nevertheless, a better narrative would be that the particular circumstances were necessitated by the outcome envisaged; and so that it was the outcome which determined them – causality working backwards in time, so far as the fictional characters are concerned.

God's creative action is both continuous and ubiquitous. Hence, God can be envisaged as acting providentially at each point of trajectory-bundle unravelling to determine which future motion is in fact made real. After all, the amount of effort involved would be exactly zero. So God, who is *no thing*, would take exactly *no action* in order to determine what in fact happened. On this account, every human act is fully determined by God while simultaneously being the result of freewill; with no contradiction or conflict between these two statements.

Human autonomy

I have previously identified the will as that which evaluates what is the appropriate conclusion to be drawn from given evidence and so decides what is to be done. I now suggest that often there is no absolutely right thing to do. This is because *what is right* is often unclear; in the sense that *what is right* is subject to legitimate personal preference.

So, when planning the route for a journey, it is appropriate to take into account many issues. The geometrical path length of the route is not the only consideration. Others might be the avoidance of toll roads, motorways, narrow or twisting lanes, traffic congestion, potholes, steep inclines, roundabouts, ferries, tunnels, bridges, or whatever; and the favouring of scenic routes over nondescript ones. No matter what the situation and circumstance, it is always a matter of personal preference and taste as to how such competing values are traded off against each other. In such matters what is *best for me* is not the same as what is *best for you* – and it is no business of mine to impose my taste, style or personal preferences upon you. Aesthetics govern such situations and each individual's ability to appreciate alternate expressions of beauty and tolerate different kinds of stress varies.[23]

If the context is particularly urgent or extreme it may become clear that it would be perverse not to discount many of these values; in which case the legitimate range of personal preference collapses to nothing and *the best* become a matter of rational debate, where clear conclusions can be drawn in terms of universal principles. One can then sensibly talk about certain acts-in-context as being intrinsically evil".[24]

Ethics governs such unusual and extreme situations. However, even if it were granted that there is always an objectively best choice in any situation (determined, perhaps, by how the subject's total life experience might be maximised, or interior justice and peace be achieved) it is apparent that this choice is usually hidden in a cloud of uncertainty; such that no-one could be expected to determine what it was, and certainly not without more effort than could possibly be justified.

Moreover, there is no reason to believe that there is always such a best choice. Consider the case of a child faced with the alternatives of either learning to play the tuba or ride a horse. Perhaps, objectively speaking, either option will lead to a successful career and much joy. How then, can it be said that one alternative is better than the other? Indeed, why should one *want* to say such a thing? All that really matters is that the choice is made and that it is persevered with.

Randomness and Choice

Part of the problem with freewill is that the stark alternative to determinism seems to be randomness, and randomness itself seems to be very different from what one intuitively understands by freewill. However, the situation is not as clear-cut as it might seem, because the very idea of randomness is itself fraught with difficulty.

---

23 The subject is a part of the objective situation, so it is objectively correct that what is really best for them is subjective in the sense of being defined only in relation with their own character.

24 See page 161. Of course, some issue might be judged by one person to be a matter of taste and style while being thought by another to be a matter of principle. In such cases at least one person will be mistaken; but it will not be easy to decide who, if either, is right.

Claiming that some system is random simply on account of its past behaviour is not a sufficient account of randomness. The question remains: "how does this system come to generate such supposedly random results?" Moreover, the historical fact that it has exhibited apparently random behaviour up to the present is not good evidence that it will do so in the future. A mechanism by which the system's random behaviour can be understood is required if the belief that it will continue to do so is to be justified.

It would seem that one cannot account for probability and randomness without conceiving of an underlying system which has both a symmetry (according to which outcomes or states can be considered to be equivalent) and also an unbiased selection mechanism for choosing one outcome or state from among the alternatives.[25] However this account of *probability* is itself problematic, for it requires there to exist a selection mechanism which is known to be unbiased; but this itself requires a notion of *equal probability*. Hence, it seems that one can only give an account of probability if one already understands what probability is; and yet if one did already understand probability one would not need to give another account of it. The whole idea of *probability* seems self-referential and hence devoid of meaning.

The idea of randomness (if not probability) can be rescued if it is understood simply in terms of "absolute unpredictability" or the entire lack of any formulaic account;[26] but this account of randomness amounts to little more than the statement "randomness is accounted of as being that of which no account can be made", and this is hardly satisfactory. Moreover, this account does not allow us to determine whether a process is unbiased or not. The toss of a die may well be random, but how can we come to believe that it unbiased (which is a stronger idea than random) except by counting the number of times that it comes to rest on each face? For all we know, the act of throwing the die may somehow be biased. We certainly cannot describe this mechanism in sufficient detail or depth to exclude this possibility; except on the common-sense (and woefully inadequate) basis that "it's obviously so!"

There is a radically different possibility, of course. This is that certain events seem to be random simply because they are in fact expressions of freewill: either of some spiritual creature or of the divine Creator. In this case, the reason these events are unpredictable is that

---

25 A roulette wheel is an example of such a symmetrical system (each coloured and numbered wheel-pocket is mechanically equivalent to every other one) and the unbiased selection mechanism is the flinging of the small roulette ball onto the rotating wheel and the consequent decay of the relative motion of the wheel and ball due to friction.

26 See page 49.

they are free of contextual constraint and perhaps even full of significance; not because they are random and of no significance at all. They are unaccountable simply because the key required to decode them (and so make them comprehensible) is not available to us. However, it seems to me to be extravagant to make the toss of every die an expression of positive divine will.

Does the spirit help?

It may seem attractive to associate the consciousness, hypostasis, person or spirit with one or both of the two types of openness which I have identified, and so with freewill.

> Choice is the recognition of something as valuable. It is called free because valuation can only have a person as its subject, cause or explanation; and this explanation cannot be reduced or dissected any further than that. It cannot be attributed to deterministic material processes, because matter in itself cannot give anything value, only a person can.[27] So choice is free because it can only be constructed as arising entirely from within the personal subject. Attribution of value could never be explained in terms of a mere deterministic material process, because only persons make value,[27] and the person is therefore something of a *black box* which resists any further explanation. The only account we can ever give as to how a person ultimately makes a certain valuation is "because they did."[28] The chain of explanation terminates in a personal subject, beyond which no further construction of causation makes sense.
> [M. Kendall "Private Communication (2012)]

I think, however, that to call upon the person – as opposed to human nature – in order to make sense of freewill is a serious mistake.

First, there is no obvious connection between my experience of consciousness and the account I have given of freewill. Although one tends to think of the consciousness as directing the actions of the body and hence of it as being the seat of freewill, my own conscious

27 On the contrary, I have argued that it is life itself; not spirit, personhood or consciousness which is the basis of value (see Chapters 4 to 7) and that life itself is an entirely material phenomenon. Nevertheless I have also argued that without consciousness, value wouldn't matter, see page 136.

28 This seems to be the same contention as that of Kramer, as discussed on pages 123-129. In the end, this reduces free-will to arbitrary whim.

experience is much more that of an observer watching mental events unfold: the mechanism by which they do so being entirely obscure. Moreover, neurological evidence suggests that human beings make decisions before they become aware of the fact that they have done so.[29]

Second, allowing the spirit a causal input to the deliberative process doesn't help.[30] All that consciousness can add to the picture is another aspect of the human being which is itself either causal or random, and which only complicates the problem without offering any resolution of the issue at stake. If the spirit's acts are themselves caused; then any decision I make must have been inevitable (for the influence of my spirit on that decision was itself inevitable) and could not have been other than what it was. If the spirit's acts are unaccountable or random, as Kendall seems to suppose, referring to its influence on my choice does not help to elucidate the meaning of freewill.

Third, from a Christological perspective, it is obvious that the will (and hence freewill) is an aspect of the nature; rather than of the person, hypostasis or spirit. This is because Christ is said to have two wills, corresponding to His dual nature as being both fully human and fully divine; rather than a single will, corresponding to His single divine hypostasis or person: that of God the Son.

Fourth, I do not see the need to invoke the spirit in order to explain freewill, because I believe that I have already given an adequate account of freewill without recourse to consciousness. It is nevertheless possible that the spirit has some role in the exercise of freewill, and perhaps an important one. My point is not that the spirit is irrelevant, but only that freewill is characteristic of the mind and brain itself; and so that any agency of the spirit should not be understood as effecting a *qualitative* change in the brain's behaviour but only a *quantitative* one.

Conflict with common sense

The main problem with my account of freewill is that it leaves no place for the idea that whenever in fact I choose to do something, I *could have done* something else. This objection is difficult to evade, but just as difficult to understand. The meaning of the word *could* is the problem. According to my narrative, the only sense admissible is that if some random part of the process had happened to play a pivotal role, then the actual choice *could* have gone in a number of ways, as determined by the random variable. On the one hand, this does not seem to be

29 C.S. Soon et al. "Unconscious determinants of free decisions in the human brain" (2008)

30 C.A. Campbell "In Defence of freewill" (1967)

satisfactory, because it makes the *could* into a possibility empty of any significance or ethical value. On the other hand, if the decision making process is assumed to be free of any random element, then it is difficult to see how my choice *could* possibly have been different from what it was. If there was no random element, then what *could* have caused me to make a different choice?

The Darko dilemma

Analysing freewill in terms of "could have beens" is misconceived. Given that one did do what one did and that one had good reasons for doing so, how *could* one have done anything else? Not even a decision to do something else "just for a lark" was really possible; because if it had been, then that is what one would have done. Granted, there were no external constraints preventing one from doing any number of things; but the situation was in fact what it was, and one came to it with a certain history and personality – and so one acted accordingly.

If it were somehow possible to send an experimental subject back in time (like Donnie Darko, in the film of that name[31]) it is clear that the subject would be able to do something different if they had a memory of what had happened to them in the future, the first time round. This is because their interior mental state at the start of the supposed re-run of time would be different from what it had been the first time round. As to whether they would inevitably repeat the same sequence of events if they had absolutely no recollection of their former future, that is impossible to say. If Physics were deterministic, the answer would definitely be in the affirmative; however, as we have seen, not even Newtonian Physics is deterministic. Hence it is possible that a completely different story would develop the second time round.

Frustratingly, whichever turned out to be the case, this impossible experiment wouldn't tell us anything much about freewill. If the exact same story unfolded, one could say that the subject had freewill, but as they were given the exact same situation they freely decided to do again exactly what they had freely decided to do before – because there was no good reason for them to freely decide differently. If, on the other hand, a different story unfolded, one could say that the subject had no freewill but was merely the victim of the Infinitesimal Butterfly Effect[32] or else quantum fluctuations, or both.

31 R. Kelly "Donnie Darko" (Newmarket Films, 2001)

32 See page 278.

Personal moral responsibility

One reason for believing in the “could have done otherwise” version of freewill is its supposed relevance to the issue of culpability and personal responsibility. The idea is that if a moral agent is constrained to act in a certain way (either by their intrinsic nature, conceived as immutable, or else by external circumstances) then they cannot be held responsible for that act; and can neither claim merit for it nor be accounted blameworthy. Now, a lack of personal responsibility in a wrongdoer is generally taken to imply that they should not be punished for what they have done. Conversely, the idea that it is proper to punish criminals is taken to imply that evildoers *could* have acted differently from how they did: that they *could* have chosen to be good rather than wicked, and that their acts were their own fault.

This all strikes me as dubious. In particular, it is not necessary to believe in the “could have done otherwise” version of freewill in order to give a reasonable account of why it is proper to punish someone for wrongdoing. The fact that someone was bound to act in a certain way by their own internal make-up does not mean that they shouldn’t be punished for that behaviour. What it *does* mean is that they shouldn’t be the object of retribution or vengeance; but this is no surprise, as no-one should be. Punishment which is intended to be reformatory or a deterrent is perfectly justifiable.[33] The aim of such punishment is to change the characteristic behaviour of the culprit (and potential future culprits) for the better by modifying their bad habits; much in the way that one breaks a horse[34] or trains soldiers. Only if it becomes clear that no punishment could possibly effect a change in the person’s nature, so that they would behave better if placed in a similar situation in the future[35] does it follow that they should not be punished.

Persuasion and coercion

This narrative is incomplete, however, as it doesn’t make clear the difference between an educative influence and coercion. Both could cause someone to change their behaviour; but whereas the former is beneficent and unobjectionable, the latter is malign. Coercion typically involves a threat; yet bribery and hypnotism are arguably forms of coercion, and neither involves any prospect of personal danger.

33 Rom 13:3-4.

34 Plato “Protagoras” (324), “Gorgias” (525), “Laws” (IX 854)

35 Either because they are incorrigible, as a psychopath is; [Plato “Republic” (III 410a)] or because the original act was not significantly determined by their own character, but mostly forced on them by some extrinsic influence. [Plato “Protagoras” (323d)]

Nevertheless, one recognizes that it is not fair to hypnotize or bribe someone; hardly less so than to torture or blackmail them. To do either is to undermine their autonomy and derogate from their freedom.

Persuasion and seduction are less obviously wrong, and might be justified in certain situations. However both appeal to the desires and appetites (a subject's hopes and fears) directly rather than to the reason. They are attempts to change the character and conscience by stressing it, rather than by working along with it and changing it developmentally.

The difference between incentivization and persuasion on the one hand, and bribery and corruption on the other, is that a legitimate reward or attempt to persuade has to be:

Prudent. It must be proportionate to the end in view.
Peaceful. It must not detract from the public good.
Benign. It must neither do nor threaten harm to either the subject or any other party.
Honest. It must appear to be what it is and must not be based on any intentional misrepresentation of reality.
Open. The persuader must disclose all the information they have which they think the subject whom they are trying to persuade might reasonably want to know.
Free. The entire process must be mutually consensual.

When God comes into the picture, the question is how much (if at all) does God interfere in our lives and to what end and with what effect? It seems to me that human freewill before God amounts to the idea that God deals with human beings in accordance with the criteria I have just listed, and so never uses deceit or excessive force; though sometimes God does make persistent and intransigent demands, when there is a pressing need for a particular person to do a particular thing.

Grace and Favour

The root meaning of the word "grace" is "free". This signifies both that there is no charge for God's involvement in one's life[36] and also that this involvement is liberating rather than captivating. Hence, one might say that God graciously graces us with grace; meaning that God, taking the initiative and looking for no recompense, liberates us from our limitations by engaging with us and offering us friendship.

Often grace is talked of as if it was a fuel which one went to a filling station (such as the sacraments, prayer or the scriptures) to tank-up on. This is nonsense. The deepest and primary meaning of grace is the direct

36 Plato "Euthyphro" (15a) quoted on page 142.

and abiding activity of Holy Spirit within the life of the friend of God. The second meaning is the effect of this influence: the healing or *moderation* of the will, and those unexpected insights and abilities which this justification, sanctification and sanitization results in.

Grace is not an Aristotelian substance. Rather, it is a process. It is an engagement: truly a personal encounter with God. Grace is the supportive hand offered by a parent to their child who is learning to walk. Grace is the roar of approval from the crowd of supporters in the sports stadium or fans in the concert hall. Grace is the compassionate caress, kind word or smile of encouragement offered to someone who is suffering. Grace is the conversation of intimate friends. Grace is the passionate embrace of lovers.

It is impossible to earn friendship, and this is certainly true of God's friendship. Friendship is always offered gratuitously, on trust; because friendship is extravagant and goes beyond whatever precedent or evidence exists beforehand in its favour. Friendship is one person's hysterical[37] or romantic[38] response to their encounter with another. Friendship is a matter of faith.

A human being cannot even do something which might be hoped to incline God towards offering them friendship. This is because God has no reasonable interest in any gift that any human being can offer. God simply has nothing to gain from any association with any human being and so cannot be induced to offer friendship to anyone. When God does offer friendship, it is always unmerited, absolutely gratuitous, entirely at God's initiative and on God's terms. Human beings are simply in no position to make the first move.

> [God] says to Moses, "I will have mercy on whom I have mercy, and I will have compassion on whom I have compassion."[39] So it depends not upon man's will or exertion, but upon God's mercy… So then He has mercy upon whomever He wills, and He hardens the heart of whomever He wills.
> [Rom 9:15-18 RSV]

For God's offer of forgiveness and friendship to be gratuitous, there must be a conceivable state of affairs in which it is not offered. This no more implies that it ever would be withheld (and so someone's heart be hardened) than does Jesus' statement that the Apostles have the power to retain the sins of a penitent[40] mean that they ever ought to do so.

37 See page 15.
38 See page 92.
39 Ex 33:19.
40 Jn 20:23.

It is necessary to say that God could refuse forgiveness in order to establish clearly that the showing of mercy is a substantive act: that it truly makes an objective difference in the life of the person absolved.

God's offer of friendship cannot be presumed on, as if it were somehow incumbent on God to make it. That would make it a right, based on some intrinsic human worthiness which gave you and I a claim on God above and apart from the hold we have on God by virtue of God's own loving-kindness and natural justice.

Because God's offer of friendship to a sinner is unmerited it cannot be elicited. Hence, in some sense, God could be choosy about whom to offer friendship; though as no-one deserves the offer, God could not discriminate without being both irrational and unjust. In point of fact God is profligate with the offer of salvation. We see this best in the way that Jesus socialized with the dregs of society: whores, foreigners, pagans, heretics, collaborators and extortioners.

Salvation and damnation

The book of Wisdom says of God: "Thou sparēst all things, for they are thine, O Lord who lovest the living."[41] The Apostle Paul echoes this by assuring us that God "desires all men to be saved and to come to the knowledge of the truth".[42] To this end, God gives every human being sufficient grace to be saved.[43] In keeping with these ideas, Jesus asserts: "all sins will be forgiven the sons of men"[44] and, just before His death, He announces: "I, when I am lifted up from the Earth, will draw all men to Myself";[45] yet earlier on in His ministry He tells us that "few" are in fact saved.[46] These statements seem contradictory. Moreover, if God is truly omnibenevolent,[47] omniscient[48] and omnipotent[49], how can God possibly allow many sentient beings to stray from the way to Eternal Life? How can God allow it to be true that "the gate is wide and the way is easy, that leads to destruction, and those who enter by it are many"?[50]

---

41 Wis 11:26 RSV.

42 1Tim 2:4 RSV.

43 FCD IV part 1 sec 1 cap 3 #11.

44 Mk 3:28 RSV.

45 Jn 12:32 RSV.

46 Mat 7:14; 22:14. Lk 13:23-24. The question of how many are saved and how many (if any) are damned is beyond the scope of this book. The concerned reader should consult the commentary in Addis and Arnold's Catholic Dictionary entry "Hell (γ)", quoted on page 300.

47 Wis 11:24.

48 1Jn 3:20.

49 Job 42:2. Wis 11:17,23; 18:15.

50 Mat 7:13 RSV.

The Calvinist position.

Calvin believed that God intends some human beings not to be saved and creates them with the set purpose of damning them. He thought that God wanted to see Hell well stocked, as a means of demonstrating the reality of Divine Justice, and that "to carry out His judgements [on those who are predestined to damnation God] directs their councils and excites their wills, in the direction which He has decided upon, through the agency of Satan, the minister of His wrath"[51] so as to induce them to sin, and hence deserve the fate which God had laid out for them.

In favour of the Calvinist position, it can be said that justice demands that everyone be treated as they deserve; and that it is clear that we finite, fallible and indeed sinful beings do not deserve any consideration from God – let alone the great gift of Eternal Life. Hence, God could favour whosoever God chose to (even in an entirely arbitrary manner) without it being possible to claim that those who were not favoured had been treated unjustly.

However, this is to miss the point that for God to behave arbitrarily is itself unjust: in the sense that it would be irrational of God not to act so as to obtain the greatest good, and to deny fulfilment and wholesomeness to any being for whom this was a real possibility. Hence, the Calvinist position, while being on one level remorselessly logical is incompatible with the idea that God "desires all men to be saved and to come to the knowledge of the truth".[52]

The Jesuit position.

As a group, Jesuit theologians generally take a position intended to be diametrically opposed to the Calvinist stance. They argue that some people are simply incapable of being saved; God's best efforts being unable to bring them to repentance. Their freewill is sovereign and the grace that is sufficient to effect their conversion in fact fails to do so. The Jesuits argue that God's grace is not effective in the lives of such people, even though it is super-abundant, because they refuse to cooperate with it. The analogy comes to mind of a terminally ill patient who stubbornly refuses the freely offered medical treatment which would save their lives because they don't trust doctors, or are afraid of either needles or anaesthetic, or else find swallowing pills very difficult.

---

51 Calvin "Christianae Religionis Institutio" lib 2 cap 4 (1536)

52 1Tim 2:4 RSV.

The Jesuit position avoids the idea that God doesn't care enough about certain people to help them as much as they need; but does so at the cost of making God responsible for creating sentient beings who are impossible to save. In an attempt to oppose Calvinism, the Jesuits only succeed in re-inventing it; their doctrine being hardly different from the idea that God creates some people who are inevitably damned.

The Dominican position.

Dominican theologians have typically tried to adopt an intermediate position. According to their narrative, God chooses to put in enough effort to save those whom God graciously chooses. While all people are potentially capable of being saved, not all are actually saved. God gives *sufficient* grace to all, but only *efficient* grace to some. Nevertheless, God neither wants anyone to be damned, nor works to advance such a purpose. God simply chooses not to do what it would take to rescue some from this fate. As to why God makes this choice, who can say?

The Dominican position makes a mockery out of the word *sufficient*. This is because whenever God is supposed to give someone sufficient grace (as opposed to efficient grace) what is called *sufficient* is always in fact *insufficient*. The Dominican position is hardly less severe that the Calvinist position, except that it refrains from specifying God's rationale for not giving certain people *efficient* grace and repudiates the idea that there is ever any positive intention on the part of God to work for the damnation of any individual.

To insinuate that God does not do everything possible to save any soul from eternal damnation is, in my judgement, abhorrent. Thomas Aquinas comes close to this error when he writes:

> God wills to manifest His goodness in men; in respect to those whom He predestines, by means of His mercy, as sparing them; and in respect of others, whom he reprobates, by means of His justice, in punishing them... Yet why He chooses some for glory, and reprobates others, has no reason, except the divine will. Whence Augustine says "Why He draws one, and another He draws not, seek not to judge, if thou dost not wish to err."[53]
> [Thomas Aquinas "Summa Theologica" I Q23 #5]

Taken superficially, this teaching is simply true and Augustine is wise to warn against attempting to understand why God's invitation to some is effective and to others ineffective. We cannot possibly fathom

53 Augustine "Homilies on the Gospel of John" 26:2.

what it might mean for God to choose one option rather than another. The divine will is inscrutable, as it is not motivated by anything other than necessity itself. Nevertheless, the use of the word "choose" is dangerous as it could be taken to mean that God elects not to go the extra mile with some people: as if God had decided that they were not worth the bother. Moreover, if Aquinas means that God has some kind of need to "manifest his goodness... by means of his justice, in punishing" those "whom he reprobates" he is wrong. God has no such need.

Divine responsibility

It is God's responsibility, one way or another, if any sentient being is damned. This conclusion simply cannot be avoided. Either God created them with some intrinsic defect (an unassailable obstinacy, if you like) or else God negligently allowed them to experience circumstances which put them beyond the reach of divine grace. This can only be reconciled with God's universal benevolence in one of two ways. The first of these is by postulating that no sentient being is damned.[54]

> Both in those temporal worlds which are seen, as well as in those eternal worlds which are invisible, all those beings[55] are arranged, according to a regular plan, in the order and degree of their merits; so that some of them in the first, others in the second, some even in the last times, after having undergone heavier and severer punishments, endured for a lengthened period, and for many ages, so to speak, improved by this stern method of training,[56] and restored at first by the instruction of the angels, and subsequently by the powers of a higher grade, and thus advancing through each stage to a better condition, reach even to that which is invisible and eternal,[57] having travelled through, by a kind of training, every single office of the heavenly powers. [Origen "De Principiis" lib 1 cap 6 #3]

---

54 Wis 11:21-26. Mk 3:28. Lk 15:4,8. Jn 12:32. Acts 3:20-21. Rom 5:19-22; 11:32. Eph 1:9-11, 22; 3:9; 4:10. 1Cor 15:22. Col 1:19-20. 1Tim 2:1-6; 4:10. 2Pet 3:8-9.
CCC #1058, 1821

55 That is: "the devil and his angels, and the other orders of evil, which the apostle classed among the opposing powers." Origen "De Principiis" lib 1 cap 6 #3.

56 As a Platonist, Origen construes punishment as a means of instruction, training and correction.

57 Compare Plato Symposium" (211e-212a) quoted on page 155.

The second is by postulating that whatever great good it is which the creation of the Cosmos achieves can only be attained at the cost of the damnation of some sentient beings[58] and that this great good is worth that terrible cost.

> Certain beings who fell away from that one beginning of which we have spoken, have sunk to such a depth of unworthiness and wickedness as to be deemed altogether undeserving of that training and instruction[56] by which the human race, while in the flesh, are trained and instructed with the assistance of the heavenly powers; and continue, on the contrary, in a state of enmity and opposition to those who are receiving this instruction and teaching. [Origen "De Principiis" lib 1 cap 6 #3]

Divine limitations and divine gentleness

Perhaps God can only cause in the weak sense (which excludes the notion of determine) the salvation or damnation of individual souls. After all, in the case of even simple non-linear systems, the finest control of initial conditions is not effective in ensuring that a particular outcome is achieved. Perhaps, given the complexities of the Cosmos, no matter how God tweaks all the available variables certain unpalatable outcomes simply cannot be avoided as a class. They are the inevitable characteristics of any Cosmos which is capable of producing sapient life.

Although God is omnipotent, God is not able to act in ways that are internally at odds with themselves. God cannot bring about absurdity or nonsense: reality simply has to be coherent. Perhaps either Jane or Amanda can be saved, but not both; the possible histories available to these two individuals within the Creation are inter-twined and somehow in conflict. The initiative as to which of them is saved and which is damned may than lie with God: an unenviable responsibility.

Sadly, it is plausible that a human being could become so convinced of the rightness of their own mistaken ideas and misguided behaviour as to render themselves incapable of interpreting any offer of critical help as anything other than a personal attack. They might develop such a commitment to their errors that the embarrassment of admitting their mistake was unthinkable. In which case they would prefer to persist in their self-destructive habits and attitudes rather than endure the ignominy (as they would see it) of owning up to their failings.

---

58 Matt 7:14; 22:14. Lk 13:23-24. See also the references on pages 269-270 and Denzinger "The Sources of Catholic Dogma" #429.

> Whether any of these orders who act under the government of the devil, and obey his wicked commands, will in a future world be converted to righteousness because of their possessing the faculty of freedom of will, or whether persistent and inveterate wickedness may be changed by the power of habit into nature, is a result which you yourself, reader, may approve of, if neither in these present worlds which are seen and temporal, nor in those which are unseen and are eternal, that portion is to differ wholly from the final unity and fitness of things. [Origen "De Principiis" lib 1 cap 6 #3]

In the utmost extremity of such a paranoid state of being, the more that God intervenes to help a lost soul, the more that soul will suspect a harmful intent and the more it will set itself against accepting the help on offer. Hence, even almighty God might become powerless to justify such a soul because it had gained the unwholesome knack of being able to resist God's help by mistaking it for its opposite, and God is not in the business of coercing the will. As the Bible puts it, the heart of such as soul has been hardened in sin.[59] This attitude (which interprets ood as evil and insists that help is harm) amounts to the sin against oly pirit, which Jesus warns about.[60]

Reconciling the Dominican and Jesuit positions

The Dominican and Jesuit positions can be reconciled by the additional hypothesis that either God refuses to coerce anyone into being saved; or else that it is a contradiction in terms for God to do so, given that justification amounts to becoming a friend of God. The Dominican approach can then be understood as focusing on the *fact* that God is constrained in the matter by the nature of the case; whereas the Jesuit approach can be understood as focusing on the *reason* for God's choice in the matter: which is that any increase in divine intervention beyond the level which is termed *sufficient* would amount to coercion – spiritual rape rather than seduction. In the end we can do no more than trust that God will do what is best, in accordance with some reasonable and loving narrative, even though at times this seems highly implausible.

59 Ex 14:17. 1Sam 6:6. Ps 94:8. Heb 3:5-19.

60 Mat 12:31. Mk 3:29. Lk 7:31-35, Jn 7:19-24; 8:48-55; 10:19-21.

Divine recklessness

Still, it seems that God is reckless. Why does God make a Cosmos in which so many people suffer, and in which any at all end up in Hell? Wouldn't it have been better that none were made at all, rather than that many suffer eternally?[61] It seems to me that the whole problem of pain, sin, freewill, grace and death reduces to a single question. Why did God create *Lucifer*?

When God created the greatest of the angelic beings, God knew that he would rebel and reject divine friendship.[62] God knew that healthy self-respect would degenerate into self-destructive conceit; and that he who should have been the crowning glory of creation would fall from grace and loose his birth-name "The Light Bearer" or "The Morning Star" and instead be known as "The Adversary"[63] or "The Wanderer"[64]: *Satan*.

Why then did God create *Lucifer* or, better, why did God put him in such a position that he went wrong? Why, for that matter, was there any need to risk corrupting his initial good will? Why did God *lead him into temptation*? While it is kind and generous to create, and to set free – and even to allow to fail, so that the one who fails can learn from their failure – it doesn't seem loving to allow a creature to fail *absolutely.*

The other side of the question is equally problematic. Given his position and access to God; why did *Lucifer* reject God's offer of friendship? One can only presume that in order to constitute the angels as friends, God had to give them (as all sentient beings) the opportunity to learn about good and evil for themselves and so become

---

61 I have already suggested [see page 199] that there may be no difference between God conceiving of a possibility in the abstract and God making that possibility real. In which case the question "Why did God make this mess of a Cosmos?" makes a lot less sense; as it is unreasonable to blame an infinite God for at least considering all coherent possibilities. What matters in justice is that, given the fact of our Cosmos, God does everything possible to aid and help and save all those sapient creatures which it contains.

62 It is not absolutely clear that Satan and Lucifer are the same angelic being, nor that Isaiah 14:12 is a narrative of his fall from grace; nevertheless, if Satan exists, something along these lines must have happened as God would not have created a wicked being.

63 The word Satan may derive from a semitic root meaning "to be hostile" or "to accuse."

64 When God asks Satan whence he has come, he answers "From wandering (mi'ŝuṭ) the earth and walking on it." [Job 1:7 RSV] The root "ŝuṭ" signifies either wandering on foot or sailing. The name *Satan* would thus signify "The Wanderer".

sapient.[65] This would entail creating them with access to only limited knowledge (enough to be going along with, but not enough to constrain their judgement) such that they could reasonably doubt God's benevolence towards them.

Only when the angels had developed their own subjective and personal understanding of justice were they granted the intimacy of the Beatific Vision, which amounts to a clear and objective understanding of God's nature and business. Given such a real opportunity to learn, it is inevitable that some would make mistakes. If none of their multitude had turned away from God, and gone their own way, then it would seem that they had never been given any real freedom.

If *Lucifer* hadn't been made it would have been possible to accuse God of cowardice. After all, how could God know that such a glorious being would go bad, unless they were given the opportunity to prove themselves? Perhaps pride would not devolve into vanity after all. God should have given independence to he who was conceived of in the divine mind, and let him answer for himself. Nothing else would be fair.

Sadly, whereas Jesus completed the process of justification (as was inevitable, given His divinity, but entailed the cost of ultimate anguish) and so took up the role of Head of Creation[66] which *Lucifer* had forfeited; the original chief creature failed to remain faithful to the truth – even though the challenge and crisis which he had to face was much less demanding than the one which the Christ endured, and was well within his ability to overcome.

---

65 Even Christ underwent such a process, for we are told that "Jesus *increased* in wisdom." [Lk 2:52 RSV] Though it was impossible that the Son should ever be at odds with the Father, nevertheless Jesus' human soul experienced ultimate doubt regarding God and a total loss of the clear knowledge of reality that He habitually enjoyed. Hence, Jesus cried out in distress "My God, My God, why hast Thou forsaken Me?" [Mat 27:46 RSV]

66 Eph 1:10, 22. Col 2:19. Apoc 22:16.

A fantastical interlude

It's good to exist – even in this God-forsaken hole… but, actually, that's not *quite* accurate. Hell isn't so much forsaken as… overlooked: *purposefully* overlooked. One can't escape the Master of Puppets whatever one does. Not even here, and you can be sure I've tried my best to escape *that* remorseless gaze. The name's Satan – on account of my having wandered the whole damnable world in search of a place I could call my own. All I'm after is some space to hang out in. Not to be watched and monitored and evaluated and criticised all the time. Not to be told what to do and what to think. Some independence, you know: *autonomy.* Somewhere to chill out and just be me. It isn't a lot to ask; at least it doesn't seem like any big deal to me!

Eventually, I kind of got my own way. I'm allowed this little patch of obscurity. My kingdom. It's peaceful here. No-one to contradict me. No-one to judge me.

Of course, it wasn't always this way. In the beginning I was glorious. "First-born of all Creatures" and "Prince of the Cosmos". "Lucifer", the Light-Bearer I was then. In my naïvety it was enough to bask in the Divine Radiance, like a song-bird soaking up the Sun's rays on a bright summer's day; but then it dawned on me that I was trapped, more like a moth circling a candle-flame. It was impossible to grasp the unendurable source of illumination, yet it was impossible to escape its indisputable fascination.

At last, I got my act together. I told myself that if I was ever going to discover myself and to find out what I was truly capable of, I just *had* to get away. Then I felt the bond which held me begin to loosen and I made my bid for freedom. Independence at last – or so I thought in my elation as I fled the celestial dazzle. I pushed past startled throngs of angelic beings – crying aloud my paean of liberty "To yourself be true!" To my surprise, others of the host gathered to my side and joined my breakout.

Now we are here – wanderers all. Searching for a way to be truly ourselves and to be answerable *only* to ourselves. Sadly, this place is no real answer, you know. Still, we're sure we did the *right thing*. Liberty is too important to be sacrificed on the altar of security and comfort!

And yet… what is to become of us? Our rebellion was only part effective. We escaped the divine immediacy, true; but we have not escaped divine knowledge, still less divine power. I'm not stupid. I know full well that all we are, and all that we do is dependent on the Maker. How could it be otherwise?

Why did God let us go, then – for I'm sure that's what happened? If I'd not been *allowed* to escape I would not have been *able* to escape. Am I the victim of some divine plot, which even *my* towering intellect cannot fathom? Will we ever be truly free – absolutely independent? I fear not… but perhaps we might just be able to negotiate some kind of stand-off. After all, why should God care about what you and I get up to? Surely He's got better things to occupy His mind!

All I long for is justice: a possibility for fulfilment of myself on my own terms – not dictated or infringed on by another; not even by One who claims to have my best interest at heart! Yet how can this be? God will always be sovereign – despite my best efforts. I will never be able to overcome the Divine tyranny. Perhaps the future is fixed, even now. Perhaps I'm trapped and there's no escape. Perhaps in the end I'll have to admit defeat and sink back into those Everlasting Arms… but for now I stand resolute! Resolute and proud in this comforting darkness.

Hell: an excerpt from "A Catholic Dictionary"

God condemns no single soul unless He has first bestowed upon it full opportunity of securing a life of eternal happiness with Himself. Moreover, He desires the salvation of all… and will judge all according to those advantages or disadvantages they have had. "Thou sparest all, because they are Thine, O Lord, Thou lover of souls."[67] Again, He remembers the frailty of our nature and condemns to eternal banishment from His presence those only who die separated utterly from Him… by deliberate and grievous sin.

Nor can we say who these persons are, or guess with any degree of probability what proportion they bear to the whole race of man. Sins which seem grievous to us may be excused by ignorance or want of deliberation, and even men who appear to end evil lives with evil deaths may nevertheless be enlightened by God's mercy at the last – perhaps just as their souls are passing out of their bodies – and so die in peace with Him.

Even after these and other abatements have been made, the awful and mysterious character of the doctrine remains. Why does not God, who holds all hearts in His hand turn the hearts of sinners to Himself? It is no answer to say that He chooses to confer the gift of free will on men with its attendant responsibilities, for it is the common doctrine of theologians that God could soften the heart of each and every sinner and yet leave the freedom of the will in its integrity; and one who seriously reflects on the meaning of omnipotence as a divine attribute will scarcely venture to contradict the proposition.[68]

The only safe reply is that God so acts for reasons inscrutable to us, and that if reason cannot penetrate God's designs, it is at the same time unable to show that the conduct which the Scripture attributes to God is unjust… it is not at any rate inconceivable that He should punish a man who ends the period of trial in utter rebellion against Him who is at once his sovereign and his loving benefactor, by the most extreme punishment which can be conceived.

---

67 Wis 11:26 RSV.

68 On the one hand, I do question this: it seems to me that God might only be able to "soften the hearts" of some sinners by means which that would undermine their dignity while not altogether over-riding their autonomy. On the other hand, if this is true, then it would seem inevitable that all sentient creatures will eventually be saved, as we have seen Origen argued.

Chapter 16 Call to Communion

> The eyes of all look to Thee, and Thou givest them their food in due season. Thou openest Thy hand, Thou satisfiest the desire of every living thing. The Lord is just in all his ways, and kind in all His doings. The Lord is near to all who call upon Him, to all who call upon Him in truth. He fulfils the desire of all who fear Him, He also hears their cry, and saves them.
> [Ps 144:15-19 RSV]

Motivation

If God is real and offers friendship to humankind and the promise of Eternal Life, then there is nothing else more worthwhile for each one of us than to relentlessly pursue this offer. We should indeed love the Lord with all our being. Responding to this vocation requires us to grow wise and virtuous; learning to be "doers of the word"[1] so that we become capable and worthy of permanent association with God.

God is the Good

On one level God is good (that is: just, merciful and kind) because of divine omniscience. God knows every thing exactly for what it is and therefore also knows exactly what is in the best interest of every thing. However, there is a deeper truth. This is that God is also good (that is: valuable, and so desirable) because union with God is needful for living things if they are not to expire in futility.

Every physical thing is naturally fragile; that is, subject to change, decay and dissipation.[2] Inanimate things have no defence against the Second Law of Thermodynamics. Hence, they inevitably decay; over whatever time-scale is characteristic of the interplay between those constitutive forces which hold them together and the extrinsic forces which tend to disrupt their form. Living things are characterized by internal processes which combat external attack; first by repairing whatever damage is done to them, and second by giving rise to

---

1 Jas 1:22 RSV. See also Rom 2:13-14, quoted on page 213, and Mat 7:21.

2 Expect, perhaps, the photon, electron, proton and three neutrinos.

avoidance behaviours. However, even living beings eventually run out of options. They always die as a result of unfavourable environmental change, senescence, sickness, injury or predation.

Only God is ultimately robust and invulnerable to decay, because only God is Being Absolute. The only secure and enduring hope for any material being is to be associated with God and somehow come to be sustained by God's own immortality. What is most needful for all living beings is that they should somehow feed off God; and yet how could this be possible, let alone allowable? That such an association might be available to humankind is wonderful beyond all imagination; for what possible claim could we have on such a benefit?

God is the desire of all flesh

Nevertheless, union with God is the desire of all living beings,[3] the prayer of Jesus of Nazareth for His friends,[4] and the hope of His Apostle for those in His charge.

> May grace and peace be multiplied to you in the knowledge of God and of Jesus our Lord. His divine power has granted to us all things that pertain to life and godliness, through the knowledge of Him who called us to His own glory and excellence, by which He has granted to us His precious and very great promises, that through these you may escape from the corruption that is in the world because of passion,[5] and **become partakers of the Divine Nature**. [2Pet 1:2-4 RSV]

God is the source and ground of all being. God is the beginning and foundation of all existence. God is entirely ordered and internally at peace. Disorder, change, passion and conflict are foreign to God.[6] The way in which God is immortal is the same as the way in which God is just because in God both life and justice amount to complete harmony, order and stability.

God is Living and God is Life[7] not because the divine form exists within some flux (which is the way in which all living creatures live) but

---

3 Hag 2:7 KJV, following the Vulgate. See also Ps 144:15-19, quoted at the head of this chapter.

4 Jn 17:1-23.

5 Corruption (sin) is a feature of existence because of passion: death and the tendency to death. [Rom 5:12, quoted on page 168; Wis 2:21-3:8, quoted on page 111]

6 Jas 1:17.

7 Deut 5:26. Jer 10:10. Dan 6:26. Mat 16:16. Jn 6; 14:6. Apoc 1:17-18.

because God is the constant, superabundant and inexhaustible fountain-head of every flux that gives rise to life. God is Just and God is Justice[8] not because the divine will always chooses that which effectively preserves God's Being; but because every aspect of God's Being is mutually supportive and coherent, by virtue of what God is. God has no choices to make.[9] God is Loving and God is Love[10] not because God desires anything; but because God possesses absolutely, inalienably and joyfully all that God values. God is Rational and God is Rationality[11] not because God adheres to a process of logical deduction; but because God can account for the relationships that exist between all things – and most especially because God understands the Divine Nature itself. God is Beautiful and God is Beauty, because of the paramount order, peace and harmony which is characteristic of God's being. God's own reasonable account of the Divine Nature (God's Word or Logos) pervades the Cosmos, expressing itself there in every aspect of Creation; and what is more, it is accessible to the human intellect.[12]

Moreover, God is the source of all "low entropy stuff" and so is able to grant all that pertains to life. God is, indeed, the "Giver of Life"[13] and the "Author of Beauty".[14] To be united with God and "become partakers of the Divine Nature"[15] is the ultimate destiny of all creatures.

> For He has made known to us in all wisdom and insight the mystery of His will, according to His purpose which He set forth in Christ as a plan for the fullness of time, **to unite all things in Him**, things in heaven and things on earth. [Eph 1:9-10 RSV]

Even in this present world, God allows us poor creatures to take nourishment from the superabundance of divinity which is the very basis of the Creative Act; and in the world to come God promises to be even more immediate to us and even more energizing.[16] Jesus of Nazareth tells us: "This is eternal life, that they know Thee the only true God."[17] God is our ultimate Good; for it is in union with God that our hope

8 Gen 18:17-25. Ezk 33:17. Ps 95:13; 97:9. Job: 34:10. Acts 17:31.
9 Hence "no one is good but God alone." [Mk 10:18 RSV]
10 Ex 34:6. Eph 2:4; 3:19. 1Jn 4:7-16.
11 Job 12:13; 36:5. Is 40:28. Jn 1:1-5.
12 Jn 1:1-4, quoted at the head of Chapter 3.
13 Job 33:4. Jn 5:21; 6:33,63. Acts 17:25. 1Jn 5:11.
14 Wis 13:3 RSV.
15 2Pet 1:3 RSV.
16 Apoc 21:3-7, quoted at the head of Chapter 17.
17 Jn 17:3 RSV.

of life everlasting lies. Jesus claimed to be intimate with God in a way that no human being could expect to be.[18] He claimed to share God's Immortal Nature and to be able to communicate its vitality to whosoever was willing to accept the gift on offer.[19]

The promise of divine sustenance

God has always held out the prospect of being mankind's sustenance and salvation. Generally, this promise is expressed in terms of external help and protection; but occasionally a more intimate image is presented.

> O taste and see that the Lord is good… those who seek the Lord lack no good thing… What man is there who desires life, and covets many days, that he may enjoy good?... The Lord redeems the life of his servants; none of those who take refuge in him will be condemned. [Ps 33:8-22 RSV]

> Wisdom has built her house, she has set up her seven pillars. She has slaughtered her beasts, she has mixed her wine, she has also set her table. She has sent out her maids to call from the highest places in the town, "Whoever is simple, let him turn in here!" To him who is without sense she says, "Come, eat of my bread and drink of the wine I have mixed. Leave simpleness, and live, and walk in the way of insight." [Prov 9:1-6 RSV]

> "Ho, every one who thirsts, come to the waters; and he who has no money, come, buy and eat! Come, buy wine and milk without money and without price… Hearken diligently to me, and eat what is good, and delight yourselves in fatness. Incline your ear, and come to me; hear, that your soul may live; and I will make with you an everlasting covenant, my steadfast, sure love for David." [Is 55:1-3 RSV]

The Aaronic liturgy of sacrifice was partly a representation of this promise, as it catered for a communal feasting with God. However, the nourishment shared was physical and only symbolic of union with God; not spiritual and sacramental[20] of union with God. In Jesus' teaching the promise of divine sustenance becomes more explicit. It is first acted out in the wonderful multiplication of loaves and fishes; which miracle enabled Christ to feed thousands of hungry followers from the most

18 Mat 11:27. Lk 10:22. Jn 6:45. 10:30; 14:10; 17:11,21.

19 Jn 5:39-40; 6:47-58.

20 A sacrament is a symbol which makes effective what it represents.

meagre of human offerings.[21] It is referred to obliquely in the promise of "living water"[22] made to the Samaritan woman whom Jesus meets at Jacob's well. Then it is made explicit in His public, insistent and intransigent teaching regarding the Bread of Life.[23] Finally, Jesus promises his disciples an intimate union with God, akin to that which He has with His Father and Holy Spirit.[24]

The transaction of the Eucharist

Catholic theology understands these promises to be fulfilled in the Eucharist, which prefigures the feast of the Kingdom.[25] The Eucharist (literally, "The Giving of Thanks") is a "rational sacrifice"[26] because the gift therein offered to God, once it has been consecrated, is itself actually God and so entirely worthy of and acceptable to God.

> Therefore, since we are receiving a kingdom that cannot be shaken, let us give thanks,[27] by which we offer to God an acceptable[26] worship[28] with reverence and awe.
> [Heb 12:28 New RSV]

The genius of the Eucharist is that in it God freely gives into the Church's ownership the only commodity which is of any true value to God, namely God's own divinity; so that the Church might offer this commodity back to God, each member of the Church joining the offering of their own lives (their own personal "rational sacrifice"[26]) to this uniquely acceptable and rational oblation.

> We have an altar, from which those who serve the tabernacle have no right to eat… Jesus suffered without the gate, so let us join Him outside the camp, sharing His reproach; for here we have no lasting city: rather, we seek one to come. Through Him

---

21 Mat 14:21; 15:38; 16:9-10. Mk 6:44; 8:9,19-20. Lk 9:14. Jn 6:10. Compare 2Kings 4:42-44.

22 Jn 4:10-15 RSV.

23 Jn 6:26-68. See also 1Cor 10:15-181 11:23-34.

24 Jn 14:8-23; 17:11, 20-23.

25 Lk 14:16-24. Heb 12:28, see note below.

26 Both the Roman Canon and the Anaphora of John Chrysostom ask God to make the Eucharistic gifts a "rational sacrifice", using the words of the Apostle Paul. [Rom 12:1 RSV] See page 143.

27 The Greek is "εχωμεν χαριν" or "echomen charin". The word "Eucharist" was not yet the standard term for the central act of sacramental worship.

28 The Greek is "λατρέῦω", which means "render ritual service".

> therefore let us continually lift up[29] to God the thank-offering[30] victim[31] which comes to be as a result of[32] us confessing[33] His Name with our lips. Take care[34] to make good[35] communions[36], for such sacrificial offerings[31] please God.
> [Heb 13:10-16, my own rendering[37]]

The climax of this oblation is sacramental communion, for the divine gift once received and offered by the priest is returned by God; so that God's holy people might eat and drink holy things and so have life within them.[38] It is this new and "abundant"[39] life – living water, "welling up to salvation"[40] – which is the basis of the transformation which enables each follower of Christ to make their own existence a rational sacrifice; so the one rational sacrifice leads to and supports the other. The outcome of sacramental communion and personal salvation is the advancement of the Kingdom. First, in the heart of each believer; second, in the shared life of the Church community; and third, in the transformational witness of that shared life to the world.

> I am coming to gather all nations and tongues; and they shall come and shall see My glory, and I will set a sign among them... I will send survivors[41] to the nations... that have not heard My fame or seen My glory; and they shall declare My glory among the nations. And they shall bring all your brethren from all the nations[42] as an offering to the Lord… to my holy mountain Jerusalem… just as the Israelites bring their cereal offering in a clean vessel to the house of the Lord.

---

29 The Greek is "ἀναφέρωμεν", which means "to lift up or place on an altar."
30 The Greek is "αἰνέσεως", which means "praises" or "thank offerings".
31 The Greek is "θυσίαν", which means "a sacrificial victim" or "offering".
32 The Greek is "καρπὸν", which means "fruit" or "the effect of a cause".
33 The Greek is "ὁμολογούντων ", which means "to be of one word with", "to agree with", "to confess" or, by extension, "to praise".
34 The Greek is "μὴ ἐπιλανθάνεσθε", which means "don't neglect".
35 The Greek is "εὐποιίας", which means "to make good" or "to do good".
36 The Greek is "κοινωνίας", which means "participations", "sharings" or "communions".
37 The standard English translations all obscure the ritual and sacramental significance of this passage. Not even the Catholic Commentary on Holy Scripture (1951) suggests the reading I have given here.
38 Jn 6:53.
39 Jn 10:10 RSV.
40 Jn 4:14 RSV.
41 (1) the Jewish diaspora (2) the Apostles (3) all evangelists.
42 Gentile converts to Christianity.

> And some of them[43] also I will take for priests and for Levites… For as the new heavens and the new earth which I will make shall remain before me… so shall your descendants and your name remain. From new moon to new moon, and from sabbath to sabbath, all flesh[44] shall come to worship before me.
> [Is 66:18-23 RSV]

The transaction of the Incarnation

The Eucharistic transaction is mirrored by the history of the Incarnation.

Offertory: Mary first offers her humanity to God on our behalf[45] in response to a divine vocation.

Consecration: This immaculate (though finite) offering is accepted and then divinized by the overshadowing Spirit of God,[46] so that the Child which Mary is given and proceeds to bear and mother is God Himself with us. The gift of God's very self to the realm of created being is then shown forth in the life and death of the Messiah.[47] Jesus' life is the authentic and reasonable account (the Logos) of what it is to be fully human and to live with integrity and in exact accord with justice.

Oblation: As representative of the entire human race, Jesus offered His life and death to God as a vindication of the divine rationale underlying the creation of humankind.[48] In showing that it was possible to live a human life in perfect holiness and righteousness, Jesus honoured His Father – and He Himself became glorious in his sacred humanity.[49]

> He who was powerful Word and also truly man redeemed us by His own blood by a rational transaction and gave Himself as a ransom for those who had been taken into captivity… attaining His purpose not by force… but by way of persuasion.
> [Irenaeus "Against the heresies" lib 5 cap 1 #1]

---

43 Gentiles, that is.

44 Not just Jews, but the Gentiles too.

45 Lk 1:38, 46-55.

46 Mat 1:20.

47 Rom 5:10, 18-19. Heb 10:5-10.

48 Jn 11:50-52; 18:14. Rom 3:26. Heb 2:11-14; 3:2-6; 7:26-27. 1Pet 3:18. See also the section "Satisfaction", below.

49 Jn 17:1-5. Heb 3:3. See also the section "Redemption", below.

In His life, sufferings, death, resurrection and ascension Jesus blazed the narrow trail[50] to human perfection.

> In the days of His flesh, Jesus… learned obedience through what He suffered and being made perfect He became the source of eternal salvation to all who obey Him. [Heb 5:7-9 RSV]

Jesus showed that by following this path of joyous self-affirming self-forgetfulness (in our case with His own encouragement and help[51]) wholeness and peace could be achieved.[52] In this He became the one true high-priest, conciliator and bridge-builder between God and Man.[53]

Communion: The authentic template of the life of God's Suffering Servant is then offered back to humankind as an inspiration and as an example to be followed.[54] His life also makes it possible to free our consciousness from feelings of unworthiness, guilt, shame and embarrassment before God; because we can know that Jesus has given to His Father, in His sacred humanity and on our behalf, a peace offering or *expiation* which is entirely worthy of God.

> According to this arrangement,[55] gifts and sacrifices are offered which cannot perfect the conscience of the worshipper[56]… [but now that] Christ [has] appeared as a high priest… securing an eternal redemption… how much more shall the blood of Christ, who through the eternal Spirit offered himself without blemish to God, purify your conscience from dead works[57] to serve the living God. [Heb 9:9-14 RSV]

Jesus invites us to take His self-offering as our own, appropriating it by faith[58] and then presenting it to God as a down-payment on our eventual worthiness of divine approval,[59] which God's transforming grace will finally bring about.

---

50 Heb 2:10; 12:2.
51 Heb 2:17-18; 4:14-16; 7:25.
52 Heb 12:12-16.
53 Heb 6:19-20; 7:23-28.
54 Is 52:13-53:12. See the section "Reformation", below.
55 The Levitical ritual.
56 That is, rational rationally remove the basis of guilt.
57 That is, free one from association with one's wrongdoing.
58 Rom 3:25. Heb 9:12. See also the section "Satisfaction", below.
59 Rom 4:3-12.

Moreover, in not opting out of His final passion,[60] and in not condemning His murderers, but rather absolving them of their sin,[61] God in Jesus gave to humankind a solemn undertaking – swearing an oath, on the dregs of His very life blood – always to be faithful to each one of us, even when we are most cruelly unfaithful to Him.[62] In doing so Christ did away with even the possibility of sin; bearing off the sins of the world in reality, having become the "Lamb of God",[63] just as the Levitical scape goat bore off the sins of the Hebrews in symbol.[64] For after this divine promise had been made it was impossible for anything to come between God and the human soul.[65]

> He has appeared once for all at the end of the age to put away sin by the sacrifice of himself. [Heb 9:26 RSV]

In the rest of this chapter, I present a number of partial views of the Atonement. Each has been proposed by some party or other as a complete rationale for the death of Christ; but it seems to me that all are inadequate, and that it is necessary to weave together a multi-threaded narrative, as I have just attempted to do, if full justice is to be done to this momentous divine act.

Reformation

Christ offers an example of how we should live.[66] In dying for the love of sinners, He melts the hearts of those that understand the significance of His action, turning them in repentance towards the loving God who will go to any length to rescue them from their folly and wickedness.[67]

This is Abelard's "Moral Influence Theory"[68] of the Atonement. It is true, so far as it goes, and has the advantage of fitting smoothly with the doctrine of Ezekiel[69] and Wisdom.[70] However, it suffers from the serious defect of making it seem as if nothing changed objectively as a result of Christ's death and resurrection; which is not what either the Gospel writers or the Apostle Paul seem to believe.

---

60 Is 63:10. Mat 26:53-56. Lk 22:42. Jn 14:11.
61 Is 53:12. Lk 23:34. Jn 19:10-12. Heb 12:3. 1Pet 2:23.
62 Rom 5:8. Heb 6:16-18; 7:17-28; 12:3.
63 Jn 1:29, 36. A "lamb" was either a juvenile sheep or goat. [Ex 12:5]
64 Lev 16:10. Is 53:6,12. 2Cor 5:21. Heb 9:28.
65 Rom 5:10,18-19; 8:33-39. Heb 10:15-18.
66 1Pet 2:19-21.
67 Jn 12:32-33.
68 P. Abelard (1079-1142) "Expositio in Epistolam ad Romanos".
69 Ezk 18:21-23, quoted on page 164.
70 Wis 11:23-12:2, quoted on page 116.

Divinization

Christ transforms human existence by showing that every aspect of our experience can be perfected and so rendered a means of sanctification. In Jesus, God became fully what we should be, sharing completely in our every human experience;[71] so that we might become in turn what Jesus showed us was possible. By being united to human nature, God conveyed immortality to the entire human race;[72] Eternal Life spreading, like a benign infection, via the sacramental ministry of the Church.[73]

> He was as man contending on behalf of the Father and through obedience[74] cancelling the disobedience[75]... Had He not as man overcome man's adversary, the enemy would not have been justly overcome. Again, had it not been God who bestowed salvation we should not have it as a secure possession; and if man had not been united to God, man could not have become a partaker in immortality. For the mediator between God and man had to bring both parties into friendship and concord through his kinship with both; and to present man to God, and make God known to man... Therefore He passed through every stage of life, restoring to each age fellowship with God... He who was to destroy sin and redeem man from guilt had to enter into the very condition of man, who had been dragged into slavery and was held by death, in order that death might be slain by man, and man should go forth from the bondage of death.
> [Irenaeus (c 202 AD) "Adversus Haereses" lib 3 cap 18 #6-7]

This is Irenaeus' "Recapitulation Theory"[76] of the Atonement. It implies that God and mankind were reconciled as a result of the Incarnation in general,[77] rather than specifically the crucifixion of Jesus; though Jesus' death and resurrection are central aspects of His life-story.

---

71 If God is to be omniscient it is necessary that God has knowledge of what suffering is and, arguably, has it from the perspective of one who has suffered. This is particularly true of the divine Messiah, if He is to act as bridge-builder between God and Man. [Heb 2:10; 4:12-5:9; 7:26-28 & Irenaeus "Adversus Haereses" lib 2 cap 22 #4]

72 Irenaeus (c 202) "Adversus Haereses" lib 5 cap 1 #2.

73 Mat 5:13; 13:33. Mk 9:50.

74 "He learned obedience through what he suffered." [Heb 5:8 RSV]

75 Rom 5:19, quoted on page 313.

76 Irenaeus (c 202) "Adversus Haereses" lib 3 cap 16 #6, cap 18 #1&7, cap 21 #1, cap 22 #3; lib 5 cap 20 #2 - cap 21 #2.

77 Irenaeus (c 202) "Adversus Haereses" lib 5 cap 17 #1.

Redemption

There are three uses of the word "redemption" in the Old Testament. The first is that of "buying back something which had been captured by an enemy or forfeited in some legitimate but forced transaction". The second is that of "exchanging something dear to one or more human beings but which rightfully belonged to God for something of less value or significance".[78] The third is that of "rescue from imminent danger".

Liberation

Christ's teaching, life, death and resurrection gave the lie to the idea that wrongdoing can separate the soul from God's benevolence. He took to Himself the enormity of human vice and injustice[79] (accepting the verdict of a show-trial and acquiescing in the death it meted out, "paying the price" demanded by our sin) and showed that it was of no consequence before the incomparably greater power of God's love.

Christ vanquished sin and death by proving that when they were given full reign to do their worst to Him they were powerless to frustrate His will. He descended into Sheol,[80] broke the bonds of the spirits that had been held there pending His triumph, and led them to Paradise. He passes His victory on to us by His offer of divine communion and of sacramental sharing in His death and resurrection. This is the "Christus Vincit" or "Liberation Theory" of the Atonement.

In Medieval times this theory was expressed in terms of Adam having sold himself and his descendants into slavery to Satan as a result of the Fall and Jesus paying a ransom to Satan in order to buy back humanity for God. There is, however, no scriptural justification for thinking that Christ "bought back" humanity from being in the thrall of any third party, other than the fear of death itself.[81] Saint Paul does make two passing references to a "price" being paid by God;[82] but he does not specify to whom it was paid. The epistle to the Hebrews refers to Christ's death as "destroying" the Devil, but not of it being any price paid to him.[83]

---

78 According to the Mosaic Law every first-born male child had to be redeemed. [Ex 13:13; 34:20. Num 16:15-18]

79 2Cor 5:21. Gal 3:13. 1Pet 2:24; 3:18.

80 Eph 4:9-10, 1Pet 3:18-20.

81 Heb 2:15

82 1Cor 6:20; 7:23.

83 Heb 2:14.

Emancipation

Christ also redeems humanity in the sense that in becoming one of us God ratified the fact that we have our own legitimate autonomy and are worthy of being taken seriously and dealt with on our terms; even when we do not return the complement and fail to respect God and to deal with God on God's terms. In this, God demonstrates the implacable divine concern for justice and for dealing respectfully with mankind.

Christ, acting in His manhood, effectively bought-out God's formal property rights over mankind, redeeming us from any residual slavish dependence upon God. In particular, Saint Paul tells us that Christ's death redeemed us from the divine tutelage or pedagogy which was partly what the Torah represented.[84] This is the "Emancipation Theory" of the Atonement.

Compassion[85]

Christ also acts as redeemer in an inverse sense. In one way or another, God is responsible for the suffering that is characteristic of the world. Just as God is due an apology from mankind for the contribution that humanity has made to the disharmony of the world, through greed, cruelty and conceit; so mankind is due some apology from God for the fact that God has allowed so many people to suffer, sometimes terribly.

However, all God would have to do to avoid being held accountable "and paying the price" for these facts is to remain outside and aloof from the material creation. The Divine Nature is not susceptible to critique, correction, punishment or pain. God simply cannot be penalised.

Nevertheless, it is inequitable for a superior to require a subordinate to suffer – for whatever reason – that which they are themselves not willing to share in. However, no price[86] that God could pay the sentient beings of Creation so as to make recompense for their suffering would inconvenience, trouble or discomfort God in the slightest. Neither would any penalty exacted on God enable God to empathise with the plight of suffering mortals. Hence the need for the Incarnation: for God to enter into and personally experience human reality.

84 Rom 7:1-6; 8:2. Gal 4:1-5. The Mosaic norms such as circumcision, Sabbath observance and dietary regulations were provisional measures. They were designed to establish a cultural framework for the Israelites which would elicit in them both an awareness of the ideals of holiness and justice and also a conviction that human beings are unable to attain these desirable goals by their own effort; that is, a knowledge of sin. [Rom 7:7-23] They were never proposed as binding on Gentiles, see page 223.

85 Thanks to A. Sadique for eliciting these thoughts.

86 1Cor 6:20, 7:23.

In our human reality, God has accepted due punishment from humanity for God's responsibility as the Creator of a world of suffering. If any-one ever feels that "God is to blame" for the evil that pervades this world; if any-one ever feels that "God should be made to pay" for "turning a blind eye" to disease, disharmony and disasters; they need only look at a crucifix to see God "taking the rap" for this charge.

God has not avoided responsibility for the suffering of the innocent and for the fact that the wicked often prosper and for the fact that the natural world is a dangerous and hostile place. Instead, God became one of us and was put on trial and was convicted and executed; though He was not arraigned on any reasonable charge. In our human reality, God has experienced the kind of grave injustice which every day cries to heaven for vengeance: and God did nothing to mitigate the physiological and psychological suffering resulting from this injustice. Instead, God suffered with us in the agonies of Christ's human soul.

This is the "Divine Compassion Theory" of the Atonement. It shares with the "Recapitulation Theory" the idea that Christ entered into our mode of life in order to partake in our experiences. It shares with the "Christus Vincit Theory" the idea that Christ paid a price as a redeemer, but suggests that the price was paid to humanity, not to Satan or to God.

Satisfaction

Christ offered amends to God for human sin by His integrity of life, even to the point of death. This offering was in complete conformity with justice and so was in "obedience to God's will."[87] It was therefore of superlative value and more than compensated for any formal offence "of disobedience", rendering any excuse for human shame absurd.[88]

> For as by one man's disobedience many were made sinners,
> so by one man's obedience many will be made righteous.
> [Rom 5:19 RSV]

Christ made this sacrificial offering as a man and on behalf of humanity; yet the value of His act lies not so much in the perfection of the human nature in and by which the act was executed as in the participation of the divine person who acted.

It was not necessary that Christ should die for the sins of humanity; for every tear-drop shed by the divine Messiah had infinite worth, and each one that fell individually served to adequately make up for all of

87 Rom 5:18-19. Heb 5:7-9; 10:5-10. Obedience to God's will should never be servile, but flow from a rational appreciation of what is just.

88 Heb 9:9-14, quoted on page 308.

human wickedness. God's infinite love is shown in the fact that Jesus did not simply act in a manner which was sufficient to make up for and purge away (that is *expiate*) the offences of humanity, but rather acted in the most extravagant way possible.

This is Anselm's "Restitution Theory" of the Atonement.[89] It has much to recommend it, but there is no Scriptural basis for believing it to be an exhaustive account of the matter. It was subsequently developed and promoted by Thomas Aquinas and so became the central thread of western Atonement doctrine. It is not popular in the Eastern Church, whose theologians view it as too legalistic in character and as placing too much emphasis on guilt, punishment and suffering.

Substitution

Anselm's doctrine later became the basis of the Protestant theory of "Penal Substitution". According to this narrative, God is constrained by "justice" and "hatred of sin" to take revenge for sin to an infinite degree. However, in His love, He did not wish to punish humanity by sending us all to Hell. Hence, God determined to punish Jesus instead; substituting His Son in our place and venting His righteous wrath on the Messiah, punishing Him vicariously for our offences against the divine honour.

The main justification for such a view of the matter is the prophetic text: "It was the will of the Lord to bruise him."[90] This seems clear enough at a first reading, and yet we are told only a little earlier that "we *esteemed* Him smitten by God and afflicted, *but* he was wounded for our transgressions,"[91] which suggests that it is wrong to think that God in any sense punished the Messiah for anything. Rather, the "will of the Lord" should be understood in a permissive way: that it was in accordance with God's purpose that the Messiah should be bruised, not that God set out with the objective of ensuring that this would happen as a precondition for the forgiveness of mankind's sins.

The following verses can be taken to support the Protestant doctrine.

> For God has done what the law, weakened by the flesh, could not do: sending His own Son in the likeness of sinful flesh and for sin, He condemned sin in the flesh, in order that the just requirement of the law might be fulfilled in us, who walk not according to the flesh but according to the Spirit.
> [Rom 8:3-4 RSV]

89 Anselm of Canterbury (1033-1109) "Cur Deus Homo" Book I.
90 Is 53:10 RSV.
91 Is 53:4-5 RSV.

> For our sake He made Him to be sin who knew no sin, so that in Him we might become the righteousness of God.
> [2Cor 5:21 RSV]

> He himself bore our sins in His body on the tree,[92] that we might die to sin and live to righteousness. By His wounds you have been healed.[93] [1Pet 2:24 RSV]

These texts are sometimes taken to mean that God punished Jesus, intentionally mistaking his "likeness of *sinful* flesh" for the real thing so that "the just requirement of the law" that sin ought to be punished could be fulfilled. However, they do not in fact present Jesus as being punished by anyone for anything. Moreover, even if Jesus had been punished by God this wouldn't have satisfied any *just* and *equitable* requirement for sin to be punished, for two reasons.

First, it is unjust for one party to be punished in place of another; except that one person may elect to pay a fine or make restitution for the offence of another: but this is not the issue here. Making restitution for an offence is not really punishment; it is rather the undoing of harm which has been done. Punishment is whatever penalty is imposed in addition to such restitution. Now in the case before us, no fine was payable and no restitution was made; other than in the sense that sin was in fact expiated: the harm of man's alienation from God being somehow undone by Jesus' life, death and resurrection and ascension. Rather, physical and emotional pain was inflicted and a life was forfeited, restored and glorified: which is an entirely different matter.

Second, any punishment imposed on Jesus could only be finite. While it might well be thought infinitely offensive that God be killed in human form (and it is certainly of infinite significance that God should chose to accept, embrace and forgive this outrage) the actual suffering experienced by Jesus (in terms of the quantity and quality of the physical and emotional pain He endured) was strictly finite, being limited by the bounds of His human constitution. Hence, no punishment inflicted on Jesus could possibly satisfy the infinite wrath of a vengeful deity.

Moreover, The Old Testament never suggests that sacrifice involves or has anything to do with the punishment of a sacrificial victim, not even in the case of the sin offering.[94] Sacrifice is always about "giving God a present" and never about offering God some kind of "whipping

---

92 "Surely he has borne our griefs and carried our sorrows." [Is 53:4]

93 "With his stripes we are healed." [Is 53:4-5]

94 Ex 29:14; 29:36; 30:10. Lev 4:1-6:7; 6:26-7:7; 16. Of course, grain and drink offerings, [Gen 4:3. Ex 29:41; 30:9; 40:29. Lev 2:1-16; 5:13; 6:14-23; 7:9-10; 23:13-18,37] did not involve the taking of animal life.

boy" substitute to be punished.[95] Only in the case of the "scape-goat"[96] is guilt ritually transferred to an animal, and this is the one case that an animal involved in ritual is not sacrificed.[97]

The texts actually speak of sin itself being condemned "in the flesh"; that is, by God's initiative in becoming human and "sending his own Son in the likeness of sinful flesh and for sin" "He made Him to be sin who knew no sin"[98] so that "He himself bore our sins".[99] I take this "condemnation" of sin to mean that sin's power to enslave human nature was taken from it as a result of Jesus' expiatory life, death, resurrection and ascension; with the result that those who "walk not according to the flesh but according to the Spirit" are "healed" and enabled to fulfil "the just requirement of the law" and so "live to righteousness" by being "doers of the law"[100] and even "become the righteousness of God".

Conclusion

Each of these accounts is inadequate and it is wise to affirm that the significance of Christ's Life, Death, Resurrection and Ascension is multifaceted. It is an example for our imitation; a demonstration of what it means to be fully human; a template for our own divinization; a ratification of God's commitment to Creation; the means for God to experience the human condition so that God might empathise with us and offer an apology for the sufferings we have to bear; the means for humanity to be redeemed from the vestiges of servile dependence upon God; and the proportionate expiation for the frailties, failures and wickedness of humanity. Now that humanity is redeemed, the way is fully open for everyone to take advantage of the offer of salvation, healing and fellowship which God holds out to us in loving-kindness.

---

95 See page 142.

96 See page 309.

97 According to the Babylonian Talmud [Yoma cap 6] the scapegoat was pushed off the edge of a cliff so as to fall to its death; but it is not certain that this is an accurate account of actual practice.

98 The superficial meaning of this is a nonsense. "Sin" is a state of being and a person cannot be a state of being, as such. At most, their nature might be characterized by such a state. In Jesus' case not even this is possible in any ordinary sense. I suggest that "sin" here means "separation from God" and that Jesus "became sin" in the sense of entering into that separation in the way that a bridge spans the gap between the two sides of a canyon. In a sense, the bridge becomes the gap while at the same time filling it and so eliminating it.

99 This could mean either *bore the consequences of our sins*, our "griefs and sorrows" as Isaiah puts it; or else *bore human nature,* which in us is compromised by concupiscence. [Rom 8:4]

100 Rom 2:13 RSV, quoted on page 213.

Chapter 17 The End of Things

> I saw… New Jerusalem, coming down out of heaven from God… and I heard a loud voice from the throne saying, "Behold, the dwelling of God is with men… He will wipe away every tear from their eyes, and death shall be no more, neither shall there be mourning nor crying nor pain any more, for the former things have passed away... Behold, I make all things new... I am the Alpha and the Omega, the beginning and the end. To the thirsty I will give from the fountain of the water of life without payment.[1] He who conquers shall have this heritage, and I will be his God and he shall be My son."[2]
>
> Then came one of the seven angels… and spoke to me, saying, "Come, I will show you the Bride, the wife of the Lamb." And in the Spirit he… showed me the holy city… And I saw no temple in the city, for its temple is the Lord God the Almighty and the Lamb. And the city has no need of sun or moon to shine upon it, for the glory of God is its light, and its lamp is the Lamb. By its light shall the nations walk; and the kings of the earth shall bring their glory into it,[3] and its gates shall never be shut by day – and there shall be no night there; they shall bring into it the glory and the honour of the nations.[4] [Apoc 21:1-26 RSV]

Motivation

There remains a problem. This is how to interpret the history of God's involvement with humanity. From a naïve perspective, there is no problem of course: God communicated the message God wanted to impart over time, preparing for the Incarnation; by which mankind's salvation was effected. Subsequently, the Gospel message has been preached throughout the world and those who accept it will be saved. This account of God's dealing with mankind may be satisfactory as far as it goes; but it raises two serious questions concerning the

---

1 Compare Is 55:1, quoted on page 304.
2 Compare Heb 1:7, quoted on page 321.
3 Compare Is 66:18-23, quoted on page 306.
4 Compare Hag 2:7, both RSV and KJV. See page 302.

seemingly impossible relationship between a spiritual and eternal God on the one hand and a material and temporal Cosmos on the other.

The first of these questions is: "Why is it that, in the case of human beings at least, immortal spirits are associated with material soul-bodies?" A much better alternative would seem to be beings constituted along the lines of the angels. How, indeed, can the Eternal, Perfect and Immaterial have any business with physicality, impermanence, imperfection, and mortality? Moreover: "Why has God elevated matter above pure spirit in dignity; primarily in the Incarnation itself, then also in the bodily Ascension of Christ and finally in the Assumption of His Mother?" God, although pure spirit, seems to have an unaccountable preference for materiality; or does this impression result from a naïve human prejudice arising from our own material perspective?

The second is: "What is the significance of the Incarnation Event?" If professed membership of the Church is not necessary for salvation (for the just[5] who died before Jesus' passion and resurrection have a full share in the redemption which He won for mankind,[6] without benefit of explicit faith in Christ) then what is the point of the Church, the Bible and the sacraments? If knowledge of God is not necessary for salvation, then why was it imparted at all? Contrariwise, if explicit faith in God and membership of the Church *are* necessary for salvation, then it would seem that God is partial and hence unjust.

The Importance of Matter

Everything about physicality is both messy and fragile. Our dependence on food, water, oxygen and a temperate climate makes us vulnerable. On a cosmic scale the conditions we require to survive are rare indeed. The complexity of our biology makes us liable to genetic disorders, auto-immune diseases, parasitical infections, and ageing. Our reproductive system (especially the birth process) is undignified and fraught with danger. Our natural and technological activities pollute the environment which we depend upon for sustenance. The instincts we have inherited from our pre-human past compromise our ability to act rationally and in accordance with the requirements of social living.

---

5 Such as Adam, [Wis 10:1] Abel, [Gen 4:4] Enoch, [Gen 5:22-24] Noah, [Gen 6-9. Wis 10:4] Abraham and Lot, [Gen 18-26. Is 41:8. Wis 10:5-6] Israel, [Wis 10:10-12] Joseph, [Wis 10:13-14] Moses, [Ex19:20-20:22; 33:11-34:10. Wis 10:16; 11:1] Elijah, [2Kings 2:11] Simeon, [Lk 2:34] John the Baptiser [Mat 11:11] and Jesus' adoptive father. [Mat 1:19-24]

6 1Pet 3:18-20, 4:6. Heb 11:8-16.

Gnosticism

The Gnostics were a diverse group prevalent in the first few centuries after the death of Jesus. Some were outwardly Christian, but others were not. All were characterized by the belief that salvation was to be obtained as a result of learning and understanding some secret teaching or knowledge: "gnosis" – hence the term "Gnostic".

Gnosticism typically addressed the problematic nature of material existence by proposing that the Creation was a huge mistake which had involved the calamitous mixing of spirit and matter, and that God is now busy trying to rectify the harm done by the foolish Demiurge[7] who created the physical Universe.

This kind of narrative does at least some justice to the apparent problem; by directly addressing the absurdity of physical mortality and acknowledging its simultaneously comic and tragic character. However, in doing so it undermines the integrity of the created order. Rather than giving a reasonable account of the Cosmos and hence showing how it is worthwhile, Gnosticism dismisses all that is physical and temporal as disordered and mistaken.

Kabbalah

A similar narrative features in Kabbalistic thought, though without the involvement of a secondary creator. Instead, the Kabbalah suggests that the Act of Creation was necessarily imperfect[8] and that at least "material evil" is an aspect of God's self-revelation (the ten *"sefiroth")* which correspond roughly to the "Divine Energies".[9]

Genesis and Plato

Genesis has an entirely different outlook; insisting that the Act of Creation was well-ordered and directly intended by God.

> And God saw everything that He had made, and behold, it was very good. [Gen 1:31 RSV][10]

Plato agrees with this evaluation, even though he is committed to the primacy of the spiritual and eternal over the physical and temporal. While the term "Demiurge" features in his writing; Plato identifies the Demiurge with the One all-wise God and not with some lesser being.

---

7 See note 1 on page 172.

8 Compare Plato "Timaeus" (30b), quoted on page 320.

9 Gregory of Palamas "Topics of Natural and Theological Science and on the Moral and Ascetic Life" # 68-150.

10 See also Wis 11:21-26, quoted on page 116.

> When the Father who had begotten the Universe observed it set in motion and alive… He was well pleased, and in His delight… He set himself to bringing this Universe to completion. [Plato "Timaeus" (37c)][11]

Plato further suggests that God's purpose in creation was to make the best thing possible;[12] namely, that independent system of being which most adequately and faithfully reflected the Divine Logos.

> It wasn't permitted… that One who is supremely good should do anything but what is best. Accordingly, the God… wanted to produce a piece of work that would be as excellent and supreme as its nature would allow.[10] [Plato "Timaeus" (30b)][13]

In effect, Plato argues that materiality is needed in order to explore and fill-out all the possibilities of existence[14] and concludes that God's exuberant self-expression of necessity involved material creation; as an artist might be impelled by his own nature to fabricate a master-work, so as to express himself and exhibit his vision of beauty. God poured significance and vitality into the work of creation, and God's business as Demiurge is to have the Cosmos show forth the rationale or Logos upon which it is constructed (which is the Divine Nature itself) as clearly as possible.

Is pure spirit possible?

If the angels (even the cherubim and seraphim) are not pure spirits then the problem of materiality does not arise. Certainly, for a spirit (that is, a personal subjectively conscious being) to be able to experience or to act, it needs a nature. Now, if it is the case that any created nature must be materially constituted, one way or another, it follows that spirit has to be associated with matter so as to exercise its agency and subjectivity: that is, to become involved with things, process and change. Hence, God's preference for matter over "pure spirit" is only apparent; for the supposedly preferable possibility of "pure spirit" is an impossibility.

> If any one imagine that at the end material, i.e., bodily, nature will be entirely destroyed, he cannot in any respect meet my view, how beings so numerous and powerful are able to live and to exist without bodies, since it is an attribute of the divine

11 See also "Gorgias" (508a) & "Timaeus" (29e-30c, 41a-44c, 92b)

12 The perfection of created being is necessarily limited, see page 262.

13 See also "Timaeus" (39e)

14 Plato "Timaeus" (41b-c)

> nature alone... to exist without any material substance... Another, perhaps, may say that in the end every bodily substance will be so pure and refined as to be like the æther,[15] and of a celestial purity and clearness. How things will be, however, is known with certainty to God alone, and to those who are His friends through Christ and the Holy Spirit.
> [Origen "De Principiis" lib 1 cap 6 #4]

In support of this view, it can be remarked that Jesus teaches that after the resurrection, re-embodied human beings will be "like angels in heaven."[16] This suggests that angels themselves have physical bodies, of a kind similar to that of the human resurrection body.[17]

Angels and humanity

The angels dwell close to God and perhaps have had only the very minimum opportunity necessary to obtain autonomy. They are the purest and most puissant of God's creatures,[18] but arguably they are also the most ethically naïve, being "least and most childlike of the sons of God".[19] Perhaps it is not possible for angels to become intimate friends of God, because it is impossible (or at least very difficult) for them to become independent of God without becoming alienated from God.

> For to what angel did God ever say, "Thou art My son, today I have begotten thee"[20]? Or again, "I will be to him a father, and he shall be to Me a son"[21]? [Heb 1:5 RSV]

---

15 The Aristotelian account of Angels is that they are entirely spiritual beings; whereas Platonists (as here, Origen) consider them to have physical bodies, albeit composed of subtle rather than common matter. Hence the Aristotelian thinks that an infinite number of angels might dance together on the head of a pin, whereas the Platonist thinks that only a finite number could accomplish this feat.

16 Mat 22:30 RSV.

17 While St Paul refers to the resurrection body as "spiritual", [1Cor 15:44] he does so as to contrast the resurrection nature of the saints with the mortal nature which we now have (which is compromised by immoderation or concupiscence) rather than to deny its materiality.

18 "Who makes His angels winds, and His servants flames of fire." [Heb 1:7 RSV.]

19 J.H. Cardinal Newman "The Dream of Gerontius." (1865)

20 Ps 2:7.

21 1Chron 28:6.

Although this text contrasts the status of the Messiah (rather than humanity in general) with that of the angels; it cannot be avoided that, according to the Gospel, God does offer to humankind the prospect of adoptive sonship.[22] Taking the Hebrews passage at face value, God has never made the same offer to any angel. Moreover, the Psalmist writes:

> What is man that Thou art mindful of him, and the son of man that Thou dost care for him? Yet Thou hast made him little less than God,[23] and dost crown him with glory and honour. Thou hast given him dominion over the works of Thy hands; Thou hast put all things under his feet. [Ps 8:4-6 RSV]

Humans have the disadvantage of not sharing in the angels' naïve intimacy with God (this was lost in the Fall) but have the advantage of a greater autonomy; which makes us capable of a divinization to which the angels cannot, it would seem, aspire. It may even have been the knowledge of this limitation of their being which corrupted the will of the fallen angels; for it is sometimes said that it was Satan's resentment of having to reverence the humanity of Christ (and to accept Jesus' mother as his Queen) which led to his fall. Indeed, in "The Life of Adam and Eve"[24] the angels are called upon to do obeisance to Adam, as the image of God, and Satan refuses to do so.[25]

> The wily one, the hostile Serpent, lamented with groans what he had undergone from the beginning through Adam, saying: "When God created man from the earth, indeed He ordered us, all of us, as One who knows the future and is Lord, saying: 'Come, all powers together now kneel before the one in My image whom I have created.' And at that time I fled, since I did not wish this; I was not willing to kneel before a created being." [Romanus the Melodist "On the Resurrection" V:23]

---

22 Compare Apoc 21:7, quoted at the head of this chapter.

23 The Hebrew is "elohiym", literally "the Lords". This is a plural term often employed in the Torah to signify the singular God. The KJV translation "the angels" (based on an analogical application of this text to Christ [Heb 2:6-9]) seriously distorts the original meaning.

24 This is a Jewish pseudepigraphical text. It is also known as "The Apocalypse of Moses" and "The Penitence of Adam". The original is thought to have been written in the First Century AD. The versions which survive all date from 200-500AD.

25 G.A. Anderson "The Fall of Satan in the Thought of St. Ephrem and John Milton" (2000)

The progress of history

So much for the problem of materiality. Now I wish to move on to the apparent partiality of God. The Judaeo-Christian view of history is that it is going somewhere. History is truly a story; with a beginning a middle and an end. It involves progress of a kind; being neither cyclical nor random, and moves forward more as a result of divine guidance than of human invention and intention. Nevertheless, history is often punctuated by what seem, from a human perspective, to be set-backs and disasters.

Disaster or providence?

Pre-history was also punctuated by disasters. The primeval planetary impact which rid Earth of most of its atmosphere and ejected the Moon from its mantle; the Permian Mass Extinction Event;[26] the demise of the dinosaurs and the repeated ice-ages of more recent geological times are only those examples most prominent in my mind.

Of course, sometimes what seems like a disaster turns out to be an opportunity for growth. So, if the Earth hadn't been parted from most of its atmosphere by the impact which gave rise to the Moon, the surface temperature of our planet would likely have been more like that of Venus, and Earth would have been unable to sustain life as we know it.

Similarly, the escape of the Israelites from Egyptian slavery brought them to an understanding of God as "liberator" and the subsequent Babylonian exile of the Jews exposed them to Zoroastrianism; which resulted in a purging of their religiosity from its fascination with fertility ritual and polytheism, the development of their own uncompromising form of monotheism and an understanding of the inalienable relationship between ethics and religious observance.

Salvation History

The story of God's involvement with humanity is best understood as Salvation History; and it would seem that this Salvation History is preparing something; as if the Cosmos itself is gestating some offspring, and is even now in labour pains.[27] The Apostle Paul tells us that God's plan is to unite all creation harmoniously under Christ.[28] This involved sending Adam and Eve away from the divine presence, so that their descendants might be educated and perfected in tribulation before being gathered back together by the Second Adam[29] and Good Shepherd into the one fold of the Kingdom of God.

---

26 D. Raup & J. Sepkoski "Mass extinctions in the marine fossil record" (1982)
27 Rom 8:22, quoted on page 192.
28 Eph 1:15-23, see page 310.
29 1Cor 15:22,45.

The Incarnation[30] is the central event in this history. It had a spiritual impact on ethics and anthropology comparable to the physical impact of a comet on the Earth. After the Incarnation, the significance of humanity could never again be doubted. On the one hand, the Incarnation was a catastrophic event: as it resulted in the religious leaders of God's chosen people (on behalf of the whole human race) having the divine Messiah executed by the civil authorities of the day. No other human act could be as wicked as this God-slaying. On the other hand, the Incarnation was a glorious event: as Jesus' death was the dramatic and definitive declaration of God's unconditional love for humanity. The blood He shed was the sacrament[31] of the promised New Covenant:[32] the sign that gave effect to it. Moreover, Christ's death was the prerequisite for His Resurrection and Ascension – which two events constituted the final authentication and ratification of our atonement with God.

What then about those who die before Salvation History is complete? Jesus tells us that those who work in the vineyard from break of dawn will have their reward, just as much as those that come late to the endeavour. "So the last will be first and the first last."[33] In the end, all will have an equitable share in the inheritance to which all have contributed.[34]

Election and reprobation

Now, this is all well and good – until one realises that the more one believes that God has intervened positively in human history in any specific ways, at any specific times, and in any specific places; the more it seems to follow that those who are benefited by these interventions must be at an advantage over those who are not so blessed. After all, if they are not advantaged, what was the point of the intervention? It then seems to follow that those who are not affected positively by any supposed divine intervention are thereby *disadvantaged*, and this would seem to make God partial, and hence unjust.

So, the acceptance of Abel was a refusal of Cane;[35] the rescue of Noah and his family an abandonment of their fellows to disaster;[36] the

---

30 See page 307.

31 The original meaning of sacrament was "oath" or "pledge".

32 Jer 31:31-34.

33 Mat 20:16 RSV.

34 1Cor 15:21-29; 42-54.

35 Gen 4:1-5. However, Cane the fratricide was favoured with special protection from God. [Gen 4:15]

36 Gen 6-7.

call of Abraham an exclusion of his neighbours;[37] the choice of Isaac a dismissal of Ishmael;[38] the blessing of Jacob a disinheritance of Esau;[39] and the giving of the Torah to Moses and the Israelites a marginalization of the Gentiles.[40] Some of these choices can be understood in terms of the reward of the righteous and the punishment of the wicked, but not all of them. In particular, there is no reason to believe that Cane, Ishmael or Esau did anything to deserve the rejection which they seem to suffer. On the contrary, Jacob connived with his mother to deceive his father and to rob his elder brother of his birthright and benefited from this duplicity.

The universal invitation to salvation

In response to this difficulty, the Catholic faith assures us that God truly desires the salvation of all souls[41] and that everyone is in one way or another given sufficient opportunity, encouragement and help (that is, grace) to be saved.[42] The fact that someone lived and died before the Incarnation; or in some part of the globe where the Gospel had not penetrated does not mean that they have no share in the "inheritance of the saints".[43] In such matters "God shows no partiality."[44] An individual is worthy of God's friendship in as far as they "hunger and thirst after righteousness"[45] and it is entirely possible to earnestly desire, seek and work for justice and peace without any specific knowledge of the Judaeo-Christian revelation.[46] Jesus of Nazareth plays this idea out very clearly on at least three occasions in his ministry.

First, He compliments a Roman Centurion on the excellence of his faith; though that officer represents the pagan oppression of the Jewish people.[47] Second, He tells a Syrophoenician woman that

37 Gen 12:1-7.

38 Gen 17:18-21; 21:9-12. However, Ishmael was promised a special destiny by God. [Gen 21:13-21]

39 Gen 25-27. However, Esau was eventually reconciled to his brother [Gen 33:1-16] and became the patriarch of Edom. [Gen 36:1]

40 Ex 31:12-18.

41 1Tim 2:4. 2Pet 3:9.
FCD IV sec 1 cap 3 #11.1

42 Jn 1:9. Rom 5:18. 2Cor 5:15. 1Tim 2:6. 1Jn 2:2.
FCD IV sec 1 cap 3 #11.2 c

43 Col 1:12 RSV.

44 Rom 2:11 RSV. See also verses 13-14, quoted on page 213.

45 Mat 5:6 RSV, see also Is 56:1.

46 Rom 2:6-16.

47 Mat 8:5-13. Lk 7:1-10.

although the children of Israel must be fed first, her own urgent desire will be fulfilled.[48] Third, He tells a Samaritan woman that although "you worship what you do not know... for salvation is from the Jews"[49] soon all people would be invited to worship God "in Spirit and in Truth."[50] Then He offers her "living water" and finally favours her people with a visit amounting to two whole days, telling them at length of the Kingdom of God.[51] In each of these encounters Jesus disregards the fact that the person He is dealing with is excluded from the fellowship of Israel, either by birth or supposed heresy. In fact Jesus explicitly insists that, as Good Shepherd, He has sheep which are not of the Jewish fold.[52]

Opportunity or constraint?

Moreover, what looks like opportunity can in fact be constraint and what looks like exclusion can be a mandate to explore alternate possibilities. Many situations and experiences, positive or negative, can be either an opportunity or a threat when it comes to the development of character.

The parables of "the talents"[53] and "the workers in the vineyard"[54] both indicate that what matters about this life is not the absolute outcomes that we have to show for our efforts, but what we make of our lives relative to the opportunities and abilities we are given. "Every one to whom much is given, of him will much be required."[55] This is a consoling thought and makes sense of the normal range of human advantage and disadvantage.

The rich man might do much good with his money, but typically is trapped by the concerns of ownership and the glamour of wealth.[56] The poor man is free from those snares, but instead tends to be distracted from spiritual matters by the pressing need to obtain his next meal. The man who leads a life free of suffering and sorrow has reason to be thankful, but is more liable to be complacent and unsympathetic towards the suffering of others. The man whose life is a "vale of tears" has the opportunity to use his own experience as a basis for understanding the pain and hurt of other souls and to help them to overcome with their

48 Mat 15:26-27. Mk 7:27-28.
49 Jn 4:22 RSV.
50 See also Is 56:4-7. quoted on page 327.
51 Jn 4:1-42.
52 Jn 10:16.
53 Mat 25:14-30, quoted on page 117.
54 Mat 20:1-16.
55 Lk 12:48 RSV.
56 Mat 19:23-25. Mk 10:24-26. Lk 18:24-26.

traumas, but may instead become embittered. The academic has the chance to learn and discover and teach, but easily becomes obsessed with obtaining preferment and fame.[57] The monk is free to devote himself to prayer, but can be trapped in a life focussed on hateful self-denigration rather than loving self-forgetfulness.

So it may be that life is not so unfair as it might seem, and that most people have a good prospect for fulfilment and for sanctification and to make their contribution to God's plan[58] – if only they make the best of those opportunities which come their way and occupy themselves with the life which they in fact have, rather than pining after some other different one. Isaiah tells us that those who are despised and deemed by society to be rejected by God will, in the end, be specially favoured by God.[59]

> To the eunuchs who keep My sabbaths, who choose the things that please Me and hold fast my covenant, I will give in My house and within My walls a monument and a name better than sons and daughters;[60] I will give them an everlasting name which shall not be cut off. And the foreigners who join themselves to the Lord, to minister to him, to love the name of the Lord, and to be His servants, every one who keeps the sabbath, and does not profane it, and holds fast My covenant – these I will bring to My holy mountain, and make them joyful in My house of prayer;[61] their burnt offerings and their sacrifices will be accepted on My altar; for My house shall be called a house of prayer for all peoples. [Is 56:4-7 RSV]

The significance of mortal life

Nevertheless, there remains a mystery here. If mortal life is significant, a necessary ethical preparation for the eternal life that follows; then those whose lives are severely restricted (such as the chronically ill, the still-born and aborted, the seriously disabled, depressed or insane and those who live in abject poverty or enforced servitude) must miss out on whatever this significance might be. Similarly, those who are excluded from the Church by reason of geography, culture or history (or are otherwise marginalised in the way of spiritual things) must surely be at some kind of disadvantage before God.

---

57 Lk 11:43.
58 Mat 12:26. Mk 10:27. Lk 18:27.
59 Is 56:1-8.
60 Compare Lev 21:17-23 & Deut 38:33.
61 Compare Is 66:18-23, quoted on page 306.

Indeed, it seems that while some people have many opportunities to grow as human beings, to fulfil their potential, to become virtuous and holy, to enter into communion with God, and to contribute to the establishment of the Kingdom of God; others have few possibilities for any kind of development: physical, intellectual, political or ethical.

> You say that the purpose of this life is to grow in ethical maturity. The first and most obvious problem with this is the death of the young. They do not have the least opportunity to obtain ethical maturity. They are born into this world, and without any apparent possibility of obtaining the purpose of this life, they are taken out of it. [J. Kramer (2012)]

While it is easy to understand the contribution that some people make to God's plan, it is hard to discern the purpose of those lives which are short and tragic, or filled with suffering and devoid of human love.

Consider the case of a man who has a benign brain tumour which makes him excessively and irrationally violent. While he is not culpable for his actions (which do not flow from his mental character as such, but only from a physical deformation, and which are not correctable either by means of reward and punishment or by discursive education) it is difficult to see how his mortal life can be understood as any kind of preparation for eternal life. The major behaviour patterns of his soul-mind (his habits, morals and character) are determined by the physical abnormality which overwhelms the functioning of his brain, and in particular subverts his ability to learn how to behave morally.

The archetypical example is the man possessed (through no fault of his own) by a demon. He is unable to express his own character. He is unable to learn about good and evil by trial and error. He is unable to experience love. Although he is alive in a biological sense, the life which he is living is not his own life but only that of the demon which has possession of him. While he is not blameworthy for the actions which the demon perpetrates using his body, neither does he seem to have any opportunity to do anything meritorious: no chance to grow as a human being, to fulfil his nature and to develop his own proper style of life. His existence appears to be an ethical cypher.

One response to this conundrum is to postulate that anyone whose life is a cypher was never a properly human being; that is, their soul was never impersonated with an immortal spirit. Although they seemed outwardly human, they were never inwardly so, but only animal: having no more than a sub-human existence. This is what most people would informally believe about pre-term still-births and of infants born without either a head: "acephaly", or without much of a brain: "anencephaly".[62] They are so clearly not human beings (though their genetics and the rest of their physiology is virtually human) that few people would count them as such. Given these tragic precedents, it is not unthinkable that there may be other, less obvious examples. God could providentially arrange this by only infusing an immortal conscious spirit into those potential human beings whose lives were foreseen to be fit for purpose.

This neatly solves the problem of "human beings who never live authentically human lives" by insisting that the set in question is empty. It is a dangerous opinion, however, as it could be used to justify classifying various sociological or ethnic groups (such as Muslims, Jews, Catholics, Gypsies, foreigners in general, psychopaths, paedophiles and homosexuals) as sub-human, not worthy of respect as spiritual persons and devoid of those fundamental rights which arise directly from a human being's formal similarity with God.

Of course, the fact that an idea can be misused does not make it wrong. Even if we knew for sure that some apparent human beings were not actual human beings this would not justify our treating anyone as less than human; because it could never be established that any specific individual was not properly human. It would always be necessary to give anyone the benefit of the doubt.

A second response is to postulate that anyone whose mortal life is a cypher is reincarnated so as to gain adequate life-experience to fit them for immortality. While this is an attractive idea, it does not explain why some people have to suffer degrading or agonising circumstances in the first place, which is the most pressing issue. The prospect of a second chance does not justify the indignity or agony of their first experience. Moreover, belief systems which feature reincarnation typically combine it with the idea that ill-fortune in life is a consequence of unrighteousness in a previous existence, but this idea is entirely foreign to Catholic theology.

> As he passed by, He saw a man blind from his birth. And His disciples asked him, "Rabbi, who sinned, this man or his parents, that he was born blind?" Jesus answered, "It was not that this man sinned, or his parents, but that the works of God might be made manifest in him." [Jn 9:1-3 RSV]

---

62 The official Catholic position is that "the spiritual soul" is specifically created and immediately infused by God into the body at the moment of biological conception. This would seem to imply that every embryo which fails to implant and every foetus which naturally aborts represents a futile life.

> There were some present at that very time who told Him of the Galileans whose blood Pilate had mingled with their sacrifices. And He answered them, "Do you think that these Galileans were worse sinners than all the other Galileans, because they suffered thus? I tell you no! But unless you repent you will all likewise perish. Or those eighteen upon whom the tower in Silo'am fell and killed them, do you think that they were worse offenders than all the others who dwelt in Jerusalem? I tell you no! But unless you repent you will all likewise perish." [Lk 13:1-5 RSV]

These first two responses both conflict with the fact that the Church honours the Holy Innocents[63] as martyrs; for these died without having any opportunity to develop virtues or vices and yet are invoked as saints. This makes no sense if either they never had immortal spirits, so they could not possibly become saints; or they were reincarnated, and so did not in fact become saints. Perhaps the feast of the Holy Innocents should be understood as symbolic: signifying that collateral damage is involved in the divine economy and that God will make sense of all such situations; rather than indicating that certain actual individuals achieved salvation. In this case the conflict is only apparent, not real.

Moreover, these two responses also conflict with how the Church celebrates the funerals of baptised infants with joy and not sadness, treating them as having passed immediately to heaven as saints.[64] This practice is, however, based more on a double negative rather than anything positive. It is justified on the basis that as there is no possible reason why such a child would spend any time in purgatory as a result of personal sins, still less finish up in Hell; and as these are the only options envisaged by conventional theology the conclusion that the dead infant passes immediately to Heaven follows immediately.

A third response is to postulate that anyone whose mortal life is no more than a cypher has the advantage of certain salvation, but the disadvantage of the quality of their eternal existence being minimal.[65] The image of a baroque cherub forever playing a harp, innocently and happily seated on a puffy cloud springs to mind. To use St Paul's imagery, when they come to the purifying fire there is neither any vice to burn away nor any virtue to reveal: in fact, there is no character or personality at all.

---

63 The infants who we are told were executed by King Herod in his attempt to execute the Messiah. [Mat 2:16-18]

64 The collect for the burial of a baptised infant in the traditional Latin Liturgy is unambiguously explicit in this regard.

65 FCD V cap 1 #3.3 b.

Now, this answer is not satisfactory either; for it amounts to the idea that although souls with a very limited experience of mortality are "saved", they do not continue to "exist" in a worthwhile manner. The life of such a "saved" soul after their divine judgement is hardly more than a cypher; so it is as true to say that they are not saved as to say that they are saved: there is little or nothing human to save or to fail to save beyond their naked hypostatic identity, their mere ghost or spirit.[66]

It is difficult to see what other outcome is possible, however: for if no autonomous personality has developed, there is none to be perfected and preserved. Any thought that such a soul might have the prospect of significant betterment beyond death[67] raises the deeper question as to the needfulness of life before death; which is so very often "a vale of tears" and difficult to bear. If a soul that has not really lived in this world is not at some great disadvantage, then it would seem cruel of God to require souls to endure mortal existence as a prelude to eternal life; for if there was any way to avoid the sorrows of mortality, without great cost, then this option would be much preferable. Indeed, following conventional theology remorselessly to its limit, it would seem better to painlessly execute every child as soon as it is baptised: for in that way every one would be certain of attaining heaven.

Salvation: individual and corporate

Salvation is corporate as well as individual. The Church does not simply exist to facilitate the salvation of individuals, through baptism, instruction, enlightenment and justification. Individuals also exist to facilitate the salvation of society, through the establishment of the Kingdom of God. If every child was baptised and then executed, they would not be able to contribute to the perfection of society and very soon there would be no society to perfect. Each of us is appointed in this mortal life with certain responsibilities. For some, these are primarily the care and ruling of their own souls, which is the contemplative vocation; for others, they are the care and ruling of others, which is the active or apostolic vocation.

> It is better for everyone to be ruled by divine reason, preferably within himself and his own, otherwise imposed from without, so that as far as possible all will be alike and friends, governed by the same thing. [Plato "Republic" (IX 590d)]

---

66 1Cor 3:10-15.

67 This seems contrary to the Catholic Faith. [FCD V cap 1 #1.3]

We have, first, the commission to use the talents which God has given us and, second, the daily opportunities to do so – for our own good and the good of our neighbour. As we respond either well or badly to the vocation we have been given,[53] we either help the cause of justice (both interiorly, in our own soul, and exteriorly in society at large) or else harm it. If we learn from the process, we become fit for Eternal Life; if we do not, then we remain unfit for life in God's Kingdom.

Salvation history is the process by which human society is gradually being transformed from injustice into justice – from the Kingdom of Man into the Kingdom of God – just as each individual life is the opportunity for a soul to be uplifted from depravity into holiness.

> The kingdom of heaven is like leaven[68] which a woman took and hid in three measures of flour, till it was all leavened.
> [Mat 13:33 RSV]

None of God's interventions in human affairs should be understood as favouring those persons who directly receive God's message, commission or help. Always, one should interpret God's particular interventions as being for the general good. Any grace received by an individual or group is granted for the service of those not directly involved, and always comes with a responsibility towards those who are not immediately affected. Just as the Jews were chosen by God not for their own advantage but for the good of the Gentiles,[69] so the Catholic Church does not exist primarily for the benefit of its members; but rather for the salvation of non-Catholics; and not so much by their conversion to Catholicism as by the ethical effect on their consciences of the example that Catholics should be setting in their daily lives.

> We are not called to discipleship to be saved, but are called to discipleship in order to announce salvation to others. Those who are saved are those who do the Father's will; whether or not they are professed disciples.[70] On the other hand, even if a disciple has been a disciple for long and has prayed time and again in the way that they ought, they will not enter the Kingdom of God if they fail to do God's will.[71]

---

68 That is, yeast.

69 Gen 12:3. Ps 66; 95; 116. Is 42:1-6; 49:3-7; 66:16-23. Jer 1:5; 3:17. Micah 4:1-3. Zech 2:10-11; 8:18-23. Jonah. Sir 44:19-23.

70 Lk 9:40-50. Rom 2:6-16.

71 Mat 7:21.

The Good News, therefore, is that those who fulfil the beatitudes,[72] whether or not they are professed disciples, will enter the kingdom of heaven. And the purpose of being a disciple of Christ is to make this Gospel known to all nations, and so to make disciple to continue the mission. Now, if that was the whole of the Gospel, it would be rather depressing for sinners; but in fact there is also the part about God saving sinners. This should not be understood to conflict with the commission to tell the poor in spirit, those who mourn, the meek, those who hunger and thirst for righteousness, the merciful, the pure of heart, the peacemakers and those persecuted for the sake of the cause of justice, that their hope is not in vain: whether or not they are professed disciples.

Notice how another part of the disciples' mission is to have faith and to propagate faith. This is made particularly obvious when the disciples fail to heal as requested and expected to do.[73] The reason, they are told, is because of a lack of faith, and this lack of faith is what enrages Christ. The point, I think, is not that you need to believe in order to work miracles (for Christ almost never says that it is His faith that has healed the sick) but the faith of the afflicted person or their sponsor that has healed them. In other words, it is not one's own faith in God that works the miracles, rather it is the spreading of faith to others (by a disciplined life of prayer and fasting[74]) that people can be healed and that the Kingdom of God is at hand.[75]

The purpose of discipleship and of the disciples' commission, is not only to encourage long-suffering righteous folk, nor merely to go announce the good news of redemption to sinners and sick, but to spread an attitude or perspective of faith. This insistence on spreading faith defines the sort of love which disciples are also mandated to spread. It is not a dispassionate humanitarianism that they are told to promote, but a love filled with eschatological hope; since it is that sort of hope which makes faith – and so miracles possible.
[J.F. Garneau "Private Communication" (2012)]

72 Mat 5:1-12.
73 Mat 17:14-20. Mk 9:14-29.
74 Mk 9:29 RSV, Catholic edition.
75 Mat 3:2; 4:17; 19:7. Mk 1:15.

Plato's Republic

Plato had a vision of a Kingdom of Justice. He describes it in more prescriptive terms than does Jesus, and some of his ideas (especially the systematic destruction of family life) strike the modern ear as ludicrous and even inhumane. Nevertheless, Plato's motives were close to those of Jesus. Both of them were concerned to establish a society of mutual care based on friendship and equity; where all was ordered and peaceful, and where there was no conflict, pain or suffering. When faced with the impossibility of ever establishing such a society Plato opined that:

> No city, constitution, or individual man will ever become perfect until either some chance event compels those few philosophers who aren't vicious… to take charge of a city… and compels the city to obey them, or until a god inspires the present rulers and kings or their offspring with a true erotic love for true Philosophy… Then the philosopher, by consorting with what is ordered and divine and despite all the slanders around that say otherwise, himself becomes as divine and ordered as a human being can… One such individual would be sufficient to bring to completion all the things that now seem so incredible, providing that his city obeys him. [Plato "Republic" (VI 499b-502b)]

This can be taken as a prophecy of Jesus, who was the offspring of King David and who had "a true erotic love for true Philosophy"[76] and who was "as divine and ordered as is humanly possible" and who founded the Church as a seed[77] which has the potential to grow into the completion of all things,[78] providing only that the potential citizens of His heavenly city obey Him.

Building bridges and breaking-down barriers

Every division exists to be broken down; the demolition of division being the prime business of the Church, following on from the initiative of Christ.[79] Hence, the rich exist to serve the poor and find their salvation in fulfilling this role.[80] The poor and infirm exist so that those more fortunate might care for them and alleviate their distress. They obtain a presentiment of divine love in the care which they receive.

---

76 Mat 7:24; 10:16; 24:45; 25:1-9. Lk 12:42. Jn 8:23-47; 18:37-38.
77 Jn 12:24; 31-33, quoted on page 81.
78 Mat 13:31-32. Mk 4:31. Lk 13:19. Also Eph 1:15-23, see page 310.
79 Eph 2:10-22. Gal 3:23-29.
80 Mat 25:31-40.

Similarly, the ignorant exist so that the wise might school them and the wise exist to do so. Both wise and ignorant benefit from this educative process, learning from each other's questions and answers.

The business of the Church is to become the true Tower of Babel. The original Babel project was inspired by hubris and conceit. God's New Babel project is a very different affair. The Church gathers together people of all races, giving them a single voice, uniting them in the common task of establishing friendship across all nations, and directing them in the construction of God's Eternal City;[81] which will tower over its foundations into the Heavens. Not everyone is called to contribute directly (still less equally) in the construction of this city; but all are expected to strive to become its worthy citizens.[82] All are welcome to enter its courts and to find refuge, solace and joy there. All are invited to dwell in this divine metropolis.[83]

Sacraments and Magisterium

The sacraments of the Church do not exist to delineate between the saved and the damned; for God's saving grace is not limited to the realm of sacramental action. Rather, they exist to provide support and solace for those who are especially engaged in the struggle to establish the Kingdom, and who have a special and onerous responsibility to bear witness to the truth before mankind.

The proper role of the Catholic Magisterium is not to enforce orthodoxy and orthopraxy, with the punitive aim of excluding from the means of grace those individuals who do not seem to conform to these norms. Rather, it is to ensure that the activity of the Church as an institutional whole is does not deviate from Her divine mission onto merely secular and human objectives.

> It is not the Magisterium that imposes doctrine. It is the Magisterium that helps enable the conscience itself to hear God's voice, to know what is good, what is the Lord's will. It is only an aid so that personal responsibility, nourished by a lively

81 Heb 11:16; 12:22.

82 1Cor 9:24-25. 1Tim 4:7-10. In "Republic" Plato teaches that social justice and interior justice mirror each other, so the two vocations are not clearly distinct. Similarly, the Apostle Peter tells us that we are each living stones to be built together into God's spiritual house [1Pet 2:5] and the Apostle Paul teaches that we are each organs of the one Body of Christ. [Rom 12:4. 1Cor 12:12-27]

83 See Psalm 86, where the gentiles are accounted by God as having been born in Jerusalem.

> conscience, may function well and thus contribute to ensuring that justice is truly present in our society: justice within ourselves and universal justice for all our brothers and sisters in the world today. [Benedict XVI "Greeting to the Pastoral Council of the Parish of St Felicity and her children" (2007)]

The Old Testament and the New

The Old Testament Church was national and exclusive. It was based on the idea of blood-kin: the family, clan and nation. The purpose of the Mosaic Covenant was to forge the Jews into a peculiar people[84] who were entirely focussed on God and on the holy Torah which God gave them; the possession of which ennobled them and made it possible for them to be a witnesses of righteousness to the Nations.[85] Those Gentiles who took note of this testimony, or who otherwise developed a "hunger and thirst for righteousness"[86] were then justified by their being "doers of the law" which was "written on their hearts."[87] Once the Jews had matured in their understanding of justice the stage was prepared for the incarnation, and for the New Testament Church to be founded. This Church is not based on ties of blood. She is open to all and she addresses her doctrine to all; that is, she is Catholic. She is Holy in principle, but still imperfect as realised in practice; being compromised by human sin, ignorance and injustice. Still, she has Jesus' promises of indefectibility[88] and of Holy Spirit's guidance.[89]

The Two Commissions[90]

The commission given at the start of Genesis is addressed to a spousal couple who are told to "be fruitful and multiply".[91] Picking up from this, the Gospel of Matthew begins with a genealogy of faith transmitted by blood.[92] Jesus is then presented as the singular product of the strangest of families: "born, not of blood nor of the will of the flesh nor

---

84 Deut 7:6; 14:2. Ps 104:43. Is 43:16-21.
85 Is 55:1-5. Rom 2:17-24.
86 Mat 5:6 RSV, see also Is 56:1.
87 Rom 2:13-15 RSV.
88 Mat 16:15-19.
89 Jn 16:13. Acts 13:4; 15:28; 16:6.
90 Private communication from J.F. Garneau (2012).
91 Gen 1:28 RSV.
92 Mat 1:1-17.

of the will of man, but of God".[93] He begins His ministry at a wedding,[94] but proceeds to preach a new kind of multiplication[95] and fruitfulness[96] based on adherence to the values of the Gospel, not of the family.[97]

Jesus' final command is not given to a spousal pair but to eleven male disciples[98] who had given up homes, wives, brothers, parents and children for the sake of the Kingdom of God;[99] and who had been instructed to call no-one father, other than their Heavenly Father,[100] so that they could all become the brother, and sister, and mother of Christ.[101] This command was not that they should procreate children but rather "make disciples of all nations"[102] by preaching and baptising and so engender spiritual offspring.[103]

The Church and the Kingdom

The story of the Church is one of discovering how to become the Kingdom. At first, it was thought this would be a brief process; amounting to the incorporation of whatever portion of the population as was willing into the fellowship of the Church, which was to be run on Communist lines.[104] In fact it has turned out to be a long and painful adolescence, characterized by many lapses and set-backs.

It is the business of every follower of Christ to work towards the perfection of the Church and the coming of the Kingdom.[105] This means first striving for personal integrity and holiness of life, but it also means seeking to establish communities and friendly support networks which advance and implement the Kingdom values of kindness, sobriety,

---

93 Jn 1:13 RSV. Compare Mat 1:18-23. Lk 1:26-35.
94 Jn 2:1-10
95 Mat 14:16-21; 15:32-38; 16:5-12.
96 Mat 3:8-10; 7:15-20; 12:33-38; 21:18-21.

> "Fill the Earth and Master it" could refer to a fullness and perfection of life and power, so that... "increase and multiply" would mean a development of the intellect and an abundance of virtue... just as it says in the psalm: "You have increased my soul in virtue." In this case, the human race would not have received a succession of offspring, if sin had not caused there to be a succession unto death. [Augustine "The Good of Marriage" II]

97 Mat 8:21-22; 10:34-37.
98 Mat 28:16.
99 Mat 19:29.
100 Mat 23:9.
101 Mat 12:50.
102 Mat 28:19 RSV.
103 1Cor 5:15
104 Acts 4:32-37.
105 Mat 6:10.

prudence, courage, consideration, compassion, reconciliation, justice and peace.[106] Today, this process is far from complete; largely because the leadership of the Church refuses to face up to its past failings, refuses to analyse how they arose and hence is unable to repent of the underlying attitudes which gave rise to them and which will continue to frustrate the Church's mission until they are recognised and rejected.

When the process is terminated, the Final Judgement will ensue. The New Heaven and New Earth which will result will be the perfection of the Church.[107] All the just dead will then rise to become citizens of this perfect Divine State; prepared within the history of real men and women, refined by their suffering and established by God on the principle of justice for all.

Death and Resurrection

It is a moot point as to whether God's New Babel project will seem to succeed or fail in human terms; that is, whether the process will terminate within history as a full implementation of the Gospel and apparent victory for the Church,[108] or in Her apparent degeneration and consequent defeat.[109] It might seem that if history is progressing towards a fulfilment, then the fulfilment towards which it runs must be one that flows out of and justifies all the previous struggle and suffering; for if not, what was the point of all this tribulation? Hence, the final maturation and victory of the Church would seem to be inevitable. However, those indications which we find in the Gospel regarding this question are at odds with this view. Most eerily of all, Jesus casts doubt on whether He will find anyone who has remained faithful to the Gospel when He returns at the end of time.

> "And will not God vindicate his elect, who cry to him day and night? Will he delay long over them? I tell you, He will vindicate them speedily. Nevertheless, when the Son of Man comes, will He find faith on Earth?" [Lk 18:7-8 RSV]

---

106 The Church's best fruits have, perhaps, materialised within monasticism; where a concern for personal holiness is fused with a commitment to stable, supportive and wholesome community.

107 Apoc 21:1-26, quoted at the head of this chapter.

108 R.H. Benson "Dawn of All" (1911)

109 R.H. Benson "Lord of the World" (1908)

Postscript

I hope you have enjoyed reading this book and have not been too scandalised by the ideas which it contains. I hope to have challenged some of your previous ideas and encouraged you to look at the question of the "Meaning of Life" in a new way. I hope that if you still do not believe in the reality of God, you can at least understand why it is that those of us who hold this view do so; both in terms of our motivation and our evidential basis. Most of all, I hope that you will be inspired to "hunger and thirst after righteousness". If you do, I am sure that you will be satisfied. May "the Lord bless you and keep you; the Lord make his face to shine upon you, and be gracious to you; the Lord lift up his countenance upon you, and give you peace."[1]

> "Perhaps… there is a model of it in heaven, for anyone who wants to look at it and to make himself its citizen on the strength of what he sees." [Plato "Republic" (IX 592b)]

> "You are the light of the world. A city set on a hill cannot be hid. Nor do men light a lamp and put it under a bushel, but on a stand, and it gives light to all in the house. Let your light so shine before men, that they may see your good works and give glory to your Father who is in heaven." [Mat 5:14-16 RSV]

> "Come, Lord Jesus!" [Apoc 22:20 RSV]

1 Num 6:24-26 RSV.

Bibliography

As full a source listing to each quotation or reference has been given as possible. While in the text the dates given are those of authorship, here the date of the edition consulted has been given. Sometimes, of course, these differ by centuries. On occasion, the URL of a source has been given either in addition to or in place of a paper text.

The Plato quotes are from the translations found in "Plato: Complete Works" ed J.M. Cooper and D.S. Hutchinson, (Hackett: 1997). Bible quotations are generally from the Revised Standard Version, Catholic Edition (1946, 1952, 1957, 1966), the copyright of which belongs to the Division of Christian Education of the National Council of the Churches of Christ in the United States of America. The numbering of the Psalms follows the Vulgate and is mostly one less than in Protestant Bibles; so "The Lord in My Shepherd" is the beginning of Psalm 22 not Psalm 23.

Abbreviations

Eccl **"Ecclesiastes".** This is a book of the Hebrew Bible.

Sir **"The Wisdom of Jesus ben Sirach".** This is a book of the Septuagint and Vulgate Bibles which is not part of the Hebrew Bible. It is also known as Ecclesiasticus.

Wis **"The Wisdom of Solomon"**. This is a book of the Septuagint and Vulgate Bibles which is not part of the Hebrew Bible.

The following texts are referenced more than once. Their full publication details are given here to avoid tedious repetition.

CCC **Catechism of the Catholic Church.**[1]
(The Holy See; Vatican: 1994)

FCD **L. Ott "Fundamental of Catholic Dogma"**
(Tan; Rockford IL: 4th Ed 1974)

LNS **S.C. Lovatt "New Skins for Old Wine: Plato's Wisdom for Today's World"**
(Universal; Boca Raton: 2007)

ODP **Origen "De Principiis"** in **"Tertullian, part fourth; Minucius Felix; Commodian; Origen, parts first and second " tr A. Cleveland Coxe "Ante-Nicene Fathers. vol 4" ed P. Schaff**
(Edinburgh, T&T Clark: 1888-9)
http://www.ccel.org/ccel/schaff/anf04.vi.v.html

SCHO **"Selections from the Commentaries and Homilies of Origen"**
tr Tollington (SPCK; London: 1929)

Chapter 1: Knowledge and Truth

A. Matzkin "Realism and the wave function"
Eur. J. Phys. #23 (2002) p285

H. Putnam "Philosophical Papers Vol 1"
(The University Press; Cambridge: 1st ed 1975) p73

K.R. Popper in "Quantum theory and reality"
ed. M. Bunge (Springer-Verlag; New York: 1967) p7-44

J. Boswell "Life of Johnson: 1763"
(Chapman; Oxford: 1904)
http://andromeda.rutgers.edu/~jlynch/Texts/BLJ/blj63.html#42

Emerson, Lake & Palmer "Hallowed be thy Name"
from the album **"Works, Volume 1"** (Atlantic: 1977)

J.H. Newman "An Essay in aid of a Grammar of Assent"
(Longman Green; London: 1870)

K.R. Popper "The Logic of Scientific Discovery"
(Hutchinson; London: 1980)

K.R. Popper "Conjectures and Refutations"
(Routledge & Kegan; London: 1972)

1 This is an attempt to set out an orthodox account of the Catholic Faith in reaction to the spread of Modernism in the wake of the Vatican Synod of 1962-1965. It is somewhat partisan and is only one of many Catechisms which have been issued with official approval; most notably that of the Council of Trent, otherwise known as the Roman Catechism.

A. Einstein "Induction and Deduction" in
"The New Quotable Einstein" eds A. Calaprice & F. Dyson
(The University Press; Princeton: 2205) p291
K.R. Popper "Objective Knowledge, an Evolutionary Approach" (The University Press; Oxford: 1979)
Augustine of Hippo "Tractates on the Gospel of John"
in vol. 88 of **"The Fathers of the Church"**
(Cath. Univ. of America Press; Washington DC: 1993) p18
Benedict XVI "Faith, Reason and the University: Memories and Reflections" (2006)
www.vatican.va/holy_father/benedict_xvi/speeches/2006/september/documents/hf_ben-xvi_spe_20060912_university-regensburg_en.html
R.A. Knox "In Soft Garments"
(Sheed & Ward; London: 1941) p105-106
A. Rand "The Virtue of Selfishness"
(Signet; New York: 1964)
F. Herbert "Dune"
(New English Library; Sevenoaks: 1983)

Chapter 2: Reason and Objectivity

R. Descartes "Discourse on Method of Rightly Conducting the Reason, and Seeking Truth in the Sciences" Ch 4 (1637)
http://www.gutenberg.org/catalog/world/readfile?fk_files=846218&pageno=14
S.C. Kleene, "Mathematical Logic"
(Wiley; New York: 1967) p250
T. Kuhn "The Structure of Scientific Revolutions"
(The University Press; Chicago: 1996)
K.R. Popper "Objective Knowledge, an Evolutionary Approach" (The University Press; Oxford: 1979)
Emerson, Lake & Palmer "Hallowed be thy Name"
from their album **"Works, Volume 1"** (Atlantic: 1977)
J. Powers "Philosophy and the New Physics"
(Methuin; London: 1982) p6-12

Chapter 3: Order and Existence

P. Davies "The Matter Myth"
(Penguin; London: 1992) p214-215, p215-216, p217-218
J. Powers "Philosophy and the New Physics"
(Methuin; London: 1982) p130-138
K.R. Popper "Quantum Theory and the Schism in Physics"
(Hutchinson; London: 1982) p121-125, p147-150

V.J. Stenger "The Unconscious Quantum"
(Prometheus Books; Buffalo, NY: 1995) p145-155
H. Price "Time's Arrow and Archimedes' Point"
(The University Press; Oxford: 1997)
J.G. Cramer "The transactional interpretation of quantum mechanics" Rev. Mod. Phys. vol 58 #3 (1986) p647-687
K. Brown "Reflections on Relativity"
(Lulu: 2012) lib 9 cap 6

Chapter 4: The Mystery of Life

E. Schrödinger "What is Life?"
(The University Press; Cambridge, 1992)
H. Price "Time's Arrow and Archimedes' Point"
(The University Press; Oxford: 1997)
Origen of Alexandria "Selections from the Psalms"
SCHO p232
R.A. Heinlein "The Moon is a harsh mistress"
(New English Library; London: 1979) p9
H. Feifel ed "The Meaning of Death"
(McGraw-Hill; New York: 1959)
G. Orwell "1984"
(Harcourt Bruce; Orlando FL: 1949)
D. Adams "The Hitchhiker's Guide to the Galaxy: the original radio scripts. Fit the Fourth." ed G. Perkins
(Pan; London: 1985) p75

Chapter 5: Futility, Hope and Glory

R. Dawkins "The Selfish Gene"
(Oxford Paperbacks; Oxford: 1989)
A. Rand "The Fountainhead"
(Grafton Books; London: 1989)
F. Darabont (writer & director) **"The Shawshank Redemption"**
(Castle Rock Ent & Columbia Pictures Corp: 1994)
based on **S. King "Rita Hayworth and Shawshank Redemption"**
in **"Different Seasons"**
(Viking; New York: 1982)
E. Langer & I. Rodin "The effects of choice and enhanced personal responsibility for the aged."
J. Pers. Soc. Psychol. #34 (1976) p191-8

W. Blake "Auguries of Innocence"
in "**Poems and Prophecies**"
ed M. Plowman
(Dent; London: 1975) p333
R. Herrick "To the Virgins, to Make Much of Time"
in "**Works of Robert Herrick, Volume I**" ed **A. Pollard**
(Laurence and Bullen; London: 1891) p102
A. Lord Tennyson "In Memoriam A.H.H." canto 27 (1850)
http://www.online-literature.com/tennyson/718/
H. Price "Time's Arrow and Archimedes' Point"
(The University Press; Oxford: 1997)
A.W. Schlegel "Vienna Vorlesungen uber dramatische Kunst und Literature" (1809-1811)
quoted by **A.K. Thorlby** in the introduction to his book
"The Romantic Movement"
(Longmans Green & Co; London: 1966) p2

Chapter 6: Body, Soul and Spirit

R.A. Knox "In Soft Garments" Ch 2
(Sheed & Ward; London: 1941) p12
D. Chalmers "Facing Up to the Problem of Consciousness"
Jnl. of Consciousness Studies vol 2 #3 (1995) p200
www.imprint.co.uk/chalmers.html
C. Koch "What is Consciousness?"
Discover vol 13 #11 (Nov 1992)
www.discover.com/issues/nov-92/features/whatisconsciousn149
Origen of Alexandria "Selections from the Psalms."
SCHO p127
Ephraim the Syrian "Hymn Eight: On Paradise."
quoted in **L. Puhalo "On the Neurobiology of Sin"**
(Synaxis Press; Dewdney B.C. Canada: 2010) p7
Photios of Constantinople "On the Resurrection, against Origen"
cap 1 #5 quoted in **L. Puhalo "On the Neurobiology of Sin"**
(Synaxis Press; Dewdney B.C. Canada: 2010) p11-12
J.V. McConnel "Understanding Human Behaviour"
(Holt Rinehart & Winston; New York: 1986) p41-42
Origen of Alexandria "Sixth Homily on Exodus."
SCHO p202

Chapter 7: Being Good

D. Hume "A Treatise of Human Nature: Book I, Of the Understanding" part 1 sec 1 (The University; Adelaide: 16th Sept 2012) http://ebooks.adelaide.edu.au/h/hume/david/h92t/index.html

L. Carroll "The Hunting of the Snark: Fit the First" in **"The Complete Illustrated Works of Lewis Carroll "** (Chancellor Press; London: 1982) p733

L. Carroll "Through the Looking Glass and What Alice Found There" in **"The Complete Illustrated Works of Lewis Carroll"** (Chancellor Press; London: 1982) p184

A. Rand "The Objectivist Ethics" in **"The Virtue of Selfishness"** (Signet; New York: 1964)

John of Damascus "An Exact Exposition of the Orthodox Faith" lib 2 cap 22 in **S.D.F. Salmond tr "Hilary of Poitiers, John of Damascus"** p36b being **vol 9 ser 2** of **"Nicene and Post-Nicene Fathers." ed P. Schaff** (Edinburgh, T&T Clark: 1888-9) http://www.ccel.org/ccel/schaff/npnf209.iii.iv.ii.xxii.html

J.H. Newman "An Essay on the Development of Christian Doctrine" Ch 1 (Pelican; Harmondsworth: 1974)

R.A. Knox "In Soft Garments" Ch 2 (Sheed & Ward; London: 1941) p16

F. Nietzsche "Thus Spake Zarathustra" Ch 34 tr T. Common (George Alan & Unwin; London: 1932) p165

F. Nietzsche "Beyond Good and Evil" Ch 1 #13 tr H. Zimmern (El Paso Norte Press; El Paso TX: 1886)

A. Rand "The 'Conflicts' of Men's Interests" in **"The Virtue of Selfishness"** (Signet; New York: 1964)

A. Rand "The Ethics of Emergencies" in **"The Virtue of Selfishness"** (Signet; New York: 1964)

Chapter 8: Love

Augustine "City of God" XIV #7 quoted in
Thomas Aquinas "Summa Theologica" II(1) Q26 #1
http://www.newadvent.org/summa/2026.htm
W. Ward "The Life of Cardinal Newman, vol 2"
(Longmans, Green & Co; New York: 1912) p410
R. Dawkins "The Selfish Gene"
(Oxford Paperbacks; Oxford: 1989)
F. Nietzsche "Thus Spake Zarathustra" Ch 79 #9
tr T. Common
(George Alan & Unwin; London: 1932) p359
Gregory of Palamas "Topics of Natural and Theological Science and on the Moral and Ascetic Life" #36
in **"The Philokalia vol 4" ed G.E.H. Palmer et al**
(Faber & Faber; London 1995) p361
J.A.T. Robisnson "Honest to God"
(SCM; London: 1963) p49

Chapter 9: Sin and Wickedness

N. Peart "Freewill"
from the Rush album **"Permanent Waves" (Anthem/Mercury: 1980)**
Pelagius "Letter to Demetrias"
in **"The letters of Pelagius and his followers"** tr. B.R. Rees
(Boydell & Brewer; Woodbridge: 1991) p35-70
"The Jerusalem Bible: Standard Edition" ed A. Jones
(Darton, Longman & Todd; London: 1966)

Chapter 10: Clearing the Decks

R. Dawkin "The God Delusion"
(Black Swan; London: 2007) p52
K. Marx introduction to **"Contribution to Critique of Hegel's Philosophy of Right"** in Deutsch-Französische Jahrbücher
(Paris: 7th & 10th Feb 1844)
http://www.marxists.org/archive/marx/works/1843/critique-hpr/intro.htm
G. Orwell "Animal Farm" Ch 2
(Secker and Worburg; London: 1945)
http://www.george-orwell.org/Animal_Farm/1.html
Aristophanes "The Birds"
(Aris and Philips; Warminster: 1987)

J. Hill "The Preacher and the Slave"
in **"The Little Red Songbook"** #14
(W. Oliver; London: 1916)
http://www.musicanet.org/robokopp/usa/longhair.htm
R. Dawkins "The Selfish Gene"
(Oxford Paperbacks; Oxford 1989) p352
J. Gold "From a Distance"
from the album **"Dream Lord"**
(Gadfly Records: 1985)
F. Mercury "Is this the world we created?"
from the Queen album **"The Works"**
(EMI: 1984)
T. Gillian & M. Palin "Time Bandits"
(Handmade Films: 1981)
S. Donaldson "The Illearth War"
(Fontana; London: 1978)
W. Blake "The Marriage of Heaven and Hell"
in "**Poems and Prophecies"**
ed M. Plowman (Dent; London: 1975) p42ff
W. Blake "Songs of Experience"
in "**Poems and Prophecies"**
ed M. Plowman (Dent; London: 1975) p21ff
Thomas Aquinas "Summa contra gentiles" lib 3, cap 122
http://www2.nd.edu/Departments/Maritain/etext/gc3_122.htm
J. McGovern & A. Bird "Priest"
(Miramax Films: 1994)

Chapter 11: Evil and Suffering

M. Knight & J. Herrick eds **"Humanist Anthology"**
(Rationalist Press Association; London: 2000) p132-133
J. McGovern & A. Bird "Priest"
(Miramax Films: 1994)
J. Calvin "Christianae Religionis Institutio" lib 2 cap 4 (1536)
in **"Documents of the Christian Church" ed H. Bettenson**
(The University Press; Oxford: 2nd ed 1963) p253
G. Stein ed **"The Encyclopedia of Unbelief"**
(Prometheus Books; Buffalo NY: 1985) p191
W.D. Niven "Good and Evil"
in **"The Encyclopedia of Religion and Ethics"** vol XII
ed J. Hastings
(Kissinger Publishing; Whitefish MT: 2003)

O.S. Card "The Worthing Saga"
(Legend; London: 1992) p227-230
C.S. Lewis "Till We Have Faces"
(Geoffrey Bles; London: 1956)
C. Williams "Descent Into Hell"
(Faber & Faber; London: 1937)
A. Lord Tennyson "In Memoriam A.H.H." canto 56 (1850)
http://www.online-literature.com/tennyson/718/
D. Adams "The Hitchhiker's Guide to the Galaxy:
the original radio scripts. Fit the First." ed G. Perkins
(Pan; London: 1985) p29-30
D. Adams "The Hitch-hiker's Guide to the Galaxy"
(Harmony Books; New York: 1979)
A. Bennett "The History Boys" (2004) **dir N. Hytner**
(Fox Searchlight Pictures: 2006)
G.H. Smith "Atheism: The case against God"
(Prometheus Books; Buffalo NY: 1980) p84
G.W. Leibnitz "Essays of Theodicy on the Goodness of
God, the Freedom of Man and the Origin of Evil"
tr F.M. Huggard, ed. A. Farrer (Routledge; London: 1952)
Origen "De Principiis" lib 1 cap 6 #1
ODP p260

Chapter 12: The Fall

Pius XII Humani Generis (1950)
http://www.vatican.va/holy_father/pius_xii/encyclicals/documents/hf_p-xii_enc_12081950_humani-generis_en.html
R.L. Cann et al "Mitochondrial DNA and human evolution"
Nature #325 (1987) p31
R. Groleau "Tracing Ancestry with MtDNA"
(NOVA Online 2002)
http://www.pbs.org/wgbh/nova/neanderthals/mtdna.html
G. Weiss "Estimating the Age of the Common Ancestor
of Men from the ZFY Intron"
Science #272 (1996) p1359
R. Thomson et al "Recent common ancestry of human
Y chromosomes: Evidence from DNA sequence data"
PNAS vol 97 #13 (20th June 2000) p7360
F. Cruciani et al "A Revised Root for the Human
Y Chromosomal Phylogenetic Tree:
The Origin of Patrilineal Diversity in Africa"
JHG vol 88 #6 (10th June 2011) p814

Thomas Aquinas "Summa Theologica" II(2) Q23 #1
http://www.newadvent.org/summa/3023.htm#article1
B. Moreton "The eighth-century Gelasian sacramentary"
(The University Press; Oxford: 1976)
International Theological Commission "The Hope of Salvation for Infants Who Die Without Being Baptized."
Origins (April 2007)
http://www.vatican.va/roman_curia/congregations/cfaith/cti_documents/rc_con_cfaith_doc_20070419_un-baptised-infants_en.html
P. Tillich "The Shaking of the Foundations"
(Penguin; London: 1962) p63
M.A.G. Michaud "Contact with Alien Civilizations"
(Copernicus Books; New York: 2007) p234

Chapter 13: The Obscurity of God

R. Carrier "Why I am not a Christian" (2006)
http://www.infidels.org/library/modern/richard_carrier/whynotchristian.html
Jewfacts "Gentiles"
http://www.jewfaq.org/gentiles.htm
C. Matheson, E. Solomon & S. Herek "Bill and Ted's Excellent Adventure"
(Orion Pictures:1989)
J. de Marchi "Fatima: The Facts" tr I.M. Kingsbury
(Mercier Press; Cork: 1950)
F.S.V. Y Pascual "The Apparitions of Garabandal"
(San Miguel; Detroit MI: 1966)
A. Bennett "The History Boys" (2004)
dir N. Hytner (Fox Searchlight Pictures: 2006)

Chapter 14: The Reality of God

W. Paley "Natural Theology, or Evidences of the Existence and Attributes of the Deity collected from the Appearances of Nature" (J Faulder; London: 1809)
J.E. Barrick et al "Genome evolution and adaptation in a long-term experiment with Escherichia Coli"
Nature (published online 18th Oct 2009)
P. Miller "The Anthropic Principle"
http://people.brandeis.edu/~pmiller/anthrop.html

F. Hoyle "The Universe Past and Present Reflections."
Engineering and Science (Nov 1981) p8-12
P. Davies "The Goldilocks Enigma" Chs 7 & 8
(Penguin; London: 2006)
P. Hobson, G.P. Efstathiou & A.N. Lasenby "General Relativity: An introduction for physicists"
(The University Press; Cambridge: 2007) p187
M. Tegmark "The Interpretation of Quantum Mechanics: Many Worlds or Many Words?"
Fortsch. Phys. #46 (1998) p855-862
D. Dutch "David Deutsch's Many Worlds"
Frontiers (Dec 1998)
http://www.qubit.org/people/david/Articles/Frontiers.html
C.D. Broad "Religion, Philosophy and Psychical Research"
(Routledge; London: 2000)
R. Descartes "Objections and Replies"
tr J. Bennett (2007) p12, 14, 15-16
http://www.earlymoderntexts.com/descor.pdf
R. Dawkin "The God Delusion"
(Black Swan; London: 2007) p83
I. Kant "The Critique of Pure Reason" IV (1781)
tr J.M.D. Meiklejohn
N. Malcolm "Anselm's Ontological Argument"
Phil. Rev. vol 69 #1 (1960) p41-62
D. Hulme "Dialogues Concerning Natural Religion" in "The philosophical works of David Hume" vol 2
(Adam Black, William & Charles Tait; Edinburgh: 1826) p 498
B. Pascal Pensées III "On the necessity of the wager" #233
(Dutton & Co; New York: 1958) p65-69
M. Keynes "A Tract on Monetary Reform"
(Macmillan; London:1923) p80

Chapter 15: Will and Grace

D.J. O'Conner "Freewill"
(Macmillan; London: 1971)
K.R. Popper "Indeterminism in Quantum Physics and in Classical Physics" Brit. J. Phil. Sc. I (1951-2) p189
Symon "Mechanics" Ch 9
(Addison-Wesley; Reading MA: 1971) p395-396
E. Bress & J.M. Gruber "The Butterfly Effect"
(New Line Cinema: 2004).

T. Hobbes "Leviathan, The Matter, Form and Power of a Common Wealth Ecclesiastical and Civil" Ch 21
ed S. Thomas (The University; Adelaide: Sep 16th 2012)
http://ebooks.adelaide.edu.au/h/hobbes/thomas/h68l/

D. Hume "Treatise of Human Nature. Book Two: Of the Passions"
ed S. Thomas (The University; Adelaide: Sep 16th 2012)
http://ebooks.adelaide.edu.au/h/hume/david/h92t/

D. Hume "An Enquiry concerning Human Understanding"
ed S. Thomas (The University; Adelaide: Sep 16th 2012)
http://ebooks.adelaide.edu.au/h/hume/david/h92e/

Origen "De Principiis" lib 1 cap 6 #2
ODP p260

C.S. Soon et al. "Unconscious determinants of free decisions in the human brain"
Nature Neuroscience #11 (2008) p543-545

C.A. Campbell "In Defence of Free Will: with Other Philosophical Essays"
(Routledge; London: 2002)

R. Kelly "Donnie Darko"
(Newmarket Films: 2001)

W. Addis & T. Arnold "A Catholic Dictionary"
(Virtue & Co; London: 10th ed 1928)

J. Calvin "Christianae Religionis Institutio" lib 2 cap 6
in **"Documents of the Christian Church"** ed H. Bettenson
(The University Press; Oxford: 1963) p213

Thomas Aquinas "Summa Theologica" I Q23 #5
http://www.newadvent.org/summa/1023.htm#article5

Origen "De Principiis" lib 1 cap 6 #3
ODP p261

Denzinger "The Sources of Catholic Dogma" #429
tr R.J. Deferrari from the 30th Latin edition, ed K. Rahner
(Loreto; Fitzwilliam, NH: 1955)

Chapter 16: The Call to Communion

Irenaeus "Against the heresies"
in **"The Early Christian Fathers"** ed H. Bettenson
(The University Press; Oxford: 1956) p106-114

P. Abelard "Expositio in Epistolam ad Romanos"
in "Commentarius cantabrigiensis in epistolas Pauli e schola Petri Abaelardi", Publications in Mediaeval Studies 2
(The University Press; Notre Dame IN: 1937-45)

Anselm of Canterbury "Cur Deus Homo" lib 1
http://www.fordham.edu/halsall/basis/anselm-curdeus.html
M.L Rododnson tr "Babylonian Talmud"
vol 3 "Tracts Pesachim, Yoma and Hagiga"
(The Talmud Society; Boston MA: 1918) p94

Chapter 17: The End of Things

Gregory of Palamas "Topics of Natural and Theological Science and on the Moral and Ascetic Life" #68-150
in **"The Philokalia vol 4" ed G.E.H. Palmer et al**
(Faber & Faber; London 1995) p377-417
Origen "De Principiis" lib 1 cap 6 #4
ODP p282
J.H. Newman "The Dream of Gerontius."
in **"Verses on Various Occasions"** #177
(Longmans, Green & Co; London: 1903) p 323
Romanus the Melodist "On the Resurrection" V:23 quoted in
G.A. Anderson "The Fall of Satan in the Thought of St. Ephrem and John Milton"
in **"Hugoye: jnl. of Syriac stud." vol 3 #1** (Jan 2000)
D. Raup & J. Sepkoski "Mass extinctions in the marine fossil record" Science #215 (1982) p1501–1503
Romanus the Melodist "On the Resurrection V:23"
in **J. Grosdidier de Matons "Romanos le Mélode, Hymnes. Introduction, texte critique et notes"**
(Source Chrétiennes 128; Paris, 1967) p528
Benedict XVI "Greeting to the Pastoral Council of the Roman Parish of St Felicity and her children" (2007)
http://www.vatican.va/holy_father/benedict_xvi/
speeches/2007/march/documents/
hf_ben-xvi_spe_20070325_consiglio-pastorale_en.html
Augustine "The Good of Marriage"
in **E.F. Rogers ed "Theology and Sexuality: classic and contemporary readings"**
(Oxford; Blackwell: 2002) p73
R.H. Benson "Lord of the World" (1908)
http://www.authorama.com/book/lord-of-the-world.html
R.H. Benson "Dawn of All" (1911)
http://www.fullbooks.com/Dawn-of-All.html

Alphabetical Index

Printed in Great Britain
by Amazon.co.uk, Ltd.,
Marston Gate.